Beyond Equity and Inclusion in Conflict Resolution

···

ACR PRACTITIONER'S GUIDE SERIES

Series Editors:

Michael Lang is a mediator with more than thirty years' experience in the areas of family, workplace, organizational, congregational, and public policy disputes. Michael is the founding director of the Master of Arts Program in Conflict Resolution at Antioch University.

Susan Terry is a pioneer in mediation and conflict education. Susan created the Mediation Program of Woodbury College, which later moved to Champlain College and became a highly respected graduate degree program.

Books in the ACR Practitioner's Guide Series are *field guides* for the benefit of practitioners actively engaged as third-party intervenors, scholars, educators, trainers, researchers, and participants in conflict resolution processes. Each book is a practical guide that illuminates thought processes that lead to action—the underlying rationale for practice decisions—rather than simply describing "what to do." Grounded in Reflective Practice principles, the books examine the application of theory and research in relation to practice choices and guide the reader/user in a deeper understanding of why we make particular choices in our work.

Association for Conflict Resolution®
VOICES, CHOICES, SOLUTIONS

About the ACR

The Association for Conflict Resolution (ACR) is a professional organization enhancing the practice and public understanding of conflict resolution. An international professional association for mediators, arbitrators, educators, and other conflict resolution practitioners, ACR works in a wide range of settings throughout the United States and around the world. Our multicultural and multidisciplinary organization offers a broad umbrella under which all forms of dispute resolution practice find a home. Website: www.acrnet.org; Twitter: @ACRgroup.

Beyond Equity and Inclusion in Conflict Resolution

Recentering the Profession

Edited by

S.Y. BOWLAND

HASSHAN BATTS

BETH ROY

MARY ADAMS TRUJILLO

A Collaboration by Practitioners Research and Scholarship Institute

ROWMAN & LITTLEFIELD
Lanham • Boulder • New York • London

Acquisitions Editor: Mark Kerr
Acquisitions Assistant: Ivy Roberts
Sales and Marketing Inquiries: textbooks@rowman.com

Credits and acknowledgments for material borrowed from other sources, and
reproduced with permission, appear on the appropriate pages within the text.

Published by Rowman & Littlefield
An imprint of The Rowman & Littlefield Publishing Group, Inc.
4501 Forbes Boulevard, Suite 200, Lanham, Maryland 20706
www.rowman.com

86-90 Paul Street, London EC2A 4NE

British Library Cataloguing in Publication Information Available

Library of Congress Cataloging-in-Publication Data
Names: Bowland, S. Y., editor.
Title: Beyond equity and inclusion in conflict resolution : recentering
    the profession / edited by S.Y. Bowland, Hasshan Batts, Beth Roy,
    Mary Adams Trujillo
Description: Lanham : Rowman & Littlefield, 2022. | Series: The ACR
    practitioner's guide series | Includes bibliographical references and index.
Identifiers: LCCN 2021062458 (print) | LCCN 2021062459 (ebook) | ISBN
    9781538164372 (cloth ; alk. paper) | ISBN 9781538164389 (paperback ; alk.
    paper) | ISBN 9781538164396 (epub)
Subjects: LCSH: Conflict management. | Discrimination. | Racism. | Equality.
Classification: LCC HM1126 .B495 2022 (print) | LCC HM1126 (ebook) |
    DDC 303.6/9—dc23/eng/20220204
LC record available at https://lccn.loc.gov/2021062458
LC ebook record available at https://lccn.loc.gov/2021062459

Contents

· ·

· ·

SECTION II · INSIGHT   111

Acknowledgments

This book is part of a movement to disrupt oppression, poverty, and inequality that exists across the world. We acknowledge that had it not been for the sacrifices of those who came before us among our ancestors and elders, neither we nor our body of work would exist.

We begin by acknowledging the context in which this book primarily occurs, the facts of stolen land and labor. Second, we acknowledge those who have given their lives so that we would be blessed with the power to breathe, read, write, and continue to share our collective stories.

Specifically, we would like to thank Gabriela Trujillo Williams, who managed this unwieldy project; Susan Weiss, who wrestled a cacophony of styles into a symphony of coherence; Susan Terry and Michael Lang, our series editors whose patience, commitment, and productive suggestions shine throughout the book; Connie Yeh, for design assistance and good questions; a bevy of volunteer editors; and, finally, all the writers and poets who gave so freely of their time, their hearts, and their wisdom.

In addition, each editor who shared the construction of the book wishes to offer their thanks:

Mary: First and foremost, I thank God for the opportunity to advance justice in this season with the beloved community, which includes my esteemed colleagues S.Y. Bowland, Hasshan Batts, and Beth Roy; Jonas, my children, grandchildren, and great-grandchildren, whose black and brown lives compel me forward; DeBorah Cannady, whose wisdom kept me focused and encouraged; Melissa O'Keefe, who is an assistant extraordinaire; and Melissa Pavlik and the staff of *Feather Bricks* at Stateville for sharing content. Much gratitude to every person who contributed by writing, listening, critiquing, coaching, researching, or praying.

May we all become the change we seek.

Beth: To bear witness to injustice grieves the heart. To be unable to find means to fight injustice corrupts the soul. My swords are my pen and my voice. I am enormously grateful to everyone who placed their talented hands on this collective sword, honed sharply with the wisdom of all who came before us.

Thanks in particular to Susan Terry, who, in the aftermath of an egregious act of racism, promptly suggested we produce a collaborative volume and pledged to get it published; to Mark Kerr at Rowman & Littlefield, who worked so openly with us to craft a contract sensitive to our contributors' wishes; to Courtney Packard and Ivy Roberts, for patiently answering all our many production questions. My life partner, Mariah, suffered through the ups and downs of the project, always supportive of the intent while also grieving, with her accustomed honesty, the strains and stresses on our daily lives. And most of all, to my co-editors: you keep my toes to the line, my mind on speed dial, my heart full, and my life enriched. Thank you!

S.Y.: Thank you beloveds for staying alive and out of jail. You managed to cling to your roots no matter the pressures. As a woman of African heritage, the countless hours of inclusion tax, invisible labor, Black tax, and personal sacrifice are recognized as labors of love, and I thank both my beloved nuclear and extended families for their patience. Special thanks to James Gleason, Sandra Bowland, James and Justus Bowland-Gleason, Barbara Bowland, James Ciccone, and Merton Simpson.

All efforts by the settlers to isolate, alienate, or eliminate me, or to colonize my mind, body, and spirit, or the minds, bodies, and spirits of my children, shall never succeed. Instead, their efforts shall continue to present opportunities to create new ways of being and becoming in the physical and spiritual realms.

I am grateful to all the contributors who have suffered similar experiences at the hands of the settlers—still dealing with the issues and pushing past the resistance to make yet another offering for a better world that is more loving to people of African heritage. I thank my colleagues Mary, Beth, and Hasshan for teaching me so much about faith. I thank you all with heartfelt gratitude, love, with appreciation for sending positive energy into the world with this literary contribution.

During the course of preparing this book, my young cousin Deangelo Antonio Jerome Saez Morgan became an ancestor. He was a wonderful, good-spirited person, loved by many.

Hasshan: To those that have been forced to spill and shed blood to create discomfort, disruption, resistance, and revolution on this journey to liberation, I read and write in hopes that the pen is mightier than the sword. To Mama Batts, who birthed, nurtured, loved, and believed in me when the world so hated me, and who continuously taught me to love myself and to be present and breathe through the asthma attacks. To S.Y. Bowland, my sister, second mother, friend, mentor, and colleague, who taught me that my first language is energy and encouraged me to listen, write, and tell the world my story. To my children and grandchildren, Nina, Nakia, Justice, Harmony, Arielle, Elijah, and Beckham, your warrior spirits drive me. To my muse and life partner, Katarah J, who continues to challenge me to see the beauty of the world, to travel often, to rest, and to leave my mark. To my life-changing PRASI family, especially Beth and Mary, nothing but love to you for your patience, guidance, and perfect mix of accountability and compassion, and to everybody in the struggle, we're in this together!

Finally, we remember those killed by state violence during the time we wrote this book. It is not lost on us that we are listing names of those murdered by white terrorism in 16 months during 2020 and early 2021, and that this book will be read for decades to come when the memory of their deaths may have faded to black. Although traditionally a hopeful group, we know that the tyranny of white supremacy and the unnumerable state-sanctioned slaughter of Black and brown bodies at the hands of police will continue. Just as Mamie Till Mobley shared, "When people saw what happened to my son, men stood up who had never stood up before," so too we share the following names to invigorate, enrage, and stimulate action, lest their names and deaths are forgotten.

2020

Albert Lee Hughes was killed on January 15, 2020, in Lawrenceville, Georgia. Officers claim Hughes was "armed with a chair," but no body-camera footage was released.

Jaquyn O'Neill Light was killed in Graham, North Carolina, on January 29, 2020. He was 20 years old, was known to his friends and family as "Meat," and had four brothers and one sister.

Barry Gedeus was killed in Fort Lauderdale, Florida, on March 6, 2020. He was 27 years old and described as a loving man whose motto was "get right with God."

Donnie Sanders was killed on March 12, 2020, in Kansas City, Missouri. He was 47 years old and was described as protective and fun to hang out with.

Mychael Johnson was killed on March 20, 2020, in Tallahassee, Florida. He was 31 years old and a graphic engineer. Johnson enjoyed reading, playing video games, and working on the computer.

Fred Brown was killed on April 23, 2020, in North Las Vegas, Nevada. He was 34 years old.

Shaun Lee Fuhr was killed on April 29, 2020, in Seattle, Washington. He was 24 years old and a father.

Yassin Mohamed was suffering from a mental health crisis at the time of his death on May 9, 2020, in Claxton, Georgia.

Wilbon Cleveland Woodard was killed on May 19, 2020, in Tallahassee, Florida. Woodward was 69 years old when he was killed. Police claimed he was armed, but no details or body camera footage were ever released.

Maurice Gordon was killed on May 23, 2020, in Bass River, New Jersey. He was 28 years old. Gordon was studying chemistry at Dutchess Community College. He was described as a warrior and someone who would lay his blood down for others to stand.

Dion Johnson was 28 when he was killed on May 25, 2020, in Phoenix, Arizona. He was one of five siblings and the father to a 14-year-old daughter. Johnson was described as a "mama's boy" and a music lover, and he was well-liked by everyone he met. He was described as being in the process of turning his life around after jail time when he was killed.

Rayshard Brooks was killed in Atlanta, Georgia, on June 12, 2020. He was married for eight years and had three daughters and a stepson.

Robert D'Lon Harris was killed on June 25, 2020, in Vinta, Oklahoma. He was 34 years old. He was a loving brother, son, and uncle. His family called him the life of the party, someone who knew no strangers, and was the protector of his family and friends.

Amir Johnson was killed on August 6, 2020, near Atlantic City, New Jersey. He was 30 years old and had been mourning the death of his fiancée.

Julian Edward Roosevelt Lewis was killed in Screven County, Georgia, on August 7, 2020. He worked as a carpenter. Lewis left a widow, Betty Lewis, behind. "He was too good to die as he did," she said.

Kurt Andras Reinhold was 42 years old when he was killed on September 23, 2020, in San Clemente, California. He suffered from mental illness and was homeless at the time of his death. His family is fighting for justice over his killing.

Mickel Erich Lewis was 39 years old when he was killed on October 2, 2020. He was driving in Kern County, California, with his girlfriend and her two teenage daughters at the time of his death.

Jonathan Price was killed in Wolf City, Texas, on October 3, 2020. Price was 31 years old at the time of his death and was trying to stop a domestic dispute. "He helped everybody in his community and had a big heart and spirit," his mother said of him.

Anthony Jones was killed on October 12, 2020, in McNairy County, Tennessee. "He used to bring strays home, and he used to play with his toys. I still remember and envision him as that same lovable little boy," his aunt said of him.

Marcellis Stinnette was 19 years old when he was killed on October 20, 2020, in Waukegan, Illinois. He was with his girlfriend and the mother of his child, who was also injured.

Casey Goodson Jr. was killed on December 4, 2020, in Columbus, Ohio. Goodson was 23 years old, described as a good man who worked at Gap and who loved his family and being a big brother.

Andre Maurice Hill was killed on December 22, 2020, in Columbus, Ohio. Andre was 47 years old, had a passion for cooking, and was trained in hotel restaurant management and culinary arts. He was a loving father, grandfather, and uncle.

2021

Carl Dorsey III was killed minutes into the new year on January 1, 2021, in Newark, New Jersey. Dorsey was a father to four children—three biological and one adopted—worked as a trucker, and was planning to start a trucking business named after his children.

Patrick Lynn Warren was 52 years old when he was killed in Killeen, Texas, on January 10, 2021. He was having mental health issues and had voluntarily gone to a hospital the day before.

Jenoah Donald was 30 years old when he was killed on February 4, 2021, in Hazel Dell, Washington. His mother and brother remember him as a loving man who worked all his life to overcome mental illness, learning disorders, and substance abuse. He liked to come up with mechanical projects and go camping.

Daverion Kinard was killed in Fontana, California, just hours before his 29th birthday on February 14, 2021.

Arnell States was killed on February 20, 2021, in Cedar Rapids, Iowa. States was 39 years old and a father of three.

Donovon W. Lynch was killed on March 26, 2021, in Virginia Beach, Virginia. Lynch was 25 years old. Lynch loved basketball, football, playing pool, and fashion. He was a volunteer and member of Faith World Ministries.

Adam Toledo was killed on March 29, 2021, in Chicago. He was 13 years old, loved to play with LEGOs, say funny jokes, and make others laugh. Adam's mother says he dreamed of being a police officer.

Daunte Wright was killed on April 11, 2021, in Brooklyn Center, Minnesota. Daunte Wright was described as a caring uncle and a wonderful father. He had an "amazing smile" and liked to drive around and listen to music "just like your average 20-year-old."

READ THIS FIRST:
A Note from the Editors

HINDSIGHT, INSIGHT, FORESIGHT: A CALL TO ACTION TO ELIMINATE RACISM IN PROFESSIONAL CONFLICT RESOLUTION PRACTICE

The creators of this book are a diverse lot. We are people of many identities and experiences. We speak in many tongues and view the world from many standpoints. Some authors are new young voices, invited by the editors to contribute their unique wisdom. Others have built relationships over years of collaboration as we've worked together to understand how racism exists in our shared work as peacemakers and to support what in our lifetime has become a profession to stand firmly in the heart of justice.

As a contribution to that effort, the editors of this volume joined together in 1998 to create a new organization called the Practitioners Research and Scholarship Institute (PRASI). We are a multicultural group of conflict transformation practitioners and writers dedicated to producing publications that reflects the full diversity of our society. Understanding that a literature widely accepted as legitimate is a fundamental gatekeeper to any profession and that such writings tend to be produced by academics in white-dominated educational institutions, PRASI's approach is to amplify voices of practitioners of color as knowledge bearers. In 2008, Syracuse University Press published the first collection of writings produced with the encouragement and support of PRASI: *Re-Centering: Culture and Knowledge in Conflict Resolution Practice*. This book was the first of its kind to speak to the experience of people of color in the field of conflict resolution and put forth the idea that lived experience is valid for knowledge claims.

The field has changed significantly since then. What was "conflict resolution" has evolved into a myriad of practices, approaches, and theoretical frameworks with names like restorative justice, strategic peacebuilding, human security, conflict transformation, and more. Traditional Western mediation today reflects multicultural, multimodal, multicontextual interventions as varied as the conflicts that necessitate their use. And yet racism, cultural dominance, and institutional oppression in conventional approaches to mediation, arbitration, and alternative dispute resolution, and even in the newer forms, still have a significant presence. Our goal is to examine and interrogate these structures, interactions, and practices to suggest directions for change.

We write this volume in a time of heightened attention to racism in America. Many organizations and institutions are committing to self-scrutiny and internal change. Practitioners and academics in the field of conflict resolution began a process of understanding dynamics that create barriers for participation of people of color and other marginalized communities, contributing to bring about significant relief. To aid this ongoing effort, a group primarily composed of practitioners and researchers of color launched a project to produce a collaboratively written volume of original essays and poems detailing where racism is present today, a vision of a truly egalitarian profession, and concrete steps that would aid in actualizing this vision. We borrow from other professions, as well as write with the larger goal of offering inspiration and a template *for* other professions as well. We write for practitioners, academics, students, young people who wish to do good in the world, oppressed people who are ready to burst with a dedication to justice, and people of all races who are ready to step forward together to bring about racial change. We hope this book will be useful beyond our immediate colleagues, serving as encouragement and guide for those seeking justice in many different walks of life. We write for anyone, of any race or heritage, who stands ready to make real progress toward equity and justice.

After framing the questions, the first section invites diverse author-practitioners to define the "field" and reflect on the location of racism and other oppressions. From their standpoints, the contributors explore whether injustice is inherent in the very process of turning conflict intervention into a professional field. They question the role of mediation, arbitration, and other practices in counteracting injustice, especially as alternative dispute resolution (ADR) and other intervention practices may fail to account sufficiently for power inequities embedded in society, thereby inviting those disabling dynamics into the room. How, for example, do patterns of racial and other injustices lace through academic credentialing, which still enables entry into careers? The academy, the gatekeeper, remains rife with barriers to the inclusion of people of color and others who are characteristically marginalized. How do organizational leadership and procedures, including those in conflict organizations, still reflect and perpetuate racial and gendered inequities?

Section II reflects critically on the contemporary field and goes further. Given projected demographics that the United States will become a majority people-of-color society by approximately 2045, conversations among diverse practitioners seek to prepare professionals for what is required for such a shift. S.Y. Bowland's powerfully lyrical guidance weaves through voices of diverse and credible messengers in the form of transcribed interviews, prose essays, and poetry, all knit together to highlight places for visionary change. This section seeks to interrogate and expand the "what, how, and why" of knowledge in the field.

The central question is, of course, can racism be eliminated? Do we, whoever "we" is, believe that to be possible? For starters, we asked practitioners of color whether they can imagine a world without racism and what that would look and feel like. Mostly, they answered that they could not imagine such a thing. Thus, our starting point in section III is to envision a world and conflict practice without racism, while also suggesting actions leading to that accomplishment. Diverse artists and poets, spiritual leaders, intergenerational activists, educators, incarcerated individuals, and health workers explore systemic and structural intersections, as well as how they might bring new awareness to get us from "here "to "there."

Authors respond to four essential questions:

- What would stand in the place of patterns and practices of omission as well as overt behavior?
- What creative methodologies can be practiced beyond the prevailing Eurocentric ones?
- How would attitudes about ownership, neutrality, and power change?
- How might restorative practices enable more just and more effective practices?

The section concludes with an analysis and opportunities for practitioner reflection.

The four editors of this book are ourselves a diverse lot. Having worked together over many years, we recognize and value the different sensibilities we bring to our collaboration. We speak and write differently. Our consciousness is couched in different perspectives deriving from different standpoints. Although we share some version of English as our first language, we draw on different wells of imagery, expression, and meaning. These differences require us to reach beyond comfort zones—efforts we willingly undertake in the context of sturdy relationships built over time.

Language and communication can be sources of conflict. In any dispute, words are of central importance in the beginning, in the middle, and at the end. Language may determine whether that end is transformative or catastrophic. The languages that animate our thoughts show up in the agreements we write, in the tones and sounds we use. Language and words deliver, create, and impact conflict culture just as they influence all of life.

Throughout this book, our contributors write in a wide variety of styles. Normally, editorial conventions homogenize language and grammatic rules.

We have resisted submitting this project to that process. For example, some authors capitalize colors when they designate identities; others do not. Some authors use phrases that have become common in academic or activist circles but may be less familiar in daily life, "white supremacist culture," for example, or "Predominantly White Institution (PWI)." At their core, processes of racism and other forms of domination oppress people by requiring submission to dominant thought as well as behavioral patterns. On the bridge of multiculturalism, those who are marginalized are required to walk far more than their share toward meeting those who reside in the center (with thanks to Roberto Chené for the metaphor). Instead of reproducing that oppression here, the editors have encouraged our authors to write in their authentic voices. You, the reader, are therefore challenged to walk across many bridges. Some of those walks will, literally and figuratively, gift you with life-changing insight, perhaps a fundamental paradigm shift. Sometimes, though, the language you read may grate against the rules you learned in school. That experience offers you an opportunity to challenge racism in the act of reading. We welcome you to meet us at the very center of the bridge.

Racism is a disease that has infected all parts of life in America. It is pervasive, it breaks down the bodies of both the perpetrator and the survivor, and ultimately it kills; it kills our potential, kills our hopes, and strangles the opportunity for us to heal our spirits and to build better relationships, organizations, and societies.

Many people question how we have gotten here. How did we get to a place where we need a whole book of narratives, interviews, poetry, and prose for a field that is centered on a desire to help and built upon traditional healing practices? Many would argue that we have lost our way as a field, and others would argue that our field has always drunk from the wells of white supremacy culture.

We know as conflict resolution practitioners, theorists, and administrators that there exist many truths; what follows are just those: honest experiences of individuals who chose or were chosen by a field intended to help people, organizations, and communities. Practitioners engage with people in conflict in their most vulnerable moments to find understanding, agreement, and relationship. Let these narratives function not so much as a blueprint, but as a what-is and how-to, a guidepost on this shared journey to wellness and liberation. We extend this healing invitation not only to those we serve but also to all who would be a witness for the helpers and healers who themselves seek to find the way.

With excitement about the opportunity afforded conflict practitioners in this moment of writing, as new awareness opens the door to real progress, we offer this work to prime the pump, to stimulate discussion, and ideally to be itself an action step on a brisk and effective walk toward justice.

SECTION I

HINDSIGHT

· ·

INTRODUCTION

Beth Roy

To write a collaborative book sharing what we've learned about racism presents itself as both an opportunity and a responsibility. For 25 years, I've had the rare pleasure of working with a talented and heartfelt group of colleagues, mostly people of color, seeking to make contributions to increasing equity in our field. Over these decades, we've grown to be friends, to care for each other beyond work. When a colleague, a righteous white woman with access to publishing resources, suggested producing a book, for all the reasons I've sketched previously, we agreed that such a project should be white people's work. So I turned to my colleagues of color, not with an invitation to collaborate, but with a request to help me sort out my ambivalence about the task.

I began activism against racism in the segregated South when I was 14. I've been at it for 66 years. I've written and given speeches and counseled and mediated for social justice—but in the moment of deciding whether to take on producing this volume, my heart and my energy flagged. At the same time, I strongly felt a responsibility to meet the moment with what I have to offer: relationships and insights gained over all those decades of effort.

My friends, my collaborators, plunged right into envisioning a shared volume. My spirits—and my energy—immediately lifted. Their generosity, wisdom, creativity, and love lie at the core of this work.

One final thing: I don't see myself as an ally to my comrades of color; I am grateful to them for allying with me. I do this work not to help them, or, more accurately, not only to protect them from racism. I do this work out of gratitude for the opportunity.

So let's plunge into the expanded possibilities offered by tragedy and come to a heightened understanding of where wrongs exist today and how to change them.

In a mixed-race group recently, a white woman, a mediator of long experience, decried some act of egregious Trumpian hypocrisy. "Whatever happened to consistency, honesty, respect?!" she raged.

A Black colleague replied in a matter-of-fact tone, "Welcome to my world."

Like all of America, the geography occupied by the profession of conflict intervention is marked by wide chasms of differing experiences. The white woman in our example lived in a world of assumed consistency. Her imagined leaders were people both readable and true. The Black woman lived in a very different reality. For her, normalcy was laced with people saying one thing and doing another. The unexpected was always to be expected.

Most of us who choose service work, whatever our background and identity, act out of a value of fairness. Perhaps that is a basic human quality. One of the first protests children mount is, "That's not fair!" How we perceive justice, however, differs dramatically across racial lines. Focused on what they believe to be their fair practices, many white practitioners and scholars find it hard to believe racism in the field continues to be a significant problem. To their eyes, the work itself rests on principles of fairness and equality. How then can its practitioners be anything other?

When the racial landscape of the nation is suddenly rifted with an earthquake of the dimensions of George Floyd's murder in 2019, when the streets exploded (yet again) into a passionate protest, white members of the conflict profession express outrage and lend heartfelt support to those in the streets. But these protestations are not necessarily supported by self-awareness. We see how police officers or white supremacists, or perhaps even teachers and medical professionals may be racist. But not us, surely not those of us who practice neutrality daily! Where can racism possibly be afoot in *our* field?

This section of our book is intended to help answer that question. It also seeks to shed light on how and why we come to dwell in such a divided landscape of consciousness. The stories we present here are not accusations. They vividly portray deep pain and other emotion. But rather than blaming, they simply share depictions of lives lived in conditions very different from those typically experienced by white Americans. Taken in combination, these stories sketch a context, a way people have come to form their worldviews through childhood discoveries of their membership in despised categories, through adult experiences of barriers to careers, of white authorities who discounted their lived knowledge and expertise. Even more, their stories speak of support by others who share their identity, and occasionally by exceptional white elders who crossed lines of race to respect and encourage them.

Preparing for mediation with the leadership of a large nonprofit organization, I asked the lone African American officer (who also, not coincidentally, was the newest member of the group) whether she felt alienated.

"Of course," she promptly replied. "I feel alienated everywhere. This is America!"

Her story of alienation threads through truthful accounts by people of color in the field of conflict resolution generally. Forming identity and learning about our place in an endless, multifaceted social hierarchy is something everyone does, no matter what social locations we occupy. For white children in America, the racial norm is sameness. Peers and leaders "look like us." White people also often struggle with contradictions involving gender, class, nationality, and origins. But children learn very basic lessons from the evidence of their eyes and the behaviors of their elders; on the fundamental level of who they're like, they learn that they fit the dominant norm. Unlike children of color, they do not experience the shock of recognition that they are hated for perceived differences. White children may rail against inequalities built into gendered ideologies or sibling hierarchies. Brothers get privileges, sisters do not, for example. Older sisters get cell phones while younger ones are still prohibited. Lessons in power follow us all wherever we go, at home and in the world. But for children of color, racial lessons more often occur not within the protected walls of the home but in public spaces, and often they take violent forms on the streets or at school as discriminatory disciplinary policies play out with racist impact. Children of color must negotiate hazards of difference, and even more emotionally stressful attitudes and behaviors, at very young ages as they make their way through everyday activities.

As we all grow up, as we move from childhood into adult lives, these disparate experiences form profound differences of context for interpreting even the most subtle types of encounters. We all share the perils of our competitive society. The more disadvantaged one is on any axis of the social hierarchy, whether race, gender, class, sexuality, or ability, the harder one must work, the more obstacles one must overcome, to achieve one's goals. All the writers in this volume have traveled these rock-strewn paths, often with much success, but also with emotional wounds and, inevitably, significant fatigue. When intense incidents of police brutality against Black people become widely known, a time when white people awaken with the question, "What's to be done?" people of color know all too well the answer. But to be called upon to provide answers, when answers have been available unheeded over decades, adds to the pain of the interaction.

Nonetheless, the writers in this section generously offer their stories. Most are grounded in the lives of the author as well as detailing professional dynamics of exclusion and oppression. Narratives of personal experience tend to be held in low regard as credible forms of scholarship. We editors disagree: all research ultimately must relate to realities on the ground. For many of our contributors, the times and topics coincide in whirls of pain. As conflict intervenors, we know the power of stories, both to educate and to heal. In the chapters that follow, authors have chosen to write their pain, as an openhearted contribution to the deepened awareness of white colleagues, but also as personal and community healing. These writers start with the roads they have walked, offering to take the reader along, and noting in compelling detail the landscape they traverse day after day.

CHAPTER 1

Who Produces Knowledge?

···

I t is a truism that we cannot know what we do not know—but we need to know that we don't know it. How are we to do that if those who do know because they live that knowledge are blocked from sharing it?

Fundamental to the production of knowledge is the question of who writes and is published. A recent uproar in the medical field involved egregious unawareness of systemic racism in that profession by the editor of the major journal in the field, the Journal of the American Medical Association (JAMA). Consequent protests revealed a dramatic failure to publish research by authors of color and others studying the impact of racism on medical outcomes. The field of conflict intervention similarly manifests a failure to include the voices of those who know.

On her way to making visible the invisibility of Black thinkers and practitioners in the conflict intervention profession, Cherise Hairston reveals the emotionally rough road she walked simply to be able to write in these times. She weaves her personal experiences into the stories of many of her fellow practitioners of African descent. Over the years, Cherise has tracked the absence of Black authors in the growing literature of the field. Her chapter richly and implicitly steps us into the realm of the politics of knowledge production. Using scholarly sensibilities, she builds her essay on very personal conversations, illuminating a crucial foundation for the continuing absence of scholars and practitioners of color in the field.

In turning to her colleagues of color, Cherise manifests another theme running throughout this book: the centrality of relationships. How people work and form friendships with colleagues is central to how people learn, practice, and sustain themselves. As writings poured into this project, the editors looked for emergent themes. This primacy of relationship is striking, a strong foundation shared by very disparate authors in many ways. The dominant culture sets people apart, especially when practicing a nascent profession in competitive circumstances; yet those who are excluded move toward others, not only in collegiality but also in friendship. Cherise's "interviews" are both research and mutual help, as African Americans navigate in ways unique to their identity the devastating emotional impacts of the historic George Floyd revelations.

—Beth Roy

···

Aggregating Wisdom, Amplifying Voices: Conflict Resolution Practitioners of African Descent

Cherise D. Hairston

Prelude

From the moment I entered the field of conflict resolution 25 years ago, I experienced a painful reality of the invisibility of practitioners of African descent and a lack of any significant scholarly research designed to aid all practitioners in providing culturally responsive conflict resolution services and processes to participants of African descent. I characterize this as neglect and view this neglect as harmful for those on the ground working to address conflict. It is detrimental to the validity and effectiveness of the field as a whole. As I argued then, and now, this continued neglect reflects the same structural oppression and violence found in the broader society (Hairston, 1999, 2008) that impacts African Americans (and other historically marginalized and oppressed groups). I am driven by a passion for conflict intervention work, a desire to leave a legacy that helps inspire and motivate others, and a moral sense of duty to contribute what I can to create accessible and inclusive organizations.

A Summer of Discontent

In July 2020, I was asked by the editors of this volume to write about the question: *What would a "perfect" conflict resolution field look like?* Unsure of my reply, I began to grapple with whether I could summon my energy to explore and write about this question.

The beginning of year 2020 started hopeful for me. In January 2020, I had just started my coaching certification program through the Co-Active Training Institute (CTI). I was coaching 10 clients in addition to working full time at the Dayton Mediation Center, a community mediation center in Dayton, Ohio. I wanted to add formal coach training to my professional conflict intervention repertoire to support the efforts of my colleagues at the Institute for the Study of Conflict Transformation, Inc. This is an organization established to "fulfill the promise of mediation," a transformative conflict intervention theory first formally articulated by Bush and Folger (1994). With coaching skills, I thought I could help these colleagues to formally develop the theory and practice of "conflict coaching from a transformative perspective." This formal coach training would also support my work as a longtime staff member at the Dayton Mediation Center.

In February 2020, my services were requested in another state, so I packed my "mediator bag," and I hopped on an airplane and traveled to provide support for a workplace conflict between employees. Meanwhile, in the same month on February 23, 2020, Ahmaud Aubery, a 25-year-old African American man, was shot 11 times and killed by two white men. I was so stunned I couldn't process the news of this tragedy. I numbed out my rage.

At the beginning of March, the news was focused on the COVID-19 pandemic and within several weeks, I was preparing to "work from home," which ultimately ended up evolving into my parent employer furloughing "nonessential" employees, of whom I was one. This was stressful enough, and the stress of "sheltering in place" made it worse. On March 13, 2020, while Breonna Taylor, another African American, lay sleeping in her bed, six bullets pierced the night with one tearing through her heart and lungs and killing her, according to news accounts.

By the time May 2020 rolled around, I was in shock from the confluence of unprecedented events in the form of "rough and raw," televised, secondhand witnessing of murders of African Americans, in addition to a health crisis never before experienced in my lifetime. This all culminated on May 25, 2020, when, already emotionally exhausted, I bore collective witness to the horrific murder of George Floyd by a police officer on television.

I'm not sure what happened between the end of May through July, but by July 2020, I was reminded of Martin Luther King's lament of a "summer of discontent" (King, 1964) and feared that all the social upheaval, anger, and rage had sent me and many others over a collective edge. Repeated mind-numbing and soul-destroying events included the murder of all kinds of despised bodies, such as unarmed African Americans killed by police (www.mappingpolice violence.org) or Black and brown people with gender-nonconforming identities (Human Rights Campaign Fund, 2020). Ubiquitous racist hate speech streamed from our political leaders. These events, coupled with the stress of the pandemic facing the world's population, left me, like so many, feeling as if I were hurtling further down an emotional and spiritual rabbit hole, leaving me in a state of "disbelief and horror" (Winters, 2020).

Then in July came the editors' invitation to write about how we might collectively reconstruct our shared profession to move significantly toward racial justice. I grappled with whether I could summon my energy to explore and write about the editors' central question: "What would a 'perfect' conflict resolution field look like?" Could I successfully traverse yet another emotional middle passage of anger, cynicism, and ultimately despair after a wicked summer of discontent?

But heartened by the idea of building my contribution around conversations with other practitioners of African descent, I took a deep breath, I plunged in. I was determined to write my personal story of how marginalization has impacted me. In addition, I selected 23 African American practitioners from within my professional network and invited them to talk with me about their experiences.

A Passion for Agape Love and Service

> To make our way, we must have firm resolve, persistence, tenacity. We must gear ourselves to work hard all the way. We can never let up.—Ralph Bunche

It is important to share what motivates me personally in my work as a conflict resolution practitioner who deeply cares about this work. It is intimately linked to my concern about social justice, especially for those whose voices and needs have been ignored and silenced. My multiple identities (African American, woman, lesbian) in several historically marginalized and oppressed groups provide me with a large amount of "skin in the game." The concerns I continue to raise are vital to my well-being and quality of life and to the lives of so many others who find their identities marginalized.

My passion for learning about and understanding the unique perspectives and varieties of practice among people of African descent will always live within my heart and soul. To have it ignored is extremely painful for my spirit. Simply, for me, a central starting place is doing what I can to interrupt what I believe is a continued pattern of social exclusion. This pattern renders the valuable contributions to the development of the field by people of African descent invisible and situated at the margins of theory and practice development. The evolution of the various fields connected to the aim of engaging conflict constructively does not benefit from the contributions of this group. I encourage a collective effort to move to the center of the field the work of historically marginalized groups. With critical and sustained action, we can bust up the deeply embedded practice of "white centering" that has used those of European descent as the referent group to which all others are compared, particularly in scholarly research (see López & Parker, 2003; Perry, 2020; Smith, 1999; Stanfield, 1994, p. 176; Tillman, 2002; Zuberi, 2001). For many of us, myself included, this means "calling out whiteness" (Wilson, 2020). It also requires creating narratives that identify, aggregate, and amplify the voices of conflict resolution practitioners of African descent.

I began work on creating new narratives in 1996 when I started a graduate degree in conflict resolution. From 2000 through 2012, I worked on a doctorate in Conflict Analysis and Resolution. The focus of my dissertation research was "African-American Conflict Resolution Professionals' Experiences with Social Exclusion." A myriad of countervailing forces precluded me from finishing my dissertation research. Not finishing my research and losing my beloved mother to cancer in 2017 shattered my heart into a million shards that I never thought I could piece back together. But the desire to fill the gap in the conflict literature has continued to occupy my thoughts. This chapter brings me an opportunity to make a small contribution to understanding the experiences of exclusion felt by African Americans in the field of conflict resolution. It feels healing to bring their experiences more fully out into the open for redress.

We need a social movement within and beyond the field of conflict resolution. To contribute to starting this movement, I am revisiting the real-world experiences of practitioners of African descent woven together through my personal lens of lived experience as a practitioner on the ground doing this work in community mediation. I do not attempt to speak for anyone but myself, but I wanted to engage in such an endeavor being lifted by their hopes and concerns, and my own desire and mission to strengthen the conflict resolution knowledge base for practical applications. The consequences of numerical underrepresentation cannot be overstated because this state of affairs has serious implications for the continued development and effectiveness of the field that has a deleterious impact of rendering invisible the significance of our contributions to the development of the field. This invisibility reinforces and reproduces the same phenomenal experiences found in the larger social, political, economic, and cultural context in which there is a denial of antiblack racism in predominantly white institutions. The persistence of continued antiblack racism will continue to render interventions to increase belongingness, inclusion, and justice tragically ineffective (Bowland, 2008; Chang et al., 2008; Edwards, 2020; Hoffman & Stallworth, 2008; Johnson & LaRue, 2009; Konrad, 2018).

BELOVED COMMUNITY-PRACTITIONERS OF AFRICAN DESCENT

Prelude

I used my professional network to help me identify practitioners of African descent currently practicing conflict resolution primarily in the United States. Over four weeks, I conducted 23 life-giving and restorative conversations. My conversations were conducted via Zoom videoconferencing or telephone, most lasting 60 minutes. In each conversation, the participant (or interviewee) and I shared a common connection that allowed for immediate rapport and trust to be present. This was an exploratory, learning action approach and part informal autoethnography. I reviewed the literature on conducting qualitative interviews for a refresher (Döringer, 2020: Fusch et al., 2018; Guest et al., 2012; Maher et al., 2018; Trujillo, 2008). To write this chapter, I relied on my notes that captured keywords and specific quotes to identify common themes and to link to existing literature, where possible. My hope, with this effort, is to continue to add to the growing body of literature written by, for, and about practitioners of African descent to spark applied empirical and nonempirical research that is useful to all practitioners.

Reflecting Back My Heart

I wanted to know how each of the practitioners I talked to was doing on a basic human level because I knew all of us had faced difficult challenges through much of 2020. I used the experience I gained back in 2008 when I conducted 20 interviews as part of my dissertation research to inform my inquiry. I wanted to know what the practitioners I talked with cared about, what they hoped for, and generally what was on their minds and in their hearts. I framed my work as grounded in "action learning with an autoethnographic undercurrent." Action learning is all about exploring knowledge and experience from the perspective of those living a certain reality. They have a valuable perspective on what's working best, and what, if anything needs to be fixed or improved. My conversations were exploratory and open-ended in nature. The group's practice areas included a wide range of traditional and innovative conflict intervention specialties such mediation, arbitration, facilitation, conflict coaching, organizational development, conflict management training, teaching and training, restorative justice practices, dialogue and deliberation work, and nonviolence based on the work of Dr. King. In many ways, my goal was to get a "pulse check" on "pain points" centered around such words and ideals as "community," "belonging," "inclusion," "self-care," and "relational ethics of care." A consistent feeling and shared sentiment from the majority of conversation partners was "thank you": *Thank you for asking about my perspective, thank you for listening to what I care about, thank you for your efforts at trying to make the field work well for everyone.*

The Power of Practitioner Perspectives

I promised each conversation partner that I would not "name names" as this research was about using their individual perspectives to surface common themes. I believe it is important to aggregate the power of their collective voices and perspectives. The chart Aggregated Practitioner Profile presents an overview of the demographics of the participants. Additionally, I'm not speaking "for" or "about" participants, but rather, I have allowed the participants' conversations to seep into my heart so that I could surface them through my perspective. I hope I have honored their voices and created a wider space for us all to understand what it takes to create inclusive organizations that foster belonging and respect for the unique contributions of us all.

Practitioner Experience	Range of Involvement in Field
Combined CR Practice Experience=390.6 Median Years of Experience=16.5 years "Youngest Tenture" Experience=1.5 years "Longest Tenure" Experience=18 years	Mediation, Arbitration, Facilitation, Teaching, Training, Systems Design, Writing/Research, Executive Director, National Boards, CR Organizational Affiliations, Policy

Aggregated Practitioner Profile

Geographic Region	Gender Expression
Midwest=9 (IL, OH, MN) Northeast=8 (MD) South=6 (FL, GA, LA, VA) West=1 (CA)	Female=15 Male=9

Amplifying Our Collective Practitioner Experiences

My conversations with practitioners were enjoyable, wide-ranging, generative, and inspiring. What was immediately apparent was the passion and commitment to this work of each person. I have highlighted the main themes from these conversations and have named the themes based on my sense of the subject matter. Where possible, I connect these ideas to the existing published literature, both empirical and nonempirical. I focus on what I feel are the most critical themes raised by my conversation partners.

Participant Conversation Themes
Walking the Talk of Building Inclusive Organizations
Representation Matters
Accomplices Not Allies
Trauma-Informed Practices
A New Vision
Pipelines and Pathways: Professional Development Pathways

Walking the Talk of Building Inclusive Organizations

People of European descent who are involved in this field cannot continue to deny that racism exists and that it impacts our interpersonal relationships and the institutional contexts in which we interact (Drakulich et al., 2020; Mosley et al., 2020; Onwuachi-Willig, 2017). Effective antiracist action is required at the interpersonal and institutional levels (Konrad, 2018, p. 23). That action must involve strategies rooted in "creating conditions of equal status, common goals, intergroup cooperation, and support of authorities." (Konrad, 2018, pp. 23–24). The need for us to learn to build inclusive organizations is urgent because the divides in communities continue and the polarization intensifies (Rogers, 2015; Stulberg, 2020). If we can't create inclusive organizations, how can we help others? Many of my conversations touched on a deeply held belief in a moral duty to intervene in injustice, which is everyone's responsibility, because, after all, "we rise by lifting others." Many of my conversations included ideas about building organizations that welcome those from marginalized communities and truly seek to create a welcoming environment. The need for true inclusion and for representation of people with diverse voices and lived experiences were emphasized.

In my conversations, I found a few people who had had positive experiences in working toward inclusive organizations. One practitioner was sought out by an organizational leader who professed honestly and directly, "We're too white" (see Arao & Clemens, 2013; Dobbin & Kalev, 2020; Ely & Thomas, 2020). While seemingly a rare occurrence, another conversation partner had a similar experience of being invited in and viewed holistically. Recognition of her capability ultimately led to her becoming the executive director of a community mediation center (see Low, 2008). The beauty of this opportunity allowed her to live her deeply held value of being of service. She was able to intensify her outreach efforts into African American communities based on her firm belief that "we can make this community better one person at a time" (see Allen & Lewis, 2016; Davis & Maldonado, 2015; Gee, 2018; Hinton, 2018).

Honoring the Impact of Our Work

Conflict resolution and restorative justice practitioners are on the ground working in powerful ways. Bridgeford (2020) is doing revolutionary work to address the Baltimore riots of 2016. In one of my conversations with a longtime practitioner who spent more than a quarter of a century as an executive director of a community mediation center, he described how he continues that work in powerful and new ways, addressing current national issues of civil unrest and injustice as experienced by African Americans in their communities (see Blackwell-Johnson, 1998). Like Tudy-Jackson (2011), several practitioners have built successful careers over the last 25 years by conducting private practices in multiple arenas rooted within and beyond their communities. Although African American entrepreneurs continue to face barriers as they build their business and private practices, this has not stopped their efforts nor their thriving (see Low, 2008; Minefee et al., 2018; Scott, 2016). It is difficult to make a living as a full-time mediator or conflict resolution practitioner. Most mediators volunteer and aren't paid. Some mediators do mediation "on the side" and also combine multiple conflict resolution–related jobs to earn a living such as training, teaching, or consulting. In general, my point is that African Americans have to take on an entrepreneurial mindset to make livable wages, to control their destiny, but even with that, we still face barriers, as the research I've cited here demonstrates. Several practitioners have diverse areas of expertise such as mediator, dialogue facilitator, teacher, and arbitrator, and can traverse those roles when needed. Two practitioners with a combined 93 years of experience in the mediation and arbitration of complex conflict situations including large-scale community conflict and legally complex conflicts are just one example of the powerful practice experience African Americans can bring to bear in their work (see Davis, 2020; Green, 2017; Johnson & LaRue, 2009; Rogers, 2015; Stulberg, 2020).

Representation Matters

Six practitioners discussed the importance of the greater representation of practitioners of African descent in the field. With fewer and fewer people of color becoming involved in the field, there is a "gap that needs to be bridged." A range of experiences contributes to this gap. Sometimes one is "the only Black guy in the room." It is a common experience during court-based mediation for almost all the participants to be African American and for almost all the mediators to be non–African American. One of the practitioners lamented that in court mediations, "race is always there." It is a challenge for him as an attorney to see African American plaintiffs being "strong-armed into decisions" by attorneys representing them. Often, the public who uses mediation, particularly in the court setting, does not expect to see African American practitioners. In a situation that is not uncommon, one practitioner reported she was not recognized as a mediator when working with a white co-mediator; she was assumed to be the notetaker, not a mediator. Underutilization of diverse neutrals has been discussed by Hoffman and Stallworth (2008), who argue that an organization can create an illusion of progress by including people of color on rosters but ultimately not selecting them. Often, those doing the selection are not comfortable with choosing African American practitioners, who may alternatively be assigned all the cases with African Americans. One practitioner expressed uncertainty about whether the practice of assigning only African American cases to African Americans is effective. It has left her wondering whether she is being limited by the assignment of these cases while other mediators are not developing their capacity to work effectively with culturally diverse participants. The issues of representation and appropriate utilization of practitioners speak to a need for culturally responsive (CR) approaches to prepare non–African American practitioners better, and to serve the specific and unique needs of diverse African American communities (see seminal works by Gunning, 1995; Hairston, 1999; Mabry, 1998; Scott, 2003).

Accomplices Not Allies

"Accomplices," as discussed by Wilson (2020), are on the front lines with people of color. They listen and learn from our experiences, engage with us, engage in inquiry by asking what our goals are and what support we need in achieving those goals. Accomplices are not often found in predominately white organizations (see Sherrod, 2020). Several practitioners expressed their concern that those running and working in predominately white institutions continue to engage in willful neglect (see Lowndes & Press, 2016). From the perspective of many of the practitioners in my conversations, there is a need to hold people of European descent in the field accountable for addressing intersectional forms of oppression, particularly in predominantly white organizations. Claiming the value of "neutrality" in the conflict resolution field is viewed as an excuse that hampers any attempts at substantive change (see Wing, 2008). Another common theme for practitioners was experiencing microaggressions—that is, racial slights and insults—constantly. Microaggressions reinforce "white privilege" or "white body supremacy," undermining any attempts at creating and sustaining true inclusion (Manakem, 2017).

Trauma-Informed Practices

Being aware of the importance of trauma in the lives of African Americans, I checked in with my conversation partners about their general well-being, particularly against the backdrop of the COVID-19 pandemic and continued racial violence toward people of African descent. Most practitioners reflected sentiments of internal tumult. "Everything's stirred up." Many of the conversations echoed the tone found in the analogy of being "swallowed whole" by the impact and trauma of the violence (Bridgeford, 2020; First et al., 2020) and the confluence of racism and the pandemic (Lui & Modir, 2020). The police violence against African Americans in this year alone was indeed traumatic. One practitioner's exasperation was apparent when he exclaimed, "I'm tired of wondering why others don't care about racial matters as I do." I could feel the impact of all the racial tumult taking a toll among my conversation partners (Johnson & McGowan, 2017; Konrad, 2018; Waldron, 2020). Expressing further injury, the same practitioner reflected, "All the talk about diversity is an insult," and he characterized all the clamoring for diversity as, "All we're doing is putting a wig on a pig," meaning that it's just an effort to look good and feel good with no real substantive change (Dobbin & Kalev, 2020; Ely & Thomas, 2020). "Black fatigue" was real across most conversations (Winters, 2020) making any type of racial healing seem impossible (Drakulich et al., 2020; Onwuachi-Willig, 2017). I appreciated many of the practitioners' perspectives that they were "not waiting around" for things to get better, but the murders this year and the civil unrest had taken their toll.

The practitioners' perspectives underscore the critical need for relationship building between police and community mediation centers. It would help reduce the need for police intervention and increase the support for mediation as an effective community-based intervention. Antiblack racial trauma is real, and several practitioners spoke directly about this experience and its impact on them. For African American professionals, there is a great need for self-care in the course of their work (see Goens-Bradley, 2020; Mosley et al., 2020; Santana, 2020; Scott, 2003; Waldron, 2020). As in the mental health profession, in conflict resolution we need culturally sensitive and appropriate research, grounded in trauma-informed theory, to build knowledge and sound strategies to mitigate the risk of further racial traumas for marginalized communities (Liu & Modir, 2020).

A New Vision

The desire for "true inclusion" and "beloved community" was an undercurrent in all my conversations. The idea of creating a field with an attitude of abundance was powerfully discussed by practitioners. This sentiment can be found in the writings of Edwards (2020), Harmon-Darrow et al. (2020), and Hooker (2020). I explored with all the practitioners what a new vision for our work would look like. There was general agreement that only sustained work can help turn things around to improve opportunities for African Americans and to make conflict resolution processes more accessible and useful (Minefee et al., 2018; Phelps-Ward & Kenney, 2018/2019; Press, 2011). I felt, as many of the practitioners did, that part of the new vision included a new mindset, one reflected in a practitioner's comment: "It's our problem together, collectively." I valued the idea also shared about "transitional justice"—that is, justice processes designed to create a just, fair, and shared future for all (Edwards, 2020; King, 1964; Lowndes & Press, 2016; Myers, 2008; Phillips, 2009; Roy, 1999). The practitioners who spoke directly to the need to do things differently reminded me that new tools, co-created by people from a diverse spectrum of perspectives, are needed. The way we have been relating to each other, using old tools, will not "dismantle the master's house" that created them in the first place (Lorde, 1984).

Pipelines and Pathways: Professional Development Pathways

In the majority of my conversations, practitioners were concerned about professional development opportunities, what I call "pipelines and pathways." This concern about opportunities is reflected in the available conflict resolution literature. Several researchers discuss the challenges of breaking into the profession of mediation (see Hoffman & Stallworth, 2008; Johnson & LaRue, 2008; Low, 2008). Several practitioners brought these concerns out in their conversations. One characterized her career as "cobbled together," "stumbling" into her work as a mediator. Another practitioner characterized his work as "gig work" (see Ogbolu et al., 2015). Like Low (2008), another worked for a significant time as a volunteer mediator before eventually finding a way to be compensated through placement on a court-connected mediation roster.

Once in established roles, practitioners often experience microaggressions by participants, attorneys, or fellow mediation colleagues (see Green, 2017; Izumi, 2010, 2017). Certification and credentialing of mediators has long been a controversial topic. In two of my conversations, practitioners spoke directly to this issue, agreeing that it was important to have a degree in conflict resolution to give one's skills credibility. This was tied directly to a belief that a degree would ensure that work is valued and compensated. Mentorship is also a key way to build a pipeline into the field as discussed across multiple conversations for this chapter. The power of mentorship should not be underestimated as multiple practitioners spoke to the importance of having support. For example, one practitioner spoke of his initial difficulty locating other African American male practitioners and being rejected by some. One practitioner, with a career spanning over 36 years, had never had the benefit of a mentor. Despite that, he has found a way to excel. For the practitioners I spoke with, sharing resources and lifting up others has been a cornerstone of their experience of abundance. They generously now share with others.

Onward and Upward: A Few Healing Balms

> What we cannot imagine cannot come into being.
>
> —hooks (2001, p. 140)

During 2020, I was heartened to see new books, *More Justice, More Peace* (Terry, 2020) and *Colorizing Restorative Justice* (Valandra & Yazzie, 2020), published. In an ongoing onslaught of racialized violence and terror purposely instigated by the president of the United States at the time, these publications were a temporary healing balm.

It's still hard to answer the question, "What would a 'perfect' conflict resolution field look like?" Amid crippling pain and trauma in 2020, once I picked my heart and mind off the ground and grounded myself, bell hooks, one of my sheroes, called out to me, specifically her book, *All About Love: New Visions.* By returning to a foundation of love, I was able to engage and operationalize my hope. I was reminded of what matters most to me: having an impact and using my gifts, talents, and resources for the highest good of most people. A "perfect" conflict resolution field would be a reflection of a perfect human society where, like in the television series *Star Trek: The Next Generation,* set in the 24th century, we have eradicated most of the ills and structural and systemic oppression. A perfect field of conflict resolution would include: (1) values for access rather than exclusion, (2) practitioners of European descent who are welcoming and know how to work with the differences found among practices of diverse multiethnic groups, (3) using its conflict resolution practices within its community of practitioners and in work with participants out in the world, and (4) building knowledge through lived experiences, co-creating strategies and interventions grounded in self-determination using relational rather than transactional interactions in the delivery of our services.

I would also hope that people all over the world in every community would have access to justice and local community mediation centers. They would work with practitioners who know how to work, collaborate, and co-create processes that are inclusive and effective (Harmon-Darrow et al., 2020) and how to help transform destructive interactional dynamics into constructive dynamics, keeping at the center participants' "voice and choice" (Folger, Bush & Della Noce, 2010). Organizations and businesses would provide conflict management, communication, and "people skills" training so that everyone can build values and skills for "Responding Effectively to Conflict" (Hairston, 2016). This training would encourage everyone to handle conflict productively regardless of their credentials or role in the organization. Those who do this work and espouse values rooted in constructive conflict engagement would be "walking our talk" (Hairston, 2016).

CONCLUSION

> The vision of a world in which all peoples will live together in peace and brotherhood may be far from realization, but it remains the noblest ideal of human existence.—Ralph Bunche

People of African descent living in the United States are a diverse group of individuals with complex, intersectional, and marginalized identities. The continued denial of this fact, a form of "racial gaslighting," cannot continue (see Konrad, 2018). How much more "collective witnessing" of killings is needed, how much more empirical evidence of structural racism is needed to finally accept, "Houston, we have a problem?" Conflict resolution organizations, like all public and private entities, must close the gap in what they say versus what they do to promote access, inclusion, and environments of belonging and safety. I end as I began with the powerful statement from the very first practitioner I interviewed back in late September, who said, "I hope something comes out of these conversations."

I hope that those committed to creating truly inclusive organizations and those in positions of influence step up and learn from the voices of practitioners of African descent in the field and those with whom they work. For me, this means two things: First, to paraphrase the poet and cultural critic Audre Lorde (1984), "using the tools of a racist patriarchy to examine the fruits of that same patriarchy" will permit only the "narrow[est] perimeters of change" and thus we cannot use "the master's tools" to create a new table. If we are to build a new foundation for a new house, we must start with ourselves and our field of conflict resolution (Hairston, 2016). Our work is both a vocation and a "ministry" in service to the highest good for those we serve. We must practice what we preach with each other.

I have sought to amplify the voices of 24 African American practitioners, including my voice, which has been woven throughout this chapter in hopes that the recent crack that has appeared in the consciousness and hearts of so many well-meaning, good-intentioned colleagues of European descent, will create a bigger opening to create new relational connections, taking responsibility for the well-being of all those working in the field. People of African descent no longer want to be invited to the conflict resolution table as an "underrepresented minority." We want to co-create a new table with others committed to walking the talk of our conflict resolution values. And when we fail, we need to try again the next day. We cannot shy away from these "difficult conversations." We have the skills and the heart and mind required. What we need now is for everyone to show up, do their part, and lovingly but uncompromisingly hold each other accountable. We must close the gap "between the values [we] claim to hold and [our] willingness to do the work of connecting thought and action, theory and practice to realize the values and thus create a more just society" (hooks, 2001, p. 90). We just have to get up and do it. We can't wait any longer.

CHAPTER 2

Who Bridges Cultural Chasms?

....

N adine Tafoya's roads traverse the indescribable beauty of the New Mexico desert and mountains. As she travels between the reservation where she lives and the cities where she works, she is also traveling a history of repeated colonizations, displacement, and intolerable economic inequality. The psychic strains she elucidates echo many of the authors' stories in this volume. Note the emotional tenor of her writing. Our authors write in multiple modes: analytic, descriptive, aspirational, autobiographical, and scholarly. But in every piece, feelings ground the story in personal experience, while each author embeds that narrative in renderings of a social landscape of inequality, exclusion, and invisible labor of translation.

—Beth Roy

....

Rage Is *Not* an Option: An Indigenous Woman's Path to Building Resiliency and Advocacy

Nadine Tafoya

I am a Native American woman living in the Southwest, a member of the Mescalero Apache Tribe. I have spent my entire life trying to read between the lines of my daily social interactions. When I enter a meeting room of my colleagues at work, I'm trying to "read" if they're welcoming me with respect and true camaraderie, or if they're oblivious to my very presence, as if I'm invisible, until I make a comment or interact with them first. When I go into a restaurant, I notice if the server glances at me and looks away or if a salesperson in a store shouts out "How are you?" to me or to the person who entered behind me. Even though this type of thing may happen a hundred times a day, week after week, year after year, and I may not consciously be aware of it, my Spirit notices and keeps a running tally.

....

Conversely, I have a real physical reaction when I leave work and head home. My home, located on the reservation, is a refuge to me. I have a sense of comfort when I enter the boundaries of my home. I begin to feel a sense of relief and calm wash over me. Not only is it stressful to navigate the hustle and bustle of the city but it's also full of cues, signs, and images of a place that is not my world. As I leave the urban areas and make my way home to the reservation, I see the beautiful wide-open spaces that mark the entrance into the reservation. I see the markers that engulf me, the Sacred mountains (the Grandmothers) that tell me I'm protected; I see the crosses on one side of the road that mark the places of a funeral procession on its way to someone's final resting place, no doubt a relative of mine. I sense the blanket of the green hillsides that meet me at the entrance of my home. If I pass a fellow driver coming down the narrow dirt road as I'm making my way to my place, I casually nod or wave. I feel like I belong. I feel like I'm part of a larger group. I'm a known piece of this landscape. I am a piece of this vibrant quilt that makes up my community. I know my place and feel comforted. Everything is familiar and reassuring. I share the culture, the language, the ancestors.

This entire place speaks to me, marking my history and revealing the tales of my People's very beginnings.

This is what it's like being a Native person. We carry our history within us. Native people sometimes say we "live in two worlds" simultaneously. I feel like I'm always switching from hearing what the world is saying to me and feeling what I'm hearing. When I'm expressing myself, I'm speaking not only for myself but for my People, both present and past. I honor that lineage of the generations that have passed and those that will come after; as Maya Angelou said, "I speak as one, but I stand with thousands."

It is this perspective that led me into doing the work of an intercultural facilitator-mediator.

As a five-year-old Native American girl, growing up on the Mescalero Apache reservation in the 1950s, I didn't experience the harshness of discrimination, prejudice, and racism until much later when my family moved to the Midwest so my father could complete his degree. Our little four-room farmhouse in Mescalero was no different than any other family living nearby where mainly our extended family and other clan relatives lived. Being part of a homogenous community afforded me a childhood filled with happy memories of playing beside a clear water creek, chasing flocks of chickens in the yard, riding horses, and camping and hiking in the mountainsides, where our house was nestled. We may have been economically "poor," but we were "rich" in having a strong Indigenous cultural foundation, a strong Christian household, and an ethic of being of service to family and community. We were taught to give back and to work hard to improve the well-being of others.

No matter how idyllic I thought my early childhood was, I came from a family that also experienced the tragedy and despair of chronic physical health issues and a myriad of mental health and substance abuse issues. Native Americans in this country experience the highest rates of health disparity issues including diabetes, cancer, heart disease, as the Indian Health Services (IHS), a federal agency, continues to be sorely underfunded and unable to address the needs of its constituents. It has been documented that IHS funding lags far behind that of the Bureau of Prisons, Medicaid/Medicare, and the Veterans Administration. Native people also show dismal numbers and high disparities in other areas. Low grade point averages and high dropout rates in education are often cited; high unemployment, low economic development opportunities, and lack of basic community infrastructure, all add layer upon layer of despair. In all areas, these kinds of disparities reflect Native Americans' poverty, being overlooked and underserved.

My mother and father were part of the "boarding school generation," forcibly removed from their families and their communities and placed in residential Indian schools created in the early 19th century. The purpose of these boarding schools was to assimilate Native people into Western society. Children were sent to boarding schools during their early formative years. Although my parents did not speak about boarding school life, the cruel and demeaning conditions that Native children had to endure have been well documented. The boarding school experiment aimed to strip Native Americans of their culture and to assimilate them into mainstream America. The children were restricted from speaking their Native language, prohibited from practicing their cultural ways, and not allowed to return home until they finished their education. When they eventually returned to the reservation, they had lost their cultural, social, and familial connections to the community. Because of the institutionalization of Native children, generations of Native adults suffered the horrific aftereffects of physical, mental, spiritual, and even sexual abuse. When finally, these individuals returned to the reservations, many suffered depression, suicidal tendencies, fear and anxiety, and chronic substance abuse. A theory known as Historical Trauma recognizes that this legacy of Indigenous people contains all the behavioral and physical features that contribute to poor mental health and intergenerational family dysfunction. There are now hundreds of books and articles describing the harshness and cruelty that took place in these boarding school institutions. The boarding schools are only one part of what Native Americans had to endure to make it to the 21st century.

My first memories of shame caused by being "different" were when I was eight years old in a third grade classroom. We had moved to the Midwest so my father could complete his theology degree and work at an Indian postgraduate institution. We lived in a small rural town that bordered the Indian vocational technical college. As only one of two Native students in my class, I remember the teacher rudely pointing out that I wasn't "clean enough" because I was an American Indian. Although there were other children of color in this mainstream school, I was singled out in my class that day. The teacher pointed his finger at me and asked me in front of the entire classroom if I used soap to wash my face and asked what kind of toothpaste I used. He asked me these questions and other embarrassing questions, and it felt like I was being interrogated; he used a tone that indicated that no matter what answers I gave, the answers would be wrong. The teacher was a middle-aged white man who was also an assistant principal of the school, a man of power and authority.

I go back to that incident because it was one of the first times I felt helpless and ashamed. This memory makes me relive how it feels to lose your voice and lose your power. This is how a narrative begins to be told about you by others. This narrative is then picked up and you begin to believe this to be true about yourself. The first time it happens to you is something never to be forgotten.

In my later years, as a young adult, I learned other narratives and negative stereotypes about Native people, labels such as the "drunken Indian" and beliefs about Natives being pathetic and weak of character. Native people are also deemed to be "relics of the past" and revered as stoic "noble savages." Hollywood, pop culture, antiquated textbooks, and more have created a historical narrative about Native people from a dominant culture perspective. All this has contributed to misinformation about Indigenous people in this country and has caused many Indigenous people to distrust non-Native people, non-Native institutions, and the federal government. When I worked with a New Mexico governmental department, my job was to create an entry for tribes to acquire state grant money for community-based behavioral health services. The tribes were hesitant to work with the state as there were no historical connections with the state. We had to create bridges and work to earn the trust of the tribes. We worked together to create a mutually beneficial outcome.

My experience is not unique among those of Black, Indigenous, or people of color (BIPOC). We have all struggled to be visible to the world around us. We have all strived to be seen and heard. At some point I came to realize that I can't afford to be angry all the time; I can't afford to be voiceless or be just okay with it all. So, it became my life's work to understand the dynamic of who gets to be heard and why, and to develop strategies that allow for people like me to get the same time and space as others. We deserve that much, and the opportunity will not be given or created unless we do it ourselves.

It has been important for me to work for that visibility for tribal voices. Our strategy includes creating processes that upset the status quo and thinking creatively about how best to allow for soft voices, long pauses, and wry humor—just a few of the qualities of Indigenous thought leaders.

As an "intercultural facilitator-mediator" I feel it is my job to set the tone of each session as we get started. I believe that I have been given a "sacred" responsibility to create a safe space for conversation to take place. I acknowledge to the participants that it is my responsibility to create that space, to ensure that all voices get heard, to listen with intent, to reframe issues as needed, and then to get out of the way. I am *not* the expert on every issue; instead, my responsibility is to create a process where various perspectives can be voiced. In addition, I feel that my most sacred obligation is to be cognizant of power dynamics. "Business as usual" is a paradigm ensuring those in power will control the conversation and the process. Some white people, for example, are accustomed to speaking in public forums. They come to the table with their titles, their credentials, and their privilege, and they feel that these characteristics allow them to speak freely and to speak often. The intercultural facilitator-mediator must notice these power dynamics and quickly assess the cultural mix of the group. Cultural nuances may come into play as culture may bump into the power dynamic. For example, some people of color, let's say Native Americans, may find it difficult to speak in a public forum. They may have to process what is being said on multiple levels. Sometimes the spoken word may need to be translated from English into a Native language, then translated back into English. This is happening in the moment, and they are also trying to muster up their response or their position. When a lively discussion is taking place, often the facilitator doesn't allow enough time or allow for silence for someone to respond as needed. Sometimes a person of color or an elder, for instance, needs to hear from someone who looks like them or speaks like them first for them to feel confident enough to voice their concerns. Being aware of this power dynamic, the intercultural facilitator or mediator may start a session by saying, "Today, we're leaving our credentials and titles at the door; today we're here to start a conversation, and we each will have an equal voice." Furthermore, the facilitator can also be explicit in letting the room know that they may be interrupted if they go on too long and that space will always be made for silent voices. In almost all instances, as an intercultural facilitator-mediator, I will always implore people to conduct the conversation with humility and awareness. It is of utmost importance to spend our time together speaking from the heart. I remind them that our time together is precious.

I have learned to be direct, to be deliberate, and to be aware of creating a sacred space for important work to be conducted. People know when the energy and the intent are to honor them and our time together. Indigenous people have gathered in this way since time immemorial and the time is now to revisit the wisdom of the elders.

CHAPTER 3

How Do Organizations Welcome—or Rebuff?

···

heryl Jamison continues themes of social analysis bound together with subjectivity as she recounts her lived experience of exclusion in organizations central to the conflict resolution field. By detailing discriminatory practices in terms of her intangible experiences when entering an institutional space, she offers the reader another compelling picture of the delicacy and ubiquity with which people of color daily traverse racial barriers. Cheryl follows her narrative by enumerating the characteristics of Whiteness that constitute those barriers. We suggest that the reader engage Cheryl's list as embedded cultural practices and assumptions, many of which privilege White people because of their familiarity while also serving people of all identities badly. If the experience of the public sector is lived exclusively within one dominant culture, then white people, lacking any alternative experience, are deprived of a lens through which to understand or protest their own oppression, as well as the oppression of others. They can only consent to conditions that harm all humans, such as alienation born of competitiveness with peers, or those subtle pressures to overwork at the expense of rich interpersonal relationships.

Cheryl assesses inclusiveness through the emotional metric of how it feels to belong and be connected. Like Nadine in Chapter 1, her method of evaluation, and therefore her decisions about where to join and where to avoid participating, are deeply embodied. If Cheryl and Nadine's realities are not yours, I invite you nonetheless to feel along with them, perhaps remembering emotional experiences of your own in other parts of your life. Most of us have somewhere, sometime, felt the discomfort of exclusion, if only from the adult world of decision-makers when we were children, or the first day in a new school. Look at your colleagues, your friends, your clients with widened eyes, imagining what emotional labor they are accomplishing in the course of what for you may be an effortless, normal day. Better yet, learn how you can share the work and welcome them to a new connected reality. (Look at Hasshan Batts's chapter on "Radical Welcome" later in this volume.) Nadine concludes her chapter with specific thoughts about methods for doing just that.

— Beth Roy

···

Achieving Belonging and Connectedness: Conflict Resolution Organizations Reimagined

Cheryl Jamison

> People will forget what you said. They will forget what you did.
> But they will never forget how you made them feel.
>
> —Maya Angelou (2014)

I am a Black female conflict practitioner and as such received numerous requests from individuals and organizations to discuss the subject of diversity or the lack thereof in the conflict resolution field. My personal and professional background provides me with abundant firsthand experience determining if an organization's words about diversity match its action.

Prior to my family moving from Chicago to Three Rivers, Michigan, when I was about nine, my world was made up entirely of Black people. I only saw White people on TV or when we ventured out of our neighborhood to other parts of Chicago. Moving to Three Rivers, a small rural town halfway between Chicago and Detroit, changed my world. In Three Rivers, White people made up most of my environment. I integrated a wide range of places including schools and the accompanying extracurricular activities, churches, social organizations, workplaces, and a 4-H club.

Growing up in a White environment taught me how to navigate this space by being a safe Black girl. I endured microaggressions before I knew they had a name. All was okay until I reached dating age; suddenly prejudice and White privilege took center stage. After several hurtful encounters, I realized I had been tolerated but had never belonged nor truly been connected with people. That realization was one of the most devasting experiences of my life. This and other similar episodes have provided me with ample knowledge about race, bias, White privilege, and White supremacy. I developed an alarm system that starts to respond when I am in danger of being harmed by a racial act.

When I consider whether I am going to get involved with an organization, I do not think about the organization's declared policy in the areas of diversity, equity, and inclusion. These words are the measurements used to determine how well an organization is doing. But they are only words on a page that can never tell the whole story or answer the question of whether the words match the organization's actions. The only way to determine if the words and numbers match the objectives and goals of diversity is through involvement.

For me, as a Black female determining if an organization is where I want to spend my time, it is not about the words diversity, equity, and inclusion; it is about the experience of what I am calling "Belonging and Connectedness."

BELONGING AND CONNECTEDNESS

How do I know if this is an organization where I can belong and be connected? Sadly, I really cannot fully answer that question until a racial incident occurs. It is not that I am surprised when something regarding race happens. History has shown me that in this country, if I am in a predominantly White organization or group, it is going to happen. The question is: what happens next? When the racial act surfaces, are there attempts to excuse or dismiss it? Are there efforts to convince me that I imagined it, that my feelings are not legitimate or that intent outweighs impact? Is there a willingness to have a difficult conversation to examine what happened, how it happened, and how we make a course correction? If the latter fails to happen, I know I never belonged nor was I ever connected.

What do I mean by a racial act? In simple terms, it is any act which a Person of Color believes to be rooted in or shaped by racial prejudice, aggression, lack of awareness, or misinformation. If a Person of Color says it is a racial act, it is a racial act: end of story. In the United States of America, no one is more adept at identifying racial acts than People of Color. I could add to the definition that it is a racial act if it disproportionally impacts People of color. Again, that is a metric and subject to interpretation. People of Color, having experienced both interpersonal and structural racism nearly every day of their lives, can identify when it happens. It is an expertise we have been forced to develop to survive.

I often wonder what an organization that makes me feel like I belong and am connected would look like. What are the elements necessary to maintain belonging and connectedness in an organization? What elements are essential for me to answer this question positively? To explain this more clearly, it is important for me to provide context, to provide a snapshot of what it is like for a Black person navigating a White organization. What follows is a composite of various incidents that have occurred during my involvement in predominately White organizations. In some instances, names have been changed.

AN ICEBREAKER BECOMES AN ICEBERG

An organization I was interested in joining was having a one-day conference. I decided to attend. A friend was going to join me, but she got sick and could not attend. My preference is not to go into these situations alone, and I considered not going. There is a certain amount of vulnerability that comes with a Person of Color attending an unfamiliar White event. There are the usual concerns that one has entering a strange environment with the added layer of race. Structural racism was created 400 years ago with the creation of this country. The conscious development of systems, policies, and laws was designed to give Whites advantages and privileges while denying the same to People of Color. Structural racism was necessary to justify owning humans. Owning humans is no longer legal, but the system designed to justify it is alive and well today.

In the end, I decided to go to the conference without my friend. When I went to the registration table to get the conference materials, I looked around to see if there were other Blacks. Checking this way serves as a quick belonging and connectedness gauge. If there are none, the feeling of isolation deepens. If there are some Blacks or other People of Color, there is promise. I proceeded to the first session, a presentation on restorative justice. For an icebreaker, the presenter asked people to state their name, say where they were from, and the origin of their last name. A look of horror spreads across my face. What does this have to do with the subject? And what am I going to say? I thought about leaving as I heard person after person talk about where their families came from and the origin of their last name. I got angry: why am I being put in this situation? Okay, he wants to know; I will tell him. It is my turn. "My name is Cheryl Jamison. My last name, well my people were enslaved, and I believe my last name is that of the Slave Master." There was an audible gasp in the room, as I looked straight ahead. The presenter was speechless and after a long pause, the workshop continued.

Answering the question brought little satisfaction. If I could have turned red, I would have been as red as a tomato. My mind was flooded with numerous times when racism had reared its ugly head, where I had to fight back a feeling of resentment, to restrain myself from acting or saying something that portrayed me as the Angry Black Female. Since there is nothing to do with those feelings, I went on.

What might have happened differently in a belonging and connected environment?

Option 1: Do not ask the question. Since the question has no relationship to the workshop content, simply omit the question. Oftentimes, workshop presenters and facilitators will ask a question that we believe is fun or interesting or both without regard for the impact the question could have on people in the audience. If there is no way to connect it to the content of the workshop, it might be advisable to leave it for another situation.

Option 2: If you really want to ask the question, since you do not know the background of those attending, at least provide a way for people to gracefully decline to answer. There may be many reasons why a person would prefer not to answer the question and not to deviate from the exercise. In your instructions, provide a way to pass. In the workshop I attended, the presenter could have acknowledged that there may be many reasons why a person might not be able to trace their history back far enough to answer the question, so it is okay to pass. You could also provide an alternative question.

The point is in an environment that is about belonging and connectedness, sensitivity is required. Giving thought to how could a question, process, or procedure affects a person's sense of belonging and connectedness is a constant.

AN INVITATION TO GET INVOLVED, SORT OF

Even though the icebreaker experience left me feeling like an outsider, because I was a Black practitioner seeking to hone my craft, I decided to join the organization. After reviewing the mission, I thought the diversity statement was not great, but I believed there might be hope. The next meeting I attended was a general members meeting. Several Black women, an Asian man, and I were talking at the refreshment table when a White man approached us and introduced himself as Mark, chair of the Program Committee. He invited us to join the committee and help develop some diversity training. After some additional conversation, the meeting started, and we went to our seats. Once the meeting ended, I told Mark I would join the committee.

Involving new members quickly is a good start to developing a belonging and connectedness atmosphere. Too often new members are left on their own to find a place to get involved. But frequently, when joining a predominately White organization, marginalized people are invited to get involved in the diversity areas. This does not happen with new White members. It is as if the diversity areas are the only areas where the knowledge, skills, and expertise of Black and Brown people can be used. This is the "sort of" mentioned earlier. I often wonder what would have happened if someone had asked Mark what other areas the Program Committee handles? Or if someone had said, I am not interested in the diversity area? A better approach would have been for Mark to invite the new members to join the Program Committee and let us determine our area of interest and involvement.

MICROAGGRESSION 101

As a member of the committee, I worked with a White male and together developed diversity workshops. As we conducted the workshops in the state and around the country, we noticed something: after the sessions, when people came up to continue the discussion, they would more frequently discuss the substance with my White male colleague than with me. When people did discuss the workshop with me, at least one or two would comment on how "well spoken you are." They marveled that I was so "articulate." Most times I smiled and said nothing. On a few occasions, I did respond with a statement like, "Thank you; going to law school helped." The whole experience left me weary and wondering, what needs to happen to change the narrative, and how long will it take for that to happen?

When people realize they inflicted these microaggressions in ways like this, they need to recognize the impact they have had, acknowledge it, apologize for it, and work on correcting the behavior—actions that are a broad stroke in creating a landscape and environment of belonging and connectedness.

As I mentioned earlier, one of the organizations I integrated was a 4-H club. Thankfully, they were not a typical club with members taking care of animals. We were involved in cooking, sewing, and public speaking. Starting in junior high, I had the opportunity to participate in multiple public speaking contests where I prepared and delivered speeches to White audiences and judges. I learned that if I wanted to win, I needed to talk White. Overall, my English was good; however, there were times the judges' critique would indicate that a word was pronounced differently or that I used a term that was less familiar to them. One time I was told by a White judge that my tone was a bit too cultural, which I interpreted to mean too Black. I made the changes and once I sounded more "White," I began winning local and state public speaking contests.

I am not unique. A lot of Black folks are bilingual with the ability to speak White or American English and Ebonics. At its most literal level, Ebonics simply means "black speech" (a blend of the words ebony "black" and phonics "sounds"). When Whites are surprised that Blacks are articulate, they are reinforcing the stereotype that the educational system for all Blacks is substandard, or no matter the education, that Blacks are not capable of learning and speaking the King's English. Generally, when faced with this microaggression, I swallow hard, resisting the urge, to prove my linguistic ability, smile, and say thank you.

INTENT VERSUS IMPACT

I was part of a team working on a program for developing convenors among leaders in business, education, politics, health care, and religion. The program included multiday workshops; one of my responsibilities was managing the logistical requirements of the workshop. One year, on the final day we invited a colleague to attend to take pictures of the group. The final session for the workshop involved the members of the team facilitating a short session with groups of participants. Each team member was supposed to be assigned a group. As participants were provided instructions and moved to their various groups, I realized that I had not been assigned a group. Instead, the individual asked to take photographs had been assigned a group to facilitate. People moved to their assigned rooms, and I was left in the general meeting room, dumbfounded. I could not understand why I was not assigned a group. Yes, I was the only Black person on the team.

I thought about packing up and leaving before people got back. Instead, I called a friend familiar with the project and vented. I stayed until the end and participated in a debriefing session in which team members discussed what happened in their respective groups. When it came to me, I said I was not assigned a group. People were surprised and when the organizer, Doris, was asked why, she gave some explanation. But honestly, I did not hear it. I just wanted to get out of there.

This incident happened on Friday, and by Monday morning I decided a conversation was in order. After calling Doris to make sure she was in the office, I went to see her. We greeted each other. I asked her to help me understand why she decided not to assign me a group to facilitate. Her response was that, since I had handled all the logistics, she thought she would give me a break. Her intent was apparently to give me a moment to relax. It was not something bad, not evil.

I explained to her the negative impact her intentions had on me. I described thinking she must not believe me to be capable of providing high-quality facilitation. I was more than capable of providing the labor necessary to secure a room, some food, and flip charts, but when it came to delivering the skills of an experienced facilitator, not so much. I was left wondering what I must do to prove that I am a highly skilled facilitator who is more than capable of facilitating a discussion with this group. Doris immediately apologized indicating she never thought about how it would look or how I would view her actions. She thanked me for taking the time and energy to have a conversation.

This productive conversation was possible because we had participated in several conversations, workshops, and role-plays related to race. There was a common foundation of "belonging" upon which to build. Too often when a person of color points out a race-related act, the response is one proclaiming positive intentions and stopping there. The White person is adamant that a good intent erases any negative impact. But it does not! White privilege means "my intentions get first billing." In an organization where belonging and connectedness are at the core, the negative impact is considered first.

TO CONFRONT OR NOT TO CONFRONT

In these situations, I have to decide whether to identify the instance to the White person or to internalize it and say nothing. The decision not to confront a racist act is not without cost. No matter the decision, to confront or not to confront, there is a cost. Emotions range from embarrassment, irritation, frustration, and alienation to rage. I'm confronted with the recognition that racism is alive and well, and also know that if I speak up, the response is unknown. What are the repercussions of confronting racism? Is the price too high? Am I tired and just do not want to deal with it? These are just some of the questions I ask before confronting a racial act. If an affected person does not feel a sense that they will be heard and respected, it is more likely they will walk away and not confront the issue. If the marginalized person does confront the act in a disrespectful environment, it is dismissed as the ravings of an angry person.

BLACK LEADERSHIP AND THE NEW LIABILITIES

During my time with one organization, I became a member of the Board of Directors and was on the Finance Committee. Like most nonprofits, the Finance Committee focused on how to increase revenue and keep expenses down. I soon become co-chair of the Finance Committee, which was chaired by the treasurer, who happened to be a Black man. It was decided that at the next membership meeting, I would discuss the financial situation with the membership. After my presentation, which included little financial jargon, a member of the committee approached me and said he was concerned because he felt I lacked the understanding of basic financial concepts necessary to be co-chair of the Finance Committee. It was as if I had been punched in the stomach. I could not catch my breath. I was disgusted, coupled with a deep feeling of once again, being an outsider.

A report was subsequently prepared by a subcommittee of the Finance Committee. Their charge was to look for funding options. The report stated that should the organization dissolve it would be the fault of the Black chairs of the Finance Committee. In their minds, the board, the committee, previous treasurers, and the history of poor financial decisions would be absolved of all and any liability. In reviewing past documentation, I found nothing placing this burden on any other leader. When the matter was brought to the attention of the board as an issue of race, all manner of excuses were made. One of the signatories to the letter said he could not imagine what would make me think "this was about race." Some of the board said it was not race, but "maybe gender," the more suitable discriminatory practice. However, there were two White men, and one White woman on the subcommittee making the report. It was not about gender, it was about race and much of the board did not want to have this difficult conversation. There was no other place to take the matter for further discussion or resolution, so it ended there.

If there had been belonging and connectedness this report would not have been written. If it had been written and attempts to discuss the matter did not result in a resolution or better understanding, there would have been another step or avenue available to resolve the matter. Once the call with the board ended, that was the end. Marginalized persons in a White organization are often left with no recourse, no place to take a complaint when it happens. It would have been helpful in this situation if an outside source could have been tapped to provide a means to reach a better resolution. I was left with an open wound that never really healed.

TALKING ABOUT RACE WILL COST MEMBERS

In 2014 I was president of the Association for Conflict Resolution (ACR). During 2014, Michael Brown was killed by police, initiating the Ferguson, Missouri, riots. I wrote a President's Message titled, "Black Lives Do Matter." In the article I asked, what is our responsibility as conflict practitioners? How do we help our communities? I did get supportive emails, but then I also received emails saying that this was not an appropriate subject for a president of a conflict resolution organization. Others said that practitioners had to be careful that they did not damage their ability to get paid in the future. Still, others expressed concern about losing members.

Then I announced that Tim Wise, antiracist writer and educator, would be the keynote speaker at ACR's 2014 Annual Conference. I was told by some that he was not appropriate nor was the topic, that he was divisive and people would never attend. In the past, the ability to select the conference keynote rested with the president. They could either make the selection or delegate that responsibility to the Conference Committee. Now, suddenly that "perk" did not rest with the president. Was this all motivated by racism? My answer is an unequivocal yes. In this case a Black president had selected a White antiracist as a keynote speaker. From my vantage point, I am sure there was a problem with the person making the selection, the person selected, and the message the person was going to deliver, all of which included race. In the end, Tim Wise spoke to an appreciative, standing-room-only crowd.

There are multiple reasons people do not want to invest time in antiracism education and dialogue. There is the notion that if we do not talk about racism, it does not exist. It is impossible to move toward racial justice if we cannot acknowledge and honestly discuss the extent of the problem. If not talking about racism would make it go away, *let there be silence*. But failure to discuss racism does not mean it does not exist or that it will magically disappear. What problem do you know that evaporates once ignored? Professor and author Ibram X. Kendi likens this to having cancer. Because it is painful and difficult, refusing to talk about it or get treatment does not make the cancer disappear. And make no mistake, America has been infected with cancer from the beginning. It is a racial cancer that has metastasized, affecting every organ. There has been no remission. It is deadly, killing millions of People of Color. Not talking about it has not stopped the spread of this cancer. It has only been by constant examination and dialogue that there has been any hope of dismantling racism. If an organization is not willing to have continuing education and discussion about race, it probably is not interested in truly developing an environment of belonging and connectedness for People of Color.

YOU MIGHT BE THE BEST PERSON; IS THERE ANYONE ELSE?

There came a point when I applied for a position with a nonprofit. I was not a stranger to this organization or the members of the board. After the interview process, the job was offered to someone else. As it happened, the person resigned after 90 days. Since there had been a national search, it was recommended to offer the job to the candidate who came in second. That was me. Some board members wanted to do another search. Others want to consider the next five candidates. As I understand it, there were no concrete objections to me; they just seemed to want someone else, anybody else.

After a couple of months of discussion, an ally called it out. The atmosphere is vastly different when a White person calls out a racist act. White to White, privilege to privilege. It is hard to dismiss as the ravings of an angry Black woman. As the discussions were described to me, the first and loudest response was, "How dare you call me racist." Others chimed in with similar statements. Quickly, the original issue got lost as people tried to assure themselves they were not racist. They had not been called racist—at least not yet. In most instances, People of Color are slow to use the r-word—racist. We understand the impact of that word. Once it is out, there is no going back. But even when we do not say the word, it has the same effect.

Once I was in a discussion in which a racial incident had taken place. A practitioner in the conversation reframed my comments to, "So you think she is a racist." I said that was a horrible reframe and did not accurately reflect my comments. It did not matter: all the person heard was my calling her a racist. One other thing: when a Person of Color does call someone a racist, there is generally no question about it. It is extremely clear.

Getting back to the discussion by the Board of Directors regarding the vacancy, I am grateful that allies did not lose sight of the original discussion and the decision before the board. Eventually, I was offered the job and I accepted. Months later there was a conversation; however, it did not include those who had the biggest objection to my getting the job. Once again, an opportunity to discuss race, implicit bias, and the impact on organizational decision-making was lost. The bigger question is why there was no process in place to handle a complaint of this nature.

ELEMENTS FOR CREATING AND MAINTAINING BELONGING AND CONNECTEDNESS

As a Black female conflict resolution practitioner and based on my many experiences, here is what I have concluded thus far. Creating an organization with an environment that is all-inclusive in all its spaces means having a system of creating and maintaining Belonging and Connectedness. Here are six elements that are critical in establishing such an organization.

1. Courage to Create a Belonging and Connectedness Environment
2. Concise and Measurable Belonging and Connectedness Goals and Objectives

3. Commitment to a Belonging and Connectedness Plan
4. Complete Involvement in the Belonging and Connectedness Plan
5. Constant Race and Antiracist Education and Dialogue
6. Conflict Resolution Processes When Belonging and Connectedness Encounter a Problem

Courage to Create an Environment of Belonging and Connectedness

> You cannot swim for new horizons until you have courage to lose sight of the shore.
>
> —William Faulkner (1929/2015)

It will take courage for an organization in the United States to face the structural racism built within its normative diversity, equity, and inclusion attempts. This new horizon of belonging and connectedness will require recognition of privilege and opportunity not voluntarily afforded to marginalized members. If there is going to be change within an organization, it will require the leadership and its members to:

A. Acknowledge and accept that being White in this country means that you have privileges that Black and Brown people do not enjoy.
B. Scrutinize and identify internal organizational systems and policies that benefit White members to the detriment of historically marginalized members.
C. Commit to learning and being responsible for your own racial education and not solely depend upon People of Color to explain racial behavior, culture, and history.
D. Be prepared to have frequent difficult conversations about race and related issues without making excuses, denials, being dismissive, or acting as the victim.

Concise and Measurable Belonging and Connectedness Goals and Objectives

> You cannot manage what you cannot measure.
> —Bill Hewlett (2012)

The results of examining the organization and individuals should include developing concise and measurable goals and objectives. Designed to gauge and quantify belonging and connectedness within the organization, the metrics must be attainable and measurable so that progress, completion, or lack of completion, can be determined. There must be a timeline and a person responsible for completing the goals. This is not the place for aspirational goals. Eradicating racism is admirable; however, it is highly unlikely that the organization can accomplish it. This is where most organizations fail. Most diversity plans include a lot of aspirational language that feels good but either cannot be measured or accomplished.

Commitment to a Belonging and Connectedness Plan

> You cannot conquer what you are not committed to.
>
> —T. D. Jakes (2016)

Once the plan is developed, there must be a commitment to follow the plan. A well-meaning organization spends resources, time, and often money to develop a great plan only to put it on the shelf. The goals are aspirational, there is no timeline and no person or committee assigned to the tasks included in the plan. When another project or "emergency" surfaces, this plan moves to the back burner and eventually off the stove. When the next race-related issue comes up, either within the organization, nationally or globally, if anyone remembers and can find the first plan, it is revisited. If it cannot be found, another plan is developed, and the cycle is repeated. In the same way that organizations are rigorous about tracking finances, meticulous in recording minutes and tracking membership numbers to determine if operational goals and objectives are met, this same commitment and attention must be given to a Belonging and Connectedness Plan.

Complete Involvement in the Belonging and Connectedness Plan

> If you are neutral in situations of injustice, you have chosen the side of the oppressor.
>
> — Desmond Tutu (2017)

Once a Belonging and Connectedness Plan has been created, all White members have a responsibility to be involved in its implementation. I know this might come as a surprise to some because too often People of Color have been burdened with the responsibility for developing and implementing the plan. In too many cases, education and dialogue in this area are left to the marginalized members—as if we can make a difference. If People of Color could dismantle systems of racial oppression, we would have done it long ago. It will take those who benefit from the system to destroy it.

One role that every White member can play is that of ally. White people can be allies to People of Color in and outside of the organization. When most people think of being an ally, they think of coming to the rescue of the marginalized individual, a kind of superhero or heroine mentality. Certainly, there are times when a word or action from a White individual greatly improves the situation. When these one-and-done situations occur, it is important for White members ideally step up and step in.

Beyond particular interventions by White allies, what is also needed are ally relationships. While I was working at the Maryland Mediation and Conflict Resolution Office, I had the opportunity to develop and deliver numerous workshops on various aspects of race with Lou Gieszl, then Deputy Director. One topic was ally relationships. After hours of discussion and having developed an organic ally relationship, we created this definition for ally:

Natural and holistic, mutually supportive and beneficial, connections among people with different dimensions of diversity.

Notice that it is not one-dimensional, it is a relationship that benefits both parties. It provides a safe space for honest discussions about race. Yes, there were times when Lou interrupted racial situations directed at me and others. Our allied relationship provided a sounding board for both of us to check in about our behavior, to talk about race-related materials as well as vent safely. This was a space that continues to afford both of us support in our antiracist endeavors. Lou is not a White savior; he is an allied partner. One-and-done incidents are going to happen in which a White person not well known to a Person of Color can be the ally, and these interventions are important. White members should be ready to step up. Complete involvement in the Belonging and Connectedness Plan requires both types of ally relationships.

Constant Race (Antiracist) Education and Dialogue

> No one is born hating another person because of the color of
> his skin, or his background, or his religion. People must learn
> to hate, and if they can learn to hate, they can be taught to love.
>
> —Nelson Mandela (2014)

Once an organization has the courage and the commitment to create an organization in which People of Color belong and are connected, there must be constant race or antiracist education and dialogue. Please notice the word "constant" as in never-ending. Participation by everyone is essential. In too many cases, education and dialogue in this area are left to the marginalized members, and little to no work is expected of White individuals. This bias is dehumanizing and exhausting. People of Color are expected to take the leadership role in race education and dialogue while having little to no voice in other areas of the organization. Let me take the liberty of speaking for all People of Color: we are tired of being the *primary* racial educator for White people.

Antiracist education can come in various forms, from informal conversations to workshops, podcasts, and written materials. In my example of working out a painful experience with my colleague Doris, the reason the conversation regarding the race-related incident was productive was because we had both participated in a series of antiracist education and dialogue events.

Conflict Resolution Processes

> Not everything that is faced can be changed; but nothing can be changed until it is faced.
>
> —James Baldwin (private comment, 1968)

Earlier, I said that the way I knew if I belonged and was connected to an organization was how the group acted when that racial thing happened. Unfortunately, it is my repeated experience that incidents are mostly handled poorly. Typically, there are no processes, or no processes trusted by People of Color. Once there is an acknowledgment that negative acts based on race are going to happen, the next logical step is to put in place a system for dealing honestly, respectfully, and responsively with what has happened. More People of Color have withdrawn their participation and left an organization because a racial act happened and there was no way to seek resolution; there was not even an avenue for discussion to take place. The system could be multilevel providing both an internal and an external process.

You might be thinking that if a Person of Color decides to stay or go based on how racial incidents are resolved, why isn't developing a conflict process enough? The reason all six components are necessary is that the first five components aid in establishing and maintaining a foundation allowing a conflict process that is respectful, void of excuses, rationalization, and misplaced victimization.

CONCLUSION

I played the clarinet for 12 years, from the fifth grade through my undergraduate program. I was a member of a marching band, an orchestra, and several ensembles. It was at times fun, tedious, frustrating, and exhilarating. The high school orchestra had won many awards at the state level, and there was enormous pressure to continue that winning tradition. I was so nervous at my first concert that our conductor assured me it meant I wanted to do a good job. This is one of the few times I have been a part of a White organization and race was not an issue for me or the organization. From the beginning, the focus was on how well I could play the right note, at the right tempo, and at the right time. What mattered was my ability to play the clarinet. This is my vision of a conflict resolution organization reimagined.

An orchestra is an interesting organization. A full orchestra can have as many as 100 musicians divided into four sections each with different instruments. When a composer writes a piece for an orchestra, they write to the strength of each instrument. Appreciating, for example, the brass section is good at fast and repeating rhythms or that flutes can produce a sound as quiet as a whisper, the composition makes use of the vast dynamic range of the instruments. No instrument is better than another: different yes, but no better. Each instrument is respected for the unique contribution needed to produce a wonderful, harmonious orchestral sound. This is belonging and connectedness in action. This is my vision of a conflict resolution organization reimagined.

CHAPTER 4

How Do Institutions Maintain Dominance (Despite Their Best Intentions)?

· ·

R oberto Chené takes the reader further into the domain of institutions. Reporting from his decades of work with nonprofit organizations, Roberto teases out the invisible power dynamics that inhibit true equity among colleagues. Applied to many of the agencies delivering services in the conflict and other professions, this analysis offers crucial lessons in how to attain true collaboration across differences. Roberto's example addresses a realm of conditioned silence in most professions: relations between practitioners and funders. His work with foundations over many years has allowed him to witness up close and with respect how "normal" operating assumptions interfere with true collaboration, however genuine the intention of funders to engender the opposite. Roberto's case study of a major foundation doing work in New Mexico offers crucial insights into ways of sharing power, and even more, lessons in how to "learn on the job" as we all struggle to know what none of us yet knows about how to work multiculturally.

—Beth Roy

· ·

The Method *Is* the Message: Shifting the Conflict Transformation Paradigm, Sharing Power

Roberto Chené

At some point over very many years of teaching and training in intercultural leadership and conflict resolution, I decided that I especially enjoyed working with organizations and coalitions whose participants were already committed to diversity and inclusion, to being allies, to eliminating racism and other forms of institutional exclusion and discrimination. Much of the reflection and analysis in this chapter is based on my work with already-committed organizations. Organizations that make a serious effort to integrate the knowledge required to dismantle oppression and frame that knowledge into their practice and relationships with each other are a key source of the knowledge we all need if we are indeed ever going to create an equitable society. The wealth of knowledge that we need lies not only in the successes of such organizations but, perhaps more significantly, in their setbacks and their conflicts.

Despite their commitment, personal growth, and best efforts, I find that such organizations can commonly fall into serious conflict by replicating to some degree the systemic inequities they have committed themselves to eliminate. Such a contradiction is not a failure if one understands that it is virtually impossible in our current social structure not to get caught in that contradiction.

Eliminating systemic exclusion is always about lifelong learning, and the expected conflicts can be seen as feedback that guides us in our next step toward actual transformation, pointing the way out of the oppressive structures in which we all find ourselves. The rise of conflict in the type of organization I've described is an integral part of the transformation process toward equity. It is the unfortunate reality that we tend to discover our biases, both personal and institutional, by offending others, which of course causes conflict. In this era of the Black Lives Matter movement in which I am writing, we need to be urgently aware that the "normal" institutions we have at our disposal are most likely inadequate for the work of creating racial equity and are often not up to the task of supporting the needed relationship building that transformative change requires. To get beyond normal we have to learn to embrace conflict creatively, because that conflict is the feedback that has within it the information that guides our work of transformation. The expectation of conflict and the ability to manage it as we work for inclusion and equity need to be included in the list of competencies that are required of anyone working for change. Diversity work is ultimately conflict resolution work. In a dysfunctional system like ours that is stratified in a dominant subordinate frame around our differences, we need to realize that we have in effect institutionalized and internalized conflict between us as a condition of living together. Why are we surprised when this often latent conflict becomes explicit? The current erosion of social norms has made the conflict less and less latent.

It is a contradiction that eliminating racism initiatives tend to be implemented in the context of existing institutional models and thus can and do fall victim to the inertia of the existing bureaucracy of which they are a part. The whole thing is a potential setup for possible failure because the very institutional structure combined with already established policies, as a rule created by white people (men) for white people, are still in place and sooner or later can force the institution back to "normal"—that is, to practices that remain systemically racist and exclusionary. I find that diversity or so-called inclusion in a normal institution results in a form of racial, gender, or ethnic mixture that is labeled diversity but does nothing to change the power dynamics or contribute to the re-creation of policy. Without an intentional and repeatedly prioritized effort to transform relationships so that they are rooted in equality rather than dominant, subordinate frames, so that the strength of those empowered relationships can collaboratively re-create policy, there is little possibility that a commitment to actual inclusion will take root and flourish in the long term. If an organization is committed to racial equity, the very intention of that commitment is both indispensable in eventually achieving the desired outcome and also problematic in that the commitment sets up an expectation and potential conflict, that, if not fully anticipated, or facilitated can undermine the effort to eventually achieve equity.

RECONCILING EXPECTATIONS AND PRACTICE

I have worked with many institutions and foundations, one of which is the W.K. Kellogg Foundation. The foundation is one of those organizations I mentioned earlier that I like to work with. Kellogg has a long track record of validating and practicing diversity and using its resources to work for inclusion and systemic change in the United States and around the world. The foundation is committed to the welfare of vulnerable families and children and has prioritized its resources in that direction. Since the 1990s I have personally benefited from a long and enriching association.

The Kellogg Foundation is a leader among foundations in developing an intentional, deeply researched antiracist approach to structural and behavioral change. The work of the foundation is framed around a concept they've named Truth, Racial Healing, and Transformation. The foundation is committed to creating an infrastructure for racial healing in the United States and beyond, and to partnering with those who share that commitment. In the list of foundations from outside the state of New Mexico, the Kellogg Foundation is the largest funder in the state. The beneficial impact of the foundation's work over many years cannot be overstated.

The work of the Kellogg Foundation in New Mexico provides, I believe, a good example of the challenges inherent in the implementation of a racially equitable and healing paradigm of institutional practice in an environment victimized by systemic racism and a long legacy of multiple colonizations. The obstacles and pitfalls are inherent in race equity work, no matter how prepared any organization or person tries to be. The challenge is to have our expectations conform with the reality of implementation.

In 2011 I was hired as a consultant to support the foundation in a renewed engagement with New Mexico. As a consultant, I was asked to interview grantees who were part of an early childhood cohort who had been working with Kellogg over a long period. The foundation wanted some insight into what grantees thought of Kellogg's ongoing efforts to support services for vulnerable children and families and, importantly, how grantees perceived the foundation's proposed approach to use a racial equity lens to focus programming on vulnerable children and families, namely Native Americans, Hispanics, African Americans, Asian Americans, and others.

After my initial role as a consultant in 2011, I was invited to be a coach-mentor in the foundation's Community Leadership Network Fellowship Program from 2014 to 2017. The fellowship was a major financial investment as well as a major success in developing a cohort of 20 diverse leaders who continue to contribute their talents to critical issues in the state. The curriculum for leadership was constructed and implemented through a racial equity lens.

Through the three years of the fellowship, I was in continual dialogue with other coach-mentors, leadership fellows, and Kellogg colleagues as we worked to implement leadership development while doing our best to understand what racial equity meant in practice. I had the luxury of being able to reflect on my coach-mentor role in the supportive context of like-minded colleagues. I was able to draw on my years of experience in intercultural leadership training and my practice in conflict resolution in a conflict transformation frame.

This chapter is a retrospective analysis that allows me to try to determine from my current vantage point what went well and what could have been more effective, going back to my initial consultancy in 2011 and the implementation initiative of the fellowship from 2014 to 2017. I am interested in what we learned through our honest and often frustrating efforts in the realm of racial equity and racial healing. As I've said earlier, we all share the constraints of being trapped in a dysfunctional system, and we need tools and perspectives to help liberate us from our constraints. We are caught in what Paulo Freire would call praxis, whereby as learners, we reflect on our experience for the sake of our transformation.

When I work with an organization on inclusion and diversity issues, I start with the successes but look forward to the areas of conflict because, as I said earlier, it is within that realm that one finds out where to create the next potential success. We all fall short in the implementation of racial equity because the task is enormous, and we are still developing the knowledge base, the skill set, and above all, the political will in our society to even admit the nature and depth of the structural inequity that we have.

INTERVIEWS

The interviews revealed the depth, complexity, and challenges faced by any organization which attempts to implement a race equity approach to community and structural change. Grantees by and large were very supportive of the race equity approach but expressed confusion about what the concept means and more importantly, what it means in practice to be following a race equity model. Many of the grantees had struggled for years with countless institutional barriers in their attempt to get services for children and families generally and children of color in particular. New Mexico is a relationship-based state; many said they believe the cornerstone of their work and those who support it must be based on mutual interaction and trust-building. Those who have been struggling for years need to be involved based on shared implementation and shared knowledge. Given the frame of race equity, this expectation of *working with* versus *working for* was very high among the grantees. They expected they would be seen as equal partners with the foundation. For years, they had experienced isolated and painful struggles. Feeling that they had been pushing against racism all along, they knew something about what kind of support they needed as well as the depth of that need. The isolation was compounded by scarce resources. Their reaction upon hearing of a race equity approach might be characterized as a skeptical, "Do you really mean it?"

Grantees were effusive in appreciating Kellogg's historical role in supporting early childhood development and were very admiring of the foundation's boldness in asserting a race equity approach in their next phase of funding. They felt nevertheless that the foundation needed to communicate more clearly and explicitly about what they meant by a race equity approach and describe in detail what they had learned or were learning about how to put the approach into practice. They also expected that there would be an explanation of how the foundation's experience with race equity would affect implementation in New Mexico and just how the foundation would approach structural change.

Many grantees wanted to have a deeper understanding of Kellogg's vision of the foundation's work in the state overall, asking for a transparent description of their sense of the big picture and what types of projects were being funded. Respondents expected Kellogg to take initiative in connecting the dots of the whole picture of their role in New Mexico, thus fostering a general knowledge of how all the pieces fit together in their systemic change efforts in the state. But many respondents felt that Kellogg had not been responsive or transparent about just how they were going about their funding work in the state. This transparency, combined with an articulation of how the funding would affect structural change, is required for building mutual trust. Respondents sought some assurance that, in the guise of providing social services, the funder would not inadvertently fund an organization that might be considered a colonizing agency. Navigating the complexities of this minefield in a colonized state requires deep dialogue. Without enough collaboration, conflicts can quickly emerge.

For example, there is a common understanding among community activists and leaders that the legacy of racism and cultural invalidation has anchored the perception that locals, especially those of color, are not as competent as those from outside the state with similar credentials. This perception that outside is better is validated when major institutions like the education department, state government, or the University of New Mexico are quick to initiate national searches for top administrators, when many in the community know full well that there are more than qualified local individuals with the right credentials and the necessary awareness of racial, ethnic, and political dynamics. The slap in the face, as many see it, is compounded when the outsider is a white person who may have the right credentials but is otherwise unqualified and unprepared to navigate our local cultural realities.

Fairly early on in the implementation process, Kellogg hired an antiracism training organization based on the East Coast to come and help establish the groundwork for their race equity approach. This decision undermined for many local leaders their confidence in the foundation's race equity model and reinforced their skepticism about the credibility of their race equity approach. The action also reinforced the perception that, despite the rhetoric of partnership, the reality was one of working for rather than with. Local practitioners of antiracism training wondered why they were not consulted and the money for this work didn't go to local trainers who already knew the social context? The agency that was hired was multicultural and knew their material but needed consultation to apply their knowledge in the local reality. This dynamic felt "colonizing in the name of racial equity" to many in the community even though the work was about undoing racism and racial healing. The incident necessitated conflict resolution among community leaders.

Reasons for skepticism were understandable. I've noticed over the years that dominant culture agencies or institutions with an intention to become more diverse often practice "recruit and abandon." Even when the intent to be more inclusive is genuine and idealistically motivated, an organization may fail to take into account the reality that those entering the organization are likely to encounter implicit or overt bias. They may also encounter an organizational culture that is totally at odds with their cultural reality. They may encounter the usually unstated assumption that they are expected to assimilate to white cultural norms, ensuring that the work of fitting into their new environment falls disproportionally on their shoulders. Even if they are successful in fitting in, the effort can be exhausting, especially if their efforts are not reciprocated. The unwelcoming culture of the host organization then results in a form of abandonment. The abandonment of those joining the organization need not be intentional; it can happen by default. When an organization declares that it believes in diversity, those who are "diverse" will often take that statement seriously and expect that the inclusion effort will be based on competent practices. It's very hurtful when one realizes that that is not the case.

Having experienced versions of "recruit and abandon" repeatedly in many different settings, grantees found it hard to believe that the foundation meant what it said. Nonetheless, by and large, they put aside their skepticism and engaged in the working relationship. Grantees understood that the challenge for such a relationship is in the implementation, and that remained to be seen.

Ultimately, given the frame of racial equity, the grantees had an expectation that the partnership offered would be coequal in particular respects. Not unaware that the mere fact that a funder by definition holds certain powers, the grantees nevertheless expected to be taken seriously for their expertise, to make collaborative decisions about what to fund or not fund in the state. They had accumulated much experience and knowledge from navigating touchy political issues related to being a multicultural state beleaguered by a legacy of multiple colonizations. The grantees lived with serious consequences such as educational disparities and chronic poverty levels disproportionately affecting people of color.

Above all, grantees were asking the foundation representatives to speak with depth and clarity about their journey in implementing racial equity within Kellogg, their organization. What have they learned, what mistakes have they made, how far do they yet have to go, and how does what they have learned influence how they are conceptualizing their work with grantees in the state? To my knowledge, this level of transparency and self-introspection was not part of the initial relationship-building engagement. Self-disclosure clearly communicated is a very important initial step in the launching of a racial equity-based approach to community change. When there is a disparity of power in a relationship, and there is an honest effort to bridge that power difference, it falls to the side with the most power to tell its story of introspection, accountability, and humility. At the personal level, this transparency is manifested by such statements as, "These are my prejudices, and this is what I'm doing about them." In the real world, people who are the target of bias don't expect to hear that it's been eliminated. They want to know that one is self-aware and proactively making progress toward transformation. Self-aware disclosure is a key ingredient in establishing that a person is credible when they say they want equity, racial or otherwise.

An aspect of the white colonization in New Mexico is that people of color are asked to tell their stories of who they are. It comes across as a "What are *you* doing here?" issue in today's political climate. The dominant white system does not feel that it has to reciprocate by telling its story since it is into that system that others are expected to assimilate. This is the context in which the grantees were asking for transparency. Given the question, "Are we working with or are we working for?" people looked for the institution to say, "We are here to reframe our relationship with you in collaboration, and we are proposing that our collaborative partnership be guided by the tenets and working assumptions of racial equity and healing." This is what we've done and learned about what we are proposing we use as a guide.

Quite simply, what is required is a self-aware acknowledgment of the power differential between the funder and the grantee and thus an explicit declaration, in a race equity frame, that through mutual trust, transparency, dialogue, and the practice of conflict transformation skills, we can try to dismantle some of the aspects of the power and privilege dynamic into which we are all systemically locked. Can we mutually, in genuine reciprocity, move toward actual equity through mutual transformation? Can we use the skills of conflict transformation to sustain our dialogue toward the creation of new racially equitable policy?

A PROBLEM AND AN OPPORTUNITY

Given the traumatic nature of historical exclusion combined with the lack of knowledge and practice in how to facilitate and create actual diversity, we should always expect a gap between a declared commitment to include others and the actual implementation of that commitment. That such a gap is a given is nothing new. But I think we need to consider that the inevitable gap is integral to the process of change. By declaring a well thought-out and researched commitment, the Kellogg Foundation set up an expectation among its grantees that finally a major institution was taking leadership to do something about a major social injustice. Maybe this time it's for real? An organization like Kellogg, or any agency for that matter, needs to decide just how deeply and at what level it wants to, or can, enter into a race equity approach. The interviews revealed the depth, complexity, and challenges of such an approach. Racism, other forms of institutionalized inequalities, and residual effects of unhealed historical trauma generate an obviously complex and conflicted social-cultural context.

I've learned that a commitment to a race equity approach requires much more time, knowledge, and resources than are usually available in our current system. On one hand, the commitment to a race equity approach sets up an unrealistic expectation from those who might benefit from such an approach. I think the unreality of the expectation is a function of the depth of the pain of the struggle and the unlimited need of the vulnerable people served. This is no longer a typical offer for funding in which the expectation of help is pretty much established. Can this race equity approach finally meet the actual need, becomes a key question. The hope for improved funding and structural change can become disproportionate to what is actually possible. In practice, race equity work draws one into a new paradigm of interaction and depth of expectation in which "normal" institutional capacity, implementation strategies, knowledge, and time availability are often not adequate to meet the new demands. On the other hand, without commitment and the resultant expectation, the path toward racial equity would not be initiated. The pitfall to be avoided is to think that there is a necessary connection between articulating a commitment to a race equity model and knowing how to put it into practice. The great frustration experienced by all sides related to the differences between the goal of racial equity and the practice was debilitating and undermined the work of making it work. The mutual understanding of just what we are doing here needs to be clearly expressed and grounded in reality. The commitment and the response set up the conditions for the dialogue and partnering that will eventually result in the actual implementation of a race equity model. If the dialogue process is working well, the tension between the commitment and the gaps in implementation is the creative place where the practice of working out racial equity can take place. Working out what race equity practices must be instituted must, of necessity, rest in a reciprocal partnership between any organization and those it serves.

A NEW RELATIONSHIP

This expectation of reciprocity sets up the possibility of both a dialogue and a conflict. The very concept of racial equity and attendant language like partnerships, racial healing, restructuring to serve the most vulnerable was assumed to mean that we can figure this out as equal partners. From the grantees' point of view, we would be glad to work *with* you. Given the power differential, however, between the foundation and the grantees, creating such a relationship was questionable. This power differential is in fact a conflict. In regular funding strategies, the relationship between funder and grantee is understood and can be free of conflict. But a race equity or diversity frame raises the stakes and expectations of the relationship. The challenge in the Black Lives Matter era is to do more to shift beyond the gap between the rhetoric and the practice. How do we facilitate the dialogue between the promise of racial equity and the practice?

> Equity theory attempts to explain relational satisfaction in terms of perceptions of fair/unfair distributions of resources within interpersonal relationships. It is considered one of the justice theories. (John Stacy Adams, https://psynso.com/adams-equity-theory/)

> Descriptively, transformation refers to how the patterns of communication and interaction are affected by conflict. It looks beyond the tension around the visible issues to the underlying changes produced by conflict; this includes patterns of how people perceive, what they desire, what they pursue and how they structure their relationships interpersonally, as well as intergroup and intragroup. Conflict changes relationships. . . . How will they use, build, and share power? How do they perceive themselves, each other, and their expectations?
>
> Prescriptively, transformation represents intervening intentionally to minimize poorly functioning communication and to maximize mutual understanding. This includes trying to bring to the surface explicitly the relational fears, hopes, and goals of the people involved. (Lederach, 2003)

The challenge confronting all who believe in racial equity and racial healing is to face the reality that there will be a gap between the rhetoric and the practice. This is no small issue. The extent of the gap can be obscured by the euphoria of the myth of celebrating diversity. The euphoria is a function of the relief that we all feel when we are at least not fighting with each other. Celebration should energize the hard work of actually working it out with each other, the mutual transformation part. A common "fear of conflict" tendency makes us not want to jeopardize the feel-good celebration part. Here is a place where the conflict transformation field needs to play a role. What expertise have we developed that can be applied at moments of critical systemic conflict like the ones the Kellogg grantees described?

Whatever skills are offered need to embody deep understandings of power dynamics. Sometimes those power dynamics have a critical impact but may not necessarily be visible. Based on many confidential interviews over the years, I have noticed in New Mexico and throughout the Southwest that the common workplace hierarchy, depending on the quality of leadership at the top of the pyramid, can trigger a conditioned subordination in people at lower levels of stratification, especially evoking the pain of unhealed historical trauma experienced by people of color. The common use of fear-based authority to manage staff triggers emotions associated with feeling dominated or colonized. An agency or institution staffed by white, credentialed professionals at the top, supervising paraprofessional people of color toward the bottom with power over their livelihood, can potentially replicate, at the micro level, the legacy of dominance associated with colonization that we see throughout the system. These organizations can be relatively benign, or they can be overtly oppressive. There are fortunately very many exceptions to what I just described. Such organizations are characterized by creative, caring, and culturally knowledgeable leadership, including white allies who are liberated from the constraints of the white stereotype that this is their world into which everyone else should fit. Others and I have worked throughout the years to help rethink and restructure such organizations. Nevertheless, the model of leadership that reinforces these aspects of dominance is more common than not. The point is that, overall and all too frequently, the workplace perpetuates the status of the dominant white culture and the subordination of cultures of color in the state. These hierarchical structures reinforce, at a deep level, the dysfunctional and dehumanized relationships that we would all want to liberate ourselves from.

Restructuring hierarchies so as not to keep perpetuating what I call bureaucratic colonization has to be an ongoing mission. The process of implementation in a race equity frame has to be able to find constructive ways to share power to contradict the inherent subordination and the historical legacy of conflict that is present when there is a power imbalance.

In the implementation of racial equity, those involved must minimize and hopefully eliminate any aspect of subordination. Approaching structural change in New Mexico and anywhere for that matter, the use of a racial equity lens means that we need to pay attention to the dynamics that can lock us, once again, into the binary of dominance and subordination that characterizes so much of intercultural interaction in a colonized social system.

There are some aspects in the funder-grantee relationship that I think lend themselves to the possibility of creating channels of shared power and collaboration that might result in a deeper relationship. For example, a common point of view I heard from staff people working for Kellogg was that they felt victimized when they were stereotyped and treated not as persons but as "deep pockets" by those seeking funding. This feeling seemed pretty pervasive. It is certainly alienating and exhausting to be in that position. For some, it had a big influence on how they felt about their work and made them feel alienated at times from those they might fund. They felt reluctant to be open with grantees or potential grantees. The fact that, as program officers, they would have to make funding decisions contributed to the tension and to the reluctance to be open about their thinking.

On the other hand, some grantees felt they were put in a one-down position or in a status of subordination by the application process. Feelings of having to beg were not uncommon. Some people of color feared that if they did not communicate the right way (meaning the white way), their application would not be taken seriously. On top of all these feelings and tensions was the wondering about who would get funded and who would miss out and whether the actual disbursement of money would trigger the internalized conflict that people of color know so well. Money is often a catalyst for escalating conflict among people who are victimized by racism and the resulting inequality. Implied in all of this is the question: Do those who have the money and power (Kellogg) know the potential harm they can do when they finally decide who gets the money and who doesn't? Did they fund that organization that we view as working against community empowerment? Why didn't they ask us our opinion before they gave them money?

The dynamics I just described are based on actual conversations. The point I want to make is that these points of view are common but are usually not part of a public conversation. The funding process continues to take place in the mode of one side making decisions and the other feeling left out. Can we share power to collaboratively make resources even more available for solving disparities? I think if we are to adhere to the concept of racial equity, we must have hard conversations about these issues and, with a sense of shared responsibility, restructure the funder-grantee relationship to resolve the inequities and tensions that can keep us alienated from mutual understanding. I think the concept of racial equity to be credible in practice must find ways to open up channels of shared power that will lead to even more channels of shared power. I don't think these channels can be opened up without the creative application of conflict transformation skills. I would further add that the reason for sharing power is to minimize and preferably, of course, to eliminate any vestiges of structural subordination. One cannot claim to be operating in a racial equity paradigm and not prioritize the elimination of dominance and subordination between human beings as the principal outcome of that racial equity work.

I find it helpful to think of this scenario as a dialogue between New Mexico as an entity and the Kellogg Foundation as the other entity attempting to establish a working relationship for mutual benefit to solve serious social issues. The issues I've outlined earlier are a reflection of actual conversations. It is very important to say that, based on my participation as a researcher and a participant supporting the engagement of these two entities, I do not doubt that all the participants in this initiative have approached it with serious and genuine intent and the effort has resulted in immense help to the New Mexico community and continues to do so.

IMPLICATIONS

In general, the practice of creating racial equity requires at a minimum the establishment of a relationship characterized by a very deep and well-anchored sense of mutual trust and ongoing dialogue. I think this is the case for any human being working for equity or for that matter just being in a relationship. The quality of the trust, however, in an intercultural environment where we are working to create racial equity must be deeper and stronger because the dynamics of exclusion and historical trauma, explicit and implicit racism as well as internalized racism are always hovering at the margins waiting to sabotage any accumulated trust. Any gains in building trust must be monitored with a laser focus. No one would disagree that establishing mutually trusting relationships is fundamental and indispensable. The questions that I believe should also be asked though are: what is the *depth* of the mutual understanding and knowledge of each other on which our trust is based? What ongoing steps are we taking to nourish and protect our relationship so that what we've created here does not slip away from us? I think it's the nourishing and strengthening of the mutual trust that can get lost in the oppressive dynamics of systems we are trying to change. When an organization chooses to become diverse, intercultural, inclusive, or nonracist, it is by definition choosing to increase conflict. The reason is that structural oppression has guaranteed that we are already in conflict. The conflict is systemic and internalized and not necessarily observable until it erupts. As a result, in an intercultural or race equity frame, we need more tools and resources to prevent the hard-won trust from slipping away. When a conflict erupts in an organization that has carefully built intercultural ally relationships, the intense escalation of emotions can obscure the sense of commonality and trust and result in the dissolution of the organization, or at least the dissolution of the cultural ally connection.

We have a saying in my culture: "Entre el dicho y el echo hay un gran tre-cho" (Between the saying and the doing there is a huge distance). I know I'm stating the obvious when I say that the distance between the rhetoric and the practice of racial equity work must be declared a necessary given. This disconnect is just the way it is. I think though there is a tendency to settle for this gap as the status quo. Why not embrace the reality of it, expect it, look forward to it, and develop the conflict transformation skills to bridge the disconnect and keep moving the process toward actual transformation? We have to choose to take this on aggressively because there exists a great deal of naïveté that assumes racial, ethnic, or gender mixture constitutes diversity or inclusion. By referring to such mixture as having created diversity, our system has created an illusion that simple mixture constitutes diversity. In reality, it constitutes the precondition that is required to eventually create diversity. Now that we are together, let's transform our relationships so that we can construct actual, inclusive policy. This is what we should be about. The illusion of diversity prevents many of us from going to the next step. To break out of the normal paradigm and eventually move into the more inclusive and functionally intercultural, racially equitable one requires that we apply the skills we have and anticipate that we will have to develop new ones, or at the least, figure out ways to broaden the pool of skilled practitioners and leaders who can take on this change effort.

PRACTICE

I mentioned earlier that race equity work draws one into a new paradigm of interaction and depth of expectation in which regular institutional capacity, implementation strategies, knowledge, and resources are not adequate to meet the new demands. Among many factors, I would like to mention one in particular. One of the major barriers I've noticed that is universal but not explicitly recognized as such is what I've come to call over the years "time oppression." Race equity work is based on building a base of mutually trusting intercultural relationships, including those across gender and other identities. This step is indispensable if we are to contradict the legacy of the external and internalized forces of exclusion which are at the heart of inequality. This type of intercultural community building takes time and aware communication skills. It also requires skilled intercultural facilitation and very often will require conflict transformation strategies to sustain and nourish the sense of community that can be very fragile in a racially or culturally diverse environment. Fostering genuine reciprocity is key to the transformation process. The problem is that in your typical workplace in the United States, there is not enough time as well as an unawareness of the need to prioritize the relationship-building part of establishing equity. Even where there is a strong commitment to inclusion, time constraints can sabotage best efforts. What happens is that the mission or work of the organization takes priority. And of course, the work is directly tied to funding: accomplish goals or lose the money!

In a conflicted society like ours, the work of building the intercultural community can be just as labor-intensive and time-consuming as the mission itself. In a sense, equity work then requires two full-time jobs. I find over and over again, under the strain of time commitments in a fast-paced society like ours, that deep inclusion work recedes to an afterthought in the scheme of getting the "actual" work done. I have seen many organizations committed to diversity nonetheless revert over time to being pretty much back to the noninclusive workplace they were when they started. The pressure of short time frames forces people to fall back on a conditioned normal. Forced time frames favor those who already have the power, whether in the workplace or in society generally.

I should add that this "regression effect" can also be fueled by a common illusion that the simple inclusion of women and people of color in a predominantly white male organization constitutes diversity. This so-called diversity works sometimes because, as a result of their systemic exclusion through racism and sexism, women and people of color tend to have the skill set of being bicultural and thus able to join a dominant culture organization and make the relationship work. By bicultural, I mean that they can function in their own cultural or gendered reality as well as in the dominant cultural reality. They can relate in the direction of the men and white people in the organization, and that ability is what generates inclusion. The organization may, but often does not, have the ability to reciprocate and relate in the other direction. Nevertheless, the organization tends to take credit for being inclusive without having to do the work of making the relationship work, and the bulk of the work falls to the women and people of color who have the bicultural skills. What appears to be diversity or inclusion can become an illusion of diversity that can quickly crumble under pressure and regress to exclusion once again.

Because of my excitement as a learner in this work, I find it very helpful to frame the work of transformation around the theme of learning. Even when the work involves mediating serious conflict, I like to stress that we are all learners in the work that we do. In my leadership role, I acknowledge that I am a learner as well and an ally wanting to share what I've learned in this work that may help solve or mitigate their issues. As learners, they can decide if what I have to offer is helpful to them. The learning frame tends to have a healing effect on a sense of exhaustion in the struggle. After all is said and done, racial equity work and conflict transformation interventions are always about healing. Given the urgency of today's multiple crises and the sense that there is not enough time, it's easy to fall victim to a sense of panic. I can't imagine, though, that it is not in our self-interest to go slowly enough to build the intercultural mutual trust that will enable us to solve global problems.

CHAPTER 5

How Is Dissension Seeded Between Diverse Groups?

···

There are three common points of entry for practicing conflict inter-vention: community mediation organizations that train volunteers; businesses that offer paid services; and academic programs that grant degrees or certification. As mediation and other forms of conflict intervention have become professionalized, admission into the privilege of earning a living by doing such heartfelt work has increasingly been vested in the academy.

Our next contributor, Pushpa Iyer, is a professor in a well-respected university. An immigrant from South Asia, part of a group often problematically described as a "model minority," her achievement of academic success and professional elevation was hard-won as she traversed many of the same experiences of racism as Black or brown peers. Yet success in the academy landed her in a painful position of privilege without protection. Her story is one of abandonment by the white leadership of her institution as she worked diligently to bring about equity in her university, and how she became the focus of anger by students who rightly protested racism as they experienced it. What her personal story suggests is something painful to regard: how predominantly white institutions, with or without intention, pit people of different racial identities against each other. In the process, white hegemony remains unchallenged.

While many of the writers in this book describe with deep gratitude how they ben-efited from being mentored by people of like background, if the demography of a field is largely white, these relationships are statistically likely to compound racial inequality. Entering the profession by earning a degree in one of the many academic programs that have been created in the past two or three decades is purported to be an equitable alternative to the more relational route. But in reality, dynamics of exclusion abound in universities.

—Beth Roy

···

Whiteness in Academia: Perspectives of a Brown Immigrant Woman

Pushpa Iyer

INTRODUCTION: WHITENESS AS A SYSTEM

Academia is a microcosm of society, and so, not surprisingly, Whiteness, as culture and ideology, dominates institutions of higher learning in the United States (Ng & Bates, 2021). Whiteness is powerful; it provides access to resources and opportunities to select individuals and groups and favors some groups over others. Black, Brown, and immigrant communities who are either kept out of the spaces of Whiteness or refuse to subscribe to this culture and ideology face many challenges and disadvantages. The subject of Whiteness in academia and how it impacts minoritized community members has been explored in-depth, but literature, whether scholarly, journalistic, or experiential, usually describes these disadvantaged communities as a monolith. Although acronyms like IBPoC (Indigenous, Black, and Person of Color) provide some ease in speaking collectively about members of certain disadvantaged communities, at the same time they erase the unique experiences and interactions of each of these communities with Whiteness (Daniel, 2020). An individual who is Black, Indigenous, or a first- or second-generation American is probably not impacted by Whiteness in the same way as me, a Brown immigrant. I believe that history, culture, power, global politics, and real-life experiences all play a role in how we, as members of diverse marginalized communities, experience and work with Whiteness. I argue that it is vital to understand the diverse experiences of the many marginalized communities (and subgroups and individuals within those communities) who interact with Whiteness in institutions of higher learning. Understanding these differences, I believe, will help us develop a more nuanced antiracism approach, which is vital to dismantling institutional Whiteness.

Whiteness and White are not synonymous. White is skin color and Whiteness is a social construct. I think of Whiteness as a system because there are many different parts to it like laws, procedures, economics, culture, and national ideology. Each of these is the interdependent and connected part of the system of Whiteness.

RACISM IN ACADEMIA: MY WORK AND STORIES THROUGH MY BROWN LENS

My two decades as a student, as a faculty member, and, briefly, as an administrator have given me insights into how racism plays out in higher education spaces.

I have experienced discrimination, and I have also witnessed others impacted by racism. I have led antiracism efforts in institutions of higher learning in the United States for almost a decade now. I have taught courses on racism and related topics, and I have prepared many students and colleagues to be better allies for racial equity. I have conducted empirical research on racism as experienced particularly by minoritized members in academia. My personal experiences and research are within predominantly white institutions (PWIs) in academia.

I am from India and as a woman, I have felt sometimes disadvantaged but no other aspects of my identity—physical, mental, class, religion, sexuality—make me lack in privilege. I belong to the highest caste group in India. I was educated in Westernized universities in India, Europe, and the United States. English is my first language in the professional world. The higher education degrees I earned were due in part to my privilege that opened doors that led to more advantages.

Despite these many aspects of my privilege, colleagues in academia have often called me "different" not because I have physical, mental, or emotional characteristics that make me different from the "norm" but because those in power (and often others not in power) in academia, view me through their lens of Whiteness, as the "other." I have asked people who have called me different what they mean, and I have never received a clear answer, so I have to infer. Many of my colleagues and students, most of whom enjoy white privilege, because of my skin color I believe, see me as the outsider, different, "presumed incompetent" (Harris & Gonzalez, 2012), too emotional for patriarchal Whiteness (Torres & Pace, 2012), and too bold for knowing how to navigate Whiteness but refusing to comply. Some racially minoritized colleagues and students see me as a person with privilege because, after all, I am a member of the model minority. Many conclude that because I have entered the spaces of Whiteness, I draw benefits from it, that I have access to resources and therefore wield power, even though I am seen to have no "real" power. Either way, I do not fit any box—I am not White, I am not Black, I am not Asian enough, I am not American, I am powerful, yet I have no power. I am the woman who refuses to accept patriarchy in spaces of Whiteness—I stick out everywhere. So yes, indeed, I am different.

I describe myself as an activist for social justice, equity, and peace. I have spent most of my time in academia as the activist I was in my life before entering higher education spaces. My formative years as an activist took shape in Gujarat state in India. I worked with a local nongovernmental organization among poor communities that were marginalized further by religious and caste divisions. I advocated and fought for justice for these communities, using my voice and my privilege. My version of activism runs parallel to my goal to be a good citizen wherever I am geographically located. In academia, I strive to be a good citizen who fights to create diverse, equitable, and inclusive spaces for all.

But trying to be a good citizen in US-based higher education spaces has been a challenge for me. I try instinctively to draw on my privileges to bring about change, but most of that privilege disappears simply because of my Brown skin. I am continually shocked to know that in America I am at the bottom of the ladder in many spaces of academia, because of my skin color and its associations with culture language, class, and nationality. In dealing with sexism and skin color–related racism, I do not know how to begin leading change. I am now advocating for myself as much as I am advocating for others who are disadvantaged and marginalized. Nothing seems more challenging than being a change agent with odds stacked against me. No longer advocating from a place of privilege has made me acutely aware of the politics of oppression among people of color. I am also learning that this politic reinforces the system of Whiteness in academia.

Indigenous, Black, Brown, international (usually immigrant), and other students and faculty with marginalized identities in a white-dominant institution share some similar experiences of discrimination. We work extra hard to prove that we can complete the work assigned to us, yet we are not trusted to carry out tasks on our own. We are usually asked to work with White and American peers and colleagues and are labeled as *uncollaborative* if we push back and seek to be known individually for our contribution. Many of our more privileged colleagues receive personal accolades, but we "succeed" only as part of a team that involves White colleagues. An international faculty member, a colleague of mine in a predominantly white institution, was invited to join a team and quickly realized they were only *tokenized* and would never be asked to take leadership even though they had years of experience in the subject area both within and outside the institution. They told me this became apparent when a new White faculty member with less experience was asked to take decision-making roles during a routine change of leadership and they were not. In my research, minoritized faculty at various PWIs reported similar experiences of being bypassed for leadership positions given to privileged faculty with equal or less experience within the same institution.

The work of international faculty and students is critiqued for many reasons, but one standard probe is how well our English language capabilities live up to American Standard English and how well our accent is understood by "Americans." Many international students reported that they are sidelined in the classrooms by both faculty and fellow students who do not have the patience to allow them to express their thoughts or to produce work in less than "impeccable" American Standard English. The assumption that only those fluent in American Standard English have something worthwhile to say is commonsense nonsensical but professionally a standard. Many African American students in my research reported that they *code switch* and keep their African American Vernacular English in the background at all times in academia (King & Kinzler, 2020).

When we face *microaggression* as a part of our everyday existence, many emotions are evoked in us. Sue et al. (2007) define racial microaggressions as "brief and commonplace daily verbal, behavioral, or environmental indignities, whether intentional or unintentional, that communicate hostile, derogatory, or negative racial slights and insults toward people of color." Microaggressions are so commonplace that many times the perpetrators are unaware of how damaging their communications are to racial minorities. We are quickly and routinely labeled as difficult or angry and, of course, unprofessional when we energetically express any form of disagreement. Constantly being tone-policed, told we're *speaking inappropriately*, as well as practicing self-censorship in self-defense, impacts one's mental and emotional well-being because Whiteness considers emotions unprofessional. *Professionalism* is a code word in PWIs to center Whiteness and its workplace practices. Professionalism relates to dress code, speech, work style, and more, basically making everything that is "different" about us unprofessional (Gray, 2019). In my research, one oft-reported story from international students is being asked to wear formal clothing for final class presentations. "Formal" is a code word for Westernized clothing such as suits. Many international students do not have suits in their wardrobe or cannot spend the money for such formal attire. This requires them to have a conversation with the faculty member about their finances or fork out the money to avoid being seen as "different," or come to class without a suit and "be different."

Whiteness operates on the *myth of meritocracy* (Appiah, 2018; Young, 1958). Those who work hard achieve success, get leadership roles, receive awards and grants, recognition for their work, and even higher pay. Those who receive success are presented as competent individuals and who are recognized purely for their merit. Coincidentally, this group is full of people who conform to Whiteness. The structure provides them with unlimited opportunities for success. Because minoritized faculty and staff do not get opportunities to do the kind of tasks tied to awards and recognition, the only people who receive those awards are those who adhere to Whiteness.

Students learn the behaviors that are rewarded and see the people who hold power in PWIs. Not surprisingly, minoritized faculty or staff rarely become role models for their students, including Black, Brown, and international students. In a discussion with a student, I, as a practitioner, explained the challenge of creatively presenting ground realities in classroom settings, particularly because many in the room do not have field experience. This male, Brown, international student, suggested that I speak to a White male American colleague—who was not a practitioner—to learn from him. Students accept the curriculum, pedagogy, and the faculty recognized and promoted by Whiteness as superior, even as they demand more diversity (Hikido & Murray, 2015).

Research points out that the myth of meritocracy in PWIs is a celebration of *White mediocracy* (Oluo, 2020). We challenge the idea that Whiteness is synonymous with excellence and point out that when Whiteness does not produce excellence, there are buffer systems to ensure that those within that space do not suffer indignity or face significant impediments to their success. I'm not suggesting that every person ascribing to Whiteness is mediocre, but it is about the system of power that allows for some people to succeed with minimal effort while others battle odds to succeed at all. The gap between those who believe in the myth of meritocracy versus those who view it through the lens of White mediocrity leads to a deep chasm in feelings of satisfaction, belonging, and trust between diverse communities within PWIs.

When we, minoritized, raise the topic of racism, those who work in the spaces defined by whiteness most often fail to engage. Being ignored leaves us feeling that our concerns are not worth discussing in the institution. Further, a legal response removes all feelings of inclusivity or belonging, and as a result, we choose not to speak much about our experiences. I have worked with many students who would highlight individual cases of discrimination privately to minoritized faculty like me but were unwilling to file a formal investigation. The gap between using legal processes versus listening to the emotional and psychological impact of racism is huge in spaces of Whiteness. PWIs usually do not have a diverse faculty, and their small number of minoritized faculty end up being the unofficial counselors for all students experiencing discrimination. Many of us have played this role for years, but this work has never been formally reviewed or rewarded during performance appraisal.

In PWIs, racially minoritized communities are often at odds with one another. This is not surprising at all given the history of manufactured tensions between Black Americans and other minorities. The history of Asian Americans is a case in point. Asian Americans who came as laborers in the 19th and 20th centuries were subject to racism and even called the "Yellow Peril" (the people who would take away the Whites' jobs). This led to many of them aligning with the oppressed Black community and fighting alongside them in the Civil War. However, over time, the political dimensions of the concept of "model minority" destroyed much of this solidarity. With the label model minority, Asian Americans were characterized as hardworking, focused on gaining an education, and not being "a problem." The goal was to turn them into a monolithic community and more importantly to assign characteristics to distinguish them from the "problematic" Black community. And this is how the White leaders in the country built racial resentment between the two communities (Lang, 2020). The model minority myth continues; Asian Americans are still the minority, still the hyphenated Americans, and much marginalized because of the label (Chow, 2017; Wu, 2015). Alcoff notes that Latino/as also shared a similar history of discrimination. Further, she argues that by putting Asian Americans, Latino/as, and other immigrant communities close (metaphorically) to Black communities, every community was marginalized as race conflicts became synonymous with Black versus White (Alcoff, 2003).

As a Brown faculty member, some of the harshest critiques leveled against my teaching, my approach, my thinking come from other racially minoritized students and colleagues. This includes Black people who pit their American-ness against my Indian-ness. African American students may find overt acceptance from international students, yet many have also complained that international (Black and Brown) students do not have any idea of American Black history or culture. My research also points to underlying tensions between the Black international community and the African American community in PWIs. The former is often accused of being too close to Whiteness while the latter is described as deviating from achieving success by overly focusing on race. My research also records the disbelief of international Black students who say, "I did not know I was Black until I came to this country." Similar sentiments are reported by White international students, especially from Europe, who are surprised that their identity is now that of being "White." American views on race and Blackness are distinctive and not universally shared (Gordon, 2012). International students who refuse to participate because they do not see why they need to get involved in the "American-problem-of-race," should know that while race has its flavor in the American context, it is not just an American problem. Besides, coming here into this country, we need to make the effort to understand the historical origins of racism. If fewer people participate in antiracism conversations, Whiteness will continue to prevail.

Another story from my research highlights an international faculty member saying that Americans (Black and White) are given a pass for not accepting another culture but they, as an immigrant faculty, are required to know and accept American culture. So, while immigrant faculty learn how to run an "American" (also characterized as Eurocentric) classroom, American or other non-American students are not expected to learn or understand the international faculty member's culture and therefore pedagogical style. Many international students report that they come to study in the United States to learn American (read: White) ways and learn from American (read: White) professors. Brown female faculty tell me that students of all shades challenge and debate the rules and procedures in their classroom, but White male and sometimes White female faculty get away with just stating their rules which are never questioned (Hikido & Murray, 2015). Even as demands for diversity go up in PWIs, international faculty and students who are "different" are constantly penalized for not being "American" enough.

Recently, I experienced hostility from a Black American student who told me to educate myself on antiracism work because I had suggested doing a webinar with Black students. The student and I were not acquainted; she was not familiar with my approach. Given the heightened racial awareness in the country (this happened soon after George Floyd's brutal killing by a male White police officer in Minneapolis), this student presumed I was incompetent and made assumptions about my intentions. Her reactions are likely related to the general dissatisfaction Black Americans feel with society unfairly expecting them to educate others by showcasing their emotions. I expressed frustration and was sharply criticized. Emotions are cultural, so my expressions of emotion and my language of emotion were distinct and separate from the Black student's emotions, making it very difficult for us to be empathetic with one another. I apologized for the hurt and pain I caused, but my apology was not heard or, perhaps, believed. I became a symbolic target of the attack, a scapegoat, while the real issue of systemic Whiteness was not addressed. I was the "powerful" Brown person, a faculty member and an administrator, even though in a corporatized education system students are the clients and have much power (Lugo-Lugo, 2012).

Too often, race conflicts are characterized as conflicts between individuals. The deeper structural issues that establish Whiteness in the institution are not up for discussion. Also, as racialized minorities in a PWI, every time there is an incident related to race, we all become a party to the conflict whether we are directly connected or impacted. It is very difficult to lead a resolution to the conflict when you are a party in the conflict. Further, the lack of power as racially minoritized persons in spaces of Whiteness means we have no leverage to lead any change. And ironically, we look up to those in power under systemic Whiteness to make this change happen. As an activist and a conflict resolution professional, I have the analysis and the tools to deal with race-based conflicts, but I do not have the space to act, heightening my frustration. I am challenged in my goal to be a good citizen in higher education spaces as my time and energy is increasingly devoted to simply "being present."

My experiences and my research confirm that when members of minority groups are pitted against each other, Whiteness always wins.

DISMANTLING INSTITUTIONAL WHITENESS BY DECENTERING WHITENESS IN PWIS

Each part of the system of institutional Whiteness requires work to become diverse, equitable, and inclusive spaces. PWIs may focus on recruiting diverse students and faculty, reexamine their policies related to evaluation, grievances, and governance, or may introduce mentoring programs to support faculty and staff. However, fundamental change to institutional Whiteness can come only when some kind of transformation happens to all parts of the system. That is, we move from increasing diversity, equity, and inclusion to *decentering Whiteness* in PWIs. Decentering "describes the act of removing the dominant perspective from its position of power and integrating it as one of multiple perspectives" (Schmidt, 2018). Decentering Whiteness can happen only when an institution makes an effort to understand the values, beliefs, and practices associated with Whiteness first and then tries to shift them from the center by incorporating values, beliefs, and practices from other racially minoritized cultures. This must be an evolving process and requires self-reflection that is responsive to the global context. The process of decentering by default will create conflict as power shifts. If decentering is done deliberately, one can prepare for it in ways that minimize the negative impacts of the conflict. I would further state that encouraging the emergence of overt racial conflicts is a step in the direction of decentering Whiteness because they shake up the status quo, a view very consistent with my perspective about and skills in conflict resolution.

But when a conflict is not managed correctly, it can lead to a breakdown in the community, create divisions, and lead to a reduced sense of belonging. To better manage these conflicts, I introduce the concept of "compassionate courage," a conflict intervention approach I've developed that emphasizes the need for both courage and compassion when working to resolve a racial conflict. I have practiced compassionate courage when I have given voice to racial conflicts, and I have trained or facilitated the process of developing courage and compassion through various racial equity initiatives in academia. From these experiences, I believe that for some it is easier to build courage and for others, compassion comes easier, but most people struggle to have both at the same time.

On a personal note, I will say that I leaned on my allies on many different occasions during my time in academia. My students, alumni, colleagues, and even the leadership at the top have been allies for me at various times when I was being racially discriminated. While I cannot say that their personal support led to systemic change, I can confidently suggest that the racially minoritized in PWIs must work to create a network of allies for themselves. It is the only kind of support system that helps us emerge from these difficult situations with the strength to face the next onslaught.

Further, decentering Whiteness can come only from a *historical perspective*; knowing how a particular group of people gained power helps us understand how and why power balance must be restored (Kean, 2020). Usually, in PWIs, there is a one-dimensional understanding of power. A one-dimensional view of power is when power lies in the hands of the decision-makers solely. In an overt conflict, decision-makers make their decision based on observable behavior. The decision-maker sees decisions as a simple count of votes, and the most strong or greater numbered opinion becomes the decision (Lorenzi, 2006). Decentering requires institutions to pay attention to all dimensions of power. Lukes describes the three dimensions as the (1) power to influence people to change their behavior, (2) power to make decisions and the power to set the context in which these decisions are made, and (3) power to manipulate people into thinking that the decisions made are good (quoted in Lorenzi, 2006). Replacing one group in power with another can be avoided by examining how Whiteness operates within all three dimensions of power. Doing this will ensure institutions are not just shifting power but transforming power; irrespective of who holds power, institutional values, beliefs, and practices will be negotiated.

To conclude, I would quote James Baldwin, who said, "Not everything that is faced can be changed, but nothing can be changed until it's faced." Let us together, and in solidarity, challenge Whiteness but with compassionate courage.

CHAPTER 6

Why Are Prestigious Positions Unequally Shared?

··

B enjamin Davis takes the themes of this section into the heart of the prestigious world of international arbitration. Once retired from a successful career in that realm, Ben took a position sharing his knowledge in an academic setting. His contribution gives us three views of how exclusion works in arbitration: a critique of statements by a white leader in the field; Ben's journey toward the work; and visions of what would remedy the severe absence of arbitrators of African descent. Ben's account emphasizes the importance of a particular form of relationship: mentorship. Many of our authors spoke with intense gratitude about the mentors who had sustained them as they followed a career path into conflict intervention. They also note the burdens of mentoring others once arrived in institutional positions; enormous amounts of time and effort are contributed daily by professionals of color to support and teach the next generation. The very personal nature of mentorship cuts two ways: in predominantly white settings, it becomes another way newcomers of color are excluded as white elders are drawn toward mentoring white students. At the same time, the few people of color who have put down roots acknowledge the intense responsibility to help others into the field, doing unacknowledged work in circumstances where their legitimacy is frequently questioned. A focus on shared mentoring of newcomers of color is one step forward that would make a large difference. (For more on the importance and the problems of mentorship, see the conversation among S.Y. Bowland, Angie Beeman, and Tsedale Melaku in the next section.)

—Beth Roy

··

The State of Rights and Dreams: Arbitrating Evidence of Racism

Benjamin Davis

REALITY OF RACISM

In 1948 when my father was a roving editor for *Ebony* magazine, he was told to go to Norman, Oklahoma, to cover the case of *Ada Sipuel v. University of Oklahoma*. Ms. Sipuel, a Black teenager from Chickasaw, Oklahoma, wanted to study at the segregated law school of the University of Oklahoma. We might call that her private dream. During a break, my father took a photo of her sitting at a desk with a stack of legal papers in front of her. In the background in intense discussion, one sees a young Thurgood Marshall, who was representing her in the case. The light on Ada Sipuel's face and her expression of determination led my sister and me to call that photo "Fighting for the Right to Dream." For Ada Sipuel was fighting for the right to have her private dream recognized by the state.

Fast-forward to 1963, and we have the famous "I Have a Dream" speech of Reverend Martin Luther King Jr. Following after *Sipuel* and *Brown v. Board of Education*, King's speech underscores Ada Sipuel's right to her dream when she sought recognition of it by the state and shifted it from a private dream to a broad public dream. Even if that now public dream was controversial, no one seriously contested King's agency to dream even though they might think his dream was a fantasy that was too far-fetched. His immense public dream was being massively resisted, but no commentator at the time seriously challenged his right to have that dream—to allow that dream to come forward and possibly to blossom in the marketplace of ideas.

Fast-forward to my dream to become an international arbitrator, something I achieved but without much affecting the rights of other Black practitioners to do the same.

FALLACIES OF PRIVILEGE

As of June 11, 2020, of the *3,434 attorneys* who appeared on their (very distinguished international arbitration practitioners) firms' websites as part of a "Legal500 top US international arbitration practice group," only *54 people* (1.5%) may be people of African descent. Seventeen of these 37 practice groups appear to have *no attorneys* who are of African descent. If this is the full picture, it would mean that there are perhaps *1,017 attorneys at the top US international arbitration practices who do not have (and perhaps never have had) a black attorney as a co-worker.*

This exchange between an interviewer and an international arbitrator associated with prestigious law firms caught my attention:

Chiann Bao: This next question is about diversity in arbitration. What are your views on the lack of diversity—ethnic diversity—in arbitration, especially those of African and African American descent, and what measures should be taken to address it?

Jan Paulsson: Well, the thing you have to have are individuals who are attracted to this type of practice. We've had some experience of very gifted individuals of diverse national backgrounds, educational backgrounds, racial backgrounds, what have you, whom we would have loved to join my firms—different firms I have been in—but who had so many offers that we were just disappointed. Several occasions like that.

At the same time, we are conscious of the fact that we have generated extremely competitive environments, and it's not a very wise idea to take someone just to look virtuous and put that somebody into an environment which is extremely competitive where they have a learning curve which from the beginning might put them ill at ease. It is not a good thing.

So you go for, you look at the individuals who are extremely competitive and the competition for them is extremely high.

I am looking forward to the day when the numbers are far greater.

I have spent a lot of time [in] Africa, and I've seen in some of the capital cities of Africa a new generation of lawyers coming up who are extremely good. So I think there is great hope that they will be attracted to arbitration.

I think in the last years maybe they tended to migrate to Europe, and the most ambitious ones have entered fields of capital finance and things like that, not so much arbitration.

Remember arbitration in leading international law firms represents even in the most active ones 3, 4, 5 percent of the turnover. It's a small area of practice. And that might explain some of this.

But I'm very optimistic about this.

—Transcript of Jan Paulsson, Neil Kaplan, and Chiann Bao interview diversity question July 2, 2020, Conversations with Neil, Delos Dispute Resolution (https://delosdr.org/index.php/past-webinars/)

C'mon man.

In my memory, the international arbitration groups in the 1980s and 1990s at Coudert Freres in Paris (as it then was) or Freshfields in Paris never had an African American lawyer hired in the international arbitration practice group during the time Paulsson was at either. Nor, I wonder, was there a nomination of an African American as an arbitrator.

Full disclosure: I declined an offer at Coudert New York, and at White and Case, New York, when I was coming out of law school as I wanted to go to Paris where my soon-to-be fiancée was and do international work from there. When I asked about starting in the Paris office with the Coudert Paris Office and the White and Case New York Office, both wanted me to start in New York. One said, "We'll see after a couple of years about Paris." I understood that answer as a polite "never going to happen." So I found a job on the business side. It turns out that in this past year or so, I have learned of a similarly situated American white man coming out of law school at the same time who had an offer from Cleary in New York. He faced the same pressure to start in New York from Cleary, and he also had a fiancée in Paris. He pitched Coudert Paris as I had, and he was directly hired at Coudert Paris. Just saying. Hmmm.

For those African Americans or Africans with a US nexus, I think this is useful information for seeing what you are up against as a person attracted to this area of practice. I know that such a statement from a distinguished international arbitration practitioner can be very discouraging to an African American. But I am writing to encourage, not to discourage you. The exchange reveals the playing field on which African American or African candidates are seeking to play when they want to work in international arbitration practice, showing the way those at the top of the field who are American whites are likely to think about them.

I do not buy the series of rationalizations in this exchange that can be summarized as:

1. *He claims his firms tried to get the unicorn but failed each time over 40 years. They were not attracted to international arbitration.*

Forty years of not attracting Black unicorns but managing to hire non-Blacks? C'mon man. Please get real.

2. *He expresses concern that they might hire someone who was not a unicorn just to be virtuous, worrying that person (note they, not us) would be ill at ease as they went down the learning curve.*

It is as if the Black unicorn had to be practice ready to be an arbitrator from the first day that they came to work in an international arbitration group. This reminds me of the adage taught I dare say to all African American children by their parents that they need to "Work twice as hard to get half as far." As to first-day readiness to be an arbitrator that would normally have matured over 10 to 15 years of practice, please note that no leader of international arbitration was practice ready on their first day. I remember them starting out buying the ICC

Arbitration book at the International Chamber of Commerce [where I served as American Legal Counsel at the International Court of Arbitration] as young attorneys. All the leaders of arbitration went down a learning curve and were mentored on that path by senior lawyers.

I remember my third day in 1986 at the ICC International Court of Arbitration when the court replaced a sole arbitrator. In two or three weeks, a case was brought between the parties at the Obergerichts des Kantons Zurich. As it was my case, I had to prepare the ICC response to the request of the Zurich Court to explain the decision. What was wonderful is that President Gaudet, Secretary-General Stephen Bond, and General Counsel Sigvard Jarvin made it clear that I was the "point man." They both expected me to, and had confidence that I would, figure it out. And so I did, with plenty of feedback from them and the other counsels at the time as I prepared the statement. We were successful in having the court administrative decision to replace the sole arbitrator accepted at the Cantonal and Swiss Supreme Court levels.

Moreover, and this part of the comment was really offensive, offering a black person a job is not about being perceived as virtuous, just like offering a job to a white person is not about one being perceived as virtuous. It is about giving that person a job. If they do the job and excel, great. If there is a difference between what the job requires and their skill set as they develop, then one finds them a path to another place.

Tying virtuousness to the act of hiring a black person is sickening. C'mon, man! Please get real.

3. *In some (distant) future, he hopes this will change.*

This "hope" for a distant future ensures a lack of diversity *now* when these leaders have the power to change that. It also ensures that the current leading practitioners do not have to be more self-reflective about their inability to recruit African Americans or Africans. These leaders let themselves off the hook, feeling no impetus to change a thing about how all this operates as they sit in their apex positions in the field. In a way, they are asking for those *after* them to do the change. But here is the rub, those after them will be the ones that they trained in the way they do things, which includes always looking for and never quite attracting the mythical black unicorn. This artful dodge is just a reproduction of hierarchy through a further generation with a feeble "hope" of change for those kept outside looking in. C'mon, man! Please get real.

4. *He notes that these top firms employ a very small group.*

Again, the comfort level issue is the priority. This view is very ironic in a field that is essentially about the capacity to do cultural gymnastics working with parties and arbitrators from around the world. C'mon, man!

5. *He suggests it's unwise even to think of these people as potential arbitrators.*

What is not said struck me: nothing about looking at African Americans or Africans to be nominated as arbitrators in responding to the question about diversity. Hiring the black unicorn, yes, but we do not get them. Nominating as an arbitrator the black unicorn who went to work somewhere else? Not even mentioned in the response. Deep. C'mon, man!

Unfortunately, the math of 1.5 percent African American lawyers in the premier international arbitration law firms shows that the route to experience in this space for blacks is a rivulet. And, even if one is in the rivulet, being appointed an arbitrator is like trying to get through the eye of the needle in that rivulet.

In 2021, this is just appalling, but it is what it is.

We can note that the International Council for Commercial Arbitration (ICCA) has a new Diversity and Inclusion Policy which actually mentions race—granted in a long list of diversities—but at least it is mentioned as part of the diversity vision presented. But, given the comments of Professor Paulsson, what can we expect if only black unicorns are deemed "worthy"?

What I suspect in this lack of diversity is that we are seeing the limits of the imaginations of the leaders of the field. They think of it as a small club. But the field has easily doubled in the number of cases over the past 20 years as has the size of cases. And the field is only in its nascent state concerning the true integration of technology. While those at the top now are digital immigrants, the digital natives below them will take this field to places unimagined. Just like I took the field to international fast-track commercial arbitration back in the early 1990s.

I can see a field full of diverse people, but what I do not see in the American part is a field full of Americans of different races. That is appalling in 2021.

Please note that within all the seriousness that is international arbitration, it is fun to work in this field. One does cultural gymnastics every day as one works with persons from around the world on difficult and complex matters under different laws, languages, and places of arbitration. If you have that international bent, there is nothing better. And there are plenty of African Americans and Africans with a US nexus with that international bent.

C'mon, folks. Get real. Use your power for something greater. Wherever you are, insist on making sure that African Americans and Africans with a US nexus are hired, promoted, and nominated as arbitrators. There are plenty of black folks as good as or better than the white folks you do hire.

(Excerpted with permission of the author and site from Benjamin G. Davis, C'mon Man: Diversity and International Arbitration Slight Return, JURIST—Academic Commentary, April 6, 2020, https://www.jurist.org/commentary/2021/04/benjamin-davis-diversity -arbitration/.)

DREAMS OF JUSTICE: MY INTERNATIONAL ORIGINS

Against this background of challenges to finding a place in international arbitration for Black candidates, I wonder how I managed to do it. It is hard to pinpoint exactly when international work became a dream for me. Being born of African American parents in Liberia, living there my first two years and then in Tunisia for four years, certainly built into me early on a need to do what I call cultural gymnastics.

In addition to the culture and language of my parents (my father was raised in segregated Atlanta, my mother in New Jersey), there was the Liberian multicultural experience and the Tunisian multicultural experience combined with a multilingual experience of English, Arabic, French, and Liberian languages.

In 1960, we moved to New Jersey. My parents were resolute on the importance of education and the importance of us getting the best education possible at the time. So they looked to put us in private schools—schools that were not particularly open to Black children.

My father had stayed behind in Tunisia finishing out his term as a State Department employee. When he wrote on official stationery to New Jersey private schools about enrolling us, the schools were very welcoming. But, when my mother showed up with my sister and they saw she was Black, suddenly there were issues. My sister's English was not good enough was one excuse. My mother filed a complaint with the New Jersey Department of Education against one school that had rejected my sister. She argued this was racial discrimination, not an issue of my sister's English aptitude. Ultimately a consent decree was entered that the school would look over my sister's application again. In the meantime, she had been accepted at another private school where I was wait-listed. I ended up integrating the school in the first grade.

In 1964, we moved to Washington, DC, where I can remember the rounds of private school visits and rejections. Ultimately, my sister integrated Sidwell Friends School, where I soon joined her. We lived in a nearly all-white neighborhood near Walter Reed Hospital. The key memory from that time was someone painting "KKK" in black on the garage door and my uncle George coming down from New York City to paint over it.

All these things taught me about the American form of multiculturalism, and I learned new types of cultural gymnastics. To get to school each day, we took three buses to get from where we lived across town to Sidwell. I am amazed today at our fortitude to do that routine every day, go to school, and come home. In addition, I was singing in the Washington Cathedral Boys Choir, which I could walk to from Sidwell. That was an exhilarating spiritual experience in that grand building. I am not sure what the role these experiences played in my becoming, but I do think that there was a great deal of me having to grow up and be independent beyond what would normally be expected of someone of those tender years.

I went on to have a variety of international educational experiences, living between Europe and the United States, and attending a series of prestigious schools culminating in Harvard for law school. I was not the greatest student, and the college advisor did not think I could get into Harvard. But my parents' view of going for the best education possible and their encouragement led me to apply. I wrote in my essay about the fights in the halls in the boys' dormitory at one of the private schools I attended. I wrote about being dragged down the hall by my balls in one of those fights. You see how that little vignette comes off the page for the reader. It did for my application and thanks to a wonderful interview with the recruiter, solid recommendations, strong scores, and good enough grades, Harvard took a chance on me.

No doubt, my rich international upbringing and unusual educational opportunities positioned me advantageously when I set foot on my career path. I picked up the *International Herald Tribune* and saw there was an opening for a legal counsel at the ICC Court of Arbitration. I contacted the two lawyers I knew in Paris to be references and they agreed. Little did I know that they were in fact gods of international commercial arbitration.

HOW TO OPEN ARBITRATION TO DIVERSITY

How would most Black lawyers just starting even aim for such a career? Absent a family connection or a relationship connection, there are very few if any common experiences that would orient someone to think of arbitration. There are no great arbitration television shows, no big-screen movies featuring a practitioner. Unless one was confronted with being in arbitration due to a dispute, the natural vision of dispute resolution is to imagine someone in court. Even if someone imagines court, they are most likely not seeing the alternative paths of mediation or court-annexed arbitration in their vision of court, seeing more of a process in front of a judge. Even if, somewhat ironically, court shows like *Judge Judy* are watched, one does not know that the structure underpinning such shows is arbitration and not a court proceeding.

Aside from experiences of peer mediation in lower schools, or a particular program in a high school, the place where one learns about the legal profession is in law school. But the integration of dispute resolution and arbitration into the standard curriculum varies from school to school. As a non-bar tested domain, the likelihood is that the litigation-directed courses focused on the court process would predominate in a law student's curriculum. Enter moot courts. While the principal moot courts are directed toward appellate advocacy before judges, moot courts such as those sponsored by the American Bar Association Law School Division Arbitration Moot Court, or the Vis International Commercial Arbitration Moot are pathways that may be available for some exposure to arbitration and possibly whet an appetite. One of the constraints for these moot courts is the process of designation of teams and the resources that are provided for these secondary moot court competitions at the law school. It may just be that, resources being what they are, these opportunities are not formally part of the student activity prospects and so students must already have enough interest to take these kinds of moot courts on in a manner that is ancillary to the recognized coursework.

In parallel with this process in the law school, there is also the external process of internships and summer jobs with practitioners. Thanks to the formal or informal mentoring programs at law firms, it is possible that students will be tasked with working on arbitration-related matters and cut their teeth that way. From this experience, the passion might also grow.

The road to building these passions—law school to internship, internship to law associate—is not clearly marked. Most firms have no formal process of rotating through departments. Is there some type of mentoring program that is either formal or informal so that the person can get exposure and utilization in the arbitration work? Even if the newcomer develops a desire to specialize in arbitration, there is a whole process of self-marketing to the institutions and those already in the field to get to the point at the appropriate time where one's expertise is sufficient to be trusted with one's first arbitration. The relentless process of marketing, doing arbitration work as an advocate or arbitrator, and being involved in the field of arbitration with the various entities that abound where arbitration practitioners gather and perfect the field becomes a lifelong path of self-promotion and self-identification to rise in the field.

Now factor in Mr. Paulssen's views, which I critiqued previously. Each of these steps to becoming an arbitrator involves building relationships with superiors who are inclined to view your talents favorably. In other words, unicorns might survive this process, but most young Black lawyers will probably not. Not surprisingly, the processes that I've described lead to a narrow, homogeneous group of people who are co-opted and rise in the field. Many of these dynamics appear interpersonal. But I'm also offering a systemic critique. Those who are underrepresented are underrepresented everywhere in society and are particularly underrepresented in the law and this subspecialty that is arbitration. Each step winnows down possible candidates: if the pool is not diverse to begin with, if racist biases induce white leaders to search for unicorns and fail to see the talent in front of them, then we reproduce a predominantly white field.

One of the remarkable features of having observed the international commercial arbitration community over the past 38 years is my coming to understand just how much the new entrants are required to pledge fealty to the more experienced members. This kind of hierarchy might not really surprise given the hierarchical nature of the law and law practice pretty much anywhere in the world. But it does strike me that the flexibility of arbitration might have in it the seeds of a more inclusive view of what is good and what is bad than that asserted by the high priests and priestesses of the club who look to their lessers in experience and years to validate their views if they want to progress.

If one can expand the club of arbitrators there is a chance that the variety of backgrounds and dispute resolution experience would interact with each other in a more pluralistic manner—a marketplace of ideas. And in that marketplace of arbitration ideas, the risk of a significant "groupthink" about what is arbitration might be tempered by the other imaginations of what is arbitration and how it is done. If we were to extend this vision to the courts that review arbitration, again the kind of pluralism within the traces of stare decisis or other traditions, might lead to further evolved imaginings of what arbitration's role can be.

So we get to a view in this section of gatekeepers at various points (law school, internships, clerkships, and practice) along the way of the arbitration vocation path. I have always dreamed of these gatekeepers revisiting their role of allocator of scarce spots and see it more as a gate opener—helping those farther down the ladder accelerate their career.

That reaching back or rising as one lifts those who are not so clearly identified from birth as eligible to come into this hierarchy is what I imagine. In this vision, the structures of co-optation become structures of acceleration even while recognizing that there may only be a limited number of seats in the hierarchy. Some may be of the view that with the expansion of the ways that one can be involved in arbitration and with the explosion of technology flattening the opportunities for experience, that in fact this new normal will take care of my concern. However, I am always reminded of the adage ascribed to Lampedusa which is that "Everything must change, so that nothing changes." Thus, while new networks develop, underneath those networks one can see evolved but nevertheless relentless hierarchies made up of persons who are insisting on their lessers pledging fealty to "their way" of doing arbitration. To not pledge such fealty is to be sidetracked away.

I have written of the color line in international commercial arbitration that is centuries old. International commercial arbitration may be viewed as a rarefied and advanced point on this color line, and one might see concern about it as less a priority than the urgent issues of poverty. However, for me, the color line I see is seamless from those in the Mississippi Delta or inner-city poverty up to those at the highest levels of the field. For when I came across the papal bulls of the mid-1400s calling upon the Kings of Spain and Portugal to perpetually enslave Africans, I realize that the process of rising to the light is a 500-year struggle. The evolution from enslaved humans being cargo (seen as horses to be thrown overboard at the whim of the captain) to full autonomy at the highest levels of international commerce and trade is for me a relentless drive to not have the limitations being placed by others on my dream limit the size of my dream. It is a process of understanding that the limits are in those gatekeepers' heads, and not limits that are inherent to who any person is.

And those limits in their heads, I have come to learn are likely more detrimental to them than they even perceive. The criteria of gatekeepers as to who is on a list and who gets to serve on an occasion may not capture quality and may be shown to be suspect. What if the person who has all the markers of a retired judgeship after many distinguished years is found to be a person with racial animus? The process of selection for that person did not capture this fatal flaw that might affect how they evaluate every party, counsel, witness, expert, or fellow arbitrator on the tribunal that they dealt with—denaturing by this exogenous animosity the quality of the arbitral decision-making.

WHAT IS TO BE DONE?

Pressure must be placed on parties and institutions to make more diverse choices. The institutions may be more amenable to doing this because of the reputational benefits of being seen as having diverse neutrals being appointed. The parties' counsel is less oriented to be this open given the obvious conservatism. However, there can be a kind of virtuous cycle where the institution takes the initial risk of naming someone as a sole arbitrator, they do well, and based on that they become acceptable or graduate into the party rosters and the rosters of other institutions. Increasing the pipeline, expanding the number of rosters one is on, and putting pressure on institutions to name one to build a reputation that will make one attractive to party rosters is the path one can follow to accelerate one's role in this arena without changing the structure or the system.

In these ways, we can reduce the impact of the variables that lead to the current structure, but we also need to change the system in which these factors operate to benefit those at the highest point in the pyramid. One first aspect is simply to increase transparency in terms of measuring who gets named as an arbitrator. The adage that if one wants it to count one must measure would let the numbers speak for themselves. The appallingly low rates of use of underrepresented persons would serve as pressure on all concerned and particularly the arbitral institutions to diversify their selections. Those diverse selections then become the fodder for enhancing the rosters of parties creating more opportunities for the nomination of the underrepresented.

A second aspect is to expand the roles beyond party or arbitrator to allow new younger entrants to gain experience in the field. A classic situation would be that of being a tribunal secretary. By assisting and observing how the arbitral tribunal operates, such a person gains a keen understanding of the complexities of being an arbitrator. It is kind of a post-degree educational program to help train the next generation. A similar comment might be made for the development of a person as an expert.

A third aspect is to take a critical look at what arbitration is doing. If it is an alternative to court proceedings, is it a satisfactory alternative? This kind of normative analysis of arbitration would hopefully reveal the biases and inadequacies of the roster and selection system so that increasing numbers of persons from the underrepresented groups would have a chance.

A fourth aspect would be to change the system. For example, updating the country's arbitration law so that it takes into account the use of information technology in arbitration. With the development of new ways to do arbitration while staying within the general confines of due process, being one who greets these new ways of doing with joy rather than trepidation may give one what is termed first-mover advantage in moving into that field.

A fifth aspect is integrating expert systems and information technology into the practice. The digital tsunami is a constant reality with which we all are confronted and one has to decide whether one is going to resist that wave or find ways to accommodate that wave or even ride it. These types of innovations may identify physical fossils—things that are done in the real world for a valid reason but which in an electronic setting are not essential and can be discarded. The information technology that we are experiencing has collided with the COVID-19 pandemic to create a situation of necessity to have to integrate technology more in arbitration. We might say that necessity is the mother of invention and so that ways of doing arbitration may blossom with the technology.

Particularly for the unfamiliar, the technology that is used may mask certain choices that lead to a certain path through the use of the technologies out of what could be multiple series of alternative paths of using the technology. That predetermined path in a sense limits the options of those using the technology. On the other hand, using nonarbitration-specific technology would run the risk of having a generic structure that is not sufficiently adapted to the specificities arbitration requires. In that sense, the experience of technology would not be a positive one, turning those who participated away from the technology. This situation is one where it is important to understand one is in an iterative process of experimentation with technology, evaluation, and adjustment that is never-ending. The tension arises when the costs of those adjustments begin to mount and it is uncertain whether one is willing to invest the next increment to get to the next level of technological sophistication.

A sixth aspect is coming to terms with whether how arbitration works is an appropriate form of justice. In the United States, the wild west of broad arbitration possibility is also a source of concern as to whether the impact is to essentially prohibit someone (a weaker party) from actually vindicating their claim. Now, inventive lawyers can address these areas of concern through inventive guerrilla lawyering by filing cookie-cutter claims against the same defendant 1,000 times where that defendant has agreed to pay the cost of the arbitration. Or, having parties submit payment notes that say that by cashing this check the other party agrees to waive the arbitration clause. The options are as inventive as the lawyers involved.

But, if these types of marginal adjustments do not end up assuaging the sense of inappropriateness of arbitration for certain types of disputes, it may be time to revisit arbitration and place it in different traces. And, at the same time, in creating silos for different types of arbitration (meaning beyond the classic domestic/international), certain identified kinds of cases could have certain rules that structure the fairness of the arbitration rather than the design being in the hands of one party who can impose it on a take it or leave it basis. Of course, there would be resistance to this, but all that means is that a process would go forward to make these adjustments in the near or far term. This is political economy rather than reflection.

CONCLUSION

At the end of the day, one comes to a question of whether it is possible to revitalize arbitration in a manner that is described in the previous sections. And can the structure and system be changed so that, on balance, we conclude that this is an appropriate form of dispute resolution that is rendering a form of justice?

In the first section, we discussed the right to dream and the process of private dreams becoming public dreams that become social change. This short chapter is my manner of expressing my dream or vision for arbitration. The hope is that this chapter might create a vision of an arbitral future full of passionate practitioners from many cultures, ethnicities, and genders helping humanity progress through their work aided by this peaceful means of dispute resolution. It is my dream, and I hope that it is sufficiently outlined that it might attract some affinity for those in and those who hope to be in this field which has been my passion for 38 years.

CHAPTER 7

How Do the Tools We Use Foster Inequality?

··

*A*rbitration and mediation are the two most accredited forms of practice in our field. In this chapter, I contribute a critique from the point of view of inclusion of normative mediation approaches. Many of the assumptions underlying these practices lie deeply embedded in mainstream culture. I argue that they not only fit badly with acculturated consciousness of many people of color, but they also do not provide the best service to white clients as well. Insistence on neutrality and discomfort with emotional expression often compound inequalities of power, layering advantages of voice over superior access to resources and other forms of privilege beyond the immediate dispute. I offer a few examples of alternative approaches to mediation practice.

—Beth Roy

· ·

The Soft Technology of Control: How Mediation Practices Perform Racism

Beth Roy

Conflict resolution is an infant profession. Unlike medicine or law, each of which established claims to professional status long ago, conflict intervention only began to set itself on a similar footing in the latter decades of the 20th century. In each of these cases, practices widespread in a general population became restricted to certain individuals who were accredited by more or less official agencies according to standards punitively enforced with increasing vigor as time went on.

All professions share certain characteristics. They reside within a framework of assumptions agreed to, explicitly or implicitly, by legitimized practitioners. These assumptions over time become codified in a body of literature and, in the cases of law and medicine, enforced by licensure. The path to entry into either field lies through academic institutions; the academy becomes the gatekeeper by teaching certain approaches and excluding others from legitimacy. Each of these elements is produced historically through social processes that narrow the range of acceptable thinking and practices. In the case of medicine, for example, curative activities that lay in the domain of women were co-opted by male physicians who laid claims to expertise based on scientific thought rather than folk wisdom. Midwifery is one example among many. This historical constriction of knowledge has consequences, some of them involving financial access as the cost of health care becomes encapsulated in a market economy, others conceptual as pharmaceutical impositions restrict nonchemical, and nonpatentable, forms of healing.

Mediation, alternative dispute resolution, conflict transformation, restorative justice, and other forms of intervention in conflict are currently on a path toward similar restriction and codification. We can see the impacts in very particular manifestations, major among them racial imbalances in who practices and who consumes these services. Professional barriers to people of color are formidable, not only because means of entry to the field are less than accessible to applicants from nondominant communities, but also because the practices themselves fit badly with those cultures.

To understand how racism exists within the newly forming profession of conflict intervention, therefore, we need to understand how the activities that have come to represent "right practices" turn off and turn away practitioners and consumers of color. Other chapters in this volume detail dynamics particular to various institutional aspects of conflict resolution. We begin with a discussion of assumptions about best practices that carry implications for *who* practices, who benefits, who is included, and who prevails.

NEUTRALITY

Neutrality is a well-debated yet persistent assumption in alternative dispute resolution (ADR) and other forms of intervention (see Wing in Trujillo et al., 2008). Trainers often equate mediator neutrality with an absence of bias. "I must not have an opinion lest I tilt the process in one party's favor." This formulation dictates a "professional" stance, a pretense that the practitioner stands outside the framework of discussion as an uninvolved facilitator of others' conversations. The idea of the value-neutral professional permeates the practices of both law and medicine.

In reality, though, no human being is a blank slate, and no process is devoid of meaning. Racial disparities in health care and outcomes provide ample evidence for that reality. Whether sitting elevated and clothed in black garb or companionably lounging in a comfortable chair opposite contending clients, the personhood of the facilitator matters. Indeed, it is read in detail by those being mediated. Who among us does not hope that authority is on our side? Who is not reading the twitch of an eyebrow for omens about the thought process—about the biases—of the intervenor? We read, intuit, interpret and craft our behavior strategically based on our perceptions. From the perspective of the participants, the person in the facilitator role is not neutral.

How this pretense to true neutrality imbalances negotiations among people of differing cultures is well-documented (see Chang, Witharana, Vargas, & Coronel in Trujillo, 2008). We imbibe fundamental worldviews quite literally with our mother's milk: bottle or breast? Fed on schedule or on-demand? Put to sleep in a cradle or in the family bed? Embraced by a multiage cohort of siblings and neighborhood peers, or left alone all day with one or two adults? Each of these conditions imparts meaning about the nature of the world to a child. These orientations may correspond to or clash with the most common construction of a mediation session. People of color and people from cultures beyond northern Europe often find the structure—time limitations, office settings, conversational turn-taking, controlled modes of emotional expression, leadership that hides its opinions—incompatible enough with their cultural norms that just walking in the door is silencing. Trusting that the mediator who sets these conditions is neutral is a stretch.

I contend that what is desirable is not neutrality but what I've dubbed "polypartiality," a demonstrated ability to hold the interests and needs of everyone involved as equally worthy of protection and potentially reconcilable in a context larger than the one framing the conflict. One of the most fundamental qualities of Eurocentric thinking is a pragmatic focus on the present moment absent of a deeper contextualization in history and culture. In the here and now, often there is no way to satisfy all needs. But if we move beyond the tendency to eclipse a larger frame, then more possibilities for reconciliation of differences can be imagined.

Among the frames most frequently eclipsed are experiences of racism. Mediators' insistence on the here and now and on neutrality may obscure the context of racist experiences that frame responses by participants of color. To claim neutrality protects intervenors within layers of cushioned unawareness. If I am neutral, then how does it matter whether I recognize how lifetimes of experiencing bias and dominance shape the perceptions of my clients of color as well as their strategies for participating in my process? Neutral facilitators may feel they are absolved from doing the hard personal work of learning about their participation in systems of racism, even though the work they do is one thread in the weave of dynamics that maintain institutional racism.

Combined with this historically narrowed, culture-bound framing of neutrality is a phenomenon well known to scholars of conflict: engagement in a fight draws the eye to the immediate dispute. We argue with more and more energy, amass more and more points in our favor, hoping to overwhelm our adversary with the legitimacy of our side. None of these efforts encourages a close examination of the history of the dispute, nor of the wider social or economic context in which it takes place (Dugan 1996). Broader inquiries lack the passion of the temporal argument. They are harder to see, more complex to communicate, less debate worthy.

In the narrow space that remains for consideration of solutions, dynamics of power inequity take over. Those disputants who assume their rights to be preeminent stand firm, while others whose histories are rife with a coerced need to bend do just that. In the presence of a neutral facilitator, those with more power win, whether that power resides in synergy with the process or in material conditions like money or political influence.

Imagine a situation in which the facilitator sees her role as describing this dynamic, providing an analytic framework for overcoming the tendency to inequality. Imagine that she can assume the role of educator, explaining to the dominant individual how they are dominating. This facilitator would also be able to argue for profound rewards in store for the more powerful disputant if they consent to share the power equally—rewards both material and spiritual. Imagine further that the facilitator is skilled in visioning and can propose a list of possible solutions that satisfy these overriding, now clearly articulated interests.

None of these roles I've sketched falls within conventional definitions of neutrality. All serve the interests of the most fundamental values of most mediators: to bring more justice into the world while also finding solutions to conflicts that equally benefit all participants.

A recent example: I was asked by a social justice organization to mediate a conflict between the executive director, a white woman, and a group of community members, most of whom were either African American or Latinx. Relationships had become so vitriolic that most of the contesting community people now refused to meet with the director. I started by interviewing each individual. I soon discovered several facts that persuaded me that mediation was not the first step needed. The community members were campaigning for the core organizational mission, grounded in values of multiculturalism and social justice, to be held to in the face of a gentrifying city and an increasingly white membership in the group. The composition of the Board of Directors had changed from predominantly grassroots members of color, to almost all white businesspeople with a greater ability to raise the money necessary to keep the organization afloat. With little awareness of the particular needs and racial dynamics of the community, they had hired an executive from a distant city. She had promptly offended several highly respected participants. Moreover, she had revised the budget to shift funds to programs that did not manifest the goals of equity.

I formed the view that the group of members and the director were fighting out a battle that was a matter of policy needing to be set by the board. When the citizens had gone to the board, they had been told that the organization was a family: everyone just needed to get along. Mediating these soured interpersonal relationships was all the board offered. When I reported back to the board leadership, I proposed a change of plan. The mediation needed was between the grassroots members and the board, not the director. She was following the instructions from her bosses as she understood them (correctly, I thought) to shift funds to those programs that would most help bring in new funding. But that goal, while of course important, conflicted with the visions and needs of the actual community they served, an understanding passionately expressed by the protesting members. Whatever healing of bruised feelings was needed, I argued, should come later, only after the core dispute over the priorities, values, and direction of the organization had been worked through by those with the power of decision as well as the responsibility for implementing the mission. I expressed strong sympathy for the dilemma the board faced and argued that my services were better used to support them to hear the concerns of the community, reassess priorities, arm wrestle with the fiscal concerns, and move forward using the energy of their dedicated membership rather than attempting to restrain it. Had I accepted a mandate of neutrality, a definition of the dispute, and a proposal for who needed to be at the table, I might have helped to soothe some tempers, but I might also have further obscured the essential nature of the organizational conflict that lay at the heart of the matter. I was very open about my values, expressed in part through my staunch respect for the organization and its historical work. After an initial session involving all the constituents where, with my help, essential truths were spoken and heard, the board undertook a review of their process, brought several of the community members who had confronted them onto the board, searched for new fundraising strategies grounded in the group's essential equity goals, and arranged coaching for the director to heighten her awareness of the racial dynamics at work. In other words, the result was not simply a meeting of hearts and minds but also an organizational renewal.

UNIFORM PRACTICES AND REGULATIONS

In this example, I moved quickly beyond the definition I had been given of what the conflict was about and who was involved. When I worked in a rural region of Bangladesh, every mediation I witnessed involved a cast of thousands. One case I witnessed in Bangladesh involved a man who had been beating his wife. The couple came to the mediation accompanied by their extended families. Neighbors crowded the windows and felt very free to voice observations and opinions. The mediator weighed in heavily, arguing vigorously for his belief in nonviolence and gender equality. Gaining too little agreement from the man, he resorted to threats of economic consequences should the violence continue. The chorus of onlookers hummed approval.

In an American context, this process would hardly qualify as mediation. It involved raw deployment of the mediator's power. But in the Bangladeshi village context, the man who mediated was a respected leader of a rural development nongovernmental organization, deeply involved in the community, and capable of wielding considerable economic and social influence. A cultural Rubicon had been crossed some years earlier: where previously domestic violence was an accepted norm, now it was not. This leader-mediator knew he expressed a new will of the community. He stood in no doubt of the dimensions of his culturally sanctioned role.

When we in the West try to establish common practices, what some may see as "best" others experience as oppression. Indeed, the remote professional may manifest the will of some segment of the community—that part influenced by the cultural dicta of the "majority" (a word that warrants quotation marks since we stand on the cusp of living in an all-minority society). But if we espouse values of equality, if in particular as facilitators, mediators, or arbitrators, we see ourselves as protectors of the rights of the "minority," then to apply one standard of mediation practice to all people and all cultures is to be complicit in enforcing domination of some over others.

Some mediators work from an elicitive approach (see chapter 7 "Shifting Paradigms"; Lederach, 2003) which rests on two principles: first, listening to the voices of everyone involved in the work to understand deeply whatever cultural contexts are involved; and second, flexibly constructing each process to fit the needs of the people who are there. This method demands humility, a deep understanding that knowledge takes multiple forms, a capacity to adapt to different modes and languages, and, above all, time. In our Western professional settings, even if an individual mediator devoutly wishes to work elicitively, chances are good they won't have the luxury of enough time.

TIME STRUCTURE

Roberto Chené coined the phrase "time oppression." Industrial time structures life in the industrial age. We eat, sleep, leave home, get to work, nag our children to accomplish morning tasks, and get to school, all according to the clock. Famously, people work to a different rhythm in predominantly agricultural societies. When I lived in India in the mid-20th century, I quickly learned that an appointment at 8 p.m. might start anywhere from 9 p.m. to 11 p.m. Nowadays, however, as India has become increasingly urbanized and organized around the global economy, start time for events has become ever stricter.

One thing we know for sure about conflict is that it is exacerbated by a scarcity of time. For a mediator who works to a tight appointment calendar, especially if that mediator must report out successes to an overseeing supervisor, the pressure to produce a settlement is great. One couple in my practice broke up after years of domestic abuse when the man chased the woman from their house, threatening her with a two-by-four. She ran next door, and the neighbor called the police. After the man had been taken away in handcuffs, a scene witnessed by many people alerted by the hullaballoo, the woman collected their four children, took shelter, and left the marriage.

Some months later, the couple appeared for their mandated temporary settlement mediation session. With no source of income and saturated in debt to friends and family, the woman was desperate to put in place an interim agreement for child support. The mediator rolled up her sleeves to begin the negotiation only to be stymied by the man's insistence that he would talk about nothing until his soon-to-be ex-wife apologized for humiliating him in front of the neighbors. Horrified, she refused. He (literally and figuratively) turned his back on the table; the mediator urged and cajoled and nervously eyed the clock as it inched toward the end of the hour. Frantically, five minutes before the time ran out, she proposed a sum and asked the woman if she would accept it. In a tearful panic, the woman said yes. The man nodded agreement and the door closed on the couple.

As she drove away, the woman realized she had just signed on to an agreement that left her choosing between feeding her children and herself. Paying rent for housing was out of the question. "How could I have been so stupid?" she cried in our next counseling session.

How often does a scenario like this play out? People most comfortable with working to the clock have a clear advantage in any time-pressured negotiation. Who are those people? They tend to be those employed in professions structured in time (think lawyers and doctors), or in businesses that demand brevity and directness (think marketing), or in research work formulated in terms of the scientific process. They are not people socialized to perceive the world intuitively, to express themselves emotionally, to need an understanding of the way pieces of the puzzle fit together, and so on. All these latter forms of seeing, hearing, and knowing are, because of socialization, more typical of women and people from more communitarian cultures, often people of color. The ways of being that best fit time-pressured, verbal, linear ways of negotiating tend to be male, white, employed in white-collar professions. These contrasts mirror cultural, social, and economic dominance in our social structure, which is therefore unintentionally and invisibly replicated in common conflict intervention processes.

In my example of the community organization, before meeting in session we spent hours interviewing stakeholders. Based on what we learned, we proposed a session for the community members, most of them people of color, to present their experience of the problem and for the board leadership, all of whom were white, to listen. Once we had agreed on the approach, we met with the members separately to coach them on how to present their perspectives truthfully and at the same time respectfully. And we met with the board to coach them on how to listen to hard truths with curiosity and openness, seeking frontiers of learning while also managing those inevitable tendencies to explain, defend, or express guilt or hurt in the face of criticism. There's a place for those feelings, but not in the moment of listening!

The success of this work was only made possible by the willingness of the participants to take expansive time—and by the ability of the facilitators to accept fees within the means of the organization to pay.

MONEY MATTERS

For as long as time, people have helped each other to resolve conflicts. Human history is motored by conflict, the modality of progress. Once we assert that only certain people are qualified to intervene and that those are the only legitimized practitioners, then questions of money become central. To devote a substantial amount of time helping others through contentious problems in a capitalist society requires a means to earn a living. In the United States, there are some publicly funded services, such as the federal Community Mediation Service and volunteer community mediation agencies that may receive judicial court funding. But as the field of fee-for-service practitioners grows, the question of who pays, how much, for how many hours become central.

My colleagues and I have always set fees on a sliding scale, starting as low as possible. Even then, people may not be able to afford our services. Through donations and other fund-raising methods, we've built a small amount of additional support. But the contradictions between providing services that increasingly eclipse the wisdom of grassroots mediators, creating a commensurate need to pay for something that belongs to us all but is available only to those with means to pay, is a social problem rarely addressed as we debate best practices.

MODES OF COMMUNICATION

As mediation becomes a paid service, its vocabulary and processes are legitimized by borrowing from other established professions, primarily the law. Legal thinking is analytic and sequential. It looks at a problem through an overlay of rules, with a clear methodology for organizing knowledge and procedures. As I've said, for many people of color—and also for many white women—ways of thinking are very different. They center the relationship, are nonlinear, organic, and seated in emotion equally with intellectual analysis. Therefore, one person may be speaking instrumentally, focusing on the end goal, while another is talking about a greater context of pain, hope, and connectedness. Laura Nader (1993) has critiqued divorce mediation, showing how contrasting ways of disputing disadvantaged women. These different perspectives also give rise to different vocabularies, and to different priorities for what needs to be expressed to move toward these different goals. With our borrowed legal vocabulary, we speak of cases, parties, interests, and so on. Many of these words are mystifying to lay participants. Even if they are understood in the context of law, they may only poorly correspond to the dynamic, interdependent nature of conflict as those involved experience it.

Add to differences in vocabulary and ways of thinking the fact that languages of origin vary widely in the United States. Our immigrant society embodies people of many different mother tongues. Even those born in the United States may have started life speaking a language other than English. My father, born into the Lower East Side of Manhattan early in the 20th century, never heard a word of English spoken until he started kindergarten at five. That experience is still common among New York Yiddish-speaking communities, as well as many places where Spanish or other languages prevail. Many children grow up bilingual (or more!); nonetheless, their language of most comfort, of wholistic and emotional communication, the language in which intimate relationship, first with parents, later with siblings and friends, may be something other than English. When we facilitate conversations monolingually, we are automatically creating the need for these multilingual participants to work harder as they translate the most intensely personal communications into English.

These mismatches in modes of communication set a framework of unequal power that shows up as an advantage or disadvantage in negotiated outcomes. The dominant culture is deeply reflected in legal and scientific thinking. Mediators who are trained to stay focused on settlement quite naturally wish to keep the conversation within "efficient" boundaries, resulting in discourse easy for linear, analytic thinkers but uncomfortable to relational, organic ones. The process in the room, therefore, replicates power dynamics in society at large, reproducing "isms" of all sorts.

How we speak reflects ways we form knowledge within specific cultural contexts, which in turn informs what we believe to be true in any conflict. People in contentious relationships define the facts, the problems, and the solutions very differently. Intervenors encourage people to "hear" each other but often lack the means to explore the underlying cultural meanings we bring to contention.

In my approach to mediation, I use a technique that allows people to formulate their smart hunches and teaches the listener how to connect the dots between his reality and the speaker's. What is the speaker picking up correctly, and what can you correct where you see the speaker going wrong? *Validating the reality* of people's perceptions is enormously powerful. It constitutes a way of bridging cultural differences, grounding relationships in material facts and exploring crucial contexts for experience and understanding.

Using these tools, each person has an opportunity to clear the air, one statement at a time. I help each listener refrain from responding so that each emotional expression stands clearly in its dignity. I also help each listener to do the very hard task of validating paranoias:

Sofia: [to Stuart] When you promised to take me along to your meetings with donors, but then only told me about the meeting with D_____ the morning it was happening, I felt angry, hurt, scared and powerless. And my paranoia is that you didn't really want me to go.

Beth: What's your hunch about why Stuart might not have wanted you to go?

Sofia: Well, I think he doesn't respect me.

Beth: Doesn't respect what about you?

Sofia: Doesn't think I'm smart enough.

Beth: Stuart, what's true and not true about that?

Stuart: It's not true at all, I think you're brilliant! That's why I hired you and offered to mentor you.

Beth: [Searching for a kernel of truth by trying a trial balloon.] Is there something else you don't respect about Sofia?

Stuart: [Squirming.] No, nothing I can think of.

I notice his body language and guess he's frightened to say something. I try out an *intuition of my own*.

Beth: Is it possible there's something about Sofia that makes you worried to introduce her to funders in general, or to D____ in particular?

Stuart: Well, D____ did make a bigoted remark once about people who speak English with an accent. I guess I have a bit of a worry about his being rude to Sofia.

I notice Sofia bristling. She begins to speak, "I can take care of myself!"

Beth: Understandable, Sofia. I'm sure you can! [Turning to Stuart, taking a risk to say what I intuit he may not be able to bring himself to say.] Stuart, you speak a highly educated, law-school-groomed English. Are *you* embarrassed about Sofia's Spanish accent?

Stuart: [Reflectively.] Not exactly embarrassed. I like the way you speak, Sofia. But I do worry that some of our funders will have judgments. True, they're supporting a social justice organization, but that doesn't mean they aren't personally biased. So I guess sometimes I don't want to take the risk of losing potential donors.

This example of my taking the risk of saying the unsayable demonstrates leadership and advocacy. Once the truth is out, something can change. Courageous truth-speaking by the mediator encourages—and sometimes enables—

participants to get to the core issues that need to be dealt with both interpersonally and, as in this case, organizationally.

ATTITUDE TOWARD EMOTION

What is most importantly given short shrift is emotion. When Ury and Fisher first proposed in *Getting to Yes* that conflict resolution requires "separating the people from the problem," many people of color objected strenuously. How can those things be separated? they asked. The people *are* the problem; the problem is all about the people. Translating the dictum into the management of emotion to get beyond it does grave injustice to what relationally focused people experience as essential to any resolution of conflict.

Emotional expression serves multiple functions in conflict resolution processes where any kind of relationship is involved—and even business negotiation involves human relationships. First, expressing feelings in a setting where attention is focused on them allows the release of some of the heat. Second, every emotion comes from somewhere real; to hear and understand the root of what people are feeling is to understand their experience of the world in general and of the dispute in particular. Third, emotion often tracks lines of power. Listening closely to what disputants feel tells the mediator, and also the people involved, what the core issues are that need attention. Rather than sidelining emotion, therefore, conflict intervention that allows for people of color to present themselves as full human beings requires skill in guiding, hearing, and understanding emotional expression—not skills commonly taught to mediators.

UNDERSTANDINGS OF POWER

Most central to the rewards for facilitating emotional communication in the way I've described is gaining insight into power dynamics. All conflict implicates power in some—usually many—forms. To enter into a negotiation without understanding how power is being enacted in the process is to compound inequalities. If, as a field, we are committed to inclusion and equity, then being skilled in analyzing and addressing *inequality* is crucial. Yet training more often involves jargon such as "leave inequalities of power at the door" (as if that were possible) and "how to balance an uneven table" (as if the table were the problem).

Many years ago, Juliana Birkhoff researched the ways that mediators think about power. What she found was that lawyerly concepts of BATNA (best alternative to a negotiated agreement) dominated many conflict intervenors' operating concepts. Reading power in the very narrow frame of negotiation strategy excludes most of the dimensions on which power lives in every moment in every transaction between and among people. We *feel* more or less powerful, especially in light of the framework in which we are appearing. We *interact* more or less powerfully, depending on our comfort with the language and process to which we are confined. We command more or less power depending on how well the *culture* in the room reflects the culture within which we live outside the room. We have *access* to more or less negotiating power depending on the organizational resources at our command. We bring to the conversation more or less power depending on our *experiences of privilege or oppression* throughout our lives leading up to the moment. If none of these ways that power is in play is articulated, then embedded imbalances inevitably influence the outcome of mediation.

DEFINITION OF GOALS

How the mediator defines the goal of a given process may be very different from the desired goals of participants. In a seminal piece of research done in the Albuquerque court system in 1996, Michelle Hermann and colleagues found that "minority parties" often came away from processes conducted by white mediators with settlements lower than those awarded in comparable adjudicated cases. But they expressed greater satisfaction with the process. Why the contradiction? Because these participants appreciated being able to speak freely, and they noted satisfaction in any improvement of relationship, even if improvement was only incremental.

Do we mediate for settlements or for restoration? For getting to yes or for building relationships? To meet a goal or to engage in a process? I've posed these questions as dichotomies when they are intertwined. But if we exclude one side of that binary, we create environments less friendly to participants who live life in other than the dominant culture.

WHO SITS AT THE TABLE

How we define the nature of a conflict—is it a dispute between two individuals or a matter involving the wider community?—impacts who we invite to participate in its resolution. I've already sketched a mediation in South Asia in which multitudes participated, not just the two people most directly involved in the qualifying conflict. As an organizational mediator, I am commonly asked to mediate between two people engaged in what everyone defines as a "personality conflict": "They just don't get along, and their tension is driving everyone crazy. Please do something!" If you view conflict as involving only those actively disputing, then "doing something" means getting those two quarreling people in a room and facilitating a process.

But if you think organizationally, you question how their tensions reflect organizational dynamics. Are they competing with each other because their job descriptions are too vague and overlap? Are their working styles formed in different cultural milieus, and does the dominant style of the organization reflect one but not the other? Is there a lack of leadership, and does the resulting vacuum of power impact how everyone works? Are there unexamined differences of culture and power, an ongoing, systemic conflict that bursts to the surface in these two employees' interactions with each other?

Rather than mediating two people, I would interview everyone I can in the organization and ensure that as many as possible take part. No doubt, we'll find something in the particular relationships between the two identified disputants that needs to be worked through. But I'm equally confident that they are manifesting strains beyond their interpersonal problems. Often, not coincidentally, one of the people identified as a problem is a person of minority identity. Because of their discomforts (or more pointedly, their exclusion or oppression), they speak out and become seen as out of line. If I as a mediator take that definition at face value, then I add to the oppression of this individual, and I compound the true problem, which is institutional and enduring. More, I believe I paste over an opportunity for the organization as a whole, and for every individual in that organization, to learn and to grow toward enacting equity.

Am I imposing my goal or accomplishing theirs? In my long experience of the work, I'm not in doubt that the two are the same.

RESOLUTION, TRANSFORMATION, OR RESTORATION?

Along the way in this chapter, I've referred to these distinctions of intention. At the heart of dominant US culture is a worldview grounded in individualism. If we view conflict as an isolated event between or among particular individuals, then we isolate those people in the process of helping them resolve their differences. But if we see strains between individuals as seated in collective problems, then the intention and methods of intervention become very different.

Throughout this chapter, I've tried not to generalize too absolutely about features of "people of color." People of similar color come from very many different backgrounds, experiences, ideologies, and beliefs. To the extent we can generalize, however, when people are acculturated to a dominant culture, their worldview is invisible. The assumptions and values that comprise a worldview are so widely shared that they fall out of the realm of problematic, and therefore out of bounds for discussion.

But if you sit outside the margins of that culture, then those same values and assumptions are very evident and often oppressive. Many different factors tilt excluded peoples toward valuing community. For one thing, the need for collective protection is strong. The comfort of like-mindedness is equally desired. I am only sketching a few differences in lived experience here, naming them to call into question our assumptions as conflict resolvers about what we are bringing people together to do.

Paradoxically, in my counseling work, one of the most common goals for white clients is to make a community. For while we may not have experienced collectivity in our places of origin, we know that we miss it as adults. When people of color come to counseling, they more often are seeking support as they negotiate cross-cultural relationships, both in their intimate lives and in their workplaces.

When we define the purpose, the structure, the language, and the style of mediation monoculturally, we enter into the basic conflict people come to us to solve. We become part of the problem rather than its solution. We may then wonder why clients don't come to us for our services. We believe our problem is outreach, when in fact it is not. Our problem is unawareness of our limited consciousness, embedded as we may be in a cultural frame so dominant as to become invisible.

CHAPTER 8

When Do Cultural Borrowings (Dis)Honor the Lenders?

· ·

T he raw materials we mediators have at our command are talk and truth. Professional practices impose limits on how true the voices we mold into agreements can be. In the limited time at our command, we guide participants to be clear and concise. We press people to express their interests, to nego- tiate solutions. What is often lost in that process is personhood. Our understanding of each other may be too thin for true comprehension. Possible solutions end up left under the table, never truly considered because they lie beyond the realm of a genuine relation- ship. We may hear surface truths but not the deeper ones within which creativity and lasting agreement lie.

No voice rings more true than the one speaking personal truth. We offer this vivid example of the power of humanizing stories by New Mexican mediator Lucy Moore.

—Beth Roy

· ·

Cultural Appropriation vs. Cultural Learning

Lucy Moore

I live in Santa Fe, New Mexico, a beautiful place in so many ways. The climate, the landscape, the adobe architecture, and the cultural richness—all this has made Santa Fe a magnet for refugees from mainstream America. For centuries Santa Fe has been a haven for those looking for a fresh start. In the 16th and 17th centuries, the Spanish came looking for gold and converts to Catholicism. Later and continuing today, waves of Anglos have come looking for business opportunities, relief from the hectic pace of modern life, or freedom from the constraints and expectations of family and society. Many seek spiritual meaning

· ·

in the cultural and religious experiences available from Native and Hispanic communities that have kept alive traditional practices that are hundreds, and in some cases thousands, of years old.

The stage is set for exploitation—legal, economic, and cultural. The state flag features the Zia symbol, taken without permission from the Pueblo of Zia, one of New Mexico's 22 tribal sovereign nations. Shops in Santa Fe, and elsewhere in the state, are bursting with jewelry, textiles, pottery, carvings, knick-knacks, and souvenirs claiming to be made by Native artisans. Lawsuits are brought regularly against fraudulent claims, but the exploitation goes on. Tourists and transplants alike seem to compete for the biggest squash blossom necklace, bolo tie, or belt buckle, laden with turquoise. Self-declared shamans with adopted Indian names offer healing ceremonies borrowed directly from Native practitioners. Gigantic 10,000-square-foot adobe mansions dot the hilltops outside Santa Fe. To me, they are grotesque versions of the simple adobe homes built by Native and Hispanic families with handmade adobe bricks and maintained with a new mud coating every year. These grandiose copies, often second homes, are made of modern materials covered with brown-tinted stucco and need no annual maintenance.

The wealth of these transplants, engendering entitlement, may allow them to indulge in what they see as cultural *appreciation* but what may also be called cultural *appropriation*. For some White people who are feeling devoid of cultural identity, trying on another's culture can satisfy a yearning to belong, to be surrounded by the richness, history, and spirit of that culture that seems so nurturing. But like trying on a costume, these efforts to connect and find meaning miss the mark, often trivializing at best and damaging at worst the cultural practices they claim to honor.

But who am I to be pontificating on the sins of these newcomers to New Mexico? I have only been here 45 years, and I am not being facetious. Native New Mexicans are *born* here, or better yet, like my Hispanic husband, they can trace back 16 or so generations to Mexico and Spain. The Native Americans, of course, have claims dating from time immemorial. Like many transplants, I am genuinely interested in my new, culturally rich home, and want to be as sensitive a neighbor and as good a citizen as I can be. I have learned about the landscape—geographic, political, historic, and cultural—and have many friends who continue to educate me on what it means to be a New Mexican, in both my personal and professional life.

As an environmental mediator, I am committed to creating and managing conflict resolution processes that fit the needs of my participants. Most of the conflicts I handle involve Native American tribes, often at odds with a federal, state, or local agency, an environmental organization, an industry, a neighboring community, or several of the above. The issue may be access to a sacred site, restoration of a polluted river, protection of endangered species, approval of a mining permit, or dozens of other flashpoints for conflict. I take no side in the debate and am careful to ensure that everyone at the table is treated with respect and has a voice in the outcome.

Over the years I have learned powerful lessons from Native American and Hispanic colleagues and participants about the importance of relationships and of building trust if conflicts across cultural divides are to be resolved equitably. Yet this critical step is often missing in our processes. The Anglo-based model of mediation usually practiced in the United States emphasizes the transactional part of conflict resolution. What will it take to get a deal? What do you need to be satisfied? Building relationships among the parties, showing vulnerabilities, and finding that elusive trust—these steps are often left out in the rush to find the solution to the conflict and get parties to sign on the dotted line. How the parties feel about each other at the end, how satisfied they were with the pace and the process, these questions are rarely asked.

I'm suggesting that we listen to these wise words from Native colleagues and participants and learn from them how to build trust and relationships in the mediation process. In the following, I offer one example from among many moments as a mediator when a cultural practice made a significant difference in the process.

STORIES

One Native way that has opened doors to understanding and resolution in my mediation processes is storytelling. It was a Native woman from Arizona who first taught me this. I had been asked by the National Association of Counties (NACO) to bail them out of a very tough situation. NACO is a powerful lobbying organization that includes all elected county officials in the country—sheriffs, clerks, commissioners, and so forth. A small percentage of those officials happen to be Native American, since many counties, especially in the western United States, include Indian lands within their borders.

The overlapping jurisdiction of tribes and counties had become a point of contention in the 1990s. Leadership in counties that included tribal lands claimed it was impossible to provide services when the county was denied taxation, law enforcement, and regulatory authority on Indian land. And now, some tribes were even beginning to compete with local government, setting up businesses, attracting county dollars to casinos, and levying their taxes on county citizens. It was time for Native Americans to leave their entitlements behind, said these county officials, and become "regular citizens." They petitioned NACO to initiate legislation that would abrogate treaties with tribes.

The reaction from the tribal membership of NACO was swift. This was *their* organization, too, and they naturally fought the initiative. In response, NACO formed a Task Force on County-Tribal Relations with the mandate to resolve the conflict over treaty rights and make recommendations for improved county-tribal relationships. I was asked to mediate the sixth and final meeting of the task force, their last chance to break the stalemate and reach some sort of consensus on how the organization should deal with "Indian issues."

I walked into the meeting room and saw 12 weary faces—six Native American and six Anglo. They looked exhausted and hopeless. Unsure about how I could help, I began with introductions. I knew they knew each other all too well by now, but I asked them to take their time and tell me a bit about themselves.

I called on the woman to my left, a Native American elder from Arizona. She began slowly and in a leisurely, engaging style told us about her birthplace, her family, summers herding sheep for her grandparents, the death of her father, her mother's battle with alcoholism, the time the coyotes killed her favorite sheepherding dog, years in boarding school, where she was punished for speaking her native language, how she learned to drive her brother's old pickup truck. The time was ticking away and she was only 15 years old! Should I try to hurry her along? I scanned the circle; everyone was riveted by her story. I sat back as she took us through high school, an early marriage, four children, the death of her husband while working for the railroad, life as a widow, her degree in substance abuse counseling from the community college, her political awakening in her job with the county.

Her children convinced her to run for county commissioner, so she made signs and stood out on the rural highway where you were lucky to see one vehicle an hour. She punctuated her story with laughter. To her amazement, she won, and then came the scariest moment of her life. We listeners couldn't imagine what could be scarier than the time the snake bit her baby sister, or a dozen other traumas we had heard. That moment was, she said, when she walked up the aisle to take her seat for the first time as a commissioner. Her knees were shaking, her heart was racing. "I was the first Indian ever elected," she said still amazed and laughed again. She concluded with the news that she had just been reelected for a second term and that she wasn't scared anymore, and that she loved helping everyone, Indian and non-Indians.

"Well, that's my story," she said, "and I sure appreciate you listening to me."

I looked around the table. There were smiles, looks of admiration, and some moist eyes. I thanked her for her story and moved to the next person. We continued around the table, hearing longer introductions from the Native Americans, and as we progressed the Anglo Task Force members began to open up, too, and reveal more of themselves. By the time we had completed the circle, half the day was gone. I was worried that we had only the afternoon to resolve the tough issues before us.

When the members returned from lunch, I sensed a new degree of relaxation, even friendliness. I feared that this atmosphere would fall victim to the inevitable hostilities that lay ahead. But the task force members had no trouble seeing the path they needed to take. They knew each other now at a deeper level; they had opened up and been vulnerable and honest with each other.

The mood was calm, the way was clear. I was almost extraneous; I stepped aside to let them charge forward. They agreed that no decision or rule was going to apply in all situations involving counties and tribes. Each county was different; each tribe was different. An Anglo observed that dissolving treaties was not going to happen, but suggested that there were ways counties and tribes could work together, site by site, case by case. They developed a set of steps that NACO might take to help in these individual situations, and it was a challenge for me to write their ideas fast enough on the flip chart. As I remember, we even finished early that afternoon. The group dissolved into twos and threes and straggled out of the room. The good-byes were sincere, the see-you-next-times were warm.

That "little old Indian lady," as she called herself, showed us how to build trust in a few hours with her courage, her vulnerability, and her humanity. I have treasured that gift and am always alert to the opportunity for stories to bring us together.

Allowing time for stories to unfold naturally is a luxury we (and our clients) often think we cannot afford. We all agree that openness and honesty are key to reaching a fair solution, but without taking that time to build trusting relationships, how can we expect our participants to enter into meaningful negotiations? One courageous person willing to tell a story and show vulnerability can turn a process from a stalemate into a whirlwind of progress.

We have much to learn and much to gain from Native cultures about building relationships, focusing on what is important, and taking our time. In rushing through negotiations to meet a deadline and reach a solution, we trample the moments for truly learning from each other, for relaxing, telling stories, sharing food, building trust. And we lose the chance to creatively and mutually find equitable solutions to our conflicts.

CHAPTER 9

What Do We See When We Refuse to Look Away?

···

M y fellow editor, Hasshan Batts, has a unique way of expanding my worldview with his wisdom, heart, and deep experience of both oppression and redemption. We offer the next contribution in this section, a transcribed conversation between Hasshan and Jeani Garcia, the mother of a murdered son, as a way to widen the frame of understanding from what happens "in the room" to that which lies outside the frame in the realm of greater social reality. Coming to see that which has been rendered invisible is not easy, whether invisibility is a product of intentional deception or of cultural shielding. Hasshan and Jeani lift those veils to offer profound insights into the social context for tragedy.

Pressed by the stressors of everyday practice, a reader might ask with irritation, what does the mother of a murdered 17-year-old boy have to offer that will enhance my practice? Our choice to provide this chapter rests on the belief that every piece of work we do in our shared profession, whether a restorative justice session, a divorce or commercial mediation, a university lecture, exists within an invisible context of resources available or, all too often, denied. Focusing on transactions, the tangible material apparent when we sit in the room with disputing clients, practitioners may find their attention pulled away from that which is less accessible. We may overlook underlying power dynamics, taking for granted that they lie outside the scope of the session, even though how every word is said, heard, or registered as significant is determined by those dynamics. We may forget that what's missing from the conversation is as crucial to an equitable solution as the countable resources displayed for all to see on the table. And in those absences, both in the room and outside its walls, racism resides. If we are to understand how our shared profession is implicated in discriminatory practices, we need for these and other systemic factors to become starkly visible.

Hasshan and Jeani lay bare the searing consequences of how unequal distribution of access to services and material resources impacts people in communities of color. In doing so, they speak to systemic realities for which we must account before our work can be counted toward making a more just world. Hasshan gives us a pointed critique

···

of expertise as our newly professionalizing field constructs it. Designating people like Jeani and himself "conflict revolutionaries," he contributes as well a new category to the nomenclature of the work we share.

We urge you to read this chapter, painful as it may be, as the infrastructure, mostly unexpressed but always imperative, on which all the work we do, and all the writing in this book, in fact, rests.

—Beth Roy

Kareem Was Killed Long Before the Trigger Was Pulled

Hasshan Batts and Jeani Garcia

Hasshan: When conflict practitioners focus on acts of violence as interpersonal interactions, we run the risk of missing the power of the patterns. Patterns often leave clues. It is in these clues hidden in the patterns of violence that we uncover the structural and systemic nature of the beast and it is often through telling and retelling our stories that others begin to hear their stories interwoven throughout our community and recognize they are not alone.

Violence breeds loneliness and anger, whereas healing occurs in authentic relationships and within the community. Conflict practitioners need to recognize the politics of power and weaponization of voice within the conflict resolution field that shrinks and commodifies the expressions, work, and authority of everyday people across the communities we serve. Just as pain and harm continue to be hyper-individualized by the conflict resolution field, the grassroots theorists, solutions, interventions, and champions that exist continue to be systematically ignored, whitewashed, and forgotten by the profession.

I am a conflict revolutionist, a credible messenger, and a former perpetrator and survivor of gun violence. Conflict revolution theory is grounded in healing and liberatory activism and postulates that the conflict resolution field, practices, and practitioners often harm marginalized and racialized communities by decentering the expertise of those closest to the pain. Furthermore, the field problematizes communities by ignoring grassroots solutions to our pain. Conflict revolution theory challenges allies, accomplices, and co-conspirators throughout the field to exercise their privilege by relinquishing power and lifting up the stories, solutions, and mastery of the individuals and communities we serve. The radical change that a conflict revolution calls for is grounded in authentic relationships with the stories, people, places, and experiences of harm we seek to support others in repairing.

I come from a community peppered with dual victims, so when I'm in a relationship with the mothers of the shot or the shooters, I see it as a restorative practice. Relationships and activism with the mothers who have survived gun violence and the structural violence that precedes it, I believe, allow me to atone for those I have harmed by the gun and the torment my mother experienced preparing my burial while I was living.

I make it a practice to sit with and honor mothers. I find it particularly important to learn from the joys, pain, and hopes of mothers and grandmothers across the communities that I serve. First and foremost, my survival skills growing up in the pre-gentrified Brooklyn of the 1980s, surviving multiple juvenile and adult prison systems, navigating the world of white supremacy as a Black man, and finally my training as a mediator, social worker, and community epidemiologist equipped me with the soft skills to build rapport and relationship. However, my familiarity with rejection, pain, and harm equipped me to radically listen and be in a relationship with survivors and their liberatory narratives.

Storytelling is a revolutionary act of sharing, witnessing, and affirming the interpersonal as well as the systemic nature of conflict and violence. I have sat with countless mothers such as Jeani, sat with them in emergency rooms, juvenile justice facilities, prison visiting rooms, funeral homes, and long-term care facilities.

What follows is the story of Jeani and her beloved son Kareem. Jeani has graciously and passionately shared her son's story to highlight how failing systems and lack of care from those charged with educating, protecting, and caring for our children leads to the increased burden of death across our community. As Jeani shares the story of her son's murder, I am present yet although I see Kareem's smile, I see the power of these interrelated systems to leave trails of blood across communities of color and ultimately across the world.

The individual impact of violence is real. Yet there are countless unspoken stories of violence and harm that have never been told beyond the lives touched. Every community possesses heroes and messengers without titles or credentials that routinely bring parties together, create brave spaces, actively listen, support those involved to feeling heard and to contribute to generating solutions that prevent, respond to, or mitigate acts of violence and harm. The academy and the conflict resolution field continue to ignore the voices, lived experiences, approaches, and techniques of the conflict revolutionists across our communities. The conflict resolution field has fueled a patriarchal white savior narrative that decenters the voices of racialized people and in our call to action to recenter the lives and patterns of those on the margins of the field, margins of the pain, and margins of the harm we begin by supporting them in sharing their healing stories.

I invite you to read the story that follows as an example of the death of Black boys and urge you to honor the legacy of Kareem while centering your lens on the systems that failed Kareem and his mother long before the trigger was pulled. Jeani and Kareem tell the stories of so many lost to the apathy and disinvestment of communities of color. In these countless interrelated narratives exist the evidence that systems, safety net institutions, and yes, the conflict resolution field as a whole, summarily fail many Black boys and their mothers.

Furthermore, I urge you to listen deeply for the failures in all of the points of intervention to preserve Kareem's life and importantly for the field of conflict resolution I invite you to reflect on the legacy and power of Kareem's mother, Jeani, as a skilled conflict revolutionist that doesn't require a master's degree in conflict resolution, a 40-hour mediation program and internship, a certificate or any professional credentials to care and show up and listen and heal with the countless people whose lives she impacts. Last, I remind you that our communities are full of Jeanis who go ignored by our field as they focus on resolving disputes. Why are we not collecting the data of the love they give?

DEAR MAMA: JEANI AND KAREEM

The world of conflict resolution has been known to limit racialized communities' access to voice by commodifying healing, professionalizing problem-solving, and hyper-theorizing the work of restoring relationships and resolving conflict. I would often think of my mother and the many mothers and grandmothers throughout communities of color that possess and apply the skills and wisdom to resolve family and community conflicts. All the brothers, cousins, and neighborhood youth that have experienced the healing powers of authentic relationships and community never stop to ask to see their credentials.

We practitioners do our field and the communities we serve great harm by indicating only professionals are involved in mediation and conflict resolution rather than affirming the agency of families and communities to be self-healing. In addition to attempting to control the voices of the peacemakers across the communities we serve, we sever the natural ecosystem of restorative and rejuvenating practices that hold within them the capacity to nurture and heal relationships. The lack of acknowledgment and witnessing of the power of our community healers discredits the work and perpetuates violence and harm by creating a dependency on external professionals and systems rather than the indigenous and community practices that have maintained communities for generations.

Furthermore, the world of conflict resolution continues to avoid centering the context of the people, the systems, and the problems as seen and told by the people that bear the burdens of the systems that impact their lives. On our journey to resolve conflict, to heal, to actualize agency, and to disrupt systems of white supremacy we must recenter our relationships, our stories, and our solutions. To preserve life and broaden our field to be truly inclusive of the mothers, grandmothers, aunts, and sisters across communities resolving conflict every day, we must lift up the voices of our sheroes.

Jeani is a healer, disrupter, bridge builder, and warrior. She uses the ancient power of narrative to heal, and she carries with her a medical bag/toolbox full of compassion, brilliance, and discernment to build community and repair harm. I met with Jeani and listened as she shared stories of her son Kareem who was murdered at 17 years old.

Jeani's story is one of community disinvestment and missed opportunities. As powerful as Jeani is, she was trapped in a system that disempowered her as a parent and a system that neglected to respond to the multiple points of intervention to use conflict resolution practices to save her son Kareem's life.

I asked Jeani to tell the world about her son Kareem.

Jeani: Kareem was an average young man in school. Seventeen years old, raised with four other siblings and he slowly started picking the wrong friends. I'm noticing things like him failing in school, being put into different programs at school, being taken out of the regular classroom, put into disciplinary class-rooms and settings with the so-called bad kids. That's where it started, they started segregating him into a group, and then, after some time, I found out he was in a gang, involved in the Crips, and I started reaching out for help. I started with the school, didn't get anywhere with my district, and then moved on to my government, my politicians, my police department anybody, anything that had gang or youth attached to it, I reached out and asked for help. And because Kareem had never been in trouble before, I had nowhere to turn, I got the door closed in my face. Well, he's not in trouble, they would say, so they were more interested in if they could bring Kareem in to tell on his friends. What were they up to? What are they doing? That's what they were concerned about. They weren't concerned about his safety, his future.

He was growing into a man. He's supposed to be getting help, getting out of this lifestyle. They weren't concerned about providing mentoring or any types of programs like that. And it's crazy because after Kareem died, I had a reporter who couldn't believe my experience and wanted to confirm it before she reported it. She wanted to find out. So, she took all the steps that I took and called agencies and the police department as if she was a parent. She asked questions, and the same thing happened to her. So, she wrote an article in *The Morning Call* (local newspaper). So, this is the world we live in and I got a taste of it and my son died because of it.

Hasshan: What was the time frame between you seeing the signs, asking for help, and Kareem being murdered?

Jeani: We're talking about, like, less than a year, maybe seven months. I did everything that I thought I could possibly do. I even moved from where we lived in Center City, Allentown. And I moved to the Whitehall-Allentown bor-der. Just anything I could do to make it harder for Kareem to get to his friends, to get where he wanted to hang out. And I was only living there four months when Kareem was murdered. That was my last-ditch effort to get him out of there. I didn't have money or family to send him to another state or relocate him. I'm doing the best I can, I just gotta make it harder for him, harder for him to get to his friend's house, harder for him to walk into Center City.

The issue that I have is that all the way up into the sentencing in Kareem's murder, I feel like I have been subjected to the systematic programming and oppression that all of our kids are experiencing right now. They just can't tell the story about it.

Hasshan: You're saying all of our children are experiencing it?

Jeani: All of our children. First of all, a school system that is segregating our children, because they act out or because their grades are failing. Kareem had never been in trouble before. There wasn't one educator that met Kareem and had the opportunity to teach Kareem that cared enough to say, Hey, why are your grades failing? Why are you not coming to school every day? Nobody knocked on my door and said, Why isn't your kid in school? I got those auto robo calls. Your kid skipped, he was not in attendance for fifth and sixth period. For me, I skipped school. I was like, okay, he skipped, he skipped gym, he skipped history.

Hasshan: You thought he was in the hallway playing.

Jeani: Yeah, in the hallway playing around, (or) he's in the bathroom, but when you start seeing a child changing and you're an educator and you start seeing a child, failing and their character's changing . . . (his) character didn't start changing in my house. Because when Kareem walked through those doors, he was Kareem. The little funny kid, mommy's boy, you know, Mommy, Mom, scratch my back. Mom, did you wash my clothes? So I didn't see that. He was home every night at curfew.

Hasshan: He had a curfew?

Jeani: Yes, it was eight o'clock.

Hasshan: He never missed?

Jeani: He never missed curfew, but you had to be in by six o'clock to eat. So, you can only go outside, stay in the neighborhood until eight o'clock when the lights come on. When the lights come on, you need to come home. That was for all the children in my house, not just for Kareem. I'm a single mother of five, one girl and four boys. I was hard on my older kids because I knew they had little eyes and little ears listening to everything I did with them. They were going to be influenced by what I allowed them to do, so I was very hard on them.

Going back to the educators, there wasn't one teacher that was passionate enough to take their time and notice the change of my son? He was acting out in school and skipping class, just to keep him in school while I was at work, so I knew where he was at and keep him safe.

I allowed them to segregate him more into a new school. That was my only option. (I) put him in the school that was transformed into a bad school for bad kids, kids who had attendance problems, kids who had bad grades, kids who got suspended more than once. So right there, he was segregated. Now he was accepted into that realm. He was labeled. Yeah, he was labeled, and all the difference was started in the way they treated him.

He became known for being a badass and not recognized for being a kid that's maybe facing some troubles and let's find out what's going on, let's talk to this kid and pull him to the side and let's get him some resources.

Hasshan: You're saying that there were no systems in place to support him, to mentor him? And you even went as far as to make calls? Who were you calling? What were you saying?

Jeani: So, I'm going down the list. I started with the school. Well, why is my son being segregated? Why does he have to be here? Are there any programs? What happened to the Big Brother program? Like, what programs are out here that can help? Why do you identify my son as a problem student? Where do you suggest that I get help with this problem? Because I am a single mom, I'm asking for help. And (I got) no suggestions. No advice, no resources. This is what they were going to do (transfer him to the alternative school). That was 11th grade. I'm struggling to understand what's going on. He's going to be a senior next year. Is there anybody willing to put 100% effort to help me with my kid?

Hasshan: To me, it really sounds like you're doing your work as a mother. So, when I hear you speak, I think of my mother and it's like, we don't, we don't know at 17, you don't know and you don't understand the pain that you cause, the sleepless nights the worry. We have no way of understanding that, of understanding how much you love us and how hard you worry and work to keep us safe. Your and Kareem's story mirrors so many stories of mothers fighting for their sons' lives and of so many failed systems across our community.

Jeani: Exactly. There wasn't nobody. So, we settled for that (alternative school). And as soon as he got into that school, and he got that label attached to him, it went downhill from there. It went downhill from there, everything changed with Kareem. He was fighting. He was coming home beat up with marks on (him). You could tell that he got jumped: just his attitude changed. His chest was out. He was a little tougher.

My experience as a context and content expert with gangs has taught me that youth join gangs primarily for one or a combination of three reasons: (1) Safety: When adults fail to protect youth or when placed in unsafe environments they will often bond and protect themselves. We in turn criminalize or pathologize them for seeking and providing for their basic human right of safety. (2) Belonging: We now know that rejection is violence and that when adults other, reject, remove, suspend, and expel youth for seeking help in at times destructive ways, the youth will find other ways and places to bond and belong which often leads to gangs, crime, and promiscuity; and (3) Family disruption: This is often the focus of prevention and diversion programs because it focuses the shame and blame on the youth's family of origin rather than the historically white-led systems that disinvest in and disempower the communities of color in which the youth are raised.

Kareem's journey is far from an isolated incident. I, and many of the youth I have worked with and encountered, have had the label of a child or human for that matter removed from us and relegated to alternative schools where we were criminalized, pathologized, brutalized, and labeled incorrigible by middle-class suburban white female teachers for often subjective infractions. There is a misnomer of the school-to-prison pipeline that I have experienced as a nexus. My lived experience and shared experience within the communities, schools, and juvenile justice settings in which I have worked and researched is that urban public schools are part of an oppressive predatory system that prepares youth of color for prison.

I often share how the only good that came out of the New York City public school system for me was that the violence, degradation, and dehumanization of my school experience prepared me to survive in juvenile and adult prisons. It is brutally evident how difficult it is for youth or adults that were reared in nurturing, safe, and affirming schools to adjust to criminal justice settings riddled in violence, hopelessness, and despair.

I draw the connection between Kareem's educational experience and incarceration because as suburban teachers often remind urban youth, "You're going to die in a pool of your own blood either in prison or in the streets." Kareem died at home, in his bed, and was found by a mother that loved and adored him and possessed the skills and passion to intervene.

As you read this next section, imagine had Jeani lived in a world and community that invested in conflict resolution programming that was not led by interlopers but functioned outside of the traditional hegemony and supported community empowerment. Imagine Jeani and other mothers and community members as context experts and credible messengers in partnership with community mediation centers and ADR professionals leading a conflict revolution that centers the voices of those closest to the pain. Imagine when youth in a community seek help and answers to protect themselves and youth like Kareem and Jeani and mothers and community members like her are not alone in preserving life but have a toolbox of resources, funding, and power to save our babies.

Jeani: Somebody came up to me, one of my neighbors, a young kid, Kareem's friend, and he said, I got the green light on Kareem. And I said, green light? And he said, Kareem is in a gang and I'm in a gang, too. And I got the green light on Kareem, they want me to take him out. (The rival gang leader wanted him to kill Kareem). And I can't do that, because I love him. We used to play together. We used to play manhunt together two years ago. I can't do that.

So, when Kareem came home, I confronted him, and he told me, Yo, I'm in. The first thing I did was, which was probably wrong now that I look back at it,

I rip them beads off his neck, snatched him up, and pushed him in the corner. And I was like, I'm the only person you answer to. The people in this house are your squad. We're the ones who going to ride for you.

Then it just got worse from there, and so I ended up calling the police department one day. I was so upset with Kareem that I called the police department. I said, I know that you have to have a gang unit, and my son is a gang member, and he's never been in trouble before, but I need help, because I'm gonna lose my baby.

It's bad. It's really bad at this point for me with my upbringing to call the police. I was desperate. I tell them, he's coming home beat up and all of the things that are happening to my son and the first thing they said to me, is, (If) he is on probation, call his probation officer.

He doesn't have no probation; he's never been in trouble before. They tell me they can't do nothing, unless you want to bring him down and let us have a talk with him so we could find out what him and his buddies are up to? That's the response I got. Yeah.

You know, I was torn, because of where I come from. I come from a street code, too. Maybe I should have taken him down there and let them find out what him and his buddies did. But I felt like at that time, I would have been putting him in more jeopardy. If they would have found out his mother dragged him down to the police station. forced him to talk, what would happen to him?

No, they didn't care about Kareem. They didn't care about Kareem. They told me they didn't have any resources. They never mentioned any agency like Promise Neighborhoods of the Lehigh Valley or anybody, Boys and Girls Club. Nothing. They never mentioned anything, sent me away to deal with it alone. If you want us to help you, call us, basically, call us with some information, and we'll help you. Yeah, help us solve some crimes, and I didn't have details. And even if I did at that time, I don't think I would have put my son in that type of jeopardy.

Then when he died, when he got murdered, when he got murdered, they didn't care either. It took me to solve his murder. It took me to put all the pieces of the puzzle together.

Hasshan: *I invite the reader to pause and reimagine a world where Jeani and others like her are lifted up as experts for their love, relationships, and lived experience in the communities in which they live and serve. Allentown, like all urban communities in which I have worked and lived, utilizes public dollars from a majority minoritized community to center power, knowledge, expertise, and wealth outside the urban core by creating wealth, jobs, and opportunities for suburban whites. Reimagine an Allentown where funding, decision-making, conflict resolution, and community problem-solving were centered in the hands of the credible messengers that held a symbiotic relationship with the children they reared and served. Imagine an Allentown where the lived experience of* *raising four children or successfully navigating toxic and hostile systems was enough of a credential to warrant voice, dignity, and humanity.*

Jeani searched for concern for her son Kareem in systems that systematically fail our youth, invest more in incarcerating them than educating them and reject, other, suspend, and expel them without consequence. Imagine an Allentown where there was a conflict revolution that centered the credibility of a mother as the messenger before another Kareem is murdered and another Jeanie is left to put all of the pieces of the puzzle together again.

Theoretically, the job of the police is to investigate and solve crimes. With the historical mistrust, widespread corruption, and recruitment of interlopers as overseers it is unrealistic to expect white suburban police officers without relationships and credibility within communities of color to prevent, mediate, and facilitate future acts of violence.

As you continue to read Jeani's words pay particular attention to all the potential points of intervention, had Jeani, as a context expert and credible messenger, been partnered with a content expert or conflict resolution agency to preserve the many lives lost across Allentown.

THAT FIRST SHOOTING THAT LEFT THE MAN PARALYZED

Jeani: It was definitely a bloody summer. So I'm sweating 24 hours before Kareem was murdered. Some kids from here went over to a rival neighborhood and shot up a car, which ultimately paralyzed the young man. Now, Kareem wasn't there. Kareem was supposed to be there. Kareem was not there. Kareem used the excuse that he was too high. He was too high. Let him out of the car. He was too high. He didn't want to go. And I know my son. He was scared. Yeah. He didn't want to go. Didn't want to go. He thought about it. He thought about pulling the trigger and what would happen. Yeah, the consequences. And he used the excuse to his friends that he was too high, and they let him out of the car, and he walked home that night. I remember coming home that night and seeing him, and he looked scared. You look scared, and I kept asking him what happened? What happened? What happened? I'm sorry. That was 48 hours before it I remember coming home and seeing I mean, he looks scared to death. And then I went to work. He went to school, the charter school, he went to play basketball, he went to hang out. The next day, I get a phone call coming home from work that Kareem is at Lehigh Valley Hospital because one of his friends got shot. It was the 15-year-old friend, 15-year-old friend who did the shooting the night before that left the young man paralyzed. They caught him, they caught him in the alley, and they shot him, shot him in his legs, and he was at the hospital. He survived. It was a long recovery. He's actually sitting in prison now for that shooting. That first shooting that left the man paralyzed.

After Kareem got murdered I, I was, I was numb. That was August 24, 2012. He's 17 years old, I came home from work and found my son in his bedroom. Cold, bloody. Dead. He's dead. He was dead. As soon as I felt him, I knew he was dead. Didn't know how, I didn't know from what? I didn't know from what and so I guess at that moment, I was in a state of shock. Like, I didn't even know what he could possibly be dead, it never crossed my mind that three people climbed my fire escape, opened my window, removed my air conditioner, and murdered my son as he slept.

I thought maybe he went out drinking and, you know, was regurgitating and threw up, you know, choked on his vomit or got jumped. I didn't see not one bullet hole on my son. My neighbor did because my neighbor kicked down the door because he heard me screaming. He said, "See the bullet holes."

Hasshan: Do you remember what you thought or how you felt in that moment? If you don't mind?

Jeani: Yeah, in that moment, a neighbor kicked down the door because he said, the screaming, me screaming, begging and screaming and asking for help, was so traumatic that he wanted to risk his own life, because he thought my life was at risk. He thought somebody was putting harm on me. Yeah. And he didn't hesitate to kick down my door because he thought that I was in jeopardy, like I was in urgent need of help. Because of the sounds because of the screams. Yeah. Because of the screams.

It's the first thing I see. It's the last thing I see. Every day, every day, every day. It took five years and 11 months for somebody to be charged with his murder, and then it took up until January 13, 2020, for the person to be convicted. I was cheated, I was cheated then and cheated now.

Hasshan: How do you keep going? What pushes you to do the work that you do in our community?

Jeani: I know that I got to get up because we have to fight. We got to keep fighting and if not, there's gonna be a lot more Kareems. It's gonna be a lot more killings, there's gonna be a lot more guns, and the stigma that comes with my son's murder is so heartbreaking that I can't, I just can't let it go like that. I just can't let it, I can't let my son have that stigma. And that label, that label that was attached to him. When he was pulled out of normalcy, out of that classroom, that's where the label started. Maybe even before that, if you really want to dig deep, me being a single mother, with an absent father, if you really want to dig that deep, the label that he had from birth, I don't want this to be the label for him forever. So, I gotta keep fighting and doing what I got to do out here to save our kids, save our community, and teach these parents and teach these families and get on these politicians so they got to love our kids just as much as we do. Even if they don't want to love them just as much as we do. They're definitely gonna have to, they're gonna have to act like it. Something, things got to change.

IT'S GONNA TAKE ALL OF US

Hasshan: *Does this include being led by those closest to the pain?*

The evening before I conducted Jeani's interview, she had attended a candlelight vigil memorial organized by another powerful mother and community activist, Shalon Bushkirk, who also works tirelessly to honor her son Parish's legacy. Three years to the day before, Shalon's beautiful and charismatic son, Parish Lane, was brutally murdered by a friend, feet from the homicide department.

Jeani: Last night, there was a memorial for a young man who was murdered three years ago. There was a candle-lighting vigil memorial for him at the location where he was murdered, directly across from the homicide department. Somebody came in and shot three people during that vigil at six o'clock in the evening. One is dead and two are stable but in critical condition. If that doesn't show you that we're in trouble. We didn't raise enough noise when we lost Parish 20 feet away from the homicide department. We didn't raise enough noise, we didn't do enough. Had more been done; they would have thought twice about shooting somebody 20 feet away from the homicide department again. It's gonna take all of us.

Hasshan: Who's us?

Jeani: You, me, the politicians, the educators, the parents, leadership. It's gonna take a combined effort, a collective mind, everybody sitting at the table, and focusing on how to change the mindset of these kids. I feel like we have two battles: either we're going to change the mindset of the kids because we got to act fast. Or we're going to ask the powers that be to be where we can get some money and change it ourselves. I believe I'm changing it. Every day, that I am a resource, I am somebody that you can contact for support, for a better way. I'm somebody that you can call and if I can't help you, I can lead you to somebody who is going to help you. We're going to get you help.

Hasshan: On an individual level, outside of you, what resources were available to teach Kareem and his peers, conflict resolution, problem-solving, alternative dispute resolution, violence prevention, we're talking about skills, if you can think about his school years, summer camps, whatever he was involved in?

Jeani: Amen Midnight Basketball. It was the church, they had Pastor Mike, at a program called Amen Basketball. And he would grab youth from the community, and they would be involved in these basketball tournaments. In 2010,

Kareem's team won the championship. I have his trophy upstairs. That was great. That was beautiful. I don't know whatever happened to that program after that, but that was the only program that was available. And you see, they can't say there were programs out here and we didn't get into them, because I'm not even religious and I let my son join Amen Midnight Basketball, I allowed him to join a church organization, mentorship program, and it worked. But, if I'm not mistaken, they've lost their funding and it's sad. But that's it. That's all. There wasn't a Zero Youth Violence [program]. And if there was in 2012, it was never shared with me. Yeah. And honestly speaking, I don't want to sound biased or anything, but Zero Youth Violence and Promise Neighborhood are the only two organizations that I know of personally that are meant for those that are willing to mentor kids.

We don't only have stories of trauma. At the end of my story with Kareem, there's healing too. There's healing that goes along with this with grief, healing is a state, healing is what I'm doing now. This is part of my healing, helping others, bringing awareness to my community, being supportive to other mothers who have walked in my shoes, being able to allow them to share their stories, with no judgment, being transparent, giving them a place. Because I'm gonna tell you, if you have not lost a child, you do not want to understand what it is to lose a child. And a lot of times we find comfort with each other when we can't even find comfort within our own home. Because we're supposed to walk around and still go to work, clean the house, cook the dinner, iron the clothes—while carrying that trauma.

Mother to Mother, the healing love that I am creating is giving mothers a place where we can get together and we can let it all out. And we laugh, and we cry.

Hasshan: And we laugh and we cry. What is Mother to Mother?

Jeani: I saw Mother to Mother as a support group for parents, initially mothers but now parents, who have lost their children to gun violence and drug overdose. I couldn't find a support group after losing Kareem. I craved a support group, and I couldn't find one where I felt comfortable sharing my story and not getting the side-eye, because I lost my son to gun violence, gang violence. I was judged even though nobody verbally said it. I felt the energy in the room that I was judged. My story didn't matter. My son's life didn't matter. When my son died of cancer, but your son was in a gang and got murdered, like, that's his fault.

Hasshan: Your loss was less?

Jeani: My loss is less. So I decided to start this group, this mother support group and, unfortunately, we have gained a lot of members of the support group. It is definitely a place where mothers can talk about everything, the court proceedings, the trial process, the initial shock, all stages of grieving. We were grieving a little bit different than those other losses that mothers experience.

Yeah, obviously we know, as parents we got to take some responsibility. We got to take responsibility (for) these kids. We need mentoring. We need people to step up; that's how we're strong, black and brown men, black and brown women. People in our community who look like us, who walk like us, who live in the same elements as we do. We need them to stand up. We need the backing from the government side of it. We need to be backed by them. We need everybody in on this, everyone, we need the village to take care of itself.

Hasshan: What about problem-solving the conflict resolution skills? Where do kids learn that so if someone gets shot, all these kids learn how to mediate, how to prevent retaliation, how to have conversations, how to resolve conflict together? Who teaches them those survival and community-building skills?

Jeani: The only way that's gonna change is every if every parent in this community, especially if you have your kids in the school, demand(s) the change. You know, we can't wait until something happens in the city for us to get loud. Demand things to change, it has to be consistent. I see it every day, being a leader in this community, that we get crazy when something happens. And then it dies down. I can't do it by myself. I could walk up and down the street and carry signs and, and demand things and pull strings to get things in legislation and beg for money. But, you know, we're stronger together. It takes a village.

Hasshan: Powerful. Your story is powerful. Beautiful. Thank you, Jeani. Kareem is beautiful. His story is beautiful. You keep it alive. I will do my best to honor you and him and continue to capture the beauty you share.

Jeani: It is up to us to want to heal, not a doctor, not a system; we got to want to heal, it starts with us. I don't want to walk around allowing this trauma to affect me every day to the point where I become part of the poison in my community because I could very easily have taken that route. And I don't want to be part of the poison, I want to be part of the solution. And so therefore, I got to heal. And I got to want to heal.

Hasshan: What is Kareem's full name?

Jeani: Kareem Sean Fed.

Hasshan: What's a story or an attribute you want the world to know? When you think of your son? What do you want the world to know about him?

Jeani: Loyal. Kareem was so loyal. And so funny. I want everybody to know that my son could have been the next Kevin Hart. He was really that funny. And he was so smart, where he did not have to study for a test, he aced it. Every time, we would literally sit around and play dictionary games with me and my kids.

And Kareem would always know the definition of a word and how to spell it correctly. Wow! He was just an amazing brother and an amazing uncle. When I think about Kareem, I think about how much he loved, how much he loved his family that he used to tell his little brother. You know, when he started getting in this gang life, he used to tell his little brother, Don't tell nobody. You're my brother. I don't want nobody to know we're brothers, because I do stuff. I'm involved in stuff and I don't want nothing ever happened to you. I don't want nobody to ever know.

They wanted my son Hassan to join the gang, and they were telling Kareem to pull Hassan in, and he pushed back and was like, Nah, nah, not my baby. Not my baby brother. That's what I want everybody to know about Kareem. When I know that Kareem's name is not attached to the stigma anymore, it'll be attached to what I do.

I would take it all back to have my son. All those sleepless nights because I've had plenty of sleepless nights and plenty of tears and plenty of running up in people's houses and getting my son. Plenty of running him down. Um, yeah, Hasshan, you don't have like, you have no idea.

Hasshan: No, I don't. I have no idea.

Jeani is a champion across our community; she is known by those in crisis and conflict. Jeani mediates family tensions, gang conflicts, and landlord-tenant disputes to prevent injuries and harm in her community. Jeani also responds to every act of violence in our community to prevent retaliation and to provide support to mothers and family members in mourning. Yet Jeani is not recognized or qualified to lead a mediation center, mediate a court dispute, or be recognized and compensated for her contributions to healing her community.

It is time to retell the stories of the heroes across our communities, to lift up and recognize the Jeanis across our community as assets and context experts that are steeped in deep relationships, skills, and communities of practice in helping, healing, and restoring balance. As Jeani reminds us, it's going to take all of us and for all of us to contribute, it is going to require conflict resolution practitioners to decolonize our field, interrogate power, and invite nontraditional theorists and practitioners to contribute to demystifying the canons of knowledge and voice.

CHAPTER 10

How Do White People Benefit from Challenging Racism?

....

inally, I end this section with a very personal message from me, a white editor, to our white readers. As we transition into the next section, a rich collection of voices in prose, conversation, and poetry compiled by S.Y. Bowland, I offer this passionate appeal to recognize how we all share an interest in racial equity, because we all benefit from the social changes necessary to create justice. To overcome the oppression of one is to dismantle the many forms of oppression we too suffer.

—Beth Roy

....

Letter from a White Editor to Her White Readers

Beth Roy

Why am I, a white woman of advanced years, some stature in the world, and a career as a mediator, participating in writing a book about overcoming racism?

Although I hope that many different categories of people will read this book, I wish to have an impact on white readers who seek roles in the compelling work of making our shared world a more just one. The reason I write is because I, like you, deplore racism. Beyond that reaction to injustice, I also write for the well-being of white people. I deeply believe, whatever our heritage and station in life, we are all damaged by racism. Some of the ways we're hurt are very different; others are shared by people of all but the most elite stations in life.

Every day I deplore racism, but only occasionally does an event break through the steady cadence of everyday life to remind me what that means. I watch a video of George Floyd dying beneath the murderous knee of a white policeman. I read a headline announcing the acquittal of four white officers who shot to death an innocent immigrant from Africa named Amadou Diallo. A counseling client, a six-foot-something, powerfully built Black man, asks my help to deal with overwhelming fear when he walks the streets of the city. I cast about for something to do. I join a protest. I urge friends and families to write letters to people in power. I write a letter-to-the-editor, an essay, a book.

For me, awareness of racism may be occasional. I understand that my colleagues and friends of color have the opposite experience: for them, racism *is* the everyday event. And, in very different ways but for shared reasons, so it is for me, so it is for you, the reader who is white. For many of us, however, awareness of our injuries is elusive. We cling to scant privileges, real but providing far, far weaker well-being than we all, of whatever identity, deserve, and that tenuous hold on well-being, sometimes in fact only the promise and the myth of well-being, obscures a very different reality. Those who are truly privileged are the wealthy. Racism impoverishes most of us, materially and morally, while it benefits the rich.

Yes, there are privileges intrinsic to white skin. Peggy McIntosh's backpack *is* still stuffed with them. But the price of those privileges vastly outweighs the benefits. White job applicants have an advantage over applicants of color (despite decades of affirmative action and pressure for companies to "diversify" workforces). But the jobs they get provide no secure tenure, are inadequately compensated, and tie employees to expensive health care that should be free and universal.

White people can count on greater safety in public spaces, especially from the police. But whether white or any other race, citizens live lives bounded by structures of the state that limit options, expose us to toxins that poison our health, leave us vulnerable to aging without security, send our children to under-resourced schools, expose us to hazards of unrepaired infrastructures, and, above all, destine us all to environmental disaster.

Underlying all those material deficits, whiteness traps white people in tortured relationships to our integrity. The moral distortions of enjoying benefits from a social structure built on genocide and slavery underlie every ethical moment in which we live. Looking away from the realities of our bloody history imprisons us in clouds of ignorance about the realities of racial oppression today.

So why do we white people of good conscience not more often, more forcefully step forward and declare ourselves? I believe one central reason is that we fear the conflict inherent in acknowledging our inevitable complicity. Even when we have tools for engaging conflict constructively, even when we offer those tools to help others, we look away from the reality of our participation in unacknowledged injustices. To do otherwise requires us to deal with responsibility and with the pain of inconsistency. If we are good, justice-loving individuals, how do we face the apparent powerlessness and searing shame that we perpetuate injustice in ways we cannot even begin to understand?

And so we retreat into silence—and leave the speech acts to people of color. When they do speak out, it is with the other side of white fear: often long-smoldering anger. Then *they* are labeled the problem. Pained by that label, they may give up speaking, whereupon we retreat again into clouds of denial and troubled unawareness. In one more way, we have become enlisted in consent to those same systems of injustice we abhor. The emotional discomforts for all of us, of whatever identity, lie just beneath the surface, erupting once more when the next egregious act of violence breaks through compounded silences into public space.

Having accepted this silencing, we've abandoned one form of power we might otherwise embrace. But to speak out against injustice requires power. Agency, the exercise of potentiality, rests on a sense of stability. If the ground on which I stand quakes, I must cling to whatever holds me up. Where is the energy, the generosity, the breadth of vision, needed to connect my lived reality with another's? Trouble narrows the vision. Powerlessness feeds narcissism. In troubled times, consciousness withdraws into the emotions of the moment. Immediacy overwhelms the will to support others.

We dwell in a culture of the individual. Most currents in this sea in which we Americans arduously row our separate boats move us away from others, toward the lie that we each are responsible for our reality. All these limitations on awareness blur the reality that we are all in this boat together; we all need to row as companions if we are ever to reach a beachhead of justice.

SECTION II

INSIGHT

· · · · · · · · · · · · · · · · · · · ·

We

Rubye Howard Braye

Today we are one
in the universe where what I hold forth for me
is held forth for you

I cannot run ahead and leave you
for what I am and how I decide to be for me
I am for you

I cannot hide what I know in me
thinking that I am concealing precious information from you
for what I know and treasure for me
I know and also treasure for you

I cannot do for me
without doing for you
for in doing for me
I realize that I always do for you

No being
no knowing
no doing is ever without you

Our collective is our oneness
and this truth keeps me
ever reminded of us as
we were, are, and will be

> We are the oneness that is ever being
> We are the oneness that is ever knowing
> We are the oneness that is ever doing
>
> Forever I am grateful for us

INTRODUCTION

One Story: Many Experiences

S.Y. Bowland

This story highlights the journey of one, but it could be the story of many. It is common to desire to enter a field to make life better. I entered the field of conflict resolution as a way of working for justice and peace when I saw and felt the disproportionate impact of the judicial system. I saw the black community disproportionately and adversely impacted by the social and emotional trauma of people being locked up, people being killed, and people turning on each other. I saw police mistreating people, and I saw that behavior being emulated in the health, educational, housing, and social systems and structures. I saw that lack of access to resources resulted in limitations for the entire community.

The fact that I am a mother of two young African men has made this struggle ongoing from their births. In the early 1990s, my first step into the field was to bite my tongue and get training to work with the courts. The way the system was set up, the courts and the designers of the field would not let you just go out there and get involved in the court system without training. The structures did not value or recognize the skills one brought to the profession. I could not understand, though, why there would be white trainers and white facilitators to engage in a system where over 50 to 90% of the population was black or brown.

As community people, we were already engaged in problem-solving, in working with young people, and getting young people the skills that we thought were necessary for them to survive these Mean Streets. Evidently, those in charge never listened to any of the evaluations, because I would state what I thought were the programs' limitations—not using the leaders in that community as resources to create and construct the curriculum necessary for engagement. It was very disappointing. So, what we had and have are barriers to entrance and access for the most affected communities.

What has shaped my professional conflict resolution relationships, presence, and philosophy most are the experiences of appropriate appreciation along with misappropriation. Let me give some examples. People, particularly leaders, want to "hear your stories" because they know you know something they haven't heard or experienced. Then, the next thing you know, what you thought was building a relationship, they were mining you for information that was eventually misappropriated. When practitioners of color began having these conversations, some people took those ideas and started running with them. I came along with added information and ideas that had worked in my community. Few acknowledged efforts and explored blending ideas and strategies for resolving conflicts. The traditional professional literature and the politics of knowledge seek to make me and others like me invisible, romanticize us, and then ignore our voices.

In my case, the predominately white leadership ignored what they heard, said that I did not need to be present, or that the contributions I was making were outside of their ability to comprehend. They did not know how to include my way of thinking. Instead of asking for help, they excluded me. Although I am specifically talking about my experience, this is the story for many. To meet various needs, token individuals of color would be identified. Thusly, there would be a few people queued into the top, either because of who they are, where they are, or who they know. Those in position to hire contact the people that they know, and black people and people of color are not usually in those circles. In the end, to be excluded from income and advancement in the field drove some away.

Most all the court systems and the designated agencies that offered mediation or other conflict resolution practices required training and payment of a lot of money to become mediators or trainers, but then they just want trained mediators to volunteer. Then when the jobs came, they would not hire you. I know people who have been in the field for years and have been relegated to strictly volunteer work. Are they going to feed their family? I have seen it happen to others, and they have seen it happen to me. If you are outspoken, you get labeled as a troublemaker and are further excluded

That is happening in this very moment by saying Black Lives Matter. But then again, how often are practitioners of color being asked to give their time, service, and knowledge for free, with no responsibility liability or accountability for the others, who simply disseminate what they learned and benefit financially? Who is primarily asked to perform invisible labor or pay the black tax? I have observed people in the field get hurt. I have seen it with my own eyes. It goes unaddressed, in a field of conflict resolution practitioners. I have seen people of color be what I would call mistreated in the field and did my best to interrupt it. Thus, the expressions of making things complicated often follow me. Here is an example: An Asian colleague worked hard to support the field of conflict resolution in many ways. She was faithful as a volunteer mediator and contributor of service to the field. Seldom did she get calls for paying mediation opportunities. She had to seek a different path for financial survival. We had many conversations about these issues and expressed these concerns where we could. Conferences can be cost-prohibitive including registration, travel, meals, and accommodations, not to mention the cost of getting professional attire.

I saw another striking situation with a different woman of color. She was asked to serve on a conflict resolution board. She accepted and started her service. At the conflict resolution organization's annual conference during a meal, she joined the leadership at the reserved table. The organization gave out awards, made announcements, and recognized people: the usual pomp and circumstance of such an event. Sitting at a nearby table, I could see laughter and friendliness exchanged among them. The executive director went on stage, announced the names of the board members, and her name was not called. The happiness on her face disappeared. I knew that look and had seen it many times. It was the look of, "What just happened? Did I miss something?"

Seeing the distress on her face, I waited around to approach her, to see if she was okay. I thought she was holding back tears. Well, those tears came as we talked. After the room was almost empty, she approached the executive director and asked, "What just happened, how come you didn't call my name? I thought that I was on the board."

The executive director replied, "We just couldn't understand you. We didn't know what you were saying. You know how you talk in circles; it wasn't a good fit."

The person of color asked, "Why did you lead me on? Why am I sitting at this table as a board member happily and innocently thinking I'm sharing leadership? How can your office remove me just like that: no conversation or notice? I started believing, I started engaging, and then you want to just toss me out like that?"

I stayed with her for a while, as she cried, expressed disappointment, and so on. We stayed in touch until she died. I have seen that with my own eyes more than once. I've observed it and experienced it. The people in the system allow many types of collective mis-engagement of knowledge and information, instead of learning together in relationships and findings ways to stay connected that provide time for healing. I remember there being workshops at conferences to address racial conflicts and concerns.

To increase the inclusion stories of African Americans is likely to increase the inclusion of many; it always has. We know inclusion is to draw in, to invite. Acknowledgment is a way to include. A welcoming environment is an accepting one. We can recognize other ways of knowing and being together in peace. We are aiming for a point of reconciliation, a point of restorative practice, a vision for a more inclusive field and world. How do we want to move forward together and present ourselves in the world to do better?

In this section of the book, you are invited to seize the conversation. Consider starting a relationship and discovering where you connect with the author. See how you might be involved differently in the future. We invite you to enjoy the points of contradiction, notice the teachable moments, and above all be inspired to act toward building an equitable profession and a just world. Some of the voices here are poetic while others are more discursive. In my "story of many," I write of the frequency with which people of color are told that we are not understood, get messages of being invisible, and not hearing our voices. Let us value each other. We know, but rarely have an opportunity to express to listening ears how our cultures socialize us; my culture welcomed me not only to talk differently but also to think differently. Educational indoctrination doesn't work. Stop trying to do it. My experience of thinking and feeling is together; the two are not separate. A richness lies here if it is embraced. The experience of going the extra mile, of doing the unpaid labor to reach across the chasm of multiculturalism way beyond the halfway point of shared labor, is at the heart of so many of our stories. This section offers an opportunity to share the work, to embrace the diversity of the voices that follow.

The first section presented many ways in which racism infects the field of conflict resolution. They range from the exclusion of people of color from the formation of a knowledge base to the ways people of color are left unpartnered as we traverse cultural distances. Authors present their stories of struggle in predominantly white institutions and of the failures of even the most progressive organizations to genuinely share power. All these accounts are framed in the context of greater violence besetting communities of color. It is a dramatic failure of our field when we do not value, heed, or even to respect, voices speaking crucial truths learned through painful—and unique—experiences. As a community of problem solvers, where do we go to solve and address the concerns known to and expressed among and between us?

The conversational voices in this section are interconnected. The writers and speakers are united in wanting change now. The visions that organize this section reflect the pattern that emerged from the conversational interviews. In the stories that follow, readers are allowed to value, respect, and honor the differences among us, noting the points of irritation and moving into understanding and change. These pages contain real-life experiences. Some hold fast to promise, others to hope, and many to faith for a more multi-real field. The editors aim for spaces of interaction in literature, knowledge, practice, theory, scholarship, philosophy, and for relationships.

A few of the inquiries that the interviewees were asked are: What would you like for us and the world to know about you? How do you see yourself in the world today? How do you envision a more inclusive conflict resolution field? How can we get there, and do you believe we can get there? What do you have to say about what you see going on in the world today? What are your summary thoughts for us today? Please feel free to include how to address race matters.

In essence, these conversations are a philosophical engagement. The people speak from a wish for some rationale and reason behind the mistreatment of so many and the resistance to share power, wisdom, and resources. These questions are present around peacemaking and conflict resolution. The depth of the responses is inclusive of life itself. Many experiences people recount are personal, and sometimes they brought about quick action for change. Life impacts conflict and methodologies, conflicts impact life. We do not have one without the other.

Between grieving the injustices of today and creating the world we desire tomorrow lies the fertile territory of vision. Presented here are writings that speak to a series of visionary areas:

- Vision of Inclusive Knowledge: The Path of the Credible Messenger
- Vision of Expansive Culture: The Path of Spirit in People and Conflict
- Vision of Power-Sharing Organizations: The Path of Responsibly Handling Power
- Vision of Welcoming Institutions: The Path of Healing
- Vision of Equitable Practices: The Path of Mentorship and Leadership
- Vision of Seeing the Invisible Context of Oppression: The Path of Freedom from Violence
- Vision of Action: The Path of Enlightenment or Path of Vision of a World of Humanity, Cleansed of Hate Speech and Violence

As you read these chapters you join the authors in a philosophical journey beyond equity and inclusion. A first step is examining the value system. To understand how to do that, we need to stand in moments of contradiction, viewing them as teachable moments for action and change. This section is an opportunity to take a deep breath and stretch your mind and heart to challenge reactions one might be inclined to criticize and reject. Consider this an opportunity to move forward together beyond equity and inclusion. Stay involved. Keep your eye on the prize. Hold on. Conflict practitioners know part of the skill of the trade is to practice the art of believing what you hear, no matter how hard it is to listen.

THE MEDIATOR MESSAGE

For Good and Necessary Trouble

In Memory of Honorable Congressman John Lewis

S.Y. Bowland

It is now noted and required:
A mediator must have the skill to
Raise the questions:
How am I neutral? and is being neutral here
Complicit?
How would I
make, create, stand for,
account for, be present for and document:
"Good and Necessary Trouble"?
In appreciation.
Thank you.

CHAPTER 11

Vision of Inclusive Knowledge

The Art of the Credible Messenger

I've been thinking about an example of the art of being a credible messenger in conflict resolution. The concept is known as a reliable person who carries messages. A credible messenger captures the importance of building bridges and other ways for people to exist with one another to solve problems. A credible messenger serves to carry important information from one group to another so there can be harmony or unity.

Along this path, one can leave behind greed, theft, and domination, all those forms of coercion that rob us of collective power. One can embrace the chance to move beyond hindrances, especially that of the unindoctrinated mind. The voice of the credible messenger reminds us that we are all challenged in many ways.

We begin with excerpts from a conversation I recorded recently with Maria Volpe, a professor at John Jay College of Criminal Justice–City University of New York and a superb caretaker of the mediation field. I began by telling her what I'd been thinking about credible messengers, and that I see her as a credible messenger extraordinaire. Surprised, she protested, and then went on to reconsider how the description fit her.

—S.Y. Bowland

Embracing the Good: Taking a Risk

Maria Volpe

S.Y.: How would you describe the credible messenger art form as a useful conflict resolution skill? Do you see yourself using this skill in the world of ADR or conflict resolution? How are you a credible messenger?

Maria: I think that credible messengers need to be people who are seen as approachable, people who will listen to others, who will take time with others. I often say that most people can get from point A to point B on campus in a pretty short amount of time. However, it always takes me forever to walk the same distance because I stop to talk to people all along the way and people will stop me over most anything. So it's that kind of approachability that is so important for someone who connects with individuals and to whom people go.

In one of our research projects, a research subject talked about the importance of the likability factor. It's really hard to put your finger on that, but you know it when you see it. It's like when you approach some persons and you say, "Gee, I like that person." For some people, being likeable is really hard to do. It is who they are that grates on others. And for some of us, we just find ourselves doing things that make it easy for people to talk to us.

Among other things, we listen to others and pay attention to what they're saying. I often say it's important to be a code switcher because you sometimes have to listen to different people differently or interact with people differently, in short, try to find out where they're coming from since we can't be an expert in everything. I think it's really important for us to expose ourselves to as many different cultures and peoples as we can because it gives us a frame of reference for interacting with others in the future, sort of like money in the bank. When you have this vast reserve of cultural money in the bank, you're able to deal with virtually anyone and everyone because you just have a wealth of knowledge, skills, experiences, and perceptions that help you to understand what's really important to people.

I know some people are very impatient with taking the time to connect spontaneously in real time. It requires a lot of patience and persistence to be able to work with people and meet them where they are. To do so, sometimes we have to be risk-takers. Some people will automatically not interact with someone who reminds them of someone else they have known. That's not the way I interact with people. I try to embrace whoever I'm dealing with and try to find the good in everyone.

I also think that someone who's going to be what you refer to as a "credible messenger" needs to be reliable and responsive. We all know what it feels like when we are trying to reach out to someone and they don't respond to our communications, regardless of means used, phone, email, in person, etc. As a credible messenger, you also have to be someone who people can rely on. Whether it's my students or others, I do try to be as responsive as I possibly can. That's who I am. It's my way of being credible. Some individuals will say, "Oh, I'm not going to deal with that. Make them wait." Well, I know that I don't like to wait for people to get back to me. So, in some ways, it's like, practice what you preach. You know how you feel when people don't treat you well. I'm not going to dish out some of that.

SYB: How did you learn to be that way?

MV: It's hard to pinpoint when our approach to how we manage our lives begins. I've always been able to work with others. I've known the importance of being approachable, likable, or able to code switch, being a bit of a risk-taker with situations that others might avoid or might not otherwise deal with. It's important to be reliable. It's part of how we gain trust.

There are some basic elements of a credible messenger that cut across contexts: someone who is there for people, someone who is a good listener, someone who is reliable, someone who is approachable, someone who people feel comfortable with who they know will come through for them. It almost doesn't matter whether you're on the streets or in the suites.

Sometimes we have to deliver messages that people don't like. However, if they know you and trust you, they know that you're not going to hurt them. They know you're not being, for lack of a better word, mean-spirited, or just doing something to get them. It may actually be in their best interest.

There are some people with whom you feel comfortable being around and others with whom you just don't. Sometimes your credibility comes via membership in a certain group. The person receiving the message knows that if you're a member of x organization or you're a member or former member of a certain group, that you're someone who they can trust.

Trust is often a hard thing to gain, it's something that isn't just handed to you. It may take years to gain people's trust. People have to be able to rely on you. If they think that you're not being honest, or that you're flip-flopping, or that you're not being sincere, they won't trust you. You're just not going to be effective in any context, whether it's in a family, in a religious congregation, in a business, a community setting, or most anywhere you are interacting.

I think people who are resourceful are more likely to be effective, credible messengers. When people need information, they go to people who have the information, and if they don't have it, they will get it for you. I think a credible messenger is a resourceful, approachable person who can be trusted by those with whom they interact.

It would be great if we had thousands of credible messengers in the field of conflict resolution, namely people who are believable or resourceful, who can be relied upon. But I'm not sure how we scale up to that point. We can try to teach skills that are essential for being a credible messenger. I think it is possible to some extent to train people; for sure, training can help. But a lot of being a credible messenger requires adherence to certain values which include recognizing that each person is worthy of respect and trying to make sure that you come through for people regardless of who they are. Some of that is hard to teach.

To get to the point where we have credible messengers, I think that we may have to think about how we embrace cultural values in such a way that people will have that reserve to draw upon, regardless of the situation. Once one's learned skills get tested, their default qualities will surface. And those default qualities really have to rest on certain values, beliefs, principles. Their skills won't be enough to get them through a situation. I think those who are credible messengers might be in a wonderful position to be role models so that others will see that it is possible to treat everyone with respect, and to show how one can be resourceful. If one doesn't have the information, s/he can figure out how to get it for people. I don't think there's an easy answer to how we're going to create a world with lots of credible messengers without thinking about how we address some of those basic values.

Some people think that making a difference has to be some major undertaking, but, you know, it's really like those little acts of kindness every day. You do the little things that you sometimes do that make a difference with anyone. Some people will go out of their way to help others. And there are others who just don't.

SYB: Any suggestions on how to expand the lessons of credible messengers to our current national conversation about inclusivity? And, any suggestions for the field?

MV: We're immersed in a national discourse around diversity and inclusiveness. I was raised in a very diverse community. Being with people who are different was always the norm, contributed to feeling comfortable with differences and figuring out how to be inclusive of everyone because that was just the way it was. I encourage everyone to always stretch themselves.

For the field to be more inclusive, it means that we need to have structures that support inclusiveness. We have to create structures that will reward individuals for doing the work. And in our society, that means having some way for individuals to be compensated. It's hard for someone to do full-time peacemaking work if they're not being compensated for it. To keep thinking that individuals are going to do this work as volunteers for free, I think that means that a lot of people just won't be able to do it on a full-time basis. If we're talking about people being peacemakers in everyday life, those individuals are people who are able to interact with others, go to, and be effective in the everyday world.

SYB: How do we get to the point where our structures and our systems make sure that people's needs are taken care of and that the access to resources is equitable?

MV: A lot of our differences are over inequality and injustice. To sort that out is hard work. And a lot of people who are interested in conflict resolution or peacemaking don't always address some of those fundamental aspects. They don't understand what triggers people or what kinds of conflicts we have. And without understanding that, it's going to be really hard to have broad-based peacemakers. So that's a tough one.

I do think on an individual level, people can be more peaceful. But how do we get there? We probably need to teach and support all kinds of values. On a larger societal scale, I think we need to pay attention to distribution of resources, the kind of existing structures, etc. There's a parable I love that recounts how fish that are swimming in a stream meet up with an older fish who asks, "How's the water, boys?" The two younger fish look at each other and say, "What the hell is water?" Well, since they're always in it, they're breathing it, inhaling it, swimming in it, they don't know what the water is. Sometimes because we are living, breathing, inhaling the culture, the structures of our society, we don't see what's causing the kinds of challenges we experience.

I think we are seeing a lot of activity around trying to be more inclusive. In the past, there have been promises or pledges to address the lack of diversity in the dispute resolution field. There have been some scholarships to reach out to underrepresented groups, as well as a variety of programs of mentoring programs. Where we see our biggest red flag is with diversity in those positions where there's a need for years and years of experience, or at least that's what's been requested for certain positions. And we know, some of the underrepresented groups aren't always well represented in some of those roles. We have got to work harder in creating the pipelines so people looking for candidates can't say, "Well, we can't find individuals."

One of the emerging problems is that a significant pipeline of individuals interested in conflict resolution work seems to come from the legal field. If the legal field is not inclusive and representative, it's going to limit who enters the broader conflict resolution field. Part of the problem is the field doesn't have its own identity. It's not like some other fields where there's a college you go to or a specific major that you pursue. A lot of people enter the field from a wide range of different disciplines, traditions, cultures, life experiences, and professional disciplines. As a result, we are all over the place. There are no boundaries regarding what is even defined as the field. We have no way of putting our arms around the field.

Twenty or 30 years ago, the field was younger and smaller and there were efforts to identify what would be meaningful criteria for accountability. In the last 10 years, the field has expanded and become more amorphous. Not only are we including conflict resolution, peacemaking, dispute resolution, but other processes and specialties as restorative justice, social justice, and transformative justice. How do we put our arms around everything?

SYB: When you imagine the field has had success with inclusion, what's the image that comes to your mind?

MV: The image is a mosaic. All of us would accept and welcome each other as members of the field. We would see each other as equals. We would have a field that "walks its talk," an expression that comes to mind for me. We talk about empowerment, we talk about providing forums for people to be able to express themselves—we will truly have to walk our talk when it comes to working with all those with whom we interact in the course of doing conflict resolution–related work. In short, we would be serving as role models of the way all could be in an ideal world.

. . . .

Writing a Multicultural Choir

Dwight L. Wilson

I am concerned with a multicultural choir of voices. My vision requires expanded voices. I researched the art of writing as expressed by a multicultural selection of approximately 75 writers. In my youth, I was a jazz critic and a disc jockey on three separate stations, and my youngest son has cut three hip-hop recordings. I added words about the creative process from more than 100 jazz musicians and hip-hop artists.

Because I also write poetry, for tips on poetics, I turned to Yale University professor and leading literary critic. He recommended 103 poets and 379 poems. Who was included? No one who looks like Maya Angelou or Paul Laurence Dunbar. No one who looks like Pablo Neruda or Julia de Burgos. No one who looks like Joy Harjo or Leslie Marmon Silko. No one who looks like Kimiko Hahn or Vijay Seshadri.

We are not talking about marginalizing: this is literary cleansing. Check your bookshelves. I'm not upset because I hate white men. In my collections of stories, there are 10 white male heroes: four farmers, a merchant, a trapper, a blacksmith, a business tycoon, a physician, and an author. My unapologetic criticism is because I love all people, especially those who are excluded from the conversation. Any educator knows that's one of the definitions of social bullying.

Inclusion is a moral imperative like who shall live, not a personal choice like Colgate or Crest. These deliberate omissions point to why there needs to be a reckoning on race with more than the Ku Klux Klan and Proud Boys. When the cultural leaders also disrespect our art, this wounded nation is being choked from the right and from the left, from the ones fearful of replacing those on the bottom and from the ones on top who claim to be sensitive to justice.

How should you attempt to shape your writing? One size does not fit all, and no single writer fits mine. Let's be clear, mostly men who were from European backgrounds found media support and book publishers. The media and publications are also largely under the control of men from the same cultures. Together they have formed the rules of engagement for writers. The vast majority of writers dance to definitions that are more cultural than God-ordained. God utilizes more than Random House English. As a former English teacher and Humanities Chair in high-end educational institutions, I know but do not worship their rules. "I am who I am and I shall be who I shall be." My old sociology professor said, "There is no such thing as objectivity." I own my subjectivity as a leader who seeks accountability and understands, without inclusion, this country cannot retain a position of world leadership.

•••

As one credible messenger to another, Hasshan Batts, I recognize the struggle we have had to be respected in the boardrooms and in the courtrooms. To do that, we've had to name ourselves, to respect ourselves, to build the bridges, and then to cross them far more than halfway when others wouldn't meet us in the middle.

—S.Y. Bowland

•••

Message to Credible Messengers

Hasshan Batts

Those that know me know me, see me, feel me and hear my story
I know these streets cause I am the streets and somewhat of the streets
I know this pain because it's in me
systems, family, community and self inflicted
It's in me and they told me it is me
The fractured narratives of disinvested communities
inequities and disparities
Broken pipelines of promise
Prison detours
Rejections, expulsions, retentions and solitary confinement
I know this pain through experience
I know these people through authentic relationships
I've known these courts of injustice since birth
Toxic systems designed to destroy, misguide and oppress
Designed to derail a community, a people, a boy of promise
Systems intended to remove the good that exist, remove the labels of
greatness and redefine the nature of the man
Self sustaining systems of oppression and cross sector industrial complexes
Ignoring, silencing and muting the voices of those that matter most
Carriers of creative solutions
Riots narrating solutions of peace, wellness and liberation
But these streets see through the lies
And witness the credibility of my message

•••

As a credible messenger, you must learn to code switch, interpret symbols, and disobey some rules.

—S.Y. Bowland

. . . .

What Rule Do You Need an Exception To?

S.Y. Bowland

I need an exception to the Rule(s)
You too?
That rule messed up my life and yours
It killed ancestors young and old
It killed people's soul(s)
It prevents and destroys housing, health care, education.
Communication, financial gain opportunities and more.
I am a songbird tired of carrying this Rule Message on my Feathers
   and in my soul.
These Rules—Exclude
These Rules—keeps us out
I am tired of these rules that deny freedom. Aren't you too!
Get to know your neighbor, build healing relationships, develop
   new paths and create a better world.
Let freedom reign not rules.

CHAPTER 12

Vision of Expansive Culture

....

The Path of Spirit in People and Conflict

*M*any years ago, I met Jeff Hitchcock at a national conference and recognized him as a dedicated advocate for racial justice. A white man who is a member of a multiracial family, Jeff has devoted a lifetime to understanding the nature of dominant culture as well as engaging in activism toward building a truly multicultural world. In this edited transcript of my recent conversation with him, he shares his vision of cultural inclusion and the work he and his colleagues have accomplished over the decades. I see his work as an effort to address the interpersonal conflicts surfacing as race matters on a social and systematic level toward the eradication of racism.

—S.Y. Bowland

....

Responsibilities of a White Justice Fighter

Jeff Hitchcock

I cofounded an organization called Center for the Study of White American Culture. We are in our 26th year. That's primarily my vehicle for the work that I do. The other cofounder is my wife and partner, Dr. Charley B. Flint, who is an afro-descendant as she identifies racially. We are a mixed-race, interracial couple. We've been together for over 40 years. We connected in the mid-1970s, when we were both graduate students at Rutgers.

I recently celebrated my 70th birthday. If you want to know my story, there's a lot to it, a lot of ground to cover. I was raised Quaker, with a consciousness of

....

social justice. Even being married to a black feminist sociologist, it took me a while to get a good handle on what structural racism is and how it manifests in our society. In my 30s or 40s, it was no secret to me that racism existed, but I still had a sense of it as being individual acts; I did not see the structural component quite clearly. I knew it was something that needed to be worked against, to be opposed, to be resisted.

I had this image of my two very young boys at that time growing up and saying, "Well, what did you do about all this, Daddy?" I would be compelled to respond by mentioning several relevant aspects of my history. I did not particularly know what my role would be in that whole process. There came a point when I got a master's degree in social psychology at Rutgers and then later on a master's in business administration. These were points where I saw my culture in operation, how white culture works. Other white people had not seen it as well. At that point, I understood that people of color generally do have an appreciation of what is going on. There was a task to be done of unmasking and bringing into the public discussion the idea of white American culture and how that operates. I came around to the point of saying, "Well, I want to set up an educational nonprofit to start doing this sort of consciousness-raising work." I talked to Charley about it, and she said that it seemed like a promising idea back in 1995.

We decided to call it Center for the Study of White American Culture in a very intentional way. There's a particular dynamic that plays out in our society, in white or mainstream culture. One is to be white supremacist, and the other is to be colorblind. And if you're not one, then you're presumed to be the other. Colorblind ideology does not allow us to name race. By default, people who are functioning within a colorblind framework say that if a person's naming race, they must be a white supremacist. So, we had a lot of dissension coming our way.

Our stance is that there is a third way of going about things, which is to name race in order to work against it. You can't operate on something unless you can see it and you can name it. You can be race-conscious. In fact, you *need* to be race-conscious if you're going to see structural racism and work toward racial justice. Our name is part of our work. Some people get it, even though it may push some people away. Twenty-five years ago, there weren't a lot of people doing this work. Nowadays, it's become much more commonplace. It has even been co-opted in many ways, by academia, or even the trade publishers now.

We have built up a lot of social capital over time, with our name, and with our approach. It was about the concept, and not about me as an individual. I tend to be a shy individual; my name was not important. But I did feel a need and imperative to put the concept out there. Putting the concept out there was the first part of our approach and it still is.

Second, I've always tried to work collaboratively. We have built a good network over time. Now, things have changed a little bit. We're starting to operate with some financial resources. This is strange after all this time, but it's a welcome thing. And we're able to build or have more continuity with people who are working as part of our organization. And so that's feeling really good.

The biggest obstacle is resistance, especially when working on racial justice. Many times, over the years, we would have somebody, maybe a white person, or a person of color working within the organization, who would get what we're doing and saying. This is great, really needed and there would be good discussions. But then at that point, it would die. We need the commitment from key decision-makers to be sure our work is properly presented and followed up, and that takes time.

We authored a paper called "Decentering Whiteness and Building Multiracial Community." That is still our philosophy. The term decentering whiteness has become exceedingly popular. It just means that our society is centered on white culture and white values. That whiteness needs to be taken out of the center and marginalized. We need to build a multiracial culture in the center. We use the term multiracial because we want to keep the emphasis on race and on racial structure. Our goal is to change the racial structure of the country. As part of that process, we will also become multiracial. We want to keep our eye on that prize.

Another point that we make is that these two things are dependent on each other, you can't do one without the other. You can't take white culture out of the center; you can't decenter it unless you put something else in the center. And we're saying that needs to be a multiracial culture. It's very unlikely that any single monoracial/cultural group is going to displace whiteness. We need some sort of multiracial fusion to occupy that central space. There is going to be some sort of centralization of powers and some sort of central values to any particular society or culture. We want those to be multiracial.

Now, as to the question of, what are multiracial values? We don't exactly know. That is work that still needs to be done. We do know that no single racial group can answer that question. Instead, it's got to be some collaborative process. There is some learning there, particularly for white people, which is that whatever that central culture is, we are not going to be the ones who have the final say on it. No one culture can set up or create a multiracial culture.

There is a little bit of irony because people say, "Oh well, you're centering it by naming it." That's not really true. You center it by just assuming it's a standard and letting it operate without making it visible. When you start to make it visible, when you name it, then that brings it to consciousness. What other cultures are involved? What is their relationship? It allows people to have a discussion. That is very key. You need to name it, and you need to also name other cultures.

I had a Google alert set for the term "decentering whiteness"; very often, what's involved is some place in the arts, like a dance group, or new museum putting on an exhibition, or even setting up an entire season, where it features artists of color, as a means of decentering whiteness. The political right wing is pushing back against this, but many private schools have engaged in the idea of decentering whiteness in their curriculum by bringing in voices of people of color. Sometimes it goes under the name of decolonization as well, which is a whole area in and of itself. A good approach is to critically look at who is actually setting up the curriculum, and who is actually creating that program for use. My guess is that in many cases, it's predominantly white people who are doing it. So then is it truly decentering whiteness? They need to get some color in their boardrooms and among the decision-makers. I would look critically at that. We feel that you're not going to be decentering whiteness until you have a critical mass of people of color who are present in a decision-making capacity. That goes hand in hand with building a multiracial community.

Our biggest success is just being and surviving in doing racial justice work. A second success is raising the level of public discussion and awareness of white culture, white American culture. We are a part of the history of change in racial justice work. When we started out, we were advocating for the need for a white, antiracist identity as an alternative means for white people to identify themselves racially. When we were first doing that some people said, "What the hell is that?" I'm talking about racial justice activists who are deeply engaged in working for racial justice and equity. White activists in many cases did not understand that concept. We were out there pushing it. Now it is commonplace, at least to the extent that people talk about white antiracist culture. There are shared concepts about what somebody should do as a white antiracist, the idea of following the leadership of people of color and being in accountable relationships. That is a success.

Again, we were out there taking shots 25 years ago. We have been able to step into the recent change of consciousness in the country. People are starting to come to us. That's a new experience. The logistics and the practicalities of taking on the work are more manageable. Maintaining a stance of integrity is something we have had to measure. We don't want everybody's money. It is a hard decision, but we have declined clients, even when we were working on a shoestring budget.

• •

In a very different voice, we next present a portrait of a very different cultural experience. Johnnie Mitchell, activist and author, gives us the gift of knowledge about the unique world of her origins, a little-known history of an intentional community formed from adversity and the power of survival on the shores of an Atlantic island.

—S.Y. Bowland

• •

The Jig Is Up! Movement: Past, Present, and Future

Johnnie Mitchell

As the leader of The Jig Is Up! Movement to Dismantle the Caste System of Race and Racism in America, I am going to tell the truth, the whole truth, and nothing but the truth. I am going to tell you what I know about the past, what happens during my lifetime, and what I see for the future.

When I woke up to myself, I was on an island where everybody looked the same. If there was royalty, I was born into the royal family. I was born to the beloved Lucinda Jones Frazier Patterson and John Wesley Patterson of Hilton Head Island, South Carolina. Everybody on the island knew me for many reasons: (1) I was born to the beloved teacher on the island who had been married for 16 years and did not have any children; (2) My father was one of the very few people on the island with a car; so he knew everybody on the island, and everybody knew him and his wife and their miracle child; and (3) I was precocious and didn't act as if I belonged there.

How my parents got me there is pretty miraculous. During the time of my birth in 1946, most women approaching their 40th year were having their last child, while my mother was still hoping and praying for her first. She found a "white" fertility doctor in Savannah, Georgia, who got her with child. Through all obstacles, she was able to bring me into this world.

When we were brought here and enslaved and put on the plantations, a group of people was left on the islands. The ships that came from Africa, of course, landed at ports. The ports were where the Africans coming were settled along the coast, along the way up from North Carolina down to Florida. And when the Africans were put out, some were taken as far I guess, as Texas, Louisiana, wherever slavery existed. But there was a group of us who were distributed on the islands off the coast of North Carolina, South Carolina, Georgia, and Florida. And because of the isolation of the islands, we were able to maintain our African culture. For example, the Africans were collected from different villages, different countries in Africa, speaking different languages, different religions, different everything. When we were brought here, they didn't teach us English, English was a new language to us. Christianity was new to us. And they didn't spend the time to teach us anything, they just put us there and told us what our jobs were to do with the cotton and Indigo and rice cultivation.

When we got here, along the South Carolina, North Carolina, Georgia, and Florida coast, it looked pretty much like Africa. We knew immediately what to do, how to survive. And then we created our own language because we had to use the different languages put together with some English that we heard from the overseers and working in the big house. We heard a little English and we put it all together. Today that language is called Gullah Geechee. My family, for the most part, happens to have been located on Hilton Head Island. During the Civil War, Hilton Head Island became the headquarters for the Union Army.

The Union Army captured that area very early. All the slave owners, the plantation owners, and overseers all ran away for their lives. And they left the slaves, the Africans on the plantations. Since the Union Army wasn't interested in having slaves, and Abraham Lincoln was saying the Civil War wasn't about freeing them, we were in this in-between status that they called contrabands of war. But they allowed us to work for the Union Army, allowing us to earn a little bit of money. It's the same economic system that it is today. They paid the white people, let's say $1, and they paid us maybe 25 cents. But we were able to put our money together. Nevertheless, something magnificent comes about during this time. There was a Union officer by the name of Ormsby Mitchel. Ormsby Mitchel turned out to be a real Christian. And I guess you could say a true Christian, he really believed that all people were people, and that we, you know, were all made from God. And so he said, even though Abraham Lincoln says that the Civil War is not about ending slavery, that he believed at the end of the war, we were going to be free. And that if we were going to be free, we were going to need some basic things to be able to survive in America after the war, and he believed the number one thing we would need was education. Second in importance was religion.

He proposed the idea of forming a village where we would get the opportunity to have education and practice living in a free society. And it was called Mitchellville (in South Carolina). However, just to show how powerful an idea can be, his idea is why I'm here today, able to speak and think about the next step in our march to freedom as a human. He died before the village was completed because that was the reason why the whites were not permanent residents of the area. He died of malaria. We were left to really run the plantations and to manage and do everything even though we were still, you know, enslaved. He decided, as soon as the Union Army captured this, that area, Hilton Head and that whole area, and the slave owners and the other whites ran away from the island to save their lives. Then we were left there and people from all around came to us. They came to the Hilton Head to get the protection of the Union Army as well as a pre-freedom status.

We were pseudo-free, even though on paper, you aren't free, but there were no slave masters or owners. You could now work with the Union Army and earn money for your family. And so this town called Mitchellville became probably the first freedmen's village. And that's something that, you know, many people have heard about the Port Royal Experiment. So we were that Port Royal Experiment. And so the first public education school system was started in that town on Hilton Head of Mitchellville, where public education was provided; the first place where compulsory education was enforced. And then the first church, a Baptist Church was started, and then the first Methodist Church was started. In this town, Mitchellville families were given a plot of land, a house, and a place for gardening. It was run with its own governmental structure. General Ormsby Mitchel delivered a very historical speech to the first residents of Mitchellville, one that I would put right up there with the Gettysburg Address by President Lincoln. I am credited with unearthing the story of Mitchellville; and when I organized the first National Freedom Day

Celebration on Hilton Head, his speech was read at the program. National Freedom Day is another historical day that I uncovered. That's a beautiful history. I organized the first National Freedom Day celebration and used that opportunity to bring together the family members of General Ormsby Mitchel. We brought them to Hilton Head for the celebration. That may have been the first time that the people on Hilton Head or anywhere really knew the history. I was the only one who had researched it, realized the significance, and the relevance of it for us to embrace. So, Mitchellville is where public education starts. And my family adopted it. It became about, was about, you know, everything was about who was able to get a good education. And we were able to get a great education, and then *Brown v The Board of Education* came on board, and we dismantled the black school system, and put our children in the hands of what I call the KKK.

Today, we have the opportunity to go to Harvard and Princeton and all the top universities, but they don't have the knowledge that we who went through the black school system have and the knowledge that we need now to be able to experience and, attempt to get true freedom. That's another thing in a historical walk, um, that I forgot to mention. Harriet Tubman said when she was getting an award for, you know, saving so many slaves, and she said she "could have saved so many more if they only knew that they were slaves." If you think about that, that's again where we are today. America is a slave to the shackles of race and racism. I say, "the jig is up"—let's free America by dismantling the system of race and racism; and return *all* of us to the human race.

I invite you to a "nonracial America." Now, I hope we have reached a time where everybody, blacks and whites, will work together to bring all Americans back into the *human* family, as brothers and sisters.

As you may or may not know, no one wants to be called a "racist." Well, to not be a racist means you have to give up your status as a White person or a Black person. To become free, you have to embrace the theory that there is only one race, the human race.

And I will get to laugh with my grandchildren, and hopefully, my great-grandchildren will be able to laugh about a time when we had to check a race box that would determine every aspect of our lives. They will laugh and want to know, "What did that mean, your 'race'—the color of your skin, your hair texture? Was America ever that self-indulged?" Education will be valued, and the spirit of knowledge, wisdom, courage, and compassion will have spread throughout the planet; and as a Buddhist (who believes we come back), I'll be back as the new baby in the family! Won't it be grand!

• •

When a moment becomes a movement, the energy of universe and spirit are inevitably behind it.

—S.Y. Bowland

Vision for Justice

Michelle Armster

A Vision for Justice

Long, long time ago
Or was it last year
Or was it yesterday
A seed was planted
A seed
A seed was planted
A justice tree seed
But how will it grow
This justice tree
When the ground is poisoned
With lies and broken treaties
How will it grow
When water spills the blood of African and indigenous blood
How will it grow
When the stories of settlers is the sun that scorches the earth,
    burns our backs and denies our tears

And
We

Know

That Our stories are not the same
And we know

That justice is a verb

And WE know

That it is all about the babies
Taking care of the babies
The babies until the 7th generations
The babies we must love
In ourselves
In our homes
In our communities
In the streets

Bearing witness
Creating Brave spaces
Learning from the past to see the future
Sankofa
Telling our stories

And
Then
Maybe then

This moment becomes a movement

CHAPTER 13

Vision of Power-Sharing Organizations

....

The Path of Responsible Handlers of Power

D r. John Henrik Clarke reminds me to be a responsible handler of power. Many of the organizations in which individuals take part expound principles of equity. At the same time, too often leaders fail to recognize the ways that domination is deeply embedded in their daily practices. This contradiction between intention and reality may be invisible to those living within dominant cultural norms—hierarchy seems natural and inevitable—but it is a source of daily indignity to people living within marginalized cultures.

Having met each other at a retreat sponsored by the Religious Society of Friends (Quakers), the authors of this next essay decided to come together to consider our responsibilities toward and opportunities for decolonizing minds by providing insight into our values and experiences in our separate journeys. We have roots in Native, African, Asian, and Latin cultures, and we gave our gifts to this chapter in many ways, but we all resonate here as one voice.

tom kunesh is a mixed-blood lakota from Minnesota. He is active in Tennessee native politics of historical preservation and interpretation and studies decolonizing religion and family history.

S.Y. Bowland is an african american from Harlem, New York, with expertise in conflict resolution, restorative practices, and alternative dispute resolution with emphasis on African indigenous praxis.

jiche is a corean american ecofeminist activist, poet, and postcolonial educator of liberatory praxis and mind-body reintegration in Chicago, Illinois.

....

Diego James Navarro is a hispanic/latino educator working with formerly incarcerated and other adult students using liberation and social justice research for cultures of dignity in California.

Jorge Morales is an elder human being, quaker, and zen practitioner in San Jose, California.

—S.Y. Bowland

. . . .

Achieving Solidarity in Decolonization: Dialogue Among Friends of Color

tom kunesh, S.Y. Bowland, jiche, Jorge Morales, and Diego Navarro

Following a Friends of Color retreat in October 2020, a diverse handful of Friends of Color began meeting to share and study what decolonization means for us. "Decolonizing the mind," a concept introduced in 1986 by Ngũgĩ wa Thiong'o, has become a central theme in our weekly gatherings where we reflect on personal and ancestral narratives related to colonization from different regions of the globe. We learn from and honor each other's cultural and spiritual heritages, expanding our perspectives and wisdom. In seeking the truth behind the narrative of colonialism we have come to see how much of our ethnic histories have been appropriated and erased by the colonials who deemed themselves the masters, then rewrote or entirely omitted our stories in the history books used in our US settler school systems, government structures, and media. Our solidarity stands on the understanding of the danger in accommodating everyone's story to a single story (Chimamanda Ngozi Adichie's "The Danger of a Single Story"); and such self-awareness is usually a sigh of relief for the community.

We hold space for each other on our individual journeys of decolonizing the mind with the understanding that heart is central to this practice. One method we use is sharing our narratives, which strengthens the conviction that spirit manifests in multitudinous ways. We recognize our unity as children, not stewards, of Mother Earth, explained by agroecologist Vandana Shiva as the only true identity we have (navdanya.org). We thus explore diversity of friendship as living decolonizing praxis that is harmonious with the ecology of the natural world. The focus on accountability in an article by Eve Tuck and K. Wayne Yang ("Decolonization Is Not a Metaphor," 2012) us as Friends of Color to refer to ourselves as Decolonizing for Action.

On May 1, 2021, we were invited to join a virtual conference held by another group of Friends who had formed around the decolonizing question with the intent to learn about similar efforts by other Friends. Decolonizing Quakers was an ad hoc group of predominantly white Friends who had begun meeting online in the spring of 2018 to promote indigenous concerns following a gathering at Pendle Hill. Several weeks after their first meeting, the group named themselves Decolonizing Quakers (DQ), declaring their primary focus to be in "Seeking Right Relationship with Indigenous Peoples." On their website, decolonizingquakers.org, DQ members collect resources and publicize educational programs related to indigenous history and sovereignty rights.

In the event called "Decolonizing Quakers Invites You to Continue Working Toward Right Relationship with Indigenous Peoples," the hosts demonstrated an openness to hearing our voices and understanding our approach to decolonizing which is radically different from the traditional approach. Our work in Decolonizing for Action differs from the programmatic focus and cultural definitions of DQ in that we started with listening and sharing our own stories in a safe, compassionate, and restorative space created and shared by Friends of Color. We consider trust and relationship-building foundational to the work of hearing others' histories, herstories, and their stories related to colonization and assimilation that often involve intergenerational trauma. Herein lies a query of why Decolonizing [White] Friends might create more work for People of Color.

Each group was allotted two minutes to address the participants of the May 1 DQ event, and we decided to split our time between us to ensure the presence of multicultural voices.

S.Y.: We each speak and take some comfort while bearing our responsibility to just listen, hearing the truth given to us from our loved ones and ancestors. To me this is only possible with the presence of spirit. I hear our ancestors sharing through us. I feel the release of the unspoken pain. Then, I discover we are in healing relationships with each other. We see, feel, witness, and experience the essence of our presence in the moment with one another. Recognizing the joyful interconnectedness of Ubuntu. Ubuntu is an African perspective, representing the essence of being human in relationship, with the world and each other. I am because we are; we are because I am. Only together—I through you and you through me—do we achieve our common goal of decolonization. The Saturday gathering of Decolonizing Quakers was refreshing. It was a pleasure to be with Friends who seek to address the impacts of colonization and the desire to create change by decentering white-bodied perspectives. To decenter the white dominant norm is most important in this journey.

Ji: Historically the descendants of white settlers have maintained the privilege of framing most discussions of "what to do with the Natives," but in calling us together as "Decolonizing Quakers" we are offered a sacred opportunity for critical and collaborative self-reflection on what colonization means and on what decolonization entails. Has there been critical self-reflection on what the repercussions of colonization have been on all nonwhite-identified, nonbinary peoples, particularly within the diverse communities of Quakers presently settled on Turtle Island? If the intention for "right relationship" is genuine, the first priority must be on authentic collaboration with representation beyond the settler/native power binary, in humble acceptance of the sovereignty of all peoples to determine what is needed for their own healing and restoration. It is ours to decide whether to open to the sacred opportunity of the present by listening, with honest conversations about impact and action demonstrating accountability. We can begin practicing in the here and now the sacred connection and transformative action that "right relationship" entails.

Diego: Again, our focus is on decolonizing the mindset of colonization. We've been inquiring into and deconstructing our mindsets and our experiences of assimilation, racism, cultural appropriation, othering and being colonized. In this solidarity, we better understand the ways we have been and will always be in a healthy healing relationship.

In closure, our experiences show that decolonization has a different meaning to white-bodied people. To them, seeking "right relationship" is tantamount to befriending and learning from Native American peoples as honorary guests. This is not our perspective nor that of other Peoples of Color. As other Peoples of Color who have been colonized, who are equally engaged in decolonizing our lives and our Quakerism, this is not our perspective. Decolonization impacts and must represent the presence of multiple cultures and voices adversely impacted by the settler narrative.

The queries offered by the steering committee included:

- What does "decolonizing" mean to you?
- What could "decolonizing" mean for your meeting? For Quakers in general? How are you or your meeting working toward "right relationship with Indigenous Peoples," within or outside of the meeting? (Or how might you like to be?)
- Are you already doing something, thinking about something, heard about something?
- What challenges have you seen or experienced so far?
- What challenges do you think you or Quakers might face?

• •

Women Like Me

Celeste Brock

Women like me
Ordinary women, human women,
Poor, or rising, or . . . with endless accomplishments.
Mothers, daughters
Sisters, aunts, cousins
GRANDMOTHERS—

All of these share grief—
The grief of murdered sons
The fear of murdered sons
The fear of what might happen any day, any night.

I see these women
and the magnificence of who some are.
What we can become is limitless,
bordered only by restrictions put upon us by . . .
When I hear or see what women society calls Black go through
the anger rises in my throat, a fulsome beast engorging so I cannot breathe.
This rage I feel is a living thing, growing, pulsing,
fed by the knowledge of ignorance, hatred, fear . . . that word again.
What we have in common is fear.
What we all share is fear.

What would the world look like if our magnificence were UNbounded?
If we knew our success depended on no one else but US?
White people, LISTEN!
Black folks are not holding YOU down,
do not hate you out of hand,
only wish for ALL of us to be free of chains.
Freedom for Blacks means freedom for ALL of us.

What would the day and night look like if we LOVED one another?
What would WE look like? What would we FEEL like?
Who would we all be? Magnificent?

. . . .

Bring Your Magnificence

S.Y. Bowland

To find it—listen to
The rhythms of soul

The rhythms of soul
The universe awaits our gifts
It hungers for our unified presence
It swirls the senses of unknown smells of Joy and Prance

The Rhythms of my soul
The stars await our gathering
It demands our dance of engagement
It sings the verses to all of my songs

The Rhythms of your soul
The darkness awaits your light
It demands the brilliant illumination
It swings to unheard beats of intellectual love

The Rhythms of our souls
The World awaits our presentation
It demands an opening night
It captures all that is visible for the glimpse of night

I behold the evidence of things hoped for
And yet unseen
Will you join me in the dance
in the dark
under the moon
and be a part of instead of apart?
new beginnings

The Rhythms of our Souls
Be bold cause only
you know
what goals

Is this your magnificence?
Bring your magnificence!

· ·

Frank Hall embraces the belief that the ancestors can guide a better future for all, if we but listen to them.

—S.Y. Bowland

· ·

ancestors

Frank Eugene Hall

may the words of my mouth
and the meditations of my heart
be acceptable to you o ancestors
who have known the roots of my beginning
and who have felt along the way
that things were changing
that good things might stay
but things that did not serve the soul
would fail

CHAPTER 14

Vision of Welcoming Institutions

··

The Path of Healing

W hen we speak of institutional racism, heads nod but eyes often glaze. If individuals are the distinct foreground in our awareness of social reality, institutions are the background, vague entities that blur within a frame that is both too close and too distant. Yet they are the place in which discrimination is deeply embedded, the site of needed social change. Where we can see foreground and background in distinct relationships to each other is in the stories of those most harshly affected.

Diane Ciccone is an accomplished attorney and conflict resolution expert. Throughout a long career as an attorney, she has encountered dual indignities of sexism and racism. Her determination to assert her dignity is woven through the stories she offers here, testimony to the power vested in us all to overcome discrimination in the unwelcoming institution we daily encounter.

—S.Y. Bowland

···

Dignity, Respect, and Healing in a Diseased World

Diane Ciccone

I had the privilege of clerking for Jane Bolin, the first African American female judge in the United States. She believed that respect is essential: "I will demand respect!" My lesson from her is, if you can't respect me, then I will not interact with you. Culturally, that means holding yourself in such a way that, if someone wants to deal with you, they must come in the manner and fashion you have set as your personal parameters. Very early on in my legal career, I faced a need for that philosophy because I was always one of the first in the door. It was either racism or sexism.

I'm a black female, so it was present in my profession constantly. There was always overt and covert discrimination directed toward me in the workplace. My intellect, work ethic, and abilities were always questioned, and I was as capable as my white counterparts. Early in my career, there was always the underlying need to excel for oneself and to prove to others that I was just as good as if not better than my white counterparts. The need to dispel the bigotry was always present.

I don't experience it now or, more precisely, I don't think about or react to it now, because I have proven myself and I really don't care what others think. It's the wisdom, I suppose, that comes with age, not letting the negative behaviors seep into your consciousness. I can't remember a time when I haven't faced sexism and racism.

But earlier in my life, it was important not just for my own self-gratification but especially to prove to the naysayers that I was more competent than those who I worked with or came into contact with.

If you are going to interact with me you have to approach me with the respect I command. If you don't, I just don't deal with you anymore. I mean, I'm at a point in my career I can pick and choose who I want to interact with; my position as an administrative law judge comes with a basic level of respect. Of course, you will always have a few who think they can talk to you any way they please. Those folks, you put in their place quickly. And they usually correct their behavior.

I tell younger lawyers to always be self-confident, to always work from a power of strength. I tell them they should always have allies, have people you can surround yourself with, at your kitchen table, who will encourage you, support you not to take anybody's crap. And then, of course, the other thing is, know how to choose your battles. You need to always have that personal line, that you don't let anyone cross. You must take care of your physical, mental, and spiritual health as well. You have to figure out what you can and cannot take, and what you will and will not allow, in terms of how people deal with you: what they say to you, what you are willing to put up with. That's very individual; some people can handle situations differently, they'll let things slide off their back. Now I'm at a point in my life to let things slide off my back.

To give you an example: there was a time when I was a trial attorney. We were picking a jury, but we were in the lawyers' room. There was an older white male attorney who I knew, I'd had a bunch of cases with him. He called me sweetie, or something like that. And I knew that he wasn't being derogatory because we had developed a relationship. He had a daughter the same age as

I was. Because he was an older person, I simply said to him very politely, "You know, that's okay. But make sure when we're in front of the jury, you address me by my name." It was a way that I made it very clear it was not acceptable. But it was okay. I wasn't going to make a mountain out of a molehill, and he respected that.

So I think it's those kinds of little things that you really have to address. I could have blown it up and made it a real big deal. Or I could have taken the tact that I did take, which is to say, Okay, all right. Just don't do that.

However, if someone crosses the line that you have set for yourself, you deal with them in the manner that suits the situation and your comfort level. But always stay true to yourself.

SYB: What are ways that people have approached you and discussed the politics we're experiencing right now, especially the Black Lives Matter movement?

DC: The people that I am generally exposed to are mostly like-minded. But what I found is that even my white colleagues and friends, there's a point at which they don't get it. And when they reach that point, then you have to decide, do you want to educate them or let them continue to be blinded by their white privilege? What I usually do, if I sense that they are willing and can accept it, then I will speak to it. But you don't want to talk to the wall if someone's not going to understand it.

Here's an example: We were walking one day, and I was telling them about my concern about the possible violence that may ensue, with this whole nonsense with the Proud Boys and that kind of stuff. And they were like, well, no, what do you mean violence? And so I had to say, we may not see it here in the suburbs where we live. But I'm concerned that it's a real threat to people that look like me in urban areas. They still couldn't understand why I would be nervous about the eruption of violence. And I had to say, well, you see what happened in Michigan; if they're willing to do that to their own, what are they going to do to us? Just because you think you're liberal, that doesn't mean that you truly understand race relations. Sometimes you have to tell them exactly how it is. There's a way we talk to each other and a way that we talk to them. And sometimes you have to break it down to them to let them completely understand and really pierce their white privilege, so they understand what it is to live in our skin, and what it is that they can do to change how they think and interact with Black folks.

SYB: But we've told them that already 1,000 times! If you keep doing the same thing and expecting a different result, is the learning curve too long or short, and for whom?

DC: That's true. That's why I say to you, there are times I don't bother. But sometimes it's the one time someone will really listen, and then I will say it again.

You're right. You want to be hopeful that things are going to change. But what we're dealing with in this country is 400 years old. I don't want to say very little is changed, because there has been change. But a lot of it's been cosmetic. Yes, I know, 100 years ago, you and I would not have been able to have the professions that we've had. I do understand that. But how much of it is really changed when we're still so often not considered humans in this country? Our bodies are disposable. Our men are completely disposable. There isn't any place where you can go, anything you can do, where you feel protected. From that perspective, very little has changed. But then on the other side, you have to have some sort of hope. You have to have some sort of hope that things could change, that they are changing.

For me, history has always been important. By studying the past, we can employ what worked, avoid future pitfalls, and develop modern strategies based on the current level of oppression. But we also need to rejoice in our legacy and our struggles. I don't believe we should shy away from the pain of the past. We need to use that pain to strengthen our resolve. Each generation has its own set of issues, but they're really similar to past generations. And so, if we can look at past generations and see what they've done to survive and maneuver, it gives us something to build on, whether we tweak it or find it doesn't work. The white culture sees us as inferior, but when you look at our history, you look at what we've done in this country, in the world, it's a very rich legacy. It's something to be proud of.

SYB: Let's talk about ways of surviving the racial struggle. How do you build your own strength? In addition to your immediate family, where do you find support?

DC: I think it is of the utmost importance that we turn inward. As a community, we need to be self-healing, and self-sufficient. We need to provide for ourselves; many of us live in food and health deserts. Individually and as a community, we must learn to grow as much of our own food as possible. We must demand quality food choices in our neighborhoods. Personally, we need to be mindful of what we eat and drink. One must understand the effect of a poor diet on one's health.

We need to build economic strength. The one thing we lost with integration is self-contained communities that were thriving. We need to buy Black, bank Black, work Black.

We need to work on conflict resolution to reduce the violence among ourselves. We need to teach our children our glorious history, give them the tools for them to survive and excel.

We need to honor and provide shelter for our elders. Essentially, to strive to live by the seven principles of Kwanzaa on both the personal and community level. The principles should be a way of life.

By having strong communities and folks that work together, we will have more tools to shield ourselves from the physical, emotional, and spiritual ravages of the "isms," from white privilege and its tentacles.

. . . .

As we engage the legal system, many decisions are made before the evidence is known, and thus "The Verdict."

—S.Y. Bowland

. . . .

Verdict

Mary L. Jones Wade

Three days before the verdict, a thought tried to make its way to me,
my surface, the place that holds my heart and spirit.
My mind resisted, it was too uncomfortable, if that is the word?
Or was it my mind? Could it have been my heart, unwilling to feel?
sympathy, and empathy for one who had done such a dastardly deed?
Could it have been my spirit saying no, you have violated the truth of
the commonality of Spirit that uplifts the meaning and practice of humanity?

But I thought, no, was it will, no, was it feeling no.
Whatever it was it persisted. It inched and inched and inched.
The I in me kept pushing it down, but it continued to inch its way up,
haltingly, yet with persistence until the day it broke through.

The verdict, GUILTY, GUILTY, GUILTY. Then as my heart calmed,
my mind began to settle from sheer exhaustion of prolonged
celebration and joy. It appeared again, up from deep within
some part of me.
What was it? Was it wonder; then why?
What causes the light in the eyes of a newborn baby,
the wonder of a searching soul, the reaching for comfort
and humanity to go out?

What causes one to go cold, unfeeling, blank?
What rejection, indoctrination, abuse, initiation led to
dismissing of one's own humanity, so that it could not
phantom or feel the humanity of another?
What prevents the mingling and co-mingling of the inner
longing for life?

What prevents one from seeing the self as real,
and valuable to the human struggle for life?

And why are we afraid to feel and care for one whose inability
or unwillingness to feel the deepest longing of one's own being
and the cry of another, for life?
Can it be that in our inner belly we too have lost or are losing sight,
our sense, our hunger, our grip on the sanctity of our own life?
And therefore, is the preciousness of all life and the urgency for the forward
motion of life lost?
Have we indeed lost the sway of the rhythm of life with all our sisters and
brothers, humanity, and creation as a whole?

PERHAPS WE TOO ARE GUILTY.

CHAPTER 15

Vision of Equitable Practices

··

The Path of Mentorship and Leadership

W hat we learn in this chapter is that even when people have achieved the highest traditional educational degrees, those who are marginalized are still hindered by the same forms of oppression they encountered on the way to gaining those degrees, as well as some new ones.

Angie Beeman and Tsedale M. Melaku are leaders in their field. Their lived experience guided their research into the phenomenon of hidden labor required of oppressed people everywhere.

—S.Y. Bowland

· ·

In Search of Academic Freedom: To Censor Word or Deed: Why Do We Ask the Question?

Angie Beeman and Tsedale M. Melaku

Tsedale M. Melaku: I grew up in the Bronx, in New York City, with my parents and three siblings. I am an Ethiopian-born naturalized citizen. My parents sought asylum in the United States in the early 1980s, coming here with nothing but their children and dreams of a better life. They constantly emphasized the importance of education. I went to public schools in the Bronx, until high school when I entered an all-girls Catholic school, Aquinas High School. From there, I attended New York University and majored in sociology and Africana studies, with a minor in psychology. All my life I wanted to be a doctor, but after an incident in college, I decided that being a lawyer would be the better step for me. However, I quickly learned after working at a corporate firm that that's not where I wanted to be. At the advice of my husband, I ended up in a PhD program in sociology while working full time at a law firm. I was lucky enough to be able to turn my sociological gaze toward the environments in which I worked. In so doing, I decided to do research centering the experiences of Black women, and particularly Black women lawyers. Presently, I am a postdoctoral research fellow with the Institute for Research on the African Diaspora in the Americas and the Caribbean at the Graduate Center, City University of New York.

Looking at the experiences of women of color and wanting to hear their particular stories and journeys is what makes being a sociologist or researcher worth it for me. Utilizing a Black feminist thought perspective in my practice, I value knowledge production derived from narratives and stories, which is why I want to center my work in collecting that kind of history and knowledge from Black, Indigenous, and people of color (BIPOC). That's where I'm situated. I'm presently working on my second book that looks at diversity and workplace stratification, while also researching the experiences of BIPOC professionals in organizations and the impact of COVID-19, racial upheaval, and political polarization on their trajectories.

I'm so lucky to have had the opportunity to meet Angie, and to produce work engaging not only our experiences, but the experiences of women of color generally, in organizations that we've been a part of and that we've researched. I would love to continue lifting those voices in the work that I do—supporting [BIPOC] and not just talking about it but actually doing it, and getting other people to pick up that work that oftentimes overburdens us and is not valued. This unrecognized, and uncompensated invisible labor, significantly disadvantages BIPOC professionals. We are forced to pay an inclusion tax, in the form of additional resources "spent" including emotional, cognitive, relational, and financial labor expended to be in these spaces, as well as to resist and or adhere to dominant norms. This is exhausting. I want to continue pushing others to pick up that work and get dirty doing it.

Angie Beeman: I agree. It's great to hear these stories. I can find a piece of myself in all of your stories. SY, when you say, you're the person who's always the one, it sounds like we're a bunch of troublemakers. [Everyone laughs.] I found my people! I am also that person, who often points out inequality. I often ask, "Why is it always me? Why do I always end up in these situations?" My husband says, "That's why you're always so exhausted. It's because you see through things that other people ignore."

I attribute that to my life experiences. When you grow up working class and as a woman of color, of course, you're going to be positioned differently. One of my professors said women see through BS a lot more easily than men. Working-class people see things a lot more easily, and people of color, and women of color. When you're at the intersections of those, of course you're going to see things differently.

My mother is from Korea, she came over to the United States in her 20s. My mother faced a lot of trauma, coming from Korea to the United States. For me growing up, I saw that trauma, and I experienced that trauma, even though I didn't quite know how to articulate it. I grew up in Somerset County, Pennsylvania, a predominantly white area. That town is very class-divided— it's Appalachia—so you have the working class like I was, and then you have people who are much worse off than me. Then you have the people who are doctors. So it's not all poor European Americans. It's a mixture.

My father has his own story about growing up working poor, joining the army, and then ending up in Vietnam. That was his way out. And then he met my mom. He worked very hard for us.

Looking back, I can now understand my experiences as determined by social class but also intersecting with racism and sexism, living in a predominantly white coal mining town. I was always called "the chink." And then, of course, I'm a woman. My mother faced gender inequality in Korea and this intersected with racial inequalities in the United States. I saw her pushing back against them all the time, but also reproducing them. For instance, she would say "Kelly [Angie's brother] doesn't do the laundry, he's a boy." But then she would also tell me these stories about how she would push against these gendered ideologies when she was a young girl. I also saw her fighting against racial bigotry that she encountered in her everyday life, when people would discount her and make fun of her accent. Yet she didn't want me to fight these things.

SYB: Being born and raised in Harlem, I had a lot of support. The people around me realized that I was different, but they supported me.

AB: Neither of my parents have college educations. They stressed to me, "You're not going to get out of this town, you're not going to make it unless you take your education seriously." That push from my parents and seeing the work that they did, working-class labor, and their telling me you don't want to have to do this, that was the urge that I had to [be different]. I got a scholarship to Indiana University of Pennsylvania, which is a working-class school. There were some really good mentors in the sociology program. SY is talking about her community. There were people [at IUP] who really believed in me. They had these race and ethnic relations classes; there were two that I remember, two classes on racism. They were taught by Herbert Hunter, an African American man. He was very stern, very serious. But I liked that he was teaching racism in a serious way. That "racism is something that my students are going to think about in my class!"

He became my mentor. I could just pop into his office and theorize with him and share experiences that I had with racism, and he would listen. He was always there. He was just so supportive. He was also assigned as my mentor—they would assign students of color with different mentors. After him, I just continued to have mentors who were usually African American or Asian American.

Herbert Hunter gave me articles to read by Noel Cazenave, who was at UConn. After reading these I thought, "I want to go work with Noel Cazenave." So, then I went to get my PhD at UConn, which was a completely different situation than IUP. I mean, I was amazed that they had food trucks on campus. [Laughter.] Wow, I didn't know college could be like this! [Laughs.] I requested Dr. Cazenave to be my advisor, but the university put me with somebody else. I wondered if it was because they didn't really like Dr. Cazenave. He was the one who created the white racism course. He was seen as a troublemaker. He now has a course called Killing African Americans and a book by the same title. He's very outspoken. I made sure to meet with him. I said, "I requested you to advise me." He said, "I didn't hear anything about that." [Laughs.] I still talk to him until this day. He got me through grad school.

TS: When I began my doctoral studies at the Graduate Center, it was distressing for me to recognize that you barely see people of color in faculty positions within a city university, and I wondered why that is? How can we be a city university that prides ourselves on diversity and being focused on equity and justice, on providing access and opportunity to the children of city workers and to all communities within New York City, and yet not have a representation of faculty who would reflect that? Coming in as a grad student and being one of two Black students in my cohort of 28, I was like, wow! And being the only self-identifying Black woman! I didn't understand.

As a graduate student, I ended up working with Dr. Jerry G. Watts. He was an amazing, Black male, incredible scholar, thoughtful human being, generous person, and my champion, and what he did was [pauses, tears].

SYB: There is pain in your story.

TS: He [still tears] opened a door for me to see the value in the work that I was doing. He gave me an opportunity to not only just be myself, but he valued my intellectual journey and the humanity in the work that I was doing, and the interest that I had in looking at the experiences of Black woman. He recognized that I myself as a Black woman, in a predominantly white space, was important and valued.

This is very emotional for me because he died right before I graduated, right before my defense. I spent six, seven years working with him. He was someone who fought the establishment, he stood up for students and particularly students of color, who he saw consistently marginalized and silenced and left out, really excluded in a way that oftentimes makes other people devalue our presence, and our intellectual capacity. Losing someone like that at any stage of your life is just devastating.

I'm standing on the shoulders of giants. Yeah, I was very, very fortunate to have that time with Dr. Watts. And then, of course, to be lifted by Dr. Erica Chito Childs. At the worst moments, she just pulled me out of darkness. And I think the reason why she was able to do that, and the reason why I was able to trust her, is because she had built a relationship with me, because she valued my work. She valued me as a student.

There is so much about being recognized and supported by individuals in the system. How critical that is, and how much it's about not just being recognized and valued, but actually building a relationship where people show up for you at those critical moments.

SYB: You've told these stories about the attention you got, the door being always open, the conversation being always available to you; wasn't that hidden labor on the part of your mentors? What was the added burden to them of being the one person you could turn to for that kind of support on a mostly white faculty?

AB: I know the burden my mentors had because I'm experiencing it now. I am that mentor. Mentorship is not valued. In fact, I'll share the story of how I was basically punished for mentoring people of color. First, let me give you some history.

At UConn, they threw graduate students into teaching right away; you have your own class. UConn is a predominately white institution; I was always the one, as a graduate student instructor, taking on that added work, and then going and doing service work at the Women's Center and working to bring faculty of color together, to create spaces that would support instructors in general. That's the labor I was already engaged in, being one of the few people of color and simply caring about these issues. I thought that it was my duty to do that. And then that just continued throughout my work. White faculty would send me students to over-tally [i.e., more than the capacity of a class], especially if they were people of color. I had an incident recently, where I had already accepted enough over tallies in this class; a white faculty member sent me a student saying, "Well, I thought you would want the student because they're the president of the African American Association." And I'm thinking, "Maybe you should take that student, then; maybe you should care." I also have to manage my workload.

And then also, I am a faculty mentor. Our former dean would assign senior faculty of color with junior faculty to be a mentor, but without any reward. And my chair at the time didn't even know that I was a faculty mentor, she was surprised to learn. I'm doing all this extra work to make the college look good, and I'm not getting any recognition for it at all. I'm happy to do it because I had those mentors and I need to pass it on. But in no way is it being valued.

I was once retaliated against for being the mentor of a Black woman who was in her first job. We developed such a strong, very close mentor-mentee relationship. We're very good friends now. But she left her first job, because of the hostility she faced. One of the things that she wrote when she left was, "My mentor cannot mentor me." She was talking about me and the hostility I was facing. "I've seen her work be disrespected, right in front of me. I see this woman of color being treated in disrespectful ways. Why would I seek tenure in an institution like this?"

There's an expectation that we're doing that work for the university, but then that's never taken into consideration. The time that we are expected to dedicate to this service work can then hurt our ability to publish. That's the invisible labor, which we've all experienced with regard to mentorship. If you don't do it, you're punished. If you do it, you're punished as well, if it hurts your research. And particularly, I think, if you're a woman, or a woman of color, you're punished for doing that extra service. So, there's all these layers to it.

What I would do if I was in a position of authority in these institutions, I would put my money where my mouth is. Some institutions are receiving funds to address racism through these diversity initiatives. Okay, so who is being hired as a result? Have you valued their work? How do you amplify the work of faculty of color? I have talked about how we will email people in our institutions to say, "Hey, I published this article, I gave this talk." And yet, they're not advertising it, but they're advertising the work of the white folks who are doing similar kinds of talks. I would make sure to amplify the work of faculty of color, if I'm saying that I care about this message of "diversity" and antiracism.

. . . .

How are we in the world?

S.Y. Bowland

The world is loving we are kind
The world is at peace we are gentle
The world is a mess we are damaged
The world is mean we are confused
The world is violent we lose ourselves
The world is a terror who am I where am I
The world is unbalanced I am isolated
The people are uninformed I am alienated
Don't box me in—who am I—I am lost—I become a monster —

What type of monster are you!
Capitalist
Socialist
Marxist
Memeist
Individualist

Whoever and whatever we become, we can find our way to the
    place where we always wanted to be.

CHAPTER 16

Vision of Seeing the Invisible Context of Oppression

....

Vision of Freedom from Violence

W omen are and always have been responsible for creating and nurturing community. jiche is a credible messenger who speaks in
the voices of many cultures, bringing knowledge and relationship
across profound distances. In her daily roles, she is a professor, a restorative justice facilitator, and a spiritual practitioner. Ji is also an outsider poet, writer, and urban educator
yogi in Chicago.

—S.Y. Bowland

....

The Mudang Sends the Missionary Home: Practicing Critical Humility in Intercultural Peace and Justice Work

jiche

Decolonizing is perhaps the more straightforward name for "transformative
justice," a phrase that seems to remain in a magical sphere. The social and psychological work of decolonizing equally involves our bodies, the material forms
upon which our bodies live, and their organizing systems. It is the struggle to
achieve the means for healthy bodies and a clean earth that ground the undertaking of decolonizing our minds. Without this definitive grounding, "transformative justice" is easily conflated with the increasing demands for professionalized
peace and justice workers by governmental and nongovernmental agencies

....

(NGOs), and the possibility for critical humility is often lost. When this happens, the institutional apparatus perpetuates its colonial violence in euphemized forms. We consider how critical humility is a necessary practice within the peace and conflict fields variously called restorative justice (RJ), transformative justice (TJ), mediation, and alternative dispute resolution (ADR). This work is a thought-stream opened from reading the accounts of women elders who had experienced militarized sexual violence during World War II, and dedicated to the grandmothers past and present who have given the gift of testimony despite being silenced by guilt, shame, and buried stories.

Grandma Gil
(13 when abducted, Corea):
After thinking about it,
I realize I did not sin
It was they who sinned

Grandma Adela
(14 when abducted, Philippines):
When I came home I got sick
I was ashamed
I hid from people
I couldn't eat
I couldn't sleep
I did not tell my father
I told my mother
She told me not to tell my brothers
I did not even tell my husband
Even today I repent for not telling him
I try to forget it
But it's there always

Cao Hei Mao
(18 when abducted, China)
The pain of when they bind your feet—it breaks your bones
We had backbreaking work in the fields every day
They attacked our village and we were surrounded
They took me and we walked in the dark at night
Two years later I returned home
I was damaged so badly
I couldn't have children

Women bear the burden of community
How are the children
This may be difficult to integrate into schemas

Who dares to advise when problems confound us at home
Home is private
Its contract does not end
We can't fly home from home and show pictures
We are implicated
What do we mean by *relationship* when mother is stuck in an abusive marriage
Which of her children defy the rule of the father
Family is the last frontier

Swiftly decolonizing our intellectual frameworks is an acute necessity in the Anthropocene, and the visionary excavations this entails call for unusual collaboration as we refine our solitary aims into a liberatory life flow of actions. The testimonies of survivors of the Japanese Imperial Army's rape stations throughout World War II—which in principle are not peculiar to Japan as a colonial power—speak to the comprehensive legacy of trauma as well as an indefatigable human need for truth-telling. How to hold and contain truth-telling spaces, as well as contextual analyses of both the conflicting parties and the theory of change assumed by facilitators, are the foci of peace and justice curriculums. However, especially when we are referring to "transformative justice," a new priority must be to examine individual and community conflicts from the perspective of empire. The facilitators themselves are not somehow exempt from nor do they transcend hegemonic structures.

A task for those of us waking up from the mythology of white supremacist patriarchy is in owning our own bodies, then relinquishing all notions of ownership when realizing our basic earthiness. For white and honorary white bodies among us who, influenced by a progressive education or else somehow become aware of having reaped unearned social capital and material privileges from work that perpetuates colonial structures, ours is a similar priority but in different terms: to go home. Going home means to step into the vulnerable unknown, the true New World of humility grounding critical analysis to include self when approaching these excavations of indigenous health and justice restoration practices that are neither new nor ours to claim. Going home also means to apply this practical knowledge still mostly in the reserves of privilege to already-existent communities always within our reach—kin, colleague, neighbor, religious community, and metropole are the ground zeroes for transformative justice that do not require a round-trip ticket. Going home also frankly means to stop meddling in cultural domains in which we did not grow up that makes us conflict tourists, not experts. Folks already apply their ways or are busy refinding or refining them, otherwise we and they wouldn't have survived for this long under centuries of brutality and consciousness warping. Going home means that by pausing to observe the chronic validation-seeking and obfuscating of origins methods and aims, we can let these wearisome habits go and find our own truth, reconciliation and rest. Going home for all bodies means developing sustained attention within our bodies. Perhaps when the descendants of settlers, natives, slaves, and immigrants do a little healing and find all unearned privileges reprehensible enough to throw them off, we can share our journeys as ironic co-conspirators, and when spirit rises, as co-visionary friends working to repair our most profound harms to our M/mother(s). Critical humility is not a feeling or a posturing but a praxis of transformation toward liberation from a 500-year-old dismembering ideology.

JICHE (WE/US/KIN) INTRO

There was no preconceived order to the journey recounted here, nor plan of how it would transpire; it merely unfolded of necessity, serendipity, and some imagination.

Mother moved us to the United States when we were toddlers, and we settled into an immigrant Catholic neighborhood on the northwest side of Chicago with mostly Polish and Latinx and a sprinkling of others like us. Ethnic ties became dissociated from the two Coreas (precolonial, anglicized spelling) and ancestors who had known two imperialist wars with its masses of souls abruptly and permanently separated from their families. The selective forgetfulness that is the bromide of American life was consented to in relief by our mother who had been a child in the burgeoning years of the ROK (the Republic of Korea, or South Korea). Thus "my people" became those existentially ungrounded urbanites, much of whose shared metanarratives came from pop culture with its shallow multicultural referents, and our connection to the land hindered by miles and miles of horizontal walls laid over ground. But atop these built sites we ran fast and shouted exuberantly at our teammates playing freeze-tag as the streetlamps dimmed and mother's sonorous voice beckoned us to come home.

Who can understand another body's trauma except through its discordant dedication to safety? Mother declined to narrate the confusion of sorrow from a literary father who had abandoned his *yangban* wife and five young children in the postwar years, mistaking respite in a teahouse for love. Instead mother used her magical storytelling art to enliven old Confucian folktales and conjure the early Christians martyred in Corea when it had been a myopic dustbin of ignorance and insularity from the new world owned by the imperialists. The wealth of tales hailing principled suffering compared to the dearth of kinflesh narratives alienated us from body and land, as well as the repercussions in our family dynamics of unnamed intergenerational trauma, and made navigating young adulthood a fraught iconoclastic experience, as it is for so many youth coming of age in America. Searching for our ethnic history in the curriculum offered in a Midwestern university in the late 1980s was an exercise in despair.

On some level we understood that pharmaceuticals and talk therapy could not begin to address a pain as incommensurable as a haunting, and thoroughly disillusioned with the low-grade depressions normalized in a predatory economic culture, we finally abandoned it to wander both at home and abroad in search of self. After a decade of white-collar migrant work interspersed with long travels, during which we saved enough to immerse ourselves in search of viable cultural alternatives teaching EFL, we returned to Chicago for graduate studies in critical theory and began teaching in its sprawling community college system. It was 2008. Familiar with the working-class immigrant and Black cultures that maintained the cityscape, we found we could begin to teach. We knew the daily hustle to navigate the sly appeals and selective constraints of neoliberalism, and we shared cultural and geographical referents, for this was home. Though grad school had provided tools and a setting for intellectual survival, the territorial hostilities inherent in capitalist schooling felt unsafe and incompatible, and this developed a sensitivity for the processes by which public learning took place. About this time, having completed training as *yoga siromani* we began experimenting with embodied practices in our classrooms, developing a somatic praxis toward full integration with critical content.

As postcolonial realists, we take to heart Fanon's exhortations to the native intellectual in *The Wretched of the Earth* to disentangle from the moral and psychological wasteland of white-centric culture. In so doing, he warns against the reactive sentimentality upon achieving a colonialist education which idealizes a precolonial past that even the natives have superseded. Our starting ground then, which we find profoundly rich with covert herstory, theirstory, and ourstory, are those voices abandoned by history by which we find where we actually are in a creative dance of fragment and fusion in the work of liberation of body, mind, and spirit. We consider our work a praxis of critical healing communities to quicken the waning of a settler regime that has actively suppressed the humanity of all those who toil within it.

We write at present with media reports fresh in the mind of the mass shootings in three massage parlors in Georgia, touting the image of yet another white male supremacist and circulating his immediate explanation to eliminate sexual temptation, while the six Chinese and Corean women among the eight killed remain faceless and voiceless, and whose names are misspelled or disordered. Then to an audience already dissipated from regular news of gun violence, Georgia is superseded within weeks by two more shootings in Colorado and California, and finally dismissed in the main by an investigative reporter who validates the killer's stated motive by finding that in one of the three Asian massage parlors, criminal charges of prostitution had occurred six years prior to the shootings. The selective quasi-Christian moralizing validates a patriarchal sexual norm of the privatization of women's bodies and evokes wartime tropes of Asian women compelled into prostitution. The compounded vulnerabilities of women and nonbinary people in the United States also at the intersections of class, race, citizenship status, and language speak to patriarchal violence as the operative of imperialism, settler colonialism, and war.

THE WORLD'S LARGEST SEX TRAFFICKING PROGRAM

The historical references in this section come mostly from transnational feminist scholars whose analysis was their cultural home, such as Dai Sil Kim-Gibson for her 1999 publication and documentary, *Silence Broken*, which was my introduction to these buried herstories, Margaret Stetz and Bonnie B. C. Oh, editors of the 2001 anthology, *Legacies of the Comfort Women of World War II*, and Tiffany Hsiung and Christopher Kang, whose 2017 interactive web project *The Space We Hold* is the most dignified online process for testimony I have yet seen, with appreciation for their careful renaming of the survivors of wartime sexual violence to the "grandmothers."

In 1991, Kim Hak Sun was the first grandmother to come forward in a small class action suit to tell of the rape camps installed by the Japanese imperial state up to and during World War II. A conservative estimate of over 200,000 women and girls as young as nine in Korea, China, the Philippines, Indonesia, and Indochina (now called Cambodia, Laos, Burma, Thailand, and Vietnam) were forced into years of sexual servitude for Japanese officers and recruits stationed across Asia, a program euphemistically called "comfort women" by its officials. The women's suit came forward in Tokyo District Court demanding a legal accounting, reparations for the elderly women survivors, most of whom by then were deceased, and the revision of Japanese schoolbooks to name the sexual enslavement of women in its colonial and occupied territories. Seoul, Manila, Berlin, and San Francisco had convened conferences and erected memorials to the victims since numerous documented accounts and a lawsuit were brought to the United Nations the year following Kim Hak Sun's public testimony in Tokyo.

The military defeat and economic triumph of Japan had followed a century of emulating Western imperialists, only to be spurned by the West in the first half of the 20th century starting with the Russo-Japanese War and later earning geopolitical status as Honorary Whites by the Apartheid regime in South Africa. Evasions and suppressions by Japanese officials regarding the enforced recruitment of women's bodies as military supplies have included the offer of remuneration out of private funds that was summarily rejected by the survivors, and diplomatic terminations with the European and US municipalities that had agreed to memorialize the survivors of the military rape camps. Other evasive tactics included the issuance of equivocal apologies, patriarchal oversight of national history books, and manipulation of media language used to refer to the sexual enslavement program.

The half measures, denial, and delay tactics of the Japanese government relied to a great degree on the silencing power of gendered shame and the sheer passing of time in hopes the testimonies of these women would be buried along with their bodies. Due to the agency-building work of feminist scholars, activists, allies, and artists around the world, particularly those whose ancestors were based in the testifying cultures, the opposite of these official anticipations has occurred. In the internet era, the strategies of feminists with cultural roots in the affected countries have moved beyond academic documentation to expanding the traditional boundaries and potentialities of the mediums and meaning of art and healing.

What then are the ramifications for healing in the west which underlie the largely unknown narratives of the poor and elderly women across Asia who bear the weight of silenced testimonies and others like them? With hegemonies regularized in the home, workplace, and communities, and a media that thrives on besieging the public with fearful brutalities, what are our priorities as practitioners of peace processes that are viable alternatives to the carceral state but whose comparative positionality is as privileged members of the state? What does whole healing mean when we're talking about embodied historical trauma? Have we seen palpable satisfaction, release or liberation occur enabling the capacity for joy and self-actualization to flourish? What are the theories of change by ADR experts when it comes to intercultural engagements where we cannot call home?

THE PROFESSIONALIZATION OF PEACE AND JUSTICE MOVEMENTS

The rapid professionalization of restorative justice as an arm of the peace and justice movements began developing in the United States in the early 1990s with state endorsement in the form of mandated alternatives to its burgeoning carceral system. Largely in the hands of private Christian universities, the majority of RJ trainings are led and populated by the privileged descendants of white settlers, with a practical emphasis on truth-telling in which victim narratives are heard and documented with bodies representing conflicting polarities.

Academic RJ trainings, transitioning in name to "transformative justice" to include structural and systemic analysis, include a broader contextualized model for conflict that remains externalized. Due to increasing co-optations by the carceral state of practices originally based on indigenous community restoration practices preceding European settlement and the subsequent American colonial regime, the academic trainings emphasize logocentric productions which easily adapt to the legal construct of the settler state. The product then reifies rather than works to dismantle the white supremacist heteropatriarchy of settler colonialism, the structures of which are profound causal factors for the violence inherent in the global reach of state-sanctioned peace and justice work. The subsequent danger in reproducing a missionary model of addressing local and regional conflict as the setting for personal salvation is to starve the essence of RJ work, which is in restoring humanity among all members of a community by preserving the requisite dignity in relationship. Like weeds pushing up through cracks in the asphalt, however, such ideals do occur but have a hard time proliferating under the weight of unchallenged structures.

Contemporaries in the United States who inhabit an intersectional psychological space as women of color can begin by considering ritual paradigms indigenous to the testifying communities which include dance, poetry, art, communing with the natural world, and in the case of the *mudang*, hilarity stories for revelation, consciousness-building, and regeneration. Cutting-edge narrative technologies such as Hsiung and Kang's *The Space We Hold*, the truth-telling work of Gibson's *Silence Broken*, and the native symbolism of the bronze memorials erected around the world to honor the victims of wartime sexual violence should probe the assumptions that underlie our talk-as-therapy logocentrism and urge deeper self-reflection and more rigorous critical analyses of our theories of change.

The artistic testimonial documentation, along with multiple indigenous and native sacred paradigms to embody the women's narratives into visual, ritual, and musical forms continue the creation of safe and dignified containers to transpose the shame of trauma narratives that otherwise render the victims extremely vulnerable to social stigma, especially women at the intersections of multiple oppressive systems. It is for this reason that the only women quietly granted reparations by the Japanese government following World War II were European white settlers who had resided in what was then the Dutch Indies to the exclusion of the Indo-Dutch and Indonesian women who had also been extensively sexually exploited by the colonial Dutch army. Much of the first-hand accounts of the Dutch women in the wartime tribunal documents following World War II are sealed until 2025.

Here the captive narratives and dangling threads of herstories from beyond can braid into our frayed ends in a schema surely more mysterious than can be exposited in rational language, for synthesis is a felt sense. Thus one among many possible replacements for the colonial missionary model is the multifaceted indigenous methodology of a shaman, whose role in Corea has sometimes been filled by male eunuchs but mostly by unconventional women called *mudang*. The medium or *mudang* in rural precolonial Corea had long been filled by women assigned shamanic powers due to trauma, and Jinil Yoo and Pál Koudela have documented in Sesŭmmu (2014) how the *mudang* are distinct among shamanic practitioners in their use of only the percussion, ritual recitation and movement to move into a trance state without the use of psychotropic drugs. This point is added to encourage the reader to understand that shamanic rituals are indigenous and thus distinct according to their cultures and geographies, and that shamanism is not to be systematized transculturally.

We offer a comparison chart for ADR models:

Mudang	Missionary
A sister who has experienced trauma and brought into the training among women	A brother who has been institutionally trained
Indigenous, accepted within the cultural origins of the victims	Patriarchal, colonialist, touristic, expert model
A medium, an empty vessel, a channel for expressive catharsis	An interceder, facilitator of forgiveness, understanding or restoration
Ancestors	God
Embodied, restoration/healing is a ritual act; calling upon ancestor spirits before the survivors	Forgiveness
Music, percussion, chant (nonverbal, rhythmic, collective processing, rocking the body)	Prayer, circle process, verbal accountings
Ritual: universal variants of rhythm/percussion, fire/candle, water/oblations, wail/chant	Religious: culturally embedded and not easily grafted onto a foreign culture
Transmutation	Translation
Intersectional	Mythical norm
Heretical: *heresy* of choice	Missionary: theology
Trauma treatment engages the entire organism	Verbal treatment may remain cognitive
Hilarity rituals where humor heals	Humor does not correspond; jokes fail in translation
Shamanic training depends upon the land and the indigenous belief systems/culture which emerge from it	Even shamanism is institutionalized and certified

The *mudang* voices in chant the cries and comforts of our ancestors, symbolic metaphoric speech not unlike poetry but contained to mark the storytelling as a ritual act of embodied healing that crosses the boundaries of present currents and history. As an outgrowth of indigenous culture and thus untranslatable to practitioners raised with a more objectified world view, we must be careful not to reproduce a colonial pattern and turn these rituals into an idealized parapoetics that display "ancestral worship," "animist," or "primitive" proclivities and thus affirm the rational dominance of the Western spectator. Likewise, academic RJ training, accessible to mostly white and honorary white liberals, presume the facilitator as the healing expert in a cultural context and history that is foreign to or already otherized by the facilitator, an ignorance that does not seem to be of central import within facilitator trainings aside from hovering references to power dynamics and colonization. In intercultural practice, externalizing these structural analyses maintains the white-bodied privilege of not having to understand the nuances and ancient histories of "ethnic peoples" whose communities are a part of larger societies struggling with profound gender constraints of heteropatriarchy and the violent disorderings of an imported or internalized racial hegemony. The blood, shame, and silence of our ancestors are unearthed and manifest in trauma bodies in unspeakable ways.

The *mudang* model also brings into focus the invisible people at the frontlines of struggle and vulnerability, such as elderly, low-income, non-English-speaking, impaired, and disabled brown women who yet survived years of separation from family, physical abuse and medical neglect, guilt, shame, and social pariah status—when we do not begin with and center the voices of these women and gather their/our ancestors, we miss a tremendous opportunity for transformation of self, other, society, and land into interactive agents—opening our suppressed imaginations beyond known place to a world where restoration becomes as ordinary as talking around the kitchen table or while walking alongside a stranger.

When we accept a model of restoration of forgiveness of past sins to bring about individual salvation with the same patriarchal colonial model of foreigners who do not dream in our languages nor recognize ordinarily women-led ways, we miss an opportunity for connection and healing not only as women abandoned by patriarchal history, but also across class and national boundaries with collaboratives now requisite on a planetary scale. Those abandoned by history continue to rise, but not in the sense of supremacy or dominance by which we in the West conceive of as power, with geopolitical regimes upheld by avid followers of the materialist and transactional capitalist worldview. But that among those whose personal and political sovereignty continue to be systematically attacked, leadership rises to determine the terms and processes of what healing and restoration mean for them/us.

Practicing critical humility is to acknowledge the profound failures of this colonial model to maintain even a livable relationship with the life forms on which humanity depends, presently in a crisis of extinction. Those who understand what is at stake in our dread of addressing our problems at home, in the avoidance mechanism of looking forever elsewhere, and the maintenance of the soothing familiarity of divisive colonial structures, can take Fanon's counsel to heart to "put off aping this Europe that never stops talking about humanity yet brutalizes [them] at every turn."

Critical humility means that when we recognize how our privileges continue to harm the living world, we move beyond naming and framing to acts of genuine accountability in stepping aside from front center and foreground. In logistical terms this means material restoration and reparations through redistribution of land and wealth, social restoration and reparations in the form of free and relevant education that normalizes somatic practices, prioritizes intimate understanding of one's bioregion, and facilitates the study and sharing of the wisdom and experience of many civilizations on how to coexist joyfully with maximum diversity and minimal harm, and to achieve the above, genuine political and organizational participatory planning that prioritizes those needs determined by the most disenfranchised among the frontline, Indigenous, and People of Color.

The social praxis of critical humility is a conscious moving away from the patronizing expert guidance presumed in the colonial model, and moving toward the genuine sovereignty and dignity of all those historically oppressed and marginalized by the legacy of colonialism, to allow maturity and self-discovery to flourish on their own when patriarchal hindrances and false austerities are removed. The global reach of our communications can enable discernment of our most fundamental political allegiance to earth sovereignty. Thus while affirming the right to make and learn from our own mistakes, this perspective is not akin to a state's rights formulation but most akin to contemporary permaculturist principles for global communities.

For the decent people who aspire to be social healers in training in TJ, RJ, ADR, and mediation, one can consider that when an agent is contracted to work in a culture foreign to one's own, a decolonizing approach is to refuse such privileges by redirecting resources and training to the healers and community organizers already doing this work within it, starting with the women. A host of questions will arise, perhaps some not without existential anxieties, but these are the right ones to start with. When practical necessity calls for engaging directly as a triage facilitator, it is important to prepare oneself internally to be more like an empty vessel, willing and capable of being or creating a container for the transmutation of past harms, not an expert or agent for reconciliation, forgiveness or any other spiritual undertaking. It is helpful to remember how mystification has and still causes myriads to suffer greatly, and that it is no exaggeration to say that life depends upon the sacred mission of this generation to decolonize both internally and externally. It is time to let go of what we have been trained to expect, and re-envision what we may have only tasted but have never seen. Sacredness is not innate in any mythologized body nor encapsulated in performative gestures but a vivid experience of presence and humility when we awaken to our interdependence and connection with the living world.

CHAPTER 17

Vision of Action

....

Path of Vision of a World of Humanity, Cleansed of Hate Speech and Violence

*T**he mouth of a nation shows the soul of its people. That truth is what I heard when I talked with James Ciccone. I was surprised when James agreed to speak with me. He is an attorney and an accomplished author, as well as a businessman with an office on 42nd Street in New York City. When he said he was honored to speak with me, I had to catch my breath.*

—S.Y. Bowland

• •

An End to Myths and Hypocrisy: How Hate Speech Protects White Supremacist Ideology and Kills People of Color

James Ciccone

I'd like to say that I am flattered that you have asked me to comment on the threshold issues you have framed in such a thoughtful way. It's November 18, 2020. And it is the first time in my life that I have been so honored. I'm busy working on two new novels and a short story. I was invited to contribute the short story to an anthology of the top living Western writers, which is quite obviously a huge compliment. My new release, *Stagecoach Justice*, is a story about a black female protagonist in the Montana Territory of the 1800s. Interestingly, black female protagonists have been systematically excluded from the mainstream of Western literature to the point of invisibility, and this slight has

....

been perpetrated by writers who claim to insist upon historical accuracy. This work follows the release of my debut novel last summer, *A Good Day to Die*. And the thrust of these books is to spotlight the historical record as it relates to the cruel and hideous racial situation in the States as it existed during the Old West and to invite readers to accept the challenge of comparing the situation that existed in the 1800s with the situation that exists today.

Furthermore, I'd like to say from the outset that I am not at all interested in appealing to stereotypes or expectations or euphemisms. Instead, I believe the reader may profit from direct statements of fact on the issues of the day. I am all too familiar with the black intellectual's need to first dispel the stereotype that black men or women must be perceived as visceral and emotional to be real. However, I can assure you that I am real. Black men and women can, and often do, relate to the world on a purely intellectual level, a Hegelian dialectical ascent or descent, if you will. If that bothers you, that is your problem, not mine. Whether such a man or woman is visible or invisible is up to the reader. Frankly, I could care less. If you are looking for a man interested in appealing to stereotypes to gain an audience, you have clearly come to the wrong place. Again, I could care less, and the longer I persist, the more direct I have become. I am a 65-year-old mixed-race man, and I have dealt with myths and stereotypes for years, even where, as here, there is pressure to fit into a particular racial category and deny other parts of my heritage as a mixed-race person.

I imagine many thoughtful readers feel the same way since we are all unique individuals when we really bother to examine our lives from cultural, racial, sexual, intellectual, and all other standpoints, right? In other words, there is societal pressure to be one or the other, but never both. For example, there is pressure to believe embracing more than a single racial category triggers a "paradox" or a category of "racial otherness." This is not true. It has never been true. It is fiction. Moreover, there is pressure to fit into all sorts of other categories, so it is convenient to exclude diversity as it relates to race, class, sexual orientation, gender, physical challenge, emotional challenge, and the rest. If you are asking to meet me, that is the person you would meet, a person who has extraordinarily little patience to dismiss the fictitious beliefs, if any, that cloud your mind.

Similarly, the arcs of my stories are influenced by the *sitz im leben* of the characters. Often as writers we are asked to edit history. And as Maya Angelou once profoundly stated, "history cannot be unlived." And if we simply discover and state the facts, we frequently find that the facts have an eloquent way of speaking for themselves. Conversely, when we do the opposite, when we ignore the facts, when we endeavor to edit or revise history, or we sit by passively while others edit or revise history, the doors to hypocrisy, the doors to ethnocentricity, and the doors to the rest of the porous ideologies swing wide open. As writers and intellectuals, even as descendants of ancestors who suffered the cruel and hideous racial situation enabled by porous ideologies, or for that matter, merely as academicians who respect the precepts of intellectual honesty and accept the duty to act in good faith in the service of historical accuracy. If we do not insist on historical accuracy, if we do not challenge distortions to the historical record, how on earth would we expect succeeding generations to draw reasonable inferences?

And so that is the way that I approach these threshold questions. And that is my ambition in this interview today. My ambition is to state clearly the historical record on these crucial questions relating to the cruel and hideous racial situation that exists in the country, and more importantly, the cruel and hideous racial situation that existed during the Western expansion of the 1800s, the period covered by my stories. The reader may connect the linkages concerning how the racial situation remained unchanged while the rest of the sectors of American society evolved rapidly, and the brilliant young people of our future may gaze at the controversy and form their opinions accordingly. Curiously, the sectors of American society relating to transportation, communication, medical care, and technology evolved rapidly from their origins in the 1800s while the question of race manages to remain unchanged. The reader is challenged to debate this issue and to explain why this is the case.

S.Y.: As the dialogue continues, I ask James what the vision is, and I understand it is learning and acting on the situation in life.

JC: Thank you very much for prompting me in that fashion; as you know, I'm not a man who typically needs to be prompted. I would begin my response by talking about the *sitz im leben*, which is German for the situation in life. And I introduce this phrase not to be showy or pedantic, but to emphasize a point. The point is anyone can go to a computer and search that phrase *sitz im leben* and get the answer. We live in the digital era, and cotton is no longer king. The internet is king. We are moving toward a global culture of borderless inclusion and diversity where the old superstitions, myths, stereotypes, state lines, and misconceptions no longer apply. We are evolving. Now, having said that, American society has evolved rapidly in many sectors, while at the same time has remained suspiciously paralyzed in other sectors. In this respect, every book that relates to the American Negro, as James Baldwin used to say, describes a racial situation that has managed, artificially, to stand in exactly the same place across centuries of American history. The point couldn't be more obvious, unless, of course, you are disposed to indulge in revisionist history, isn't that correct?

How did the racial situation remain in exactly the same place after all these years while everything else evolved? And what specifically is the issue? The issue is white supremacist ideology, that porous, diseased ideology, and the tools prescribed to reinforce it, chapter and verse, namely, demonization, marginalization, stereotypes, myths, and hate speech. So, there you have it, a target.

Ban the ideology, and ban the tools prescribed to reinforce the ideology, and you have eradicated the problem in each of its manifestations. Furthermore, it requires only a single line of federal legislation and zero dollars of expenditures. Simply ban hate speech in all of its manifestations as a start. If we don't learn to define inclusion as the promotion of an environment where a diverse population may thrive, we really are not speaking the same language and cannot even measure goals related to change and recovery.

You might ask, well, what's the cure? We all can acknowledge the stacks of books in the library on the issue of white supremacist ideology, the myth of white heterosexual male superiority, *ad nauseam*. There isn't that much written on the cure. Well, the internet itself, and the exchange, the free exchange of information is the cure. The facts themselves are the cure. The historical record accurately stated is the cure. We look at the flawed reasoning the States have employed to protect this ideology. And when I say the flawed reasoning, I talk about the line of Supreme Court cases that have ruled that hate speech is protected by the First Amendment. And those cases, I would call the *Brandenburg v. Ohio* line of cases. Brandenburg was decided in 1969. But there's an entire line of Supreme Court cases that contain the flawed or impoverished reasoning that hate speech intended to denigrate is protected by the First Amendment.

I would argue that hate speech is no more protected by the First Amendment than the Second Amendment protects a person's right to use a gun to commit the crime of murder. One does not have the right to denigrate a citizen; there is no such right.

The secret to understanding the Supreme Court's legacy of wrongly decided cases around the issue of race, whether it is *Dred Scott, Plessy v. Ferguson,* or *Brandenburg,* is the court relies on extra-constitutional authority for these decisions. It considers the ideal of white supremacist ideology paramount to constitutional authority, and it has no problem shamelessly ignoring the dictates of strict construction and the four corners of the Constitution to do so. For those readers who doubt the concept of extra-constitutional authority and analysis, I would ask where precisely do you find the constitutional authority for the president to conduct foreign affairs? The answer is no such authority exists anywhere within the four corners of the Constitution. It is an extra-constitutional grant of power.

Similarly, the court's suspect rulings relating to race are extra-constitutional acknowledgments that white supremacist ideology is paramount to the Constitution. If one were truly interested in eradicating systemic racism, overruling this hypocrisy the court keeps hidden in chambers might be an excellent place to start, don't you agree? Banning hate speech in no way diminishes or dilutes the sweep of First Amendment protections in a free and democratic society. The Second Amendment protects the right to bear arms, but it does not protect the right to commit a crime with those arms. Similarly, the First Amendment protects the freedom of speech, but does not protect the right to use speech to denigrate others. Speech used in this fashion is tantamount to a crime. There are bans on hate speech all across the globe. Why are the States so intent on using tortured reasoning to evade the ban and leave the door open to subject little children to being denigrated by the use of hate speech in our society? Germany doesn't have a problem criminalizing hate speech, given its history. Conversely, the United States does. In the 1960s when the United Nations adopted a covenant banning hate speech, one of the countries that objected to that treaty was the United States. And then only 10 years or so thereafter, the United States reluctantly endorsed the treaty, but with one very important condition. The treaty would only take effect in the United States to the extent that it was not in conflict with Supreme Court decisions. And as we know, the Supreme Court had previously ruled that hate speech was protected by the First Amendment.

And here is another point regarding the importance of language: in 2020, we hear the words diversity and inclusion used loosely. And until we define what those words mean, we cannot set goals in terms of progress or change. Next, we cannot measure our success in moving toward those goals. And see, we create all sorts of loopholes for slippery politicians, whether they are Democrats, Republicans, liberals, independents, conservatives, or others to evade accountability. When it comes to the question of race, what is indisputable, is there is a racial divide in the country, a statistical divide. What is indisputable is there is hypocrisy in the country that has existed for hundreds of years that has been embraced by the Supreme Court. So, when we don't define the terms, and we leave the loopholes open for slippery politicians to slip through, we do a disservice to ourselves. That is why I am focusing this interview on language, language skills, hate speech, where it relates to diversity. These political questions are more urgent than literary questions. What do we mean by diversity if we don't define the term to include racial diversity, diversity of sexual orientation, diversity of gender, diversity, of geographic origin, diversity of religious belief, diversity of thought, and so on? We rob ourselves of a very important coalition if we don't define the term expansively.

The second term that needs to be defined, which our slippery politicians repeatedly leave vague, is the word inclusion. What does inclusion mean? It has to be developed, defined broadly for not just recruiting a diverse population, but also creating an environment that is friendly to the diverse population. If you only define it as recruiting a diverse population, you can see that you really don't have change. All you've done is you've selected some magic negros or magic homosexuals or magic whoever and you place them in the same hostile environment where meaningful change cannot occur.

The Supreme Court has been politicized by both the left and the right. And the forsaken brother is the African American who still languishes and who still suffers from the racial divide. We suffer in terms of income; we suffer in terms of standard housing: we suffer in terms of education. We suffer across the board, and that suffering has been largely ignored.

S.Y.: Something different needs to happen and we need to be change agents: How will you change a rule? How will you change a custom? Or work toward the change you want to be and see?

James: For the country to evolve, it has to do something about the myths and the hypocrisy, not to mention that over 50% of the population has been excluded for how many years now? I mean, it's time for these old men to get out of the way, and let the young people lead, let those brilliant black people lead, let women come forward and lead, and so on. When we see women in leadership capacities, we know we are making progress. But so long as 50% or more of the resources in the country have been excluded, and then when we add the 20% of the people in the country who are of color, we are talking about a set of myths that has managed to exclude us all essentially, aren't we? Well, we're talking about a very sad situation, aren't we?

SYB: Who gets to make those definitions? Who is at the table?

JC: The internet is the clear and imminent threat to prevailing myths and hypocrisy that defend exclusion, isn't it? That thin thread must finally snap, and when it snaps, the whole reservoir of human rights inherent in the dignity of the human condition will finally be respected. We will escape the oppression of the *Brandenburg* line of cases.

SYB: We're talking today while we're all facing the COVID-19 pandemic. We see how racism has impacted who gets sick, who dies. What's your best analysis on how to move forward to address the health questions that are coming up before us at this time?

JC: With any issue relating to health, the first step toward healing is to acknowledge that you have a problem. If you're in denial, and don't see the cure, if you don't seek treatment, you'll never heal. Arguably, the country has grown used to the statistical racial divide that exists in our country. We need to acknowledge that white supremacy is not an ideology, it is a disease, and we need to look at the cure for the disease. Arguably the first step is free of charge. Ban hate speech, criminalize it. That would be the first step forward because that begins to change the entire psychology of the country.

The evolution of the racial situation has been so slow. We've seen a quote-unquote black president, and we have heard very, very intelligent people argue that we were moving into a postracial era, which was not true. Probably we will not see it in our lifetime.

Typically, what happens in movements and protests is there is a festering long-term cause followed by a short-term trigger. Now, if there's a predisposing event, something that triggers outrage and dissent, we may see that evolution in our lifetime. If not, the arc of how this racial issue has evolved over the hundreds of years, and where it continues to exist today, will not change appreciably. When we see George Floyd murdered on videotape in 2020, and we watch passively as the perpetrators investigate and prosecute themselves, instead of having them held accountable by a special prosecutor and independent investigators, the chorus of outrage in 2020 is precisely the same as it was in 1950, in 1850, in 1750, and in 1650. The evolution has been very, very, very slow.

. . . .

Where Can I Say It?

Laurie F. Childers

Where can I say it, that it will make a difference?
that the future, and maybe the present, will be better?
I cannot make the past different.
Where can I say it? And say it often enough
with sincerity and conviction,
with empathy and power,
with respect and influence?
I'm going to say it now.
In this small moment, in this very place.
I am sorry.
I am sorry it all happened.
I am sorry your bountiful land—this land—and ancestral lives were stolen,
by lethal diseases, then with intention
by weapons of deceit, by the force of lies, by murder, by fear.
I am sorry.
I lament the theft of good people from their land.
Freedom robbed, and that of their children.
Families wrenched apart.
I grieve for everyone since for whom the birthright of dignity and belonging
has been an ongoing struggle to maintain
in a place such as this
where we proclaim freedom and the pursuit of happiness
as inalienable rights.
I'm saying it now, and I'll say it again.
I hate what happened.
I loathe what happened in the times of our ancestors.
I loathe the injustices since.
I abhor the injustices happening now, today's cruelties
that come from those same lies,
those same lies that fog our eyes to what is everyday reality for millions
and millions of people.
As if there must be a reason — a reasonable reason —
for enslavement rape beatings lynching redlining

incarceration or even
death for a broken taillight
for selling single cigarettes
for holding a toy
while black

As if anything in the land of the free could justify
genocidal massacres, broken treaties, forced marches, smallpox infected
    blankets, uranium poisoning,
prison or bullets
for standing ones ground
for protecting the water
for loving sacred land
while red

As if my orphaned ancestors crossed an ocean to create the home of the brave
    but today,
we fear newcomers,
we draw the line and raise the wall, and we pull children from parents
for seeking safety from guns we ship south
for seeking asylum from countries we invaded and dictators we armed
for working our farms
for cleaning our homes
while brown.

As if detention camps and internment camps and concentration camps based
    on race or religion
can ever, ever be justified.

So let me say it again.
I am sorry it all happened this way, and sorry the train is still on that track.
I am sorry it took me this long to see through the fog.
I am an unwitting beneficiary of centuries of
genocide, enslavement, cold-blooded murder, and theft, and I would trade
    every advantage
in a heartbeat
to have had our ancestors' encounters been permeated with equality and
    respect.
I call for us to behave justly, NOW. To recognize dignity, NOW.
And, please, let me say this, too, because
even if the underlying lie seems subtle to some, it is
so pervasive.
And it's not just morally wrong.
The justifications given were, and are, scientifically and spiritually incorrect.
They are doubly wrong.

Allow me to say that in my one little life, I have learned
that high intelligence and profound wisdom is found inside black skin and
    brown skin and red skin and
every rainbow shade of skin
as often as it might be found in pink skin
if not more—because others see and know things that we pink people were
    trained to be blind to.
I call upon us to shake up our optimism and cure that blindness.
I wish to proclaim, right now, that the myth of racial superiority
is an evil lie that must be dismantled
as we name it, as we blame it, as we reveal it to be the constant excuse for
invasions, colonialisms, and militarism as solutions
when really, they are the problems.
No matter who enacts them.
And let me also say, out loud, so that my ancestors can hear,
that my heart knows this:
they were wrong to fear the so-called mixing of so-called races.
The beauty of every kind of people shines in the faces of the living today.
There is no genetic racial purity to protect.
Love, respect, and compassion — they need our protection.
Love, respect, and compassion create justice. Create peace.
Let these be the gifts we give all children to carry into the future.
Because what if—what if—our ancestors had met
with mutual respect?
With love and compassion?
What world would we have inherited?
Love, respect, compassion, and justice.
Let *these* be the gifts we give all of earth's children to carry into the future.

SECTION III
FORESIGHT
· ·

INTRODUCTION

Mary Adams Trujillo

In his poem, "I Dream a World," Langston Hughes wrote:

> I dream a world where man
> No other man will scorn,
> Where love will bless the earth
> And peace its paths adorn
> I dream a world where all
> Will know sweet freedom's way,
> Where greed no longer saps the soul
> Nor avarice blights our day.
> A world I dream where black or white,
> Whatever race you be,
> Will share the bounties of the earth
> And every man is free,
> Where wretchedness will hang its head
> And joy, like a pearl,
> Attends the needs of all mankind—
> Of such I dream, my world!

Notice, though, that even as Hughes articulates this new world, his language still reflects binary gender orientation. Perhaps we who practice conflict resolution will find our vision to be similarly constrained by what we cannot imagine. But we, too, must dream. And practice.

As a follower of Jesus, I commit my hopes, my voice, and my actions to advancing the cause of peace *on earth, as it is in heaven.* May these writings serve to inform, inspire, challenge, and move our hands and feet toward a field, indeed a world, where racism no longer has a home.

· ·

In this moment, we conflict practitioners and scholars are "stuck" as we figure out how the field should look in a nonracist future. Despite the best intentions of good people, we replicate old and damaging practices. Even in the repetition of terms like "white supremacy," we reify and validate racist oppression. We find ourselves facing similar challenges and contradictions as we do this work.

- We push toward justice while operating within systems and structures that are racially unjust.
- We want to develop collaborative practices in community, but struggle with upholding individual value systems and points of view.
- We focus on protecting our professional systems, tools, and status, and run the risk of overlooking meaningful opportunities for change.
- We know that trauma lives in bodies, but may fear actively confronting the conditions that produce trauma, particularly racialized trauma.
- We want to support and raise up leadership for people of color, but hope that "we" won't have to step back.
- We recognize the implications of capitalism, yet we are simultaneously dependent on funders and philanthropic organizations.
- We work sincerely and tirelessly on behalf of others, but struggle to practice radical self-care.

In this section, artists, poets, spiritual leaders, intergenerational activists, educators, health workers, incarcerated individuals, and prison survivors grapple with these seeming paradoxes in theory and in practice. Collectively, these writers, representing a spectrum of race, ethnicity, gendered considerations, and ability orientations, get us from "here "to "there" by engaging the following questions:

1. What would stand in the place of patterns and practices of omission as well as overt behavior?
2. What creative methodologies can be practiced beyond the prevailing Eurocentric ones?
3. How would decolonizing restorative practices enable more just and more effective practices?
4. How is capitalism implicated in our practices?

Chapters in this section are arranged to mirror theory and lived experience. We are hopeful that these dialogues will invite you into deeper reflection. We conclude the book with a lexicon of terms used throughout the book and a set of questions for you, the practitioner, to chart your course toward eliminating racism.

CHAPTER 18

In the Beginning

Setting the Context

To eradicate racism, we must look at the whole story. In this chapter Mark Charles and Jonathan Webb look at the legacies of embedded, systemic, and systematic racism from diverse perspectives. Mark Charles is an author, speaker, and activist who was a candidate for the US presidency in 2020. Speaking from the intersections of faith, history, and politics, Charles walks Beth Roy and Mary Adams Trujillo through a way of examining and rectifying historical and present harms. Jonathan Webb then connects the historical dots, tracing the continuing ramifications of racist practices to contemporary public health policies, particularly in maternal and infant care. Both writers show how existing systems can be reimagined and restructured.

—Mary Adams Trujillo

Truth and (re)Conciliation

Mark Charles

Mary: Would you begin by introducing yourself traditionally?

Mark: *Ya'at'eeh. Mark Charles yinish'ye'. Tsin bikee dine' nishlih. Doo to'aheedliini ba' shi'chiin. Tsin bikee dine' da shi chei. Doo' todichini da shi nali'.*

In our Navajo culture, when we introduce ourselves, we always give our four clans. We are a matrilineal people with our identities coming from our mother's mother; my mother's mother is American of Dutch heritage. And that's why I say it's *Tsin bikee dine'*. Loosely translated, that means I'm from the "wooden shoe people." My second clan, my father's mother is *Tó'aheedlíinii*, which is "the waters that flow together." My third clan, my mother's father is also *Tsin bikee dine'*, and then my fourth clan, my father's father is *Tódich'ii'nii* and that's the Bitter Water Clan. It's one of the original clans of our Navajo people.

I introduce myself traditionally, but I also do a land acknowledgment for two purposes. One, it's to help people understand that I am a dual citizen of the United States as well as the Navajo Nation. And two, the land acknowledgment is meant to help people understand that the history of our nation did not begin when Columbus got lost at sea. There's a whole history that predates that, which is just as important and just as legitimate as the history that's after that date.

I also want to acknowledge that I am speaking today from what's now known as Washington, DC. I moved here with my family almost six years ago from the Navajo Nation. But these are the traditional lands of the Piscataway. The Piscataway Nation were living here, hunting here, farming here, fishing here, raising their families here, burying their dead here long before Columbus got lost at sea. And they are still here. I want to thank the Piscataway for being the stewards of these lands. I want to acknowledge them as the host people of these lands. I want to say publicly how humbled I am to be living on these lands today. Thank you.

Beth: Thank you, Mark. In its three sections, this book is about how to re-create a profession, in this case, conflict resolution, with no racism. The first section looks at how we are racist. The second section looks at vision using poetry and creativity, offering to change the mind frame into something dramatically different. The third piece, and this is where you fall, Mark, is about what would we need to do to actually make these visions a reality.

MAT: How did you get started in your work?

MC: I think I would start most directly when I was called to pastor a church in Denver, Colorado called the Christian Indian Center. It was a Native church established more than 30 years ago. I was the first Native pastor they had had in a few decades. In my first council meeting, the elders said that their last pastor had introduced them to the process of contextualizing worship. [Communicating the Christian Gospel within the cultural worldview of the local community] and they wanted me to continue to lead them in that process. I said, "That sounds great, but I have no clue what you're talking about." They said, "Well, there's a group that we've been in touch with called the world Christian Gathering on Indigenous peoples, and we would like to send you and your family to network with these indigenous Christians from all over the world."

I went to the conference and met with many indigenous Christians from all over the world. This is where I first met Richard Twiss and Terry LeBlanc and others like that and saw at a much broader level how most of the globe had been colonized by Western Christianity. There was almost a Renaissance going on of

Native or Indigenous Christians asking the question, how do I be a Christian as well as identify as a Native person?

So, that's really what kind of propelled me into the dialogues, starting out with contextualizing worship, but then quickly going into the discussion of, why can't we do things that affirm our culture, our worldview, or our understanding of the sacred? That then very quickly leads you into the dialogue around colonialism, and ethnocentrism, and white supremacy, and the history of the boarding schools, and then the ethnic cleansing and everything else. That opened the door to all those different dialogues.

But then, after being at the church for two years, and really beginning the process of figuring out what does it mean to be Native, specifically to be Navajo for me, and to be a Christian, my wife and I realized that if we're going to continue to lead in this capacity, in this sort of dialogue, we really need to move back to the reservation. If I'm going to really have a voice of integrity in these dialogues, I need to be back on our reservation among my own people. And so we moved back to the Navajo Nation.

I had grown up in a border town, I didn't speak my language. My grandparents were both boarding school survivors. But because they survived the boarding school, that meant they became Christians, but they did not affirm their own culture. And thus, they didn't pass it on to my father, so he didn't know it to pass it on to me. Living on the Navajo reservation, we began to realize that these injustices, these marginalizations that you hear about in the church, that you see, that you read about in books, we began to realize how very present those injustices were in current daily life on Indian reservations. One of the observations we made very quickly is that by and large, the only group of non-Natives who ever go to Indian reservations are those who come to take your picture, or those who give you charity. And oftentimes, they're the same group of people. No one wants to build a relationship with you. So I'm wrestling with the marginalization that we are literally experiencing on the Rez, I am wrestling with the theological implications of the history of the church and what it's done to our people. Through the process of contextualizing worship, I'm beginning to get exposed to more of the history of what had been happening, just beginning to understand a little bit about the Doctrine of Discovery.

Two things begin happening in me. First, I began feeling insecure. I would not describe myself as an insecure person prior to that, but I began feeling very insecure about who I was and my place in society. Before, I would never assume that I didn't get this opportunity, or I didn't have that, because I'm Native. Living on the reservation, I began to feel very insecure about who I was and my space was in the broader context.

Second, I also began to get very angry. I was talking with a lot of my non-Native friends, mostly over the phone because again, they weren't coming to the reservation. Every time we would try to talk about it, I could feel myself becoming more and more angry, and I would have to bite my tongue or hang up the phone, so I wouldn't yell at them. I learned to temper myself, I would try to talk about it more abstractly and in the third person, so I could stay engaged. That allowed me to talk about it longer, but then my friends would get defensive and soon they would drop out of the dialog. I felt clueless how to engage in conversation about this.

I was writing a letter to some of my friends for what felt like the 10th time, trying to get them to understand how I felt. I said to them in my letter, being Native American, and living on our Navajo Reservation in the middle of this country, it feels like our Native communities are this old grandmother who has a very large and very beautiful house. Years ago, some people came into our house, and they violently locked us upstairs in the bedroom. Today, our house is full of people. They're sitting on our furniture, they're eating our food, they're having a party inside our house. They've since come upstairs, and they've unlocked the door to our bedroom. But it's much later and we're tired, we're old, we're weak, we're sick. So we can't or we don't come out. But the thing that hurts us the most and that causes us the most pain is that virtually nobody from this party ever comes upstairs to see the grandmother in the bedroom. No one sits down on the bed next to her, takes her hand, and simply says thank you. Thank you for letting us be in your house. I wrote that, and I finally felt satisfied that I was expressing how I truly felt. I started sharing that metaphor with people I was living around, other Natives. Some people said to me, "You know, I've lived here all my life. It's always been a struggle to articulate how it feels. You're hitting the nail on the head." I would share that with non-Native people, and instead of getting defensive, they would come back and say, "How do we say thank you?"

At this point, I realized we were now having a very different dialogue. Instead of the very challenging dialogue of victim versus oppressor, now we're talking about what I would say is the heart of the matter, which is a reversal of roles. The United States of America is literally comprised of over 300 million undocumented immigrants, mostly from Europe, who are running around acting like they own the place, and we also have six million indigenous people who have been pushed aside to lands on the margins and are treated like unwanted guests in someone else's house.

A lot of my work is, I'm trying to acknowledge that this is where our nation is. And if we're going to fix the problem, we must reverse these roles. I want this nation of immigrants, most of them undocumented from Europe, to understand that they are guests in someone's house. And I want our Native peoples to understand that in many ways and respects, we are the host people of the land. Now, in the midst of all this, we also need to acknowledge the role of African Americans in this, which is they are neither immigrant nor indigenous. They were kidnapped, stolen from their lands, brought here, enslaved, and forced to build this nation up. So we really have three primary demographics of people who we need to begin to acknowledge were here at the founding of this nation.

And we need to understand what those roles were. How do we begin to sort those things out? I've used that metaphor around the globe to begin to try and initiate dialogue between indigenous peoples and their colonizers.

MAT: I've heard you talk elsewhere about the little-known US apology to Native people in 2009. You suggested that not only were some Congresspeople ignorant of the history, but some were afraid of what would be exposed. Would you share some of these historical points that you think people may not know?

MC: The first sentence of the book I co-authored (*Unsettling Truths*) is: "You cannot discover lands that are already inhabited." You can conquer those lands, you can steal those lands, you can colonize those lands, but you can't discover them. Unless your belief is that the people who live there are not fully human. And so that is one of the spaces where we begin. People say these lands were discovered. They were not discovered, they were ethnically cleansed, and they were stolen. When we look at the history of our country, in the lectures that I give, I show a chart I made of US history from 1776 to 2016. I color-coded it for the years that our nation was at war, and the years we were fighting Native peoples. And if you look, especially at the 19th century, which is the century we call our century of expansion, the century we added 30 new states to the union. Essentially, we completed Manifest Destiny. But if you look at the wars we fought, and the numbers of people that were there at the beginning and at the end, the 19th century was not a century of expansion. It was a century of ethnic cleansing and genocide. We literally we went across the continent—the United States of America did—and ethnically cleansed this continent to make way for white settlement, as well as for the completion of Manifest Destiny.

Look at the legacy and policies of who many consider to be our greatest president, Abraham Lincoln. His legacy says he's the one who abolished slavery and redeemed our nation. This is the legacy that we've created for Abraham Lincoln. But if you look at his writings, if you look at his language, if you look at his policies, if you look at the things he did, he is one of the most blatantly white supremacists and ethnic cleansing presidents in our nation's history. Throughout his entire public career, his speeches are littered with white supremacy, going back to the Lincoln-Douglas debate, where he says things like, "I have no intention of making voters or jurors of Negroes or allowing them to hold office or to intermarry. There's a physical difference between the white and black races, which I believe will forever forbid the two from living on terms of social and political equality. But as long as they must remain together, there should be the distinction of superior and inferior. And I as much as any other man believe that the superior position belongs to the white race." By his own admission, Abraham Lincoln was a blatant white supremacist!

The last part of his legacy is the 13th Amendment, which most people believe abolishes slavery, but it does not. The 13th Amendment reads, "Neither slavery nor involuntary servitude, except as a punishment for crime, whereas the party has been duly convicted, shall exist within the United States of America or any place subject to their jurisdiction." The 13th Amendment doesn't abolish slavery. It redefines and codifies it and protects it constitutionally, under the jurisdiction of the criminal justice system. It is a blatantly white supremacist amendment.

Lincoln's entire political career is based around white supremacy. And if you look at his policies, in 1862 he signed the Pacific Railway Act and the Homestead Act. Within two and a half years of signing those bills, he committed four of the worst ethnic cleansing massacres in our nation's history. The Bear River massacre in Utah, the Sand Creek massacre in Colorado, the hanging of the Dakota 38 and removal of the Dakota and Winnebago from Minnesota, and the long walk of the Navajo and Mescalero Apache from the territory of New Mexico. After signing those two bills, he sent the US military across the country, ethnically cleansing Native peoples from along the proposed routes of the transcontinental railway, making him one of the most genocidal presidents in our nation's history. I would even say worse than Andrew Jackson.

This is the history we don't know. This is the history that no one wants to talk about. This is the challenge: history is written by the victors. Had Nazi Germany won World War II, how would their history books have recorded the legacy of Adolf Hitler? Well, he'd be their greatest leader ever. He'd be their greatest politician ever because he brought them from obscurity and global scorn and shame to prominence and military might. Had Nazi Germany won World War II, how would their history books have recorded the Holocaust? Well, we have Holocaust deniers today, imagine if they won the war? Holocaust? What Holocaust? There was no Holocaust. What they could have done, what we could imagine they would have done with the legacy of Adolf Hitler, is exactly what we did with Abraham Lincoln. We took one of our most white supremacist and genocidal presidents and created this mythological legacy about him that is completely contrary to what he did and what he actually said. Our nation is in complete denial of what we've done.

MAT: As you went through these historical analyses and looked at foundational documents, you came to the conclusion and cited evidence to the fact that the Doctrine of Discovery is significant for the racist foundations of the US. How is this so?

MC: The Doctrine of Discovery, a papal bull established by Pope Nicholas V in the 15th century, essentially allowed European Nations to colonize Africa and enslave the African people and allowed Christopher Columbus to get lost at sea, land in a "New World" inhabited by millions, and claim to have "discovered" it. This doctrine informed him that we, the indigenous peoples, were less than human.

MAT: And from this foundation, that the Constitution of the US is systemically and systematically racist, that the Declaration of Independence is systematically racist, obviously Abraham Lincoln, systematically racist, Supreme Court decisions, particularly as they spoke to Native land cases, systematically racist. Your work is so important because you cite various instances and incidences that support these claims. So what's the answer? How do we get out of this? How do we move from this legacy of systemic and systematic racism?

MC: First of all, Western culture and society are highly individualistic, hyper-individualistic. Yet their racism and white supremacy are systemic. What this does is it allows white people to claim that they're not a part of this, right? So a white person can literally stand up and say, "Well, I don't feel racist, I don't act racist, I don't believe in white supremacy." However, because of the way they've created the system, they can still benefit from racism and white supremacy because the system was set up to do those things for them. If you read our Constitution, which begins with the words "We, the people of the United States . . . ," that sounds inclusive. But if you keep reading down to Article 1, Section 2, it never mentions women, specifically excludes Natives, counts African descendants as three-fifths of a person. In 1787 that literally leaves white men, and technically it was white land-owning men who could vote. So, our Constitution is systemically racist, sexist, and white supremacist because it was written specifically to benefit, center, and protect, not Natives, not women, not African Americans, but white men. And to this day we haven't changed that.

In his final State of the Union, President Obama, appealing to the white land-owning men of this nation, alluded to our unjust foundations when he said "We the people, our Constitution begins with these three simple words, words we've come to recognize mean all the people . . . " Really??? After eight years in the White House, President Obama knows that's not true. He knows "we the people" was not written to include Native and African people. And he knows, beyond the shadow of a doubt, that "we the people" today does not include all the people. President Obama is very, very aware of that. But he perpetuates that myth. President Biden does the same thing. He loves to misquote the Declaration of Independence. He loves to say, "We hold these truths to be self-evident that all men and women are created equal." That sounds beautiful, but that's not what the Declaration of Independence says. It, along with our Constitution, never mentions women. In 2020 Virginia became the 38th state to ratify the ERA. But because the arbitrary deadline Congress set had passed, it did not become the 28th Amendment to our Constitution. And Joe Biden knows this. He is well aware that even in the 21st century, the United States does not treat women as equal in our foundations. Why do you think he makes such a big deal about saying, "We hold these truths to be self-evident that all men and women are created equal"? That sounds beautiful, Mr. President, but that's actually not what the Declaration of Independence says.

Even past the hyper-individualism, you have to look at a much deeper level. We have a two-party system, Democrats and Republicans, but the two parties work in conjunction with each other, in partnership with each other, to maintain the status quo. And if you read our foundations, our status quo is based on racism, sexism, and white supremacy. In 2016 Donald Trump campaigned to "Make America great again." And Hillary Clinton responded by telling her supporters that, "America is great already." Cory Booker in 2016, speaking at the Democratic National Convention, in his speech endorsing Hillary Clinton, acknowledged our Declaration called Natives savages, acknowledged that our Constitution excludes women, and acknowledged the three-fifths compromise. But he ended that section of his speech by telling the audience that these things do not detract from our nation's greatness. Now, he would have never said that in a closed-door meeting with African American people, he would have never said that in a closed-door meeting with women. And he would have never said that in a closed-door meeting with Native peoples. The only reason he said it is because he knew he had political ambitions to run for president, which he did in 2020. He knew that if you want to get to the pinnacle of political leadership in the United States, you have to affirm the bipartisan myth known as American exceptionalism. I like Cory Booker; I think he has a lot of integrity. And I think he really wants to make some changes in our country. But he has tied himself to the Democratic Party. And the Democratic Party is just as white supremacist as the Republicans are. The Republicans are just more explicit, and the Democrats are more implicit. The two-party system would rather blame each other than acknowledge that the problems lie in our foundations.

MAT: This seems like a great place to talk about your candidacy for the president in 2020. What did you want to accomplish?

MC: I believe our nation needs a national dialogue on race, gender, and class, a conversation that I would put on par with the Truth and Reconciliation Commissions in South Africa, in Rwanda, and in Canada. I would, however, not call ours "truth and reconciliation." Reconciliation implies there was a previous harmony, which isn't true. I would call ours "truth and conciliation." And I believe we need to do this sooner rather than later. So that was the center plank of my platform.

I also had a 100-day plan for my presidency had I been elected. That plan was first to remove the racism, the sexism, and the white supremacy from our Constitution. Most Americans will acknowledge the United States struggles with racism, sexism, white supremacy, but they would say that we struggle with those things in spite of our foundations. Most Americans believe our foundations are inclusive, that they were written to include everybody. Even Dr. King said our foundations were a blank check. However, if you truly believe that, and I don't believe Dr. King did believe that—again, he said that to get white land-owning men on board—but if you truly think our foundations are inclusive, I challenge you to get on a Zoom call or to get in a public space or in a diverse space and read our Constitution out loud. You will be shocked at how quickly and how frequently our Constitution is not inclusive but exclusive. You will be shocked at how it is blatantly racist, and sexist, and white supremacist over and over and over and over again. The problem is, the United States of America is not racist and sexist and white supremacist *in spite of* our foundations; we're racist and sexist and white supremacist *because* of our foundations. And nobody wants to address this at that level.

This is how the two systems work. Rather than just blaming the Democrats or the Republicans, I worked very hard to lay out a bipartisan critique. I worked very hard to say so many of the things we struggle with are not due to the party, but due to our foundations. A great example of this was the lynching of George Floyd, which occurred during the 2020 campaign.

I said, why don't we start addressing this problem by ending the protection for white supremacy in our Constitution? Why if we have a problem with our law enforcement, and the criminal justice system, not only killing people of color, but massively incarcerating them and taking away their rights, why don't we address it where that problem lies, which is in our 13th Amendment, which keeps the institution of slavery and white supremacy protected in our Constitution? What if we took the clause out of the 13th Amendment? So that it reads "neither slavery nor involuntary servitude shall exist within the United States" period. No clause keeping slavery legal within our criminal justice system.

I have to go back a little bit to first address why we're so hesitant to change our foundations. Many Americans have an implicit belief that the United States is a Christian nation, and its foundations were established by God. So they could not imagine rewriting our foundations, to many that would almost be akin to rewriting the Scriptures. But that is not true!

There is not a corporation in existence today that's running off bylaws written in the 1700s. Right? They couldn't exist today, they would be sued, they would be taken to court if they tried to apply laws and corporate procedures based on the way things were in the 1700s. Yet, this is what we do with our Constitution. You cannot do that. So much has changed just in the past 250 years. I remind people, frequently, the United States of America is not God's chosen people. We do not have a land covenant with the God of Abraham. And Turtle Island (the North American continent) is not Europe's promised land. There's no such thing as a Christian Empire. And we have foundations that were written by some extremely broken, racist, sexist, and white supremacist men. These are our flawed foundations, and we absolutely have the ability to change them.

When I read the Constitution, word for word, for the first time as an adult, I was appalled at how racist, sexist, and white supremacist it was. I knew about the three-fifths compromise; and I wasn't surprised at the exclusion of Natives. But what I didn't expect was the use and the frequency of gender-specific male pronouns. I saw them so frequently I began to count them. In total there are 51 gender-specific male pronouns in the United States Constitution: who can run for office, who can hold office, even who's protected by the document. There is not a single female pronoun in the entire document. So rather than saying, let's amend this, because an amendment is essentially a footnote, I proposed that instead we edit it. I went through the Constitution using a strikethrough font, and every place I came across a gender-specific male pronoun, I either inserted a general neutral pronoun or a proper noun. And for every racist or white supremacist statement, I used the strikethrough font. The clause in the 13th Amendment, strikethrough font. I wasn't changing balance of powers, I wasn't changing checks and balances. All I was doing was removing the racist, the sexist, and the white supremacist language.

I have that version of the Constitution on my website, and I encourage people to read it because if they read it, they will be surprised at how exclusive and racist and sexist and white supremacist our Constitution is. And, then they would be further surprised to see that that changing those things doesn't actually involve this massive rewriting. It just means editing about 75 to 100 words, taking those out and, and inserting some more appropriate wording to use instead.

MAT: You're saying change the language, which is theoretically a fairly simple fix? What would come next? How else would (re)conciliation work?

MC: The much broader step is this national dialogue on race, gender, and class. One of the challenges we face in our nation's history is that we have always tended to deal with our systemic problems in silos. We dealt with the injustice of slavery in a silo, we dealt with the boarding schools and the breaking of treaties in a silo, we dealt with the mistreatment of women and sexism in our foundations in a silo.

As I began to study the Doctrine of Discovery, I realized how many of these things were interconnected. Yes, they're not as connected where we can see them, but when you look down at the foundation, they're absolutely interconnected. This is where I began to think that we need to find a way to address these issues. I came up with a national dialogue, a Truth and (re)Conciliation Commission to address all these issues. One of the primary purposes of that truth and conciliation commission is to do what I've been referencing for a long time: building a shared history and memory. George Erasmus, a Native Elder from the Dene people in Canada, used this quote "Where common memory is lacking, where people do not share the same path, there can be no real community. Where Community is to be formed, common memory must be created." That idea is so interwoven into the work and vision of what I'm trying to do. We, the United States of America, don't have a common memory. We have a white majority that remembers this mythological legacy of discovery and expansion, opportunity, and exceptionalism. And we have our communities of color, that have the lived experience of stolen lands, broken treaties, enslavement, Jim Crow laws, boarding schools, Indian massacres, segregation, mass incarceration, internment camps, families being ripped apart at our borders. There's no common memory. If we are honest, there's no point in US history, where we can look back and say, during this period we had healthy relationships or healthy community across racial lines; it doesn't exist. We've never had these things.

Part of the purpose of the Truth and Conciliation Commission is to create this common memory, decentering the voices of white land-owning men, and centering the voices of people from the margins. Then, as those stories get out, and as we create that common memory and intentionally give a platform to those voices, then we follow that up with a very direct discussion. We talk about what do we do to make sure the things that have happened in our past never happen again. What changes do we need to make? This is where I think we can learn from what happened in Canada, Rwanda, as well as in South Africa.

You know, it's now been over 25 years since the Truth and Reconciliation Commission in South Africa. They had this great apology, they had this great TRC period, they even wrote a new constitution. But now, 25, almost 30 years later, people are saying, "Nothing's changed." That's because they didn't actually address the underlying economic disparities. They have a similar sentiment in Canada, where they're saying we had this great apology, we had this honest storytelling time. But again, nothing's changing.

Yes, they did deal with boarding schools, but they didn't deal with the Doctrine of Discovery, which was at the root of the boarding schools. They didn't talk about the underlying issues. I'm adamant that when we have a truth and conciliation commission in the US, we must address land titles. Land titles are the sticking point. Because the legal precedent for land titles, as referenced by the Supreme Court as recently as 2005, is the Doctrine of Discovery and the legal understanding that Natives are savages, we must address it. As long as the title to your house, the title to your school, the title to your church, the title to your business is dependent upon a segment of this nation being legally classified as savages, we will never have a nation where we the people means all the people. But we won't get there just because one President says it already happened. Or because another President misquotes our founding documents. No. It's not that individualistic. This is a systemic problem and we need to address at the root. We must address it in our foundations.

MAT: We greatly respect and appreciate the work that you are doing. We are honored to have your voice in this volume.

• •

Birthing a Nation

Jonathan Webb

The United States, one of the richest countries in the world, has the highest maternal mortality rates among developed countries. Maternal mortality rates are significant because they provide concrete examples of the health disparities that exist in our country, and they offer insight into how our nation values the health of families based upon its treatment of mothers, babies, and birthing people. The CDC (2019) reports that Black, American Indian, and Alaska Native (AI/AN) women are two to three times more likely to die from pregnancy-related causes than white women. Further, Indigenous and African American infants are two to three times more likely than white babies to die before one year of age. Most pregnancy-related deaths are preventable, yet racial and ethnic disparities in pregnancy-related deaths have persisted over time. Each one of these maternal or child deaths represents a lost mother, wife, daughter, friend, community member, future leader, world changer, problem solver, or cure finder. We must begin prioritizing this issue because lives are dependent upon our next steps. However, to identify and implement solutions commensurate with the scale of the problem, the root cause must be called out clearly and specifically. In doing so, there has been an evolution of thinking regarding the foundational cause of the problem. Research shows that the social determinants of health (SDOH)—the conditions in the places where people live, learn, work, and play affect a wide range of health, quality of life risks and outcomes. Building upon the SDOH, the life course theory introduces the notion that birth and health outcomes for mother and baby are not simply impacted by their experience prenatally, but they are impacted by experiences throughout their lives as well as by the generational experiences of their mothers. Similarly, life experiences both impact and are impacted by health and birth outcomes. Pulling all this together, research has recognized that the environments in which people live and develop and the life experiences that impact their health and maternal and child health outcomes are influenced by racism.

Thus, to truly address racism we must shift our conversation from eliminating racial and ethnic disparities that focus and blame individuals—to eliminating the systemic, structural, and institutional inequities that produce racial disparities. We must acknowledge that these systems, structures, and institutions were not created to produce equitable outcomes for Black, Indigenous, Latinx, Pacific Islanders, and other People of Color. Research repeatedly shows us that these disparities and the inequities in our systems that produce the disparities are not accidents; they are not just "happening." These disparities are the products of systems created over time that create an advantaged group and a disadvantaged group, in part because communities of color have not had a seat at the table. What is known is that organizations and practitioners can significantly reduce racial disparities and achieve equitable outcomes by partnering with impacted communities and individuals to jointly develop the path forward.

- Call on the wisdom of communities. Women of color–led initiatives and efforts repeatedly demonstrate that when Black, Indigenous, Latinx, Asian, and other women of color set their standards for respectful care and support and create the path toward it, they meet their standards and produce more positive birth outcomes and experiences than often White women served in the same geographic area. We only need to listen, align behind, and invest in them. We have no answer that Native Americans, Latinx, and other thought leaders of color do not already possess.

- Support and promote relevant legislation (influenced by the lived experiences of impacted communities), that can positively impact systems.
- Build collaborative relationships with other [birth] equity thought leaders.
- Co-create an equitable future that shares knowledge and guidance; showing how these communities face consistent barriers to being recognized or seen by public health agencies, health care systems, funders, and policymakers.
- Blend cultural and scientific rigor in program evaluation in ways that promote consideration, respect, inclusivity, and responsiveness to the culture of the community. Organizations or community members may prefer to evaluate efforts using methodology and metrics that differ from the prescribed academic research model. Evidence should be led by lived experience and practice-based results. Scientific rigor without cultural rigor will not bring us closer to achieving justice in health.
- Equip communities and organizations to act by promoting woman-centered, high quality, community-driven, respectful, and equitable care.
- Identify what's working in women's and infant health and scale up effective practices.

In summary, there's no health equity without community co-creation. In the disabilities community, the coined phrase is "nothing about us without us."

CHAPTER 19

Shifting Paradigms

···

I n the pre-COVID days, many of us found those after-session or late-night
conversations at conferences invaluable for sharing knowledge and reflection between colleagues. In the following Zoom conversation, practitioners
S.Y. Bowland, Roberto Chené, John Paul Lederach, Beth Roy, and I mine our experiences to identify conditions that facilitate changes in thinking. More questions than
answers arise. Join in and expand on the conversation. What experiences have shifted
your thinking and practice? Respond directly in the book! (Unless you checked it out
from a library.)

   Following this conversation, read the interview with Grande Lum by Beth Roy and
S.Y. Bowland. Grande is Provost of Menlo College in Atherton, California, a position
that he assumed after training in mediation with Roger Fisher. He headed the Federal Community Relations Service under President Obama and established a mediation clinic at Hastings Law School. Lum shows how he shifted his career from conflict
intervention to higher education, illuminating the ideal qualities of a good leader, as he
developed them in the practice of mediation.

— Mary Adams Trujillo

· ·

Shifting Paradigms

Beth Roy, Roberto Chené, John Paul Lederach, S.Y. Bowland,
and Mary Trujillo

Beth: We're standing in one of those moments when shifting the paradigm of
racism in our society seems possible, because of Black Lives Matter, COVID.
So, I thought we might draw on our own experiences of being in moments of
profound change, both personally and politically, and see what we might learn
about what it takes to bring about a shift in racism now. The PRASI project
has been based on the premise that lived experience holds wisdom for us. This
moment holds knowledge and information that can be translated into political

action. I thought it would be a fun way to get into the conversation to tell our personal stories of moments of change.

I'm thinking of simple moments of language change, that had profound impacts. One of them happened to me in a time of the feminist movement. I was living in India during the period when people stopped using the word "girl" to describe grown-up women and changed "Miss" and "Mrs." to "Ms." When I came back from India, this change of vocabulary had happened, and it was jarring to my ear. It was hard to get used to, actually, but it made an enormous difference in how I experienced myself and my power in the world.

It was something that was relatively so simple, we're going through it now with pronoun changes around gender. I have all of these younger people in my world, who have changed their pronouns from gendered pronouns to "they," which the grammarian in me has a lot of trouble with, but I'm actually finding myself getting used to it. it's altering my sense of categorization, of the binary, of binaries in all kinds of other circumstances, not just around gender, but it causes me to question things that I totally took for granted before. People who identify as trans are militantly insisting on that change. I've certainly mediated more than one group where there has been profound conflict around that kind of resistance.

Roberto: Your comments trigger some thoughts, kind of on the other side of that. I've been thinking that if experientially you're disposed to change, and you have a personal connection with what it's all about, then it's meaningful, Beth, as you've described your experience. On the other side I've often thought that the language piece around political correctness requires some kind of relationship connection [to] understand why the change is coming about. If we're too polarized from each other and there's no dialogue going on—given how societies exclude people—those excluded from the meaning or the thinking or the feeling behind a change in language, all they hear is another somebody telling them what to do. So, they totally miss what the language change is about. And then it becomes fuel for anger. How do you put the interpersonal dialogue connection together with a language change? If you're just somebody out there not connected, you just see it as, who's arbitrarily telling me I have to change my language?!

BR: Yeah, I think we're seeing that a lot around issues of gendered language.

S.Y.: One important paradigm shift for me was, when I was going to Agnes Scott [a predominantly white and female institution of higher education in Georgia]. I said I was going to need childcare because I was bringing [my son] James. They said, "Oh, no problem, we'll have childcare, we'll have childcare. We're Agnes Scott." I guess I never thought anything about that whole childcare dynamic, because I hadn't had to do it. I had benefited from not having to have childcare. I didn't think much about what I wanted in a childcare provider. So when I went to go to the place to hand my son over, a white woman appeared.

[Laughs.] I was like, damn! Am I ready for this? Am I ready to hand over my baby to this person? All this stuff was going on in my head at the same time. She was fairly young and she probably never thought like I thought. I was holding on to him real tight. I don't know what messages she got nonverbally. [Laughs.] I did eventually give James over to her for childcare. But I asked myself 50 questions: What am I scared of? I don't know what happened. But she took him with a smile. And I thought to myself, the anxiety that I had that day [was like] being in the session or being able to facilitate or do whatever. It was one of those moments where I was like, What am I gonna do? I gotta do it in the moment, or I gotta make a decision.

John Paul: One of the times that I get paradigm shifts is when I get a really good, unanswerable question. By unanswerable I mean, my already invented answers no longer fit. So you have to go searching further than you might have. [Chuckles.]

In [this] case, that had to do with the shift in language. That I think most of you know that I've been an advocate of thinking in the direction of transformation instead of resolution. I felt the word resolution, while it has roots that were much broader, maybe, when it was initiated, increasingly over time in the US context, focused far too much on short-term answers to problems, but not really wanting to look at the relational transformational pieces that were combinations of structural issues and the deeper power shifts that were really about what was happening and were often related to identity.

In 1983, I was engaged to develop a leadership program around conflict resolution in Central America, that would include the countries that ran from Panama to Mexico. in that context, we did some pilot workshops to test the ideas. The very first one just made the proposal about the kinds of ideas we were thinking about to get early feedback with this set of about 30 or 40 community leaders, a lot of them, church connected in one form or another. They were locally based, but had networks of activity. At least three of the countries had open civil wars going, so when I said that we were working on a concept of developing a curriculum for and with community leaders that would focus on the kinds of conflicts they faced in conflict resolution capacity, the first question that came back shifted my whole world again. [Chuckles.] Because it came from a friend! I mean, that's one of the things I noticed, when the question doesn't come from somebody you're suspicious of, but comes from somebody you care about—that's the relational part, yes—then you're really shaken, because you can't just get rid of it. The question was really simple: "What do you mean by resolution? Because if what you mean is, you're coming down here to solve a problem without changing anything, we're not interested. We've already had too much of that going on around here."

And then, of course, in the context of his explanation, there was an additional layer that came through the meaning of his statement and his question. Metaphor often has directionality to it. He added the metaphoric language, "If you're coming *down here* to tell us how to solve problems but not change anything, we're not interested." Then suddenly, what was quite apparent was that I had very inadvertently and unintentionally been a part of a colonial project. [Laughs.] So, it's not that I'm now fighting against colonialism, it's that I'm part of it. That little phrase, "If you're solving problems, but not changing anything, we're not interested," the shift from resolution of transformation was a paradigm shift for me.

The elements were language, the context, and the relationship—who it came from—and that it created deep cognitive dissonance. You had to look at yourself and suddenly realize that your behavior was not matching up with your proposed principles and values. So you either choose to get really defensive, or you sort through life and get yourself changed. [Laughs.] I'm still at it.

BR: Yes, you make me think about a moment in a piece of work, Roberto, that you and I did together. I don't know whether you remember the mediation that we did with an organization? You remember, we were off in the country for a weekend?

RC: Oh, yeah. Right. Yeah. The facility and the buffet come to mind. I remember that.

BR: [Laughs.] The conflict centered around one of, the members of their board. The organization had been started by three white Americans doing international work. They did wonderful international work, and they recruited more and more people who were more and more diverse and more and more international. And there was more and more conflict, proving a point, Roberto, you often make. The conflict in this moment centered around a woman who was Chinese born living in the United States, who in a lot of circles would have been diagnosed as having mental health problems of some sort, but she spoke this absolutely crucial truth about the power dynamics. It's often the case, whether people can see it more clearly because they're neurologically different, or because they become neurologically altered because they see it so clearly. Who knows? But she spoke in a way that was so emotional and unintelligible, that nobody was getting her truly important message. Instead, they kept trying to control her, to manage or silence her, and the more they did that the more "out of control" she got.

I had spent a lot of time coaching her about how to say things in a way that could be heard by this largely white, dominant center to the organization. So, we're in the room, and I'm coaching her, right. She's trying hard to shape what she's saying, she's getting there, everyone is intently focused and people are beginning to hear it. And all of a sudden, a younger Chinese American woman burst into tears and ran from the room.

We immediately stopped the mediation and said, "Let's take a break." I don't remember whether you came with me, but I went after her. I asked her, "What happened? What made you so upset?" And she said, "You were doing great work; I could see it was really necessary. It was getting where it needed to go. But," she said, "I've spent my life watching my mother and my grandmother be told to talk differently from the way they would naturally express themselves. And the pain of it, I just couldn't take the pain of it anymore."

So, like you, John Paul, I thought, here we are doing this power-shifting, anti-oppression, work, and we have dominated, we have oppressed this woman! It changed the way I worked from then on. So that was one of those moments of profound shift. How much dynamics of domination intrude.

Mary: I was having a conversation recently with some women who had agreed that we were going to talk about spirituality and religion. It was significant for me because some of the people in the conversation had a different orientation to religion than I do. I also knew that it felt very important for me to be explicit, to come out, as it were. And I did. I included "Jesus" and "God," and said things that I believe but typically might not say so as not to offend or be judged. What was transformative to me was that this could have been a very contentious and judgmental conversation—I could have felt very defensive. But, I felt none of those things. It was my sense that the other people in the conversation also felt the same—we were sharing about personal beliefs. I realized that the reason we could have this conversation was because we all love and respect each other. Even though this was a new ground, we had built, as you were talking about, Roberto, some sense of mutuality and reciprocity that felt like love. [Laughs.]

And that was a paradigm shift for me. Lately, I've just been thinking more about the power of listening and the power of love, which I've said before. But this time I *heard it* and I saw it, and I felt it.

[Silence.]

BR: One of the paradigm shifts I was going to talk about was going to India and meeting people for the first time. I was 20-some-odd-years old, married to a man from India, and I was meeting all kinds of people. I realized at some point that something that I had always experienced when meeting new people wasn't happening. There was an absence reflected in the questions people were asking. They asked, "Who are your people? How far away are they? Where is that? How do they feel about your being so far away? How did *I* feel about being so far away?"

I realized that they were situating me in a context of love, to use that word. And I was prepared instead for judgment, for a competitive response: Who is this person compared to me? Is she superior or inferior, better or worse, better liked or worse, right? Growing up in white America, I had never experienced a new encounter without some aspect of competitiveness. We're saturated in competition. I didn't know that there was a world beyond—well, I knew there was some world beyond it, but I didn't know that that's what the world would be beyond. It told me this is it. This is the thing I'm seeking beyond the world I know. Well, so many people [haven't been able to have that experience and so] don't even know that they are unaware of what they dwell in.

So what do we need that we don't know we need? We need to be connected with a critical mass of people who do live in a connected way, beyond dominance. A critical mass because it's critical mass that translates personal paradigm shift into political, social, institutional paradigm shift.

MAT: And speaking of shifting, I have a question, particularly for Roberto and John Paul. When you go into these places where you are the other, in whatever way you are the other, how is it that people give you credibility to do what it is that you do?

JPL: When I was much younger and just getting initiated, I relied very much on preexisting sources of trust, by way of respect and connection. So if I was in Central America, I was with people who had been there a long time. And I might be a person that's associated with that wider organization or group, that there's at least the benefit of openness. Sometimes when I didn't have that, I could experience very quickly that I didn't have actually any entry. Four and a half decades later, a bit of gray hair. . . . But there are other reasons, in fact, I think the mythology has grown sometimes far [laughs] beyond the capacity of the person. So, this is a kind of an issue in some ways.

Here's an example of the significance of a sense of ally-ship or connection. In the 1980s, one of the major pieces of connection we had was with the mediation work internally in Nicaragua between the Miskito Sumu Rama Indians and the Sandinista government. And by virtue of that, there was quite a rallying point around the indigenous communities that linked up into North. there were significant indigenous people from North America that were very proximate to the indigenous groups that we were working with.

So I get a callback in Virginia after that process is over. I get a call out of the blue that leads me into the Mohawk nation in their standoff in Montreal, where they had dynamited and armed a bridge around a dispute that was emergent. The Mohawk, of course, cross-national borders and several provinces in Canada. They were armed to the teeth, and they had blocked the roadways into Montreal, and it was an absolute crisis. The whole of Canada was watching. The call was to come but not to talk to anybody before I came. Don't make any contact with anybody.

When I got there, there were two things that were quite clear. One was that they didn't want me to talk to anybody because they were under massive pressure to choose a mediator. What they wanted [from us] was a very simple thing. They wanted to have an in-person face-to-face conversation about how the Miskito Indians did this with the Sandinista government. They had heard because some of the Miskito Indians had visited their communities, that there were a few of us that had done some of this [work], and that that might be useful to look at. But what was clear at the bridge that made it possible for your question of legitimacy was very simply that somebody that they trusted, gave a kind of a word about it.

They absolutely did not want mediation. Because all of their experiences with mediation was that it's a new form of white people taking away their voice. But what they wanted to know was, how do you move in ways that mitigate the potential for unleashing of large-scale violence. They were afraid, and with good reason, that they were close to a kind of a mini-genocide, that they would just be run over. The barricades would be taken down, and there'd be a large-scale loss of life.

I've learned over the years is that you don't build a bridge starting in the middle. You don't start by dropping in and holding onto the keystone, the last part of the arch of the bridge. Bridges start on some shore or other. And we're terribly unconscious, unaware of the shores that we start on, and how people perceive us. The ability to be, I think, transparent and honest, there's a quality around that honesty, that doesn't pretend to have answers. And isn't kind of walking around with a briefcase approach that you're going to land on somebody else. That was it for me a lot. A lot of it is about how you're going to choose I think your word listening is exactly the key.

RC: I have a thought about that. But I also wanted to back up just a minute and say that, I was thinking, Mary, as you were speaking, I was connecting what you're saying to what Beth and John Paul had said about their experiences. What I put together listening to you, if there's some kind of trust already established and a conflict arises, because it seemed to me that was the case with both John Paul and Beth, what's key is to jump on the conflict. By jump on it, I mean to face it head-on. The conflict that comes up in the context of some trust might be a key to the paradigm shift. I learned this in a facilitation years ago, every time somebody brought up an issue, the facilitator would say, "Well, we'll get to that later; we'll put it on the agenda." By the time the agenda came, the room had melted down.

So there's something to say about as soon as the conflict comes up, you follow up on it. You go with the person who left the room, or you address it directly. So anyway, I wanted to make that connection about the conflict moment.

I like to say here, to people in New Mexico, that we're already symbols for each other. So, I just happen to be a Hispano male in New Mexico, and for some Indigenous people, I'm a Conquistador. If I go to work in a Pueblo, I need to know who I am to them, I need to know that. And then it's up to me to communicate in such a way that I let them know that I know, and then establish my credibility. In general, people, I think, are accepting until they know they shouldn't be. They see a Conquistador walk into the Pueblo, but they're gonna pay attention to how I look and how I talk and what I communicate. But you have to be self-aware. You have to know that walking into it, you're already likely, possibly, from their viewpoint, part of their problem already. So you have to know that, you can't be naive.

BR: And most of us who are white and American, we smell like the other side. It's a very interesting process, because you may not perceive yourself as that. But it can be very wise to work from the perspective not of what you think you are, but of how you smell in the world.

[Silence.]

MAT: Let's say that you were watching the news and decided, I want to go to Louisville (for protests around the death of Breonna Taylor) because I think I have something to offer. Then what?

SYB: I've been thinking a lot about, here's some black Attorney General who has finally gotten in this position. He's found a way of life, he's found acceptance, but a lot of that acceptance may not be from the black community. And here he is faced with this challenge of his work, his profession, his political party, this time of year. I just wonder where his heart is in all of this. I wonder what his mother's thinking? I wonder if he thinks about what his mother's thinking or his grandmother's thinking? And how does he not—being a real scholar of the law—not give opportunity for peace or build bridges. He finally got accepted, doesn't know what to do.

I guess the new paradigm shift for me is having to figure out how to have space for this young black man 34 years of age, career's starting off in that office, and he's Republican, and all this stuff is going on in the streets. I'm wondering, what is going on in his head? Who is his support? Who does he have around him? These are some of the questions that come to my mind.

I would want to ask him what he needs. Do you have the support that you need? If you had more freedom—there's a difference between liberation and freedom. Does this Black man really have freedom? He has obligations and his commitments to so many different values, groups, people.

Some paradigm shifts come with choice and others come as a matter of survival. But if we live in a society that often attaches a cost, time, and other variables to win a paradigm shift as a matter of survival, life or death, or convenience, what is that dynamic when there is resistance to the shift or choice or opportunity or oppression? How is the heart present? Or the spirit present in the shift? Where is the privilege in this shift? Is there an expense? And if so, to whom and why?

Yes, there are laws that we have to protect people, but what's the individual accountability and responsibility about how we see each other being treated? Because many of us have been doing so much for so long [working for justice] that we're shocked that we're still in this place.

JPL: We codify practice that is often emergent from forms of creativity. The codification that we give it, the way that it becomes a manual or a how to or the training that we provide, it often captures something of what's going on but it's placed in disembodied ways. It becomes disembodied knowledge. And what I was hearing SY say was, when it's about survival, when it's about real-life stuff, if it gets disembodied, it no longer has heart and spirit to it. And what I found in a lot of places was that the heart and spirit is there but it's not necessarily codified in the same way. It's about a way of being with others. So you, Mary, earlier mentioned the word love. And then SY came back, and the questions that she was asking the 34-year-old AG Republican, there would be ways that you could learn the technique of framing that question. What I felt you doing was that you were really re-humanizing a person. You were saying, I wonder what his grandmother thinks. Because then you're placing yourself right into the cultural nuances of a way of being with something that's very painful.

Let me start by saying, what happens when there isn't a paradigm shift? What happens when the old system just repeats itself all the time? I'm thinking about our wider field of whatever we want to call it, conflict transformation, peace, mediation, the various forms that it takes.

I feel like we've been missing a lot in our wider field, that the professionalization, which is important, moves in a direction where the heart and spirit actually doesn't come along with it always. Because it's very possible to learn the technique and the framework and the skill, but it's not easy to carry the deeper part of being human beings with each other. That's where I think we're hurting right now. We're in a lot of hurt right now. I'm not sure that a simple proposal of a process technically handled will come close to this, it's going to have to be at a point of use.

That's why it's going to have to be at a grandmotherly level in some ways.

Because for me, one of the most disheartening pieces of it is that it seems like the question that I always bumped up against that I was very frustrated by, I couldn't get a paradigm shift around, keeps coming back. Which is, we have these great things available. Why don't we have more people of color in our midst? Why aren't there more expressions of it?

MAT: But how do people of color break into mediation and negotiating and arbitrating—being involved in these kinds of disputes in a professional way? John Paul and Roberto, as you have looked back on your careers, how have you involved or integrated people of color into what you do? Where have you partnered? Where have you mentored? What opportunities have you seen? What would you do differently?

JPL: Now, maybe over the years, because I've been distant from it, maybe it has grown in exponential ways, but it's almost like I hear that question, always felt like it was the wrong question. Because the assumption was we have something that exists, we just need to get more people in. And my question went the exact opposite way: if you've seen some of the work, very early on around the notion of an elicited versus prescriptive, is it already exists, go take note of it. It's happening but it may not be in the form that you've put it in your manual, and it may not have been in the way that you would describe it.

It's not easy to shift paradigms that are set up in ways that privilege certain ways of knowing and approaching and understanding. I've benefited from much of that over my years.

We have a black caucus within Humanity United. It's very much about people who have had decades-long commitments within those communities. And so the way that it moves is that I may have a PhD and have experience in this in a lot of locations, but they have a PhD and what it's like to live in that neighborhood and what's happening. We have to find better ways of understanding, recognizing, acknowledging the sources of deep understanding that have to come together in these things. And that's not always been a part of our bigger picture.

What I learned in Central America, and particularly in Mexico, I used to work a lot with this idea that conflict has a lot of synonyms. If you go into a local neighborhood, almost anywhere in the world, and you come in saying, "We want to study your conflict." That question already places you as elite, academic, analytical, whatever it is, but mostly disembodied. Everyday people are going to use a lot of other kind of language. And precisely what was happening, which kind of connects into Louisville, is very much in the direction of who's present and how are they present? And that who and how may not follow the exact forms of what the manual say, but that's actually the well of resource.

BR: I've watched over the years how you all have operated in this world, SY and Mary and Roberto. There's so much talent and so many contributions that, as an example, you three have made, to communities of color as well as to the larger society, through the work that you're doing. If I can speak for white society, we need people of color to be doing this work from the heart, and bringing what you know to our shared society. I think that means challenging professionalism, challenging neutrality, challenging codification, challenging legitimacy through academics, challenging all of the things that construct and restrict how the work is done today, and therefore who does it.

RC: Why would people do that? [Chuckles.] Right now, just use a crude model, the work is in the possession of white professionalistic, legalistic, or therapeutic practitioners. Why would they accept the competition of people coming and offering something that so many people, socialized in the dominant community, don't even know that they need?

SYB: Reverend C. T. Vivian let me come in and observe him. I don't know if I've shared this with you, Roberto, but he would usually have a psychologist with him. And it was usually a white woman, because inevitably, from the people that will come in to get the training, he knew that that's where they were going to need to go. And he thought that they can hear it easier from a white woman than they could hear it from anyplace else. So at the end of this particular session that I was observing, each person had a chance to stand, and they would get personal feedback based upon their interactions throughout the day or the day they were together, both from C. T. Vivian and from the psychologist who would say to them, you should probably go see a psychiatrist or psychologist on this topic.

To address the same question you asked, Mary, I used to ask, how can we really be honest about the entry of black men into the field of conflict resolution mediation, if many had criminal backgrounds? And if you had a criminal background, it immediately excluded you from being a part of the process, especially if you were working with the court system. So the court completely excluded a tenth of the population. We have to come up with other ways to support the entry of young black men, with black male mentors, in a way that is beyond the court and the mediation process. And then, along the way, you've got all of these rules that people have to jump across to get ahead, none of the rules of which that community embraced or helped to create.

RC: This is a somewhat cynical way of summarizing where we are. But I think what we've created here is a picture that the paradigm shift requires a paradigm shift [chuckles] of monumental proportions. So where does that leave us?

I've been thinking or saying for years, observing New Mexico, my personal experience as well as observation, when people of color assimilate to the dominant culture, it's a lose-lose relationship. You can lose your core values, in the worst case you could lose who you are, if you're a person of color. And worse, the reason it's a lose-lose relationship, the dominant culture doesn't gain anything. It sucks up other cultures but stays the way it is. So if you have cultures that still believe in connection and community and relationship and reciprocity and *mutualidad*, the dominant culture desperately needs those values somehow to be incorporated into it as a system. What it does, it eliminates the cultures that possess those values. Then when people from those cultures assimilate into the dominant culture, it sucks you up, but it doesn't get your values. It keeps being what it is. So there's something fundamental there that we need to think about how, how would you in a paradigm shift either at the personal or systemic level, how do you help white people learn respect and reciprocity? I mean, at a deep cultural level, how do you help a culture learn the value of relationship, reciprocity, mutuality, those qualities?

Thinking of Mary's question, I think that in my experience in mediation and conflict resolution since the beginning it's been in an intercultural frame. And understanding, working with people of color, that the way we do it or try to do it is separate. You're in conflict with the dominant culture way of doing it. In our efforts to train people like say in New Mexico to teach white conflict resolvers and mediators to be more inclusive, we've been doing it for years, it hasn't made a difference. [Chuckles.] I don't know the statistics, but I don't want to look at them. [Laughs.] So we end up, I've ended up in relationships like we have now on this Zoom call, working with white allies who, through whatever happened in your life, you made a paradigm shift to bridge and working with people of color, all of us desperately believing that human beings have this capacity. But putting it into practice, or helping that shift is really an uphill battle.

I am thinking of the young, is it district attorney in the Breonna case? Somehow fear plays a big role in all of this. To make a paradigm shift, at some level you have to quit being scared in order to make a choice, as SY says, or out of survival. But somehow, if the fear isn't diminished, either at the personal level, at a systemic level, it's pretty hard to shift or want to shift.

SYB: Well, Roberto, I want to share a couple of things. The first is, when I've gone to school with people like Daniel Cameron, I always ask them to make me a promise. And that is to call me before they jump. I asked the question, always, who are you? How do you be?

Because there comes that point at which they have the paradigm shift or whatever shift they have when they realize they've been a tool. And when you realize that you've been a tool, it really questions again, freedom versus liberation? There's always that question of, what is the internal work that I have to do? Or what do I have to release, to give up, and that's a space where a lot of people don't want to go.

MAT: And how are we, whoever "we" is, how are we agents in that shifting? What's our role individually, collectively?

RC: This conversation is so supportive to me personally, that that's the value in itself. It's made me think and contemplate things that I hadn't thought about. To keep framing this or trying to get at it, what are the conditions in terms of what's going on now in this country, that lend themselves to a paradigm shift? Can we take advantage of the chaos and the growing fascism to intervene? Yeah, we have to, it's about survival. This is survival in the way SY was talking about it earlier. The choice about it is quickly disappearing. But survival demands a paradigm shift.

BR: The sociology of social movements divides, as everything in capitalism does, into a binary: there are social movements that are the product of necessity, where you can't not rebel and make major social change. And there are social movements that happen as a result of opportunity. The Russian Revolution was of necessity. Right now, I think, we're in a moment both of necessity, occasioned by the cognitive dissonance, or moral dissonance, of the cell phone documentation of these terrible, terrible, brutal killings of black people by officials of the state. And there's an opportunity because the economy's in chaos because of COVID-19. Not only are we on the cusp of fascism, but also we have an economy that's sufficiently dismantled, or pretty close, that as we recover from the pandemic, people's relationship to public space is going to be forever altered. We have an opportunity to reconstruct. I'm about to turn 80. In all these years, I haven't seen a moment that is quite as split open as this one is. I think the question really is if that's the larger social configuration, how do we in the small piece of that world we inhabit, a world of conflict intervention, how do we use it in a way, or occupy it in a way, that really makes a difference?

JPL: It's a question that's been I've been working with for a while. The question is how to elder better, because so much of this has a youthful cast? Yes, I'm actually working a lot with the notion that we need to invest in the rising generations because this is such a generational moment.

The second thought is just to your earlier question, at the level of summary. One of the shifts in paradigms that I'm picking up from this conversation is just a reminder that the starting point for the mental model shift, in some ways, should be a starting point of wealth rather than vacuum. There's too much of a vacuum that we have to somehow fill. And we don't start with the notion that actually there's extraordinary wealth in the communities, on the streets, even a wealth that can be tapped for those that rise to AG levels. If we can just find a way to start from that instead of the vacuum that we're trying to fill. I really appreciated this, this was a great conversation.

SY: Beth, can you say how you were defining paradigm shift here?

BR: I don't think we ever defined it. Really, we just used it. I would define it as a shift in the underlying framework of a set of assumptions and practices, ways of being in relationship and in other forms of consciousness.

SY: Because I was thinking, if I went out in my community and asked five people, how will they define paradigm shift, they'd be looking at me like I asked how do you define social justice? Or how do you define mediation? And then once I defined that, they will say, Oh, well, I've been doing that for years.

[Everyone laughs.]

. . . .

One Hundred Years from Now? You May Not Be There

Grande Lum

Beth: Why did you make the leap from a career in mediation to the administration of a small private college in California?

Grande: Working in the Obama administration inspired me to consider higher education leadership. Having done so much mediating and facilitating over my career fostered comfort with the conflicts and problems that one faces when one leads an organization. At Menlo College, I'm in charge of academic affairs and work closely with faculty and staff. There are times where there are faculty who disagree with each other, or maybe disagree with me, and Beth and SY, if I had not gone into mediation, I don't know whether I would have ever wanted to do something like this. I enjoy the problem-solving aspect of mediation, the ability to bring people to consensus, the ability to see the common ground in the situation, and, when you do find it, you can help people move forward. Ultimately what I truly feel at Menlo is that people are in it for the students and that is the common ground. The staff, the administrators, the faculty have very, very different perspectives on what that means, but that common ground becomes a touchstone for the work. And that certainly relates to mediation in many ways.

BR: There is a difference, though, oftentimes in an administrative position, like a provost. Your job is to make a decision, too; it is not always collaborative.

GL: Yeah, it's not always collaborative. But even then, I think there's a way in which mediation skill matters: have I heard them, have I truly heard them? I don't think every decision-maker can display that ability.

Second, it is about relationships—something I think good leaders, no matter whether they have mediation training or not, understand. I built the reputation and an actual record of being trustworthy, of not kicking people behind their backs, or being disingenuous in some way. So I think all those skills that I learned as a mediator, and as a leader in different regards, they pay off hugely, because if people see you as an honest broker, they see the dean, the provost, the president are treating people fairly, and they see you as transparent, that you share what you can (and there's a lot of things you cannot share), that helps. I'm not saying I'm perfect in any of these regards by any stretch of the imagination, but it allows me to function and to enjoy it. In some ways, I'm not sure if I'd never been a mediator that I would have ever wanted even to do this.

BR: They are so lucky to have you! I think you're talking about skills, and you are also talking about values. Are there ways that the values, the worldview that you're talking about, shows up in terms of curriculum, in terms of faculty hiring and development? Where else is it integrated into the institution? And how does that impact diversity?

GL: A little bit of history. We are in our 94th year and for many years have been a four-year college. It's started as an all-male, all-white college. It was started as a junior college and, to a certain extent, as a feeder school for Stanford University. So, who lived in the area, who could afford to go to the school? It had traditionally been all white, and usually from an upper-middle to upper-upper class, and it pretty much remained that way for awhile. I think there were some international students early on, but it's not until 1971 or 1972 when women are allowed in. (Patricia Hearst, by the way, was one of the first.) The credit goes to some of the students; the students pressured the administration to bring in more Black students in the late 1960s. Students were the ones, mostly white, mostly male students, calling for that. And some were admitted, though not in high numbers.

Over time Menlo became one of the most diverse colleges in the nation and that's partly due to the changing demographics of the Bay Area and California as a whole. It also has to do with continued focus on recruiting international students, as well. So, it is a wonderfully diverse place. And we've achieved the status of being a Hispanic Serving Institution (HSI) this year for the first time. Above 25% of our students are Latinx students, right now. We also have the Asian American Native American Pacific Islander Serving Institution (AANAPISI) status as well because we are over 10%. About 20% of our students are white (not counting international students) at this point.

In terms of curriculum development, are we providing the courses that are relevant to today's students when it comes to diversity, equity issues? Menlo is offering minors for the first time, and the very first new one is "Equity and Justice." We saw increased student interest in social justice and moved quickly to help students explore that in and outside the classroom. We had a new race and racism course developed that was team-taught this year, partly in response to George Floyd and what happened last semester. I did my guest lecture on Racism in American Law this week. We want to be responsive to the moment. Usually we wouldn't develop a course that quickly. I truly appreciate Menlo's nimbleness when circumstances call for it. And I'm not just talking about curriculum, I mean that's true at Menlo more broadly.

Our faculty and staff are diverse as well, and we know we must continue to prioritize that value. At Menlo, we continuously seek to expand on our diversity to be a more equitable and inclusive institution. A student and alumni group, Black Student Voices challenged the institution, and we have worked hard to listen, understand and act based on the serious concerns articulated. This included creating a new social justice task force at Menlo and a commitment to hire a senior diversity officer.

One shining example is the women's wrestling team at Menlo, which won our first two national championships in women's wrestling last year, and the majority of the team are people of color, and many are from the Bay Area. They and the coaches exemplify values of hard work, integrity, and joy.

We provide something special for many students, having an average class size of approximately 15 that makes an impact on your ability to know your professor, to play a leadership role, to build strong bonds for a lot of students, and that makes a huge difference. We're very proud of that.

We can, of course, do better, and that's something we constantly need to do on issues of equity and inclusion. We need to continually ask ourselves new questions as we change and adapt. How are we teaching online? Are we recognizing that some students may not have broadband, high-speed internet? Are we recognizing some of them may not have the technology? There are so many ways equity consciousness matters. Are we, even in an accounting or a math or a finance class, looking at issues of race? And sometimes that's hard. People may think racism has nothing to do with accounting, when it does.

BR: It has everything to do with accounting!

GL: Yes, it has everything to do with accounting; how we count things, how we measure things matter when it comes to race. Are we working with our professors on that? I mean, part of equity is about hiring. I've hired two deans in the last year, one in arts and sciences, one in business. In a real sense it's not just in what you do, it is in who you hire, who then impacts the next level of things. Members of the faculty and staff should be conversant on equity. They should ensure the curriculum and teaching reflects issues of diversity. Not just valuing diversity, but actually knowing how to implement, create understanding and foster collegiality. We think about that for hiring, for how we write our job descriptions, in identifying the need to lead people who have different backgrounds, and showing that we are welcoming different perspectives.

BR: You've talked about how your background in mediation has informed or steered you in this direction, Grande. I'm wondering how your personal history has also positioned you to be where you are and do what you do.

GL: My background had everything to do with getting into mediation. I went to school in San Francisco's Chinatown. I went to a Catholic school where most of my classmates—not all—were of Chinese descent. And then I went to Sacred Heart in San Francisco. And it was my first rude awakening to, *Oh, people are calling me chink,* and people are saying "You're a Jap." It was very discombobulating.

Also, I was seeing fights between every different group. I remember in the cafeteria there was a white student and a Black student just going at it—it was pretty deep. I think about it now: the majority of the kids were white, often Irish or Italian. (This wasn't St. Ignatius, which is more the elite academic school. I didn't get into St. Ignatius at the time.) At Sacred Heart, they were often the children of firefighters and police officers, which was even more striking to me. I thought, *Oh, they're supposed to be cops,* and yet the kids were so openly racist to me.

So that definitely started to form a racial consciousness that I certainly did not have in elementary school. And the pain of it was, *Wow, I'm being hated for my race!* Race isn't in your consciousness when you are among people who are like yourself. And then, all of a sudden to be a part of that was jarring to me. I didn't like it!

I ended up transferring to Lowell High School, which is sort of the Stuyvesant High School of New York, which was an academically-based high school. Even at the time, and still today, it was primarily Asian, and mostly Chinese. So it was a much more relaxed atmosphere for me from a racial standpoint, at least. We didn't have racial fights every day. By the way, part of it at Sacred Heart was that it was all male. It was also more working class. Looking back now, I also can see there were all these adolescents, hormones, ego, unformed consciousnesses going on.

One thing I remembered, I remember my history teacher at Lowell took our history class to the Presidio to the Army Museum, and there was an exhibit on the Four Hundred Forty-Second, the Japanese American army regiment that fought in World War II. I had never heard of them. I didn't know anything about it. I remember being teary-eyed when I was there thinking about how young men were fighting for a country in which their parents, siblings, and friends were interned. For me it also stirred this growing understanding in me that no matter how American you were in your heart, Asian Americans continued then and now to be seen as perpetual foreigners by many. It was amazing that even though Japan was the enemy of the US and Japanese Americans were interned, there was this group of people that decided to go fight in World War Two, and many of them died. It's the regiment that suffered the most losses and got the highest number of medals ever for any regiment. That was an astounding thing to me. I remember that.

In high school at Lowell, I started learning more about Thurgood Marshall, learning about law, and learning about civil rights in that way. I think it led to a race consciousness and a civil rights consciousness that started me to think about law school. When I went to law school, it was with the idea of being a civil rights lawyer or a district attorney or something like that. Litigation was all I knew; we had the Perry Mason sort of mindset of what a lawyer might be in those days. But I took a negotiation class from a professor named Roger Fisher, who wrote a well-known book called *Getting to Yes*. I was really surprised! I thought the class was going to be about how to make the other side cry, how to win, and how to beat the other side. But you know, his approach was very much the opposite. It was being collaborative and understanding the other side's interest and building the relationships. I really liked that.

I didn't think too much more about it. I became a teaching fellow for the class in my third year of law school. We had folks in my class, people I was teaching as a law fellow, from the African National Congress in South Africa. And we had folks from the South African government, at that time the all-white South African government. They were preparing for their constitution negotiations at the time. It was just really cool to play some small role. I enjoyed teaching, I felt very comfortable.

And I felt very comfortable being a mediator. I had the opportunity from there to join a company that was started by Roger Fisher and that launched me into the field. I went into mediation and negotiation with the idea that this was an important way for people from different backgrounds to work with each other, not to find harmony or peace, but to work. You know, change needs to be not just in law. I fully believe in that, but we also need changes in our hearts and minds and how we work together. Race and conflict resolution have always, in my mind, been tied together.

SYB: I'm wondering about another aspect of change in Menlo College, and in conflict resolution. First, change needs to be in how we do things, not just in who is there. Second, how can we sustain the experience of institutions as we see the ownership become more multicultural? It's a work in progress that we want to see sustained. We know that money is a key element. But there's a whole element about pride in education, students staying connected, having wonderful memories, and seeing themselves in the images of the leaders. And I think that you have done so much. How do you imagine that Menlo College, for example, will be 100 years from now? You may not be there. How will the institution sustain the changes you've made, especially in the face of derailment attempts? Both in education and in the field—after all, education is the gatekeeper for the field.

GL: These are important questions. I'll speak as directly as I can to the higher-ed piece. There are people from different backgrounds who are taking leadership positions at the institutions. We are seeing a number of people who are Black, Latino, Asian, who are getting leadership positions. We're doing better on faculty, but we can do better across the different disciplines. I do think these voices that bring in a different approach than the traditional paradigm that has existed have come into the universities. I think that is terrific, but how sustainable that is becomes a really tough question.

It's really hard when you don't have the funding to sustain it, so that is going to be a fundamental question. Higher education is facing an existential moment right now. When you read about the forecast for higher ed—who is going to survive these next 20 to 30 years, unless you're an elite institution with an enormous endowment and a hugely recognizable brand? Everybody else, it's going to be rough—there's going be that type of challenge.

Certainly, it's a funding question. I've been reading different new books like Kendi's *How to Be an Antiracist*. One thing I pull from there is it's not just about racism: it's about what's institutionalized. What can we actually do to change things? I'm excited that the culture of higher ed has changed in many positive ways. But sustainability is the hard question.

There are some challenges to diversity in the dispute resolution field right now. Framing yourself as a mediator is suspicious to many people of color. People view it as we need to take a side. I remember in law school, if you were interested in racial justice, you went into civil rights as an advocate. That's where the energy was, and that's where the energy is today.

Even within the field, people are questioning how do we make change? We certainly know the concerns about arbitration, the use of it by companies versus the individual, and how alternative dispute resolution mechanisms often hurt people of color and often benefit the corporate entity. I think those are all things that coalesce in why, historically, there has been less diversity in the field. I think it's great that folks like yourselves are writing about alternative theory. It was important for the Bill Urys, the Roger Fishers to do what they did. But how do we decentralize that voice? To what you're saying, SY, it's not just that we look different, but what are we going to bring that is actually different?

BR: The big critique of so much of that early work, certainly the Ury and Fisher work, is that it lacked a sufficient analysis of power. So we've seen mediation, even divorce mediation, which you would think would be the most effective, actually is not. It becomes an exercise in furthering gender imbalances, lacking an integrated power analysis. I think people of color may not come into the field because that power analysis lacking, but who is going to provide that power analysis if there aren't people of color creating the theory and practice? After all, who knows it better?

GL: I think we could use more of that discussion of power in terms of identity and culture. There has been some of that for sure: the work that you all have done, the criticism of divorce mediation, and much more. It's asking the question, who has the power to make the determination and what happens in those situations? The field needs to do more to show that there's a cogent analysis of power as it relates to identity and culture. I read a lot of Wallace Warfield's work and James Laue's work. They thought a lot about power for sure. But that work needs more light shed upon it.

The ADR field is so hard to get into in the first place. Additionally, the dispute resolution field as a whole is shrinking. You know, the court, ADR programs, are not being supported. They're being eliminated. There's all that going on too, so it's making it harder for everyone.

I have noticed that JAMS, the largest court-based, civil litigation mediation program, is starting to diversify significantly, mostly because there are more lawyers of color. There's a generation where we've had more lawyers who are women, more lawyers who are Black, more lawyers who are Asian, and that has allowed for more mediators to come back. It's been slow. But we are finally getting to a point where there is some critical mass now of mediators who are of color, mostly because there have been more lawyers of color and people who don't want to be litigators anymore, because it can be emotionally draining work, and not consistent with one's soul or personality. That is one positive sign I see.

For dispute resolution to be truly inclusive and equitable, we need more of those voices coming up within the scholarship, as well. What do we consider to be dispute resolution? When we look at the violence interruption work in Chicago and other places where people who have been former gang members are trying to stop it, that to me is dispute resolution work. But generally speaking, most people in the field don't see it as such.

Restorative justice is one place where people of color are preeminent in the field. We are applying it to break the school-to-prison pipeline, using it on criminal justice issues, victim offender issues. I think that work can serve all of society well, but certainly, especially given where it's being applied to Black and brown citizens of this country. That provides hope, that provides me some optimism.

SYB: I want to share that part of the challenge to our desire to provide more insight and information from communities of color is a dilemma that many of us face. On one hand, we feel some sense of alignment, or commitment, or loyalty, to the institutions that have given us the information to succeed in our profession, and on the other hand, we feel loyalty or commitment to the communities from which we come, where we know people would do it in a different way.

At one point in the past, we had a really strong group of mediators of color who had built deep enough relationship that we could speak truthfully with each other. What we were trained to do and what we were actually doing were two different things. Not that it was against what we had learned, but the fact was that what we were doing was not being written down or used in an informative way. Frankly, the information that our trainers were giving us about the different cultures was wrong. They were filling us with stories and narratives that, when we entered the room, were very different from what we were experiencing.

And then we were caught in the double consciousness: What do we do? Do we follow our training, or do we follow our gut? Who's going to see us, who's going to tell that we may have broken a rule? And if we really did break the rule, did we do what was best?

There's so much desire to give the field accurate information about our own cultures, but then where's the place to do that without being called out? So then instead you get, whisper, whisper, whisper: "Don't hire her, she's not going to follow the rules." We want to let those who read this book know that we're not saying the way we were trained doesn't work; we're saying we want it to work better. What we're expressing are somethings that should be known so that we can all function more fully as humans as we work through conflicts which are inevitable.

GL: SY, you made me think of how a lot of us are trained to be mediators: you want to maintain a very monotone sort of approach and be super neutral, right? Sort of de-racing, de-gendering is the approach we're taught as the ideal approach toward mediation. Mediators from different genders, different races and backgrounds have approached the work very differently and done some incredibly unique things.

I think that's right: the work of mediators of color needs to be documented, it needs to be written down, it needs to be explored in the academy, to give it respect. I would say I was really lucky to have a variety of mentors. The mediator who I really learned from the most, because I worked with her most, was an African American woman who really brought herself to the room in ways that were not your typical mediator way. I mean, she brought her righteousness, if she thought something was wrong, she would just say it in the room. She was incredibly powerful in a very different sort of way, often values-based. She spoke very plainly and truthfully, she went right at the elephant in the room, versus sometimes you would see the more traditional approach not getting at the issues so directly or openly. Initially, I found myself not naming the issue directly; that is, instinctually I did not want to go right at the issue and label it and confront it. Over time, I learned a ton from Irma and it really helped me develop my own style.

I'm very glad my book *America's Peacemakers* captures many of the CRS (Community Relations Service, a program of the Department of Justice) mediators who were people of color, and many are women. I want to honor Heidi and Guy Burgess, who interviewed many of the CRS mediators in their oral history project. Their transcripts are on the University of Colorado website. I think it's so important to document, analyze that work, because I do think many people are doing important dispute resolution work in different ways.

CHAPTER 20

Keepers of Tears

....

*I*n a previous dialogue, John Paul Lederach noted that "metaphor often has a directionality to it." In the course of developing this volume, we have observed that the writing process can be a metaphor for conflict resolution practice. Directional similarities include heightened attention to language and dialogic possibilities, creativity in problem-solving, the significance of story, and power of writing to build community. The process of writing and performance are strategies that enlarge our vision and capacity as practitioners to imagine ourselves as compassionate changemakers. While editing this volume, we have watched acts of writing evolve into forms of activist communities.*

Laurie Miller Patterson and Jada Gee are both practitioners, writers, and performers who explore process and possibilities.

—Mary Adams Trujillo

....

Writing as Conflict Resolution Practice

Laurie Miller Patterson

Nineteen eighty-five was a year of many decisions for me. In June, I finished my graduate study in literature and creative writing and decided against pursuing a PhD. I loved my colleagues, writing, many of the faculty, and the place where I lived. A values conflict got in my way: I didn't see art as an altruistic act, and I knew I needed to learn a lot in order to be of real use in the world. What I thought might work with others was what worked with me—sharing stories in whatever form I could. The storytelling work in my graduate study taught me more about how to listen to and craft stories, and it affirmed the reverence I feel for other people's experience, the connection we can build across difference and distance—and the power in that. Conflict resolution felt like a natural direction.

How is writing like conflict resolution?

Writing supports CR in my life.

Writing can offer a pull to stories, not just shaping my own but listening to, respecting, and honoring others' stories. Writing helps us see that it's rare to be in the presence of The Truth, far more likely to be in the presence of *perspectives*—varied and fascinating. Writing can help us understand others' values and experiences, and whether we see connection points or only diverging lines, we understand our fellow beings better. *Writing our own story and reading others' can help us see the humanity in each other—the place where CR can thrive.*

Writing helps us to consider the larger dynamics at work in the universe as we focus in a deeper way. We consider the tiniest grains of the components in life (my grandmother's hook to button her shoes) and the largest elements of influence (where her parents brought her to be born, her father's illness, the mores of her community). In this way, writing stretches our imagination, and imagination is essential to building "fellow feeling," essential to my ability to imagine what something I've not experienced feels like or imagine how something hurtful I do to someone else feels to that person. *Imagination is essential to empathy and to asking for forgiveness.* So . . . *writing can be an avenue to healing and connection with others—empathy that's fundamental to CR.* Our ability to find a metaphor and write about it can help us obliquely access early trauma that is presenting as a barrier to happiness, effectiveness in our jobs, and fulfillment in general. Writing, like CR, increases shared knowledge.

I entered the field of conflict resolution because I am by nature an idealist, a teacher, and an artist. I learned when I was very young to love people through the stories they shared and through the song lyrics I memorized as I listened, devotedly, through the transistor radio I kept under my pillow. Books and theatrical performances taught me about lives I would never know and nurtured my curiosity about perspectives different from mine.

My spiritual beliefs, central to my decisions, focus my attention on doing "for others," so I translated my artistic work into teaching antiracist concepts and tactics. These values, however, compromised my ability to be "neutral" in the classic sense. I saw racism and other forms of oppression as injustices with deadly consequences. I wouldn't have understood being "neutral" when facing them.

As a volunteer community mediator, I learned to listen really well. As I felt the connections between us strengthen, a little of the distance diminished. Returning to that center several years later, I functioned as the trainer in communication and CR skills.

During my work, I learned from my colleagues something much deeper and more important about stories. The way we helped people be heard and understood was to challenge the systemic racism of our city and community. We created places where people felt safe and equal, where our mediators mirrored the language of origin, race, age, and sexual orientation of parties during intake and mediation. Community mediation offered two useful tools: supporting people to identify and tell their own stories. Second, to teach people (especially those who are taught to solve problems) how to listen well to each other.

Eventually, this led me to a position as an ombuds or internal neutral in a large organization.

Organizational ombuds don't set policy or make decisions. To address systemic issues in a hierarchical organization, internal neutrals carry the stories that are sometimes kept in the shadow into the consciousness of the sometimes isolated leaders who really need to hear the stories and experiences of everyone in their organizational community. Isolation is a feature of any position in a large hierarchical organization. Internal neutrals in large organizations, through their thought partnering, training, and coaching act as the conscience of an organization and as an Ethiopian colleague describes the role, "Keeper of the People's Tears."

Did you pursue an MFA or a professional degree in writing?

My school didn't offer an MFA. We received the MA in English literature with a focus in creative writing. (I know, a little weird, but there you are.) I did get turned off pursuing the PhD during that time for lots of reasons. Here are a few: it was an all-white, all-boys club with a few females to decorate the space. Our writing was judged by lots of things other than our writing. I lost patience with that. I didn't have the energy to fight with that system the whole time I was writing. I wanted freedom. I remember thinking as I made my decision to not pursue the PhD, "What good will another book of poetry do in the world?" I wanted to have an impact on people. I found that through teaching and through coordinating tutoring programs. Now I'm picking things up again because I feel pretty free from any system. I'm not in graduate school, not subject to criticism based on anything but the writing. I like writing in this space of my life better than in that space.

How does "professional" CR practice turn off the natural mediator in you?

When I've been happy about my work in conflict resolution, often that was because we were able to influence the structures and environment that had helped to create the conflict in the first place. In large organizations, that kind of influence is rare or impossible. Therefore, all the work to improve things happens interpersonally or intrapersonally. Individuals carry the burden far more than they would if the culture and structures could be called into question. People are labeled "not team players" or "problem children" for challenging the way we do things or for calling out unintended consequences of a policy or practice. Traditional organizations that are so incredibly regulated tend to be afraid of anything new, especially if it empowers or gives further autonomy to those on the lower levels of the hierarchy. The most successful work came only when leaders knew that hierarchy itself distorts communication and buries information they need about the impact of their initiatives. Moving communication around, carrying stories around, is part of the work of a CR practitioner, but the work can only be successful when those with formal power are able and willing to listen, be changed by what they hear, remove barriers that keep a conflict going and learn from the people working at the ground levels. Worse, the structures in place that can create or escalate conflict often can't be questioned; rarely can they be restructured with their effect in mind. The hierarchy necessary in some parts of organizations can result in a concentration of power, a lack of trust among colleagues, and an ease of falling from some leader's grace into *persona non grata* status . . . all these are severe impediments to conflict resolution approaches.

Like in graduate school and in writing, I work best when I feel free to do so. There are limits to conflict resolution in my current work. I'm keeping it all very small. I'm able to listen to people and help them think through how to work in a way that offers encouragement and autonomy to the members of their teams—and how to give themselves a little grace in all this tumult. It's in the one-to-one conversations where I can do what feels useful.

· ·

Performance as Conflict Resolution Practice

Jada Gee

Jada: I've been working at the Dayton Mediation Center for a little over a year. When I attended my first training in January I wanted to hit the ground running, but luckily my supervising team told me to walk it out for a while. Now I live around the west side of Dayton. The community there is somewhat in poverty. I serve the people in the community I come from. I work for the city, and then I just go right back. And I basically serve the people that I live with. So sometimes I'll recognize them, like, oh, I've mediated for you.

This is what it's all about! It's that kind of full-circle feeling. It feels actually really great. It encourages me to know that I know what I'm doing. And I love what I'm doing. I feel really fulfilled.

So far, I've learned that the world is a walking "crisis in human interaction"—that's how we define conflict here at the Dayton Mediation Center. I am beginning to become more conscientious of my status in this society even with more pressing events going on in my life.

This year with its many circumstances, humans are now facing a universal oppressor, COVID. However, a fatal disease doesn't stop us from hurting each other. I have grieved two times over with the loss of my grandfather and the death of Breonna Taylor, and then on top of that, I am expected to be a student, an artist, an intern, and a mediator. I also realize how I may be an anomaly in the mediative world as a young Black woman.

Mary: Is this a career that you would be interested in exploring?

JG: Definitely. Plus, if I'm going to get my own practice as a drama therapist, I'll definitely use the same tools that I'm using now. Being a mediator now gives me (an opportunity) to be an active advocate, or almost, without giving [my] opinion. It allows me to speak for the unspoken. I find that with a lot of juvenile cases—that's what I feel like I specialize in, juvenile and visitation—I find that the juvenile does not speak, but they're speaking through their actions. Usually, when I mediate those cases, I feel like there's a motivation to empower that child or teenager in order for them to fully get out their . . . because they often feel very weak in the inside, so they're not gonna say anything, or they're gonna say very little. Or, they could get emotional. So I feel like I am that voice for them. [They feel that] they can't talk for themselves.

For a juvenile case, we wouldn't want two older mediators. That kind of looks like, "We're looking down on you." So, they'll put me in there and probably for a younger voice to get a point across.

MAT: How have you encountered racism in the mediation community?

JG: I would say that racism is the feeling that you're superior to someone else, and that they're inferior because of their nationality, or ethnic background. And it's that feeling of creating the other. So I haven't had a lot of experiences with [racism in mediation practice]. Maybe on the telephone, because we do auto referrals. I heard a lady say, "Oh, he's just Black and he can do whatever he wants to do." As a mediator that didn't sound good to me, but I have to push my background aside in order for her to be supported. So, I'm like, "Okay, this sounds like this has been a hard time for you now." Sometimes we like to mediator cast, as I like to call it. Oh, let's say we have a Black child, who is mediating with a white male whose store that they stole a candy bar from or something like that. So, we'll have a white male mediator and possibly a Black male just matching the demographics together so there's more comfort.

As an organization, we can pick out and acknowledge all these problems within and across racial boundaries. Right now we're in the midst of brainstorming ideas for encouraging more POC mediators. Sometimes I feel like a little encyclopedia. We (POC) basically took our stance saying that we're not going to educate you guys, you got to educate yourselves a little bit. But we're not going to educate you guys.

MAT: "You guys," meaning?

JG: It's our white counterparts, to be quite frank. We've done enough. It's like you ask a person. "Tell me about your trauma. Now make a class for it. You know, like, teach me what it was like to go through your stuff." I can't fish for you *and* give you a fish. I can't give you anything, you have to learn it for yourself. You have to show me that you are motivated to learn about the struggle. It's been a journey just getting those little problems in order. But we are collaborating and we are starting some big things, just brainstorming. We have a think tank and a do tank. So, it's about executing those ideas. They said, even though you're new, we would still like to have your voice here. I feel like sometimes people might be tired of talking. But it just only takes one conversation that could really, if it's not going to solve the whole problem entirely, it's just going to bring us to the next step, and push us in the right direction. Mediation has been done on larger scales. We can stop wars with mediation. I have to trust, just have to believe that humans have the capability of making the best decisions for themselves.

But, I'm concerned with not only racial boundaries but generational boundaries because there's not a lot of young mediators.

We need to start going into the schools. You start going into high schools and start making junior institutes and groups that bring this model of mediation into the atmosphere. I'm really passionate about that. I feel like that brings a real good feeling of accomplishment for the parties personally, to know that they can work that out and that we were there to support and affirm them.

MAT: What will change the future of the profession? How will we get "there?"

JG: Honestly, I feel like not incorporating theater into mediation would be crazy. It's just hitting all those hypotheticals, getting those possibilities, and seeing them in front of your face to really help you to make healthy choices, think better, and do right. You know, just different things.

I wrote a puppet show for the mediation center, teaching kids about transformative mediation, and how to deal with their conflict in a healthy manner. It's called "Conflict Fix It!" I want to present that to schools.

We already do role plays in mediation. They often say, oh, Shakespeare wrote *Romeo and Juliet*, and they performed in front of an audience. But is there something going on in Shakespeare's life that is projected into that play? It's all about putting that hypothetical into perspective. Theater is about showing all these possibilities and reflecting it to you in real life again. The art is an imitation of life. That's all that we're doing—bringing those hypotheticals in. We do that when we reflect as mediators.

We reflect messages that the parties are sending to us, sometimes word for word, sometimes a little paraphrase. Then in turn, they are the audience, they get empowered by their own message. So it's their message projected onto us onto them, and then it cascades to the other party to better understand them.

In my troupe, Common Good Players, we do a lot of ensemble work, where you work as a group, and then you improv and then you build ideas about what you have.

We had a gun reform rally last year a few months after the Dayton shooting, where nine people were killed in the Oregon district. In order to create a visual, we dressed up in all black and angel wings and we walked stoically to that rally. And we just stood still. Just like bringing everything into perspective, while keeping the audience engaged. It was a very surreal experience.

MAT: What was it that you wanted the audience to take from that?

JG: That we are no longer ourselves. I could have been anyone is basically what I'm saying, in that performance. We called out the names of the nine victims. I called out Lois Oglesby. I actually knew somebody who knew Lois. It meant a whole lot for me to say that. But with the different faces you see in [the audience], it could literally, it could have been you. It could have been different people downtown like I was that night. I wasn't in the Oregon district, but I was around that place. I've gone through it, and it could have been me. It could have been a whole lot of people. And that's what we wanted to say. We also wanted to say these people mattered, their lives mattered. This is what happens when we don't regulate gun laws. And this is what happens when we don't take care of our mental health as well. This is what happened, what are we going to do now?

MAT: As a group, as an ensemble, you educate yourselves about social justice issues, and then you figure out through your individual and collective imaginations, values, and a collaborative process, how to share that with other people. How, if we wanted to think about eliminating racism in the field of conflict practice, how you would take it from the thinking realm to the doing? What would this process look like as a performative piece?

JG: *It starts with just the outlandish idea. Or a metaphor you could put any place you want that snaps the audience into that atmosphere that we're trying to portray.* So, for example, there aren't a lot of POC mediators as it is. If I were to make that a performative thing, and if I were to, develop that. *First, I improv, try to feel it out, brainstorm, putting it into perspective from different lenses . . .*

Just something like black. In a circle of white. A living tableau . . .

I would imagine, whole bunch of people in a semicircle in front of the audience.

"He's just black, and he can do what he wants to do." And then you repeat that, and then you layer it on with different things.

"He's just black, and he can do what he wants to do."

A phone call about xenophobia: *"I was scared for my life, they didn't like my accent."*

"I can't get out of my house," different [words] like that layered on top of each other

And then I would say, how would I feel as a participant when *none of the mediators look like me?*

And *I look like the victim,*

or NOT the victim—I look like the perpetrator!

The mediator is not supposed to be on any side, but just seeing that underrepresentation *could really feel like blame* to someone.

I could take a few transcriptions of a mediation, or take a few experiences, or interview mediators, take those interviews, maybe record them like how we're doing now, take those experiences, and then act them out.

I'm a music person. So sometimes I like to present things through song.

Right now I created a song called narrative and longevity. It's all a cappella music. That's what I specialize in. I sing all the parts, and I beatbox as well.

So I'm just simply saying, "I've been running scared for my life,
I don't know where to hide."

And I just repeat that throughout the song. *"I've been running scared for my life,*
"I don't know where to hide.
"I've been running scared for my life,
"I don't know where to hide."

There's this like, kind of buzzing sound that I do. It's supposed to represent the police in that sense. If you were to close your eyes take all other aspects out, that's what you would hear—*attacks and victims talking all at once,* going into this weird cacophony of sound, *and then it stops.*

You can also like isolate different parts of theater, whether that be lighting, the acting itself or my case, audio. With each of these things, you could really change the whole perspective. It's powerful.

Sometimes characters or situations might be stereotypes, but things that people can identify with. People attach themselves to that character, to stay with them to root for them, or to root for the actor and hope for their problems to be resolved. Sometimes we get the audience involved as performers. Just, you know, like, there are different experiences that we're all having. We can watch the same body of work, and then get all these different interpretations. Theater relies on that mystery. Really, it's just keeping the conversation going. There's no incorrect interpretation. It's just like about having that fire going, you know?

MAT: When you do common ground or social justice theater, though, is there not some interpretation that you want people to take away?

JG: It's storytelling. Because that's what theater is. It's people telling their different stories in different ways. And it's gonna mean different things to different people.

So sometimes there could be like, a correct meaning, like in terms of racism—it's wrong. That's not even an argument. But [some things] might mean different things to different people. For example, as oppression decreases in visibility, it could get a little tricky to argue. Like with racism, I can't, hide my race. But I can conceal my religion, I can conceal my sexuality if I want to. The point is, theater allows a person to identify *themselves.*

There comes a point where a play is no longer a play meant to entertain you, it is meant to teach you something. To take action, you would have to educate yourself, and listen to people.

MAT: Last question. What is it that you think people of my generation needs absolutely to know from you?

JG: Reach out to the kids. there's not just an issue with racism, it's ageism, as well. And the kids are speaking. The kids are yelling for help. And it's, it's, it's like we're facing so many things right now. And we just need to find that one centripetal force that brings us together and addresses these problems head-on.

We've grown desensitized.

It's like this name, that name, this name, and it's happening too often. And we just let it happen. We forget that seeing black people die on social media is not normal. Seeing anyone die on social media is not normal. But we keep on seeing these things, we keep on starting these movements. But this has to be ongoing, we can't stop.

I just want the older generations to know that, yes, I am listening to you. But can you please listen to me? We're really just repeating history, we're going through the same thing. It's just important to listen to each other, and once we like, start doing that, we'll start finding similarities. And then we'll start picking up the pieces of what was lost.

I'm about getting all those misunderstandings out the way. Because often I find that being misunderstood never did anyone any good. So it's about believing each other, really, and believing in each other, to keep on with this movement, or to keep this positive momentum going.

I need that support, just know that I can only have your back as much as you have mine.

How would we do that? By simply just asking us questions, being involved in our lives. So if you want to learn about something, feel free to ask us questions.

My grandfather passed away in May, due to a stroke mixed with COVID complications. So this has been a very weird year for me. Yeah, but one thing I noticed is that he always made it to an event, no matter what the circumstance, no matter what the celebration, and I admired him for that, just for simply showing up.

It's about showing up and being present in that moment.

And then I just love that outreach.

I'm just like, simply giving a hand. I can pull you up, I can take care of you when you're feeling low. Just that feeling of mutuality, you know, and being respectful. And when you show that, I feel supported by my village. Like I have my own "village" of older women that I look up to that I admire. When the village supports me, I feel like I can support them through my resources, through my knowledge and really realize that our problems are not as different as they seem. So that's, that's what I'm kind of thinking about, like, I just need that reassurance that, "Hey, you're doing the right thing. And I'm listening to you, and I support you.

CHAPTER 21

"We need to elder better"

· ·

B y 2050, there will be more older adults than children in the United States, with an increase in life expectancy. Imagine that roles and values will have changed such that elders no longer are isolated in nursing homes. In her poem "Could We Please Give the Police to the Grandmothers" (junauda@ junauda.com), Afro-futurist poet and artist, Junauda Petrus Nash reimagines grandmothers as keepers of the law, based on love and care for all the hurt and wounded. Her world integrates music, art, beauty, as active and valued members of communities. The hoped-for outcome of this intergenerational collaboration would be that "courageous healers and wild dreamers and indefatigable warriors of sweetness and change . . . puts an end to systems" and structures of oppression.

Jada Gee, in the previous chapter, has imagined a world where older and younger people can exchange knowledge and strategies for making social change. In the context of the horrific, racist murders of Asian women in Atlanta, Elder Tomi Nagai-Rothe reflects on insights and experiences gained through her lifetime of activism.

—Mary Adams Trujillo

· ·

Digging Out After Atlanta

Tomi Nagai-Rothe

In the days following the March 16, 2021, shootings in the Metro Atlanta area, I received texts and emails from several friends asking how I was doing and how I was feeling. As an Asian American elder, their support was a balm for a very painful week. Our family friends left a handwritten note of support on the front porch. One friend brought home-cooked food, and another brought a bouquet of flowers from her garden. They were wonderful acts of love. I spent time talking with Asian American and Pacific Islander (AAPI) friends and family about what they were experiencing and trying to comfort them. Toward the end of the week, I noticed that most all the expressions of support came from my

· ·

newer People of Color (POC) and white friends. From my oldest white friends: almost nothing. It made me wonder what prevented them from understanding what I was feeling. Perhaps it is a lack of information about my personal and family history, or an assumption that my experience is not so different from theirs. Or perhaps it's because I have grown and will no longer settle for the damaging model minority narrative, and as a result my expectations of my friends have changed. I hope they will learn and grow in their understanding of (and outrage at) anti-AAPI racism. *Stop AAPI Hate* noted 3,795 hate incidents aimed at AAPI people between March 19, 2020, and February 28, 2021. The AAPI community is invisible to the dominant US white supremacist culture and our issues are rarely covered in the media. We are not supposed to be seen or take up space. Have you ever had those assumptions about your AAPI friends or colleagues? Is it annoying if they ask for something you hadn't anticipated? Do you think of them differently if they behave this way?

It has been a year of increasing violence toward AAPI people and, as a result, fear of being attacked. Yet, many non-AAPI people are unaware of this. Every day includes a new report of AAPI people being harassed and assaulted.

I was chatting with a woman at the dog park soon after the shootings when she asked about the stick I was carrying. "My walking stick," I said, then added to take advantage of the educational moment—"I'm carrying it in case I need to defend myself."

Woman: But here, really?

Tomi Nagai-Rothe: Elderly Asian people are being attacked every day. A woman was beaten and robbed in Daly City yesterday.

Woman: [Incredulously.] But was it in the daytime?

Tomi Nagai-Rothe: Yes, in broad daylight.

I suppose the idea that only people walking at night are subject to attack is somehow psychologically protective, but it's illogical to think that an elderly person would make a point of walking alone at night. And "that kind of violence can't happen here" is easier to assume than "the person in front of me could easily become the victim of violence."

My family, friends, and I have been revisited by painful racist experiences on an unending loop this past month. A waking nightmare. Violence and hate have a snowball effect as they retraumatize people who have experienced it. Reading news about the treatment of Mario Gonzalez, who was a *survivor* of one of the March 16, 2021, Atlanta shootings, compounds the pain. Mr. Gonzalez survived the shooting and was handcuffed in a squad car for four hours. He was not notified that his wife, Delaina Yaun, had died—for hours. I suspect that Mr. Gonzalez was treated this way because he is Mexican, and not White. Not only was he traumatized by the violent situation and subsequently, the murder of his wife, but he was also further traumatized by being kept in handcuffs for hours, for no discernible reason other than the fact that he is Mexican.

Over the past month, I have been thrown back to traumatic memories of growing up in an all-white Midwestern town. Walking to and from school young boys would regularly pelt me with racist catcalls: "Ching Chong Chinaman!" "Where are *you* from?" "Why don't you go back where you came from?" This last question made me perplexed and angry: I was in the town where I'd lived since age two. Even when I was older, perfect strangers would ask me, "Where are you from?" And when I told them where I lived, they would reply "But where are you *really* from?" Until I moved away from the Midwest, it seemed like someone was always reminding me that I was a perpetual foreigner— despite being a native, complete with a Midwestern accent

So, *my* question is, *What is the threshold at which this crisis of racist violence becomes both urgent and important enough to take action?* Does it need to impact 300 million people? Does it need to directly impact your child? Does your spouse need to be attacked or killed to make it urgent and important? Do *you* need to be attacked on the street or in your home? I don't mean simply violence against AAPI people. I mean violence against all POC. This is not a rhetorical question. This is a real question aimed at saving lives. When does inaction stop and outrage and engagement begin? For people of faith, the bar is higher because every major wisdom tradition centers on the Golden Rule: Treat others as you would have others treat you.

But racism doesn't exist because of mean people. It exists because "race," as a designation, was created to systematically shut out and push down POC and build wealth for European-American people. The social construct of "race" carved us up so that some could be pushed down and others (white folx) could be lifted up. Remember that there is *no significant biological difference between human beings.*

I hope that what I have written is profoundly disturbing—especially if you have been upset by recent acts of racial violence. All the news of the past month and the past year—being killed for being Black, Latino, Asian, or Indigenous— has been going on for centuries and is, in fact, *the norm* in this country. It is what this country was founded upon and what continues to fuel our economy.

You should not be surprised at all because our economic, military, workforce, policing and incarceration, and land "ownership" systems are all working *precisely* as designed: to extract as much money and control as possible from communities of color and the natural environment at whatever cost. This includes making food, medicine, and clean water difficult or impossible to access—and outright killing people. The panorama of visible and invisible violence in this country hurts me, hurts my family, and hurts millions upon millions of people who are survivors of racist violence spawned by the society that we live and breathe.

My capacity to work on projects is diminished and I need to rest more. Yet with the energy I have I am still organizing because as a person of faith, a mother, and a grandmother, I feel called to justice. The Dalai Lama was asked, "How do you find time for meditation in your busy schedule?" And he replied that meditation is the most important activity each day, and everything else must revolve around it. Unless you are incarcerated or completely incapacitated, you have control over your schedule and your priorities.

If you feel led to do something, consider these actions:

1. *If you have 5 minutes*—Reflect on which parts of this text triggered emotional reactions in you. Then answer the question, what is the threshold at which this crisis becomes both urgent and important enough for me to do something?
2. *If you have 10 minutes*—Text or email your AAPI friends and colleagues and ask how they are doing. Offer to talk (though they may not want to talk right now). Tell them you are thinking about them and send your love and support. Let them know they can reach out to you.
3. *If you have 15 minutes*—Read the latest Stop AAPI Hate Report on hate incidents aimed at AAPI folx in the United States.
4. *If you have 30 minutes*—Watch Professor Viet Than Nguyen's interview (25 minutes) on the Roots of Anti-Asian Hate from US Colonialism to Anti-China Asian Rhetoric.
5. *If you have one hour*—Attend the Asian Americans Advancing Justice Bystander Training.
6. *If you have more time and interest*, find readings and actions to take and organizations to support.

Tips on things to avoid:

1. Avoid equating your experience, if you are white, with what POC are experiencing. White folx certainly experience pain and trauma, but it is not what I am talking about here, nor is it the same.
2. Spend less time talking (or writing) and more time *listening* to friends and colleagues of color. Equity means centering voices of color: giving them more air time because they often don't get enough.
3. If you are white, avoid going to POC to process emotional reactions to anything I've written or something you have read or heard recently. (Note: sometimes the emotional response may take the form of a logical argument. Rather than writing an argument, just sit with your feelings.)

We should all be on a deep and truthful learning journey to turn away from the environment we inhabit that normalizes racism, and particularly, anti-Blackness. I am on my journey to root out any vestiges of anti-Blackness in my heart, to decolonize my body-mind-spirit, and to learn from others who carry an even heavier burden than me. I am open to hearing from anyone on this journey who has already overcome their defensiveness and fragile feelings and is interested in heartfelt dialogue. I hope that even if you have not experienced racist violence yourself, you will be moved to action.

CHAPTER 22

Transformative Pedagogies

. . . .

C ollege and university courses represent a significant entry point into the field of conflict resolution for many practitioners. Thus, teachers are ideally positioned to help students confront and eradicate racism as students prepare for careers. A transformative pedagogy offers responsibility and the opportunity to examine, confront, and interrupt unjust patterns and practices. By stepping away from Eurocentric methodologies, teachers can enable different attitudes about power. Barbara L. Jones and Mary Adams Trujillo share observations as teacher activists and suggest models for transformative teaching. Following that, Hasshan Batts introduces work from Michelle Clifton Soderstrom, Jamal Bakr, and Henry Cervantes that provides an example of transformative teaching and restorative practices in the most oppressive of environments—a maximum-security prison.

—Mary Adams Trujillo

. . . .

"We teach to change the world."

Barbara L. Jones and Mary Adams Trujillo

In her seminal work on transformative pedagogy, *Teaching to Transgress*, bell hooks describes the teachers in her elementary school:

> Almost all our teachers at Booker T. Washington were black women. They were committed to nurturing intellect so that we could become scholars, thinkers, and cultural workers—black folks who used our "minds." We learned early that our devotion to learning, to a life of the mind, was a counter-hegemonic act, a fundamental way to resist every strategy of white racist colonization. Though they did not define or articulate these practices in theoretical terms, my teachers were enacting a revolutionary pedagogy of resistance that was profoundly anticolonial. . . . Teachers worked with us and for us to ensure that we

would fulfill our intellectual destiny and by doing so, uplift the race. Our teachers were on a mission. (hooks, 1994, p. 2)

Our lived experience as black women both makes us want to and requires us to change the world. Our education and training in communication have taught us how to recognize socially learned injustice and power imbalances in interactions and relationships. The task of unlearning the -isms, including our own, has been part of our process for becoming transformative teachers. Transformative pedagogy is thus an intentional way of teaching about previously unrevealed, undetected, or inaccessible social conditions to change communities and institutions into just and equitable places for all citizens.

Our goal is to help future conflict practitioners learn to navigate the intersections of culture and power effectively. We too, have felt ourselves "on a mission."

Both of us have taught at predominately white institutions and our students have been predominately white. While there are specific strategies and concerns for teaching students of color in these institutions, we will use the word "student" to refer to students in general.

Barbara: I teach a special topics class at Wayne State University in the Peace and Conflict Studies program under the College of Liberal Arts and Sciences called "Social Justice Activism." I've taught this class since 2013 and have had the incredible opportunity to develop my course, write my curriculum, revise add, delete, edit my instruction in this class. I love the flexibility in my growth and development as it relates to social justice and social justice activism. I love this class.

I have adopted many approaches over time to student development and engagement in nuanced ways that are nurturing, holistic, and I hope, transformational. When students who don't understand and are overwhelmed with complex and complicated terms, key concepts and theories of collective action, collective identities, collective behaviors, I break down the theories by showing videos, documentaries, journal articles, textbooks, books and recommendations, and suggestions so they can see the theories, key concepts, and terms play out in examples of injustice, as well as social justice and activism. My core strategies are centered on conflict theories, key concepts, and critical analysis. I explore conflict and the struggles that precede it, with solutions based on reflective critical thinking and practical approaches to creative and collaborative problem-solving that transcends beyond my cultural norms.

I am also a restorative justice practitioner and the mother of a murdered son, so I have a unique understanding of the restorative justice process. The process allows the offender to take accountability for their actions, to offer amends to the victim (something not often seen in our traditional punitive, retributive criminal justice model for violent crimes), repair harm to the extent possible for justice to occur and to prevent future harm.

My teaching incorporates restorative justice practices with a goal of dialogue and healing not to patch up, cover-up, or conceal, but to acknowledge changed circumstances—your new life—with courage. My thought is that we cannot heal what we are not willing to confront. I see restorative justice as a way of focusing on the rules of relationship-respect and honoring dignity, repair and reconciliation, accountability, justice, healing, and peacemaking.

I try to teach students by example, experience, and curriculum that to transform the world, they must be willing to insert values that serve humanity into their morality. Moving from crisis to hope must be rooted in love, coming from an absolute place of common good, genuine support, forgiveness, compassion, and empathy.

I believe that effective and efficient teaching is comprised of two key fundamentals: grasping and reflecting on content and analyzing and articulating frameworks for justice. It is imperative that students leave my classroom with the ability to grasp and reflect on the content delivered, as well as be able to analyze and articulate what they have learned.

Mary: I come from a line of teachers. My grandmother, who was born less than a decade after slavery ended, was a teacher in rural Alabama. My mother also taught the descendants of enslaved people in the one-room schools of Alabama in the 1930s and early 1940s. I "fell" into teaching incarcerated men and women in the 1970s and 1980s. I "fell" into teaching Women Studies at the University of New Mexico. Although the "life of the mind" was heaven for me, it was in only in my final year of graduate school in the 1990s that I seriously considered academia as a career. Later I "fell" into an adjunct position at a nearby university, which led to teaching mediation, which led to developing and co-directing a conflict transformation program in Chicago. As these events were occurring, I did not and would not know until years later that I had stepped into my calling. My particular pedagogy integrates lived experience and grounded theory, each holding the other in tension. Theory can be knowledge for its own sake, while practice applies knowledge to real-life situations. Based upon critical analyses of systems and structures of power, a contemporary and future-based reflection ultimately seeks to transform social inequity through strategies and methodologies. As an outcome, praxis-based reflexivity produces a commitment to actions grounded in morality and justice, and corresponding transformative processes and practices. In this sense, knowledge and praxis, two halves of a whole, simultaneously balance and transform each other.

I noticed early on that there were very few black or brown students who signed up for the peace and conflict studies courses. My personal goal was to recruit and invite these students to take the courses. My two most successful courses were Conflict and Community and Mediation. For the mediation course, I invited guest actors to serve as disputants. Some of the disputes were explicitly racial, while some mediations just involved black or brown characters. The important thing was to normalize race, as well as examine racial attitudes in conflict resolution practice. This was important for both students of color and white students. Through intense debriefing with intentional analysis of "neutrality," students learned to distinguish between personal and systemic racism; between interpersonal disputes and systemic oppression.

The core of my approach is deep listening. Formally, I have named it Transformative Mediated Dialogue (TMD). Informally, I refer to the process as Truly, Madly, Deeply. Beginning with dyads, I teach students how to listen with their all their senses, their hearts, and their spirits. I teach them how to hear what is not said as well as what is spoken. I teach them how to read contexts, "vibes," and circumstances. Essentially, I teach students how to be fully present, bringing their whole human selves. To say this process is exciting and liberating is an understatement. Over time, we also develop and apply this knowledge and awareness at group and systemic levels.

We are both deeply invested in teaching to transform, and to transgress if we must. Our joint experience suggests that transformative teaching is grounded in and incorporates the following six components. Each of these components can be creatively adapted for face-to-face, online, and hybrid classes.

Belonging, Advocacy, and Activism in the Local Community

Teaching social justice cannot occur in a vacuum, so we suggest examining issues of justice and equity in the college or university itself, and advocating for change when possible. Some examples of institutional (in)justice issues may include use of teaching assistants, tuition increases, people of color representation in faculty, staff, governance, and curriculum, hierarchies of faculty members, staff, and service workers, promoting, funding opportunities, and resources for faculty and staff to develop professionally and personally, making the tenure system transparent, equitable admissions policies, equitable and representative hiring and promotion practices, relationships with and attitudes toward the surrounding communities, disproportionate consumption of local resources, including land usage and nonprofit tax status, provision of services to the surrounding communities, overall commitment to fiscal, environmental, and social justice. As we encourage students to investigate and get involved in the larger actions of the institution, we support them with our words and our presence in their concerns.

The Use of Socially Just Teaching practices, as Well as Effective Social Justice and Peace Pedagogy

Our core assumptions of teaching as transformative praxis include:

- Encouragement and promotion of not just "safe" but *Brave Spaces* that permit respectful, rigorous debate to both nurture connection and foster critical thinking. An authentic skillful educator is also a skillful learner.

- Recognition that learning neither begins nor ends in the classroom. Student engagement in meaningful community activities, designed in collaboration with community partners for mutual learning and benefit. (For example, an annual community conference designed and implemented by students, mediation clinics for younger students.) Learning that is contextual or experiential is most easily absorbed.
- Praxis, interactive critical engagement that incorporates real-world practical experiences, and interconnectedness must be carefully and creatively designed for specific outcomes. Experiential learning (praxis) requires both individual and community commitment.
- Encouragement and support for students to take ownership of their education in ways that will enhance, enrich, and cultivate their academic imagination and character. Teachers have a responsibility to mentor students consistently.
- Engage students in a variety of interpretive, ideological, and theoretical learning frameworks to encompass a long-range vision for cultivating their abilities.
- The community of learners is formed and sustained by mutuality and reciprocity (Chené), and there must be fun or play involved in the learning.

Our strategies and methodologies to accomplish each of these goals emphasized building relational communities within and through social activism. While we both have our own political viewpoints, we are more interested in getting students talking to and engaging deeply and authentically with each other in environments. We develop ground rules, or agreements in the first class to encourage curiosity rather than judgment; constructive disagreement rather than domination. Again, we are conscious, but not fearful of racial, class, gender differences and thus we structure opportunities to engage difference in ways that bring growth.

Black and brown students, in particular, who want to go into the field professionally see few role models who look like them. We expand the definition of conflict practitioner by bringing in examples of community figures who resolve disputes without titles. We talk about and implement concepts of *ubuntu* and other practices from communities of color. We acknowledge the indigenous origins of restorative justice circles, for example. On a practical level, we collaborate with the student career center to coordinate and arrange internships and practicum experiences to elevate students' career goals. This coordination also keeps students of color from falling through the cracks.

Assist in Integrating Social Justice Principles Across the Curriculum

As proponents of a socially just world, we often have to help our colleagues in other departments see the applicability of peace and justice work.

We must often be the voices who emphasize how peace and justice work helps to resolve conflicts in our community and world. Certainly, in today's world, all students, regardless of discipline or field, need curricula and pedagogy to explore the theories and practices of peace and justice. Virtually any course or discipline can integrate conflict analysis and resolution, conflict prevention, effective listening, understanding trauma, respect for diverse viewpoints, cultural competencies, and seeing the ways that racism and injustice affect everyone into their curriculum.

General education courses are often the first set of courses that students take and are therefore the ideal place to introduce the study of peace, social justice, and conflict practices. Even as a community member, consider creating or offering to co-teach a course that interrogates racism or social justice.

Teaching Methods and Strategies

We suggest building an inclusive pedagogy that uses multiple platforms, multiple techniques, multiple means of assessment, diverse perspectives, and, in particular the work of scholars of color. In this way, we openly address racial dynamics, racism, other oppressive behaviors, and academic exclusion of scholars of color.

The following is an example of a broad but customizable pedagogy for a Kingian nonviolence course. Overarching epistemological, ontological, and axiological questions could include:

What are the social realities that you want to cover in this course?
What are the historical roots? How does power fit in this analysis
What are we doing? What should we do about it?
What theories and values may guide our thinking?
What are intersectional issues?
Who are the primary actors (organizations, individuals, politicians, national figures)?
Where are leverage points for change (personal, community, national, global)?
What forms of conflict intervention are appropriate?
Why is the search for change important? What is the role of social change movements?

CLASSROOM STRATEGIES

Consider universal design; identify best practices for accessibility for the classroom, online environment, student services, and other areas.
Lectures, readings, intergenerational and culturally diverse guests from communities, student research, reflective essays; the discussion focused on issues raised and knowledge discovered.

Develop collaborative projects (also known as the dreaded group projects) that help students critically evaluate: How do individuals and communities make change? Who has the power and capacity to make changes in our communities? What are the areas of and where do we apply personal, private, and public/political leverage? What are the primary methods or points of intervention?

NON-CLASSROOM STRATEGIES

Experiential education, simply put, is embodied knowledge. It is, to paraphrase Audre Lorde, when the hands are put in service of a larger vision. Emerging evidence on community-based applied learning suggests that educating students with skills and competencies will be valuable now and in the future, social justice learning centers the service learning experience around questions of justice, equity, and social transformations. Examples might include:

- Mediation for elementary students, community-wide restorative justice events, summits, and conferences for special groups, like churches. With online learning, community-based learning may need to come from the students' choices based on what is safe and available.
- Sustained interactions to observe and reflect on the processes of community organizing. Example: ethnographic research and data analysis in response to organization or community need.
- Reflection and analysis of all learning. Examples: students begin with a nongraded reflection paper about why this issue is important and progress through analytic essays that reflect a survey of the literature available on this topic; how their real-world experiences match that of scholars who have studied these topics. Include regular writing throughout the course; journal keeping.

Assessment and Self-Critique

Interestingly, even though higher ed institutions require levels of assessment, social justice practitioners and educators may shy away from the formal assessment processes. This is a mistake. Assessment simply asks what did you accomplish and how do you know?

- First, what are your priorities? These should be reflected in a rubric and use language that is objectively measurable. Words like "understand" or "develop an awareness of" are neither useful nor measurable.
- Identify goals as well as strategies for growth.
- Link goals to direct outcomes of activities.

- Reflective processes, like journal keeping or personal essays, may determine qualitative outcomes.

SAMPLE ASSESSMENT OF A COMMUNITY EXPERIENTIAL EDUCATION

Example: Students work with a local housing advocacy group to design and implement a housing campaign for first-time homebuyers.

Learning objective: Students (in an economics class) will learn principles of mortgage rates. *(Observing how these rates pertain to a particular community.)*

Direct measure: Students will observe and identify steps in the mortgaging process and *how they pertain to a particular community.*

Benchmark: 80% of final exams able to identify core mortgage financing, practices, and strategies.

Indirect measure: Reflective assignments in response to writing prompts that ask students to compare and contrast observations, identify feelings associated with experience, and raise questions about larger social and economic structures and processes.

Student evaluations

BLJ: I learned a long time ago that "silent" and "listen" have the same letters for a reason. Therefore, I internalize student feedback and conduct an internal audit of my practices and core values regularly.

MAT: I confess that I never read course evaluations immediately after the course ends because I knew I can't read them objectively. Instead, I have a system that includes evaluation, including self-evaluation of students and teacher at midterm. I then make mid-course corrections suggested by students. I have learned to personalize neither complimentary nor critical responses.

The Community of Practice

Build diverse networks of mutually supportive practitioners (teachers, staff, community).

- Collectively identify the global, or "big picture," conditions you wish to change or influence students to change.
- Identify collective priorities and encourage sharing of resources.
- Assess the community's collective strengths.
- Share syllabi, resources, and exercises; offer peer observation and feedback.
- Genuinely care about and actively encourage each other's well-being.

BLJ: Students have written me heartfelt messages, notes, thank-you cards, stopping by to say hi, texting, calling, and emailing me to just say thank you for what they've learned, how it helped them see issues, conflicts, perspectives, and differences differently. They tell me what they are now doing that speaks to measures big and small. They thank me for listening to their diverse perspectives and ideas without them fearing judgment, creating safe, courageous, braves spaces toward community.

. . . .

Decentering Power, Centering Stories: Restorative Justice Pedagogies in Action

Michelle Clifton-Soderstrom, Jamal Bakr, and Henry Cervantes

Hasshan Batts: We live in a society with 3.5 million children are suspended every year. Two point four million people are incarcerated, and 7 million people are under some form of criminal justice control in any given moment. And over 50% of all marriages end in divorce; rejection, zero tolerance, retribution, and violence are the imperatives of our time. I encourage you to imagine a world where radical welcome forgiveness, healing, and restorative practices our way, a world in which we always look for the alternatives to the harshest punishments, a world in which we recognize that hurt people hurt people, and that surviving trauma impacts decision-making and brain development, and we create a community where people can show up.

Prison is a dangerous, a lonely, and a scary place. Segregation, "the hole" is a place that is even scarier because you are often left alone with all of your thoughts, memories, dreams, disappointments, and nightmares. Prison can also be reflective, and the hole can either exacerbate the loneliness one has always felt or slow you down just enough to think and reflect during the long deep moments of loneliness and silence. I began to think not only about the pain of my mother and Tupac's mother, but all of the Black mothers I had known that had buried their sons or that had lost them to a system that was designed to bury and devour us. I hadn't seen my mother in months because she decided long ago that somehow in protest to my protest of the life she envisioned and fought to create for me that by seeing me in a cage she was somehow accepting what I was becoming.

Music has a way of imprinting moments on us, it's not always about the song in front of you, but the smells, people, places, and things that get conjured up every time we hear the reminder of what once was or where we once laid. As I lay in the administrative segregation unit of a newly constructed facility in the mountains of Pennsylvania, I heard Tupac's eloquent, passionate and sincere ode to his dear mother, "Dear Mama," for the first time. Although Tupac once shared that "Mercy is for the weak, when I speak I scream" his powerful and passionate voice was full of mercy and pain and whether it from the stillness, from the stench, or from the smell of violence and pain in the air I was hyper receptive that day. I learned to hear and to feel in that moment. I believe through Tupac's story I began to develop empathy for my beautiful Black mother. Just as a toddler learns to take her first steps toward the freedom of running, I also learned to hear music that day, I learned to feel art in that cold and lonely cell. I thought about Tupac's song about how painful it was to reach out to his mother from his jail cell. He reflected that as a child, he had never expected to be in prison. I thought of the fact that I hadn't seen my mother in months, and I loved and missed her dearly, but until this point had never heard her or recognized the pain and the wounds I had caused throughout my long and eventful 19 years of existence. It began to feel like my mere existence harmed her which triggered a lifelong self-reflection of the harm done to mothers of Black boys born into a world that hates them and teaches us to hate ourselves and anyone that looks like us.

In that song I learned to begin to understand the pain I caused and the harm I was doing and I also learned through the pain of Afena Shakur to understand systems. Tupac's mother and my mother shared many journeys in their stories, but the love of their Black sons bonded them. The song helped me to understand that Tupac and I were living out an old slave narrative at the hands of a new face on an old system and that the responsibility to navigate solving the conflict of racism and hatred of Black bodies has been on the shoulders of the many mothers of our community for generations.

I was transferred to this new facility from a place in NYC called "The Tombs" which has been known to be just that. It is an old, cold dilapidated facility that is riddled with fear, conflict, and violence, and as a small youth growing up in Brooklyn during the height of the crime and crack epidemic I had mastered how to navigate. I had been in countless facilities throughout my life, however, thanks to Tupac, for the first time I began to embrace the interconnectedness of these systems and witness that regardless of the facade they were in fact all the same. Tangentially I eventually began to recognize the connectedness of the stories of pain and prejudice I had heard throughout my life, from my friends, through the stories we told, the music we listened to, and the books I had read.

Jamal Bakr, Henry Cervantes, and Michelle Clifton-Soderstrom

In *After Whiteness: An Education in Belonging*, Black theologian Willie James Jennings (2020) argues that Western education generally and theological education specifically have been distorted by two phenomena. The first is the production of the educated person as a "white, self-sufficient man, his self-sufficiency defined by possession, control, and mastery." The second is education's baptism of homogeneity and control through assimilation. These toxic phenomena emerge from racism and colonialism. They not only influence the content of higher education in North America; they also impact pedagogy and power in the classroom.

The three authors of this entry believe in the future that Jennings dares to imagine. Classrooms, in fact, offer expansive opportunities to enact an ethic of shared belonging. The authors hold to this hope, because we have collaborated with, and represent, students who are incarcerated, resisting toxic cultural influences such as Jennings names and replacing them with strategic peace-building and restorative practices. Each of the authors has a unique vantage point through which we have encountered moments absent of domination and oppression. Our entry builds a vision of classroom practices that struggles with present realities and yet also offers glimpses of a future defined by an identity of belonging and communion. The space within which we build is the classroom in the context of a maximum-security prison. After describing the program's vision and context, each author will introduce themselves and provide storied examples of what bell hooks might call teaching, or learning, to transgress—as a practice of freedom. These examples form our vision of strategic peacemaking and restorative justice birthed in educational spaces.

Despite ways institutions yield to oppressive influences, Jennings believes that education can "start again." Moreover, an antidote lies in theological education. In particular, an ethic of belonging that builds people toward each other, toward shared habitation, and ultimately communion could prove strong enough to overcome possession, control, and mastery.

North Park Theological Seminary (NPTS) launched a four-year Master of Arts in Christian Ministry degree at Stateville Correctional Center (Illinois) in fall 2018. The degree program prepares people for ministry in contexts susceptible to violence. The program currently enrolls approximately 70 inside incarcerated degree seekers and four outside, or free, degree seekers. There is significant diversity in the student body in the areas of race, ethnicity, religious background, and age. There is some diversity in the areas of free, incarcerated, religion, and class.

Given the contextual realities of prison and NPTS's vision to use theological education to help incarcerated persons build meaningful lives while in prison and upon release through formation for ministry, the curriculum integrates courses in Bible, theology, and history with emphases in conflict transformation, nonviolent communication, race relations, peacemaking, trauma, and restorative justice practices.

The program acknowledges that students from nontraditional ministry contexts and varied educational backgrounds need and desire to combine coursework and life skills to become agents of restoration. NPTS also believes that access to quality formal theological education is essential for underserved communities such as prison populations. Graduates of the program will have a well-articulated understanding of restorative justice ministry and sense of vocation through themes such as trauma, healing, race, justice, and interpersonal and community relations. Learning outcomes for participation in the program include the following:

- Comprehension of individual brokenness, interpersonal forms of violence, and systemic injustices as it shapes one's theology of ministry.
- Demonstrate skills in restorative arts (personal healing, nonviolent communication, conflict transformation, care and counseling, intersectional analyses, and the art of listening) that ground one's sense of vocational identity in God's mission.

Without exception, students in prison have experienced trauma and violence, and the curriculum helps students develop concrete practices aimed at the healing and restoration of individuals and communities. Courses are taught by racially diverse faculty, many of whom are trained in the fields of conflict transformation studies, community development, racial reconciliation, sociology, and trauma. A key aspect of the program is the community outcomes, which include integrating restorative practices both in and outside the classroom. Faculty are also expected to engage and embody these outcomes in their content, pedagogy, and outside the classroom.

Three years into the program, we offer stories that reflect on what we have learned and experienced in the prison classroom and the work building toward a sense of communion and belonging. The context for the storied examples is a collaborative faculty and student project that drew upon courses and faculty from a variety of disciplines related to conflict and communication to further knowledge about how the seminary classroom might advance four goals: (1) individual healing, (2) personal and communal agency, (3) integration of restorative practices in and outside the classroom, and (4) increased knowledge of pedagogies that engage conflict in nonviolent ways and that result in creative communication. At stake in our project is the fact that conflict can either divide or it can draw members more deeply into the community. Conflict is a particularly complicated reality in a maximum-security prison. In the prison context, structural and interpersonal conflict is heightened, and it is difficult to promote nonviolent conflict skills even in the classroom. Yet together, the racially diverse group of students and faculty built a community of belonging.

Jamal

My name is Jamal Bakr. I was raised in the "Back of the Yards" neighborhood located on the south side of Chicago. Many colors made up the ethnic confluence that was my neighborhood including Latino, African American, Polish, Lithuanian, and Arab. It is a neighborhood of poor, working-class people. It was also one of the top Chicago neighborhoods with the highest levels of gang-motivated crimes at over 300 crimes per 100,000 persons.

I am connected with both parts of my heritage which is Mexican and Palestinian. To my Arab friends, I am *Wuluk*—slang for buddy or bro—and to my Mexican friends, I am *Paisa* or countryman. I care as much about immigration and heroes like Delores Huerta as I do about the West Bank and the Prophet Muhammed. Yet I learned at an early age that existing cliques are hard to break and that I wasn't ethnically authentic in the eyes of most.

Layers of oppression run deep in urban areas throughout the United States. Growing up in "Back of the Yards," I wasn't always aware of the social constructs fueling systemic oppression impacting who I would become at the young age of 18 when I was incarcerated. This would come in hindsight. The four Is of oppression which I learned about in my conflict transformation course revealed to me just how deeply oppression is engrained in the lives of urban men of color. The brutal violence and its associated fear of living in a neighborhood where violence was a regular occurrence caused my friends and me to adopt an unhealthy expectation of a premature acceptance of death. While many, especially white, children in America grew up mimicking superheroes, I pretended to be the roughest, toughest character I could imagine. This was not only in response to the violence I witnessed. It was also a response to regular police violence against Black and brown men. This is an example of both institutional and internalized oppression. I call it "Big I, little me." My neighborhood was ground zero for the war on drugs, militarized policing, and super-predator gang members were literally children. My little brown body felt helpless every time a squad car cruised past.

Once, when I was picked up and sat in the back of a squad car with my friend, the officers ran the names of our parents. Upon discovering that my friend's father had a warrant, they asked my friend what time he would return from work. They kept my friend in the car until his father came home, at which time they traded father for son. I never saw my friend, or his father, again. This case demonstrated interpersonal violence that happened between particular police officers and particular young people.

By the age of 13, I was shot for the first time. As I lay in my hospital bed, the detectives assigned to my case pressed me on the identity of my shooter, which I did not know because he shot me in the back. Unaffiliated with any gangs at this point, I made clear that I was in the dark about who shot me and why I had been shot. Undeterred, the detective leaned in close and said he thought I knew more than I was revealing. He "recognized me" from the neighborhood implying that I was suspicious simply by being out and about in *my* neighborhood. He continued, "Why would this man shoot you unless you had it coming?" I was a 13-year-old boy, recovering from a gunshot wound to my spine, and I felt like a criminal. This was not the first time I felt like the enemy and would not be the last. The ideological oppression that all brown men are criminals, or at least dangerous, was reinforced by the detective who should have been my ally, and, tragically, I internalized this identity to an even deeper level of my psyche.

I would later be assaulted by police officers, pulling me over for a U-turn on an uncrowded street. My car would be vandalized by men in uniforms assuming that no car driven by a Mexican-Palestinian "Back of the Yards" kid could be clean. Once, when I conjured up the courage to ask why they were messing with me, the officer said "Cuz we CAN." Turning to my girlfriend, he added, "You better buy a black dress, cuz this piece of shit will be dead by the summer."

In fear, I turned to a gang for safety, and I began to embody a persona that I thought would keep the violence I feared at bay. I continued to internalize the violence and oppression around me, becoming a "soldier" in a war I knew had no end. I targeted my peers from other areas in the city in ways that reflected my trauma. I developed a ruthless ethic of self-preservation and accepted violence, even beckoning my death. I was shot other times before my incarceration, and the only end that I looked to was my demise.

I was traumatized by a racial hierarchy in this country, and it would only be natural that I would have aggressive, even violent, reactions to a racist justice system and the whiteness that continues to prop it up. Yet after my courses that focus on trauma, healing, nonviolence, and race reconciliation, I realize that I can no longer simply work to interrupt violence and advocate for healing merely in my community or among issues that only affect me. I am compelled to fight against the injustice that affects humanity as a whole. Fighting injustice isn't just about making an impact. It is about making the biggest impact possible. It isn't about selecting the injustice that correlates directly with me. It means taking on the issues that impact all humanity.

In an interaction with a white student in a recent course "Black Faith Matters," the white woman named her own biases and even her ideology of supremacy. My first response was to reassure and comfort her. I sought to protect her from what womanist theologian Chenequa Walker-Barnes (2019) calls necessary truth-telling and reinforced the unequal power dynamics that come when we modify the narrative by quelling the discomfort that comes when white people attempt to claim responsibility for racism. Because I was not used to those with power claiming responsibility, I was not accustomed to being empowered to tear down the principalities of racism. Why take such risks on those who embody the oppressor? It is easier to keep the peace because even a surface level of peace is much easier to tolerate than the threat of violence present just underneath every form of human conflict.

Sitting below the surface of this interaction was an imbalance in the power dynamic that was made apparent in our exchange. She was from the upper middle class, receiving an education at a prestigious West Coast university, and the daughter of one of the seminary deans. The realities of an uneven power dynamic in this type of dialogue, with a person who benefits willingly or unwillingly from white supremacy, do not alter the heart of the matter. Nor does it invite reconciliation.

Navigating these conflicts requires self-awareness and deep empathy. Howard Thurman wrote (1996), "We are all affected by forces, social and natural, that in some measure determine our behavior without our being able to bring to bear upon them our private will, however great or righteous it may be." Community inspires including the community of authors that I have been exposed to. In Black Lives Matter founders' memoir *When They Call You a Terrorist*, Patrisse Khan-Cullors and Asha Bandele (2019) assert that the most marginalized, traumatized, and discriminated-against people in society are often those who are the best reconcilers. I had a moment last year when I did not stand up to an officer who ridiculed an LGBTQ person. I stood silent. I later felt the need to apologize to Professor Henry and acknowledge my failure to advocate for all people. To my surprise and based on previous classroom discussions, my professor had assumed that I was married to a member of the LGBTQ community. Although I am not, I felt proud that although I had failed in the moment with the officer, I had succeeded to some measurable degree to demonstrate empathy in the classroom.

The work of reconciliation and healing is political work. It is fraught with peril. There will be times of personal failures and moral triumph in the fight for restored humanity. Though the work seems overwhelming and beyond our capacities, we must meet humanity at the place of her needs because peace, restoration, and freedom leave us with no other choice.

Michelle

I am a white woman who currently serves as dean of faculty and Professor of Theology and Ethics at North Park Theological Seminary. After years of teaching Christian social ethics at North Park, I grew tired of teaching about justice and wanted education to be a vehicle for justice. I also know theological education and the formational learning experiences embedded are good for any and all who desire to pursue God's restorative justice in contexts outside the church.

When I began teaching at Stateville, I was appalled by what I found inside and who we lock up in this country. They are disproportionately people of color. They largely come from impoverished neighborhoods. They have not had access to quality education. Many suffer from mental illness. English is often a second language. Some are sentenced to life—even death—in their youth. They are victims of sexual assault and domestic violence.

We have disappeared people with the false idea that we have disappeared the social ills they represent, according to Angela Davis. We have disappeared people through a system that is connected to inequitable sentencing laws, Black codes, convict leasing, slavery, and racism. We have, in short, used incarceration to wipe the history of racism in this country.

After being inside prison, I became more convinced that a predominately white institution has a reparative responsibility to address a broken criminal historically connected to slavery. In submitting to the paradigm of educational reparations, over ministry, charity, or other ways we name Christian work, white educators such as myself must continue to acknowledge the history of racial hierarchy in the United States. Specifically, naming the place of whiteness concerning the injustices that the US prison system perpetuates, white educators submit to those people groups we have harmed.

One example of this came on an unexpected day. It was raining, and our walk to the education building after being searched for contraband included a trek outside in the mud. I wore my raincoat, which was new and white, and when I arrived at the classroom, one of my students, William J., noted, "That's a pretty risky thing, wearing a white coat in here!" I responded quickly, brushing off his concerns and reminding him that I could just wash the soiled jacket when I got home.

A few months later, I was facilitating a Sankofa trip with an African American colleague. Sankofa is a trip that follows routes of Civil Rights Freedom Rides. The purpose is to educate participants about the history of Black-white relations in the United States through partnerships and trips to Birmingham, Jackson, Montgomery, and Memphis, among others. One of my assigned lessons was to talk about the Pettus Bridge in Selma, Alabama. When we arrived at the bridge, we walked across the bridge in silence to commemorate Bloody Sunday. It began to rain. I reached to pull my hood up but quickly I stopped.

The words of Anthony Ray Hinton—an innocent Black man incarcerated for over 30 years—flooded into my head. We had just come from Bryan Stevenson's organization, Equal Justice Initiative, and had heard Mr. Hinton's testimony about judges who sat on exonerating evidence for 15 years before finally acquitting him. When asked about the joys of being free, Mr. Hinton smiled, "I can go outside whenever I want, and feel the rain on my face. Next time it rains, I encourage all of you to get wet. I know you ladies like to protect your hair, but just let the rain fall all over you."

Hearing his words again, I continued over the bridge, letting the rain fall on me, and began my lesson on the other side. I have done my research. Edmund Pettus was a lawyer, two-time senator, son of a plantation owner. And . . . a Grand Dragon of the Ku Klux Klan. As I said these words, I froze in the realization of the symbolism of my white raincoat and the violent impact this clothing has had on Black men and women in this country.

I resisted the impulse to throw my raincoat into the river. That would be to, once again, center my white guilt rather than bear the weight of my history. I thought, at least my hood is down, thanks to Anthony Ray Hinton.

In that moment, the face of William J. also came to me. It had cost him something, to be a student of a white woman encultured by a white institution. I wondered if I had evoked racial terror in my student, and yet he had the courage to make visible what I did not see. Clothing had never been a source of terror for me.

Almost a year after I had worn that white-hooded robe in a maximum-security prison, overwhelmingly filled with Black men, I apologized to William J. He did not say, "It's okay, Michelle." He did not brush it off as the result of a well-intentioned but mistaken act. He simply said, "Thank you."

Another full year passed, with me continuing to show up and William J. working diligently in his studies. He always spoke truth, and he is always a pillar of hospitality. Though his incarceration has lasted close to 40 years and he has much reason to resent whiteness and white people, all are welcome in his company. On this particular day, it is Advent. I entered the cell blocks to make rounds and wish the students well before the Christmas break. I approach William J., who is behind bars, but we can talk. My daughter is with me. As we finish our conversation, I turn to leave the cell house, and William calls out, "Professor Michelle?" I answer him with a turn back to face him. "Yes, William?"

"I forgive you," he calls.

In that moment, my negligent use of power as a teacher became an occasion for a gift. And forgiveness, I was able to see myself as both an enemy and beloved.

Complex identity work for white educators, including awareness of how our guilt impedes, inserts, or interferes is essential to dismantling racial hierarchies and becoming a self-aware pedagogue. It is a lesson that cost William J. something, and one that I hold up as a practice of freedom—William J.'s and my own in tandem.

Henry

My name is Henry Cervantes and for the past several years I have had the honor to explore the ideas of violence and peace with the incarcerated community. I have taught courses and workshops in conflict transformation with detained men in Cook County's Department of Correction through the Sheriff's Anti-Violence Effort (SAVE) program. I also had the opportunity to teach for North Park Theological Seminary (NPTS) on nonviolent communication and conflict transformation at Stateville Correctional Center (SCC). As with most jails and prisons in the United States, both are predominately filled with African American and Latinx men. From my experiences working with incarcerated men at SCC, I believe that incarcerated persons trained in racial justice and decolonization through a restorative justice lens and nonviolent approach can and do contribute tremendously to the creation and development of beloved communities. Beloved communities defy divisions based on race, class, generation, education, and freedom. During my years teaching nonviolence to incarcerated communities, I have learned about how race studies advance racial justice, how nonviolence exists in violent environments, and how restorative justice can build, heal, and transform communities inside and beyond.

The first lesson I learned is that race education is crucial to advancing racial justice at the grassroots level. It is the key that can open doors of understanding and compassion among both privileged and marginalized groups in our society. Through North Park, incarcerated students at SCC who are primarily Black and brown take courses with primarily free white graduate students with a focus on exploring racial injustices in our society. We live in a racialized and polarized society, and it is rare to see intentional communities built across, race, class, privilege while, simultaneously, studying those very same issues. At NPTS, students not only learn about the pillars of white supremacy but also about the process of struggling against these systems. It has been a powerful experience witnessing and engaging in conversation about how these systems of racial injustice have made it possible for white people to advance historically and how those very same systems have set up barriers for Black, Indigenous, and People of Color to remain oppressed. Facilitating this educational space with the descendants of privileged and oppressed people and exploring the issues of race behind prison walls has been remarkable. My colleagues and I have witnessed firsthand how attitudes can shift and how the spirit of solidarity unfolds through communication and dialogue.

In one of our discussion activities at Stateville, we explored the four Is of oppression and their manifestation in our everyday lives. Specifically, we analyzed racism as a form of oppression that manifests in four distinct but intertwined levels: (1) Ideological, (2) Institutional, (3) Interpersonal, and (4) Internalized (Chinook Fund, 2015). At the end of one of our classes, one student mentioned that he has realized how his journey to prison resulted from both his internalization of a "less-than" belief about his personhood along with being impacted by all four forms of oppression. In one of his reflection papers, he outlined his life story noting ways the four Is of oppression influenced his thinking and actions and how all four phases work together to ensure the oppression of peoples. This was a critical moment for his own story and ability to reject his incarceration by allowing his personhood to transcend it.

The second lesson I have learned is that nonviolence is an effective tool in creating social change in violent environments. For nonviolence education to be effective, it must be grounded and relatable to students' situations, whether in a classroom or the prison cell. Through my teaching experiences at Stateville, I firmly believe that those with violent offenses can make powerful, positive, and peaceful contributions to the outside world. Incarcerated individuals can be leading change agents, but they are often overlooked by the society outside prison. Teaching in a prison is as difficult as it is rewarding since prisons place limits on the instructor and students. Additionally, some men may not be receptive to the message of peacebuilding and nonviolence or may feel that discussing these topics puts them at risk in prison. The idea of discussing peacebuilding and nonviolence in a maximum-security prison with men serving sentences for violent crimes has been criticized as absurd and pointless. However, this exact formula provides a unique opportunity to explore the hidden power of nonviolence through education with this vulnerable and marginalized population.

The very notion of nonviolence as a tool is a hard sell to individuals who have been simultaneously impacted by and perpetrators of violence in their communities. For this reason, nonviolence *must* be presented as an option to engaging in conflict while, at the same time, acknowledging that violence is the norm for many individuals and communities, especially within prison. Nonviolence education for incarcerated persons with violent offenses is not intended to make better prisoners. Rather, it is meant to develop better practitioners of peacemaking in which an adversary is not harmed. This requires knowledge, training, and skill-building in communication and de-escalation strategies. When done intentionally and thoughtfully, it can produce insightful results. After the course, one student told me that he had seen a verbal altercation escalating in the prison tier. He couldn't help but notice that he was, for the first time in his life, looking at a fight differently. He explained that before the course, he would have simply watched and accepted the fight as normal. Now, he was conscious of how conflict escalation plays out in real life. He said, "I was paying attention to their feelings and their escalating actions, and I told my celly (cellmate) about how conflict works and unfolds. I could not stop thinking about our class and telling myself that these brothers need to handle their primary and secondary emotions." Nonviolence education changes our way of looking at everyday conflicts—to the point of humanizing those who might under different mindsets be seen as only as aggressors.

As a final project, we asked students to create their rubrics and protocols for engaging in conflict in a prison context. I was overwhelmed with wonder of how they came up with ingenious ways to define violence and conflict and their abilities in role-playing scenarios for resolving and defusing potentially violent situations. Prison life can make persons very resourceful in stressful situations, and this came alive in their skit presentations. The students presented conflicts such as "You owe me two packs!"—a dispute among two men settling a bet of two bags of noodles—and "Phone Check Homie!" in which men in the yard argue about who will be next to use the phone to call his family (Waging Nonviolence, 2019). These real scenarios have the potential to create violent situations. Yet, our class met them with tangible, nonviolent solutions and recommendations. I was moved to laughter and to tears in their final presentations because of their deep analysis and exploration of how to be nonviolent in a violent world.

The final lesson I've learned is that the study and practice of restorative justice rooted in indigenous practices can build communities toward healing for marginalized communities of color. Restorative justice paradigms emerge from traditions rooted in honoring Native American Indigenous forms of conflict transformation and peacebuilding. Mainstream restorative justice often focuses primarily on harm, but the real work noted in Native American Indigenous models lifts the work of healing. Healing is at the center, and the purpose of restoration is to provide community space for healing. This includes expressing pain, naming harm, and then discovering ways to heal as a community. This requires individuals to check themselves and develop self-awareness, meaning acknowledging one's biases in a conflict. It also includes identifying one's power—either institutional or social—with other actors in a conflict. It includes asking questions, such as: Is winning necessary? How well can I listen to others with whom I am in conflict? Can we work on ourselves and challenge ourselves to better engage in resolving conflicts in a community?

This practice requires people who are skillful and who embody the principles of Indigenous restorative practices by showing respect and homage to the talking circles. As a final paper, a student wrote a reflection on our nonviolent communication course. He wrote,

> At the end of the day I agree that true peace is always possible. It requires, however, strength and courage. Peace is a choice just as violence is, but the path we take is dependent on our desire to deal with the root causes within us. If we allow ourselves to be made whole, then peace becomes a viable solution. . . . Finally as you can see I used a Native American concept on my cover page. Why? Because it reflects, in my estimation, a holistic approach that seeks to close the gaps that trauma, crisis, and violence often create. . . . The medicine wheel seeks to restore that which has been stolen, robbed, and pillaged from individuals. I believe it to be an excellent concept to practice and implemented in conflict resolution. It definitely is a tool towards non-violent determinations.

In the Lakota tradition, the medicine wheel is a sacred circle symbol divided in four quadrants representing the four directions of the universe and also the four aspects of an individual: (1) physical, (2) mental, (3) emotional, and (4) spiritual. I agree with the student's reflection that violence and oppression strip us of the four parts of our humanity. A restorative and nonviolent approach can help us recover and heal. As a student mentioned during class, the violence of the system is dehumanizing, but "Here, we humanize each other."

I learn and teach with the hopes to enrich the lives of those around me. Whether it's in the classroom or the prison cell, my deepest hope is to inspire people to realize their great power and potential. Isn't the purpose of higher education to seek truth and advance life so that our knowledge and practice make our world better? I think that only through education and our work can we improve humanity. I have been committed to teaching nonviolence in schools, in jails, and at SCC because I know the power of education and the power that exists in our community. Education has the power to open peoples' minds, and open minds combined with hope can change our society.

CONCLUSION

Anecdotal data from the instructors and students about their experiences and observations proved a rich vein for connecting pedagogy, content, and restorative goals. The faculty initially thought in terms of what they would provide to the students at Stateville and what they wanted to see as a result of their work. In retrospect, it is not surprising that the project team individually and collectively mirrored the individual and collective experiences of the men at Stateville. Both groups gave and received from each other, which is the essence of building community.

Major barriers to teaching and learning in prison include poor facilities, deliberate institutional barriers to student attendance, and a highly restrictive environment—all vestiges of racism and colonial domination. However, both students and faculty more than compensated with enthusiasm, gratitude, and goodwill. The instructors' respect for the capabilities and gifts of their colleagues was obvious. There were no apparent conflicts between instructors. Even with institutional personnel, the team modeled the positive, nonviolent communication that they wanted to instill in the student cohort. Clearly, a tone and norm of mutual trust and respect had been established.

Because of COVID-19 lockdowns, the team was only able to accomplish one of the two spring observation days and remains closed as of this writing. Classes continued via correspondence, which is not optimal. Several of the students remain in various stages of illness. Devastatingly, as members of our cohort became ill, two passed away. Partnerships with other prison programs and community groups developed informally to support incarcerated victims of COVID-19 and their families. The project team and students provided memorial services through Zoom for our two deceased students. Instructors adjusted the instructional format to a correspondence, exchanging course materials with some of the students with some irregularity and more regularly into the summer. These events showed that the outcomes hoped for had been achieved, though absolutely not in the way hoped for. Forged in our shared grief, students and instructors became a learning community, functioning as agents of healing and restoration in each other's lives.

Concerning conflict and communication, the students demonstrated the pure genius of thinking about how nonviolence can work in tough situations. Inside, this can cost them their reputation, and the team was impressed with the way they took material and did something with it in their context. Students did work and not just for the grade. They modeled Frier's pedagogy of the oppressed as opposed to the banking concept of learning. It was rewarding for them to take their education so seriously.

Some faculty discussed intense interaction with particular students. We concluded that it was a way for faculty to engage graciously and transparently while establishing credibility. Some were surprised at how Eurocentric most of their theology was given that most are people of color. When faculty brought in sources by scholars of color who had an explicit scriptural basis for justice and liberation, significant shifts happened. The team concluded that this added integrity. Similarly, the team agreed that the majority of instructors should be instructors of color. Student evaluations named specifically how empowering it was for them to see two Black women, a Black man, and a Latino instructor. For many, it was the first time they had experienced a teacher of color.

Finally, students named how meaningful the embodiment of the community was beyond the content of the courses. The wealth of our communities are trapped behind bars, and this has an impact on instructors, especially African American and Latinx. There need to be explicit conversations among faculty and with outside students. The Black women in particular had what they called a "load-bearing function."

Overall, the team and students grew in appreciation for persons outside their race or ethnicity. They indicated that this was harder than they had thought it would be. We learned that a significant part of recovery and healing is acknowledging truth, including histories. Students named that they have to be who they are because of the place they are in, but they learned to have moments of vulnerability while remaining "safe" in prison. This cultivated increased trust within the learning community. It is also important to note that the students showed an increase in anxiety, as demonstrated by more frequent leaving the room, heated discussions, threats of quitting the program, and attempts at triangulation. However, instructors navigated these situations beautifully and acceptingly. In short, the reliable presence of members of the community went a long way to combat the isolating effects of prison.

CHAPTER 23

Restorative Justice

....

What Is It Really?

O*riginating with Indigenous people, restorative circles and models have been incorporated and/or appropriated throughout the field of conflict resolution. Is restorative justice practice effective in systems of oppression? Who should lead restorative justice circles? Tonya Covington and Johonna McCants-Turner reconceptualize restorative justice in ways that include youth organizing practices and young peoples' narratives.*

—Mary Adams Trujillo

....

Sticking to Doing Things the Way We Always Have, Even When We Know It's Not Working

Tonya Covington

I'm Tonya Covington. I'm a native of Washington, DC, have lived in Morocco, Wisconsin, Massachusetts, and for the last 45 years in the enchanted state of New Mexico. In my lifetime, I have experienced a multitude of cultures, systems, conflict styles, and peacemaking—leading to a fascination with intercultural communication.

I am a restorative justice advocate, trainer, and cheerleader. Restorative justice is a hot topic right now as people look for the silver bullet (pardon the pun), that will solve all violence—especially involving youth.

I train people on the theory and practice of restorative justice in the hopes that it will become more mainstream.

The city we live in, Albuquerque, is unique. We have a majority-minority population. We are second highest in poverty rates. We have a huge problem with gun violence—especially among youth—and the president (without being asked) has just ordered federal troops to our city to "combat crime."

Against this backdrop, young men of color, from middle to high school, in a youth development program, asked for restorative justice training. These youth have housing challenges, some with incarcerated parents, most have experienced school suspension or expulsion and many of the indicators on the "Adverse Childhood Experiences" chart.

The opportunity to train a group of young men of color is rare and for me, it was quite refreshing. I longed to tell them of the indigenous roots of restorative justice, how every ancient civilization known to man, had discovered the power of sitting in a circle and discussing the issues of the village while allowing everyone to have input. I needed them to understand how important it is at this time to reclaim the ancient wisdom of people of color, at a time when people of color are disproportionately affected by the criminal justice system. I wanted to teach them that leadership was theirs for the taking—in the end they taught me a lot more.

But I was afraid that in this day of nonpersonal, digital interaction, friend-unfriend culture that it might be difficult for young men to allow themselves to be vulnerable. It also seems that our current political climate is eroding collective empathy and causing the loss of social bonds.

Seeing their excited faces boosted my resolve and I took my pom-poms and began. Our session was opened by two young indigenous men who offered blessings (in their native tongue) and cleansed us with sage.

I start each training with the basics of mediation, because it is the foundation for modern restorative justice. Both restorative justice and trauma-informed care ask the question, "What happened to you?" as opposed to "What did you do?" The answers to these two questions are markedly different.

I teach in a very interactive way. I use videos, roleplays, and always encourage lots of discussions. One of the videos I often use shows a mediation done for a group of young men—how apropos. In this scenario, a co-mediation team is conducting the session. The issue is that four college roommates share a house, and one of them has recently been drinking a lot. In his drunkenness, he has caused damage to the house, including putting a large hole in a wall. The landlord is quite upset. He has assessed the damage at $400 and said any further damage will result in all the young men being evicted. The mediation discussion centers around the payment of the damages.

I have used this video in numerous adult trainings. No matter the makeup of the training class, the comments have always been similar: comments and questions about who leads the discussion; who talks first and talks the most; how the decisions are made; and the fairness or not of the financial agreements.

However, when I showed the video to the young men of color, their reaction was quite different. One young man immediately stated, "Homie's got a problem." The others quickly joined in asking why no one was addressing

"Homie's" drinking problem. They questioned the validity of the friendships and how trivial the financial issues were. They shared stories of the consequences of not addressing the elephant in the room. The empathy and compassion of these wonderful young men was astounding.

Humans are hard-wired to connect and empathy fuels connection. Restorative justice can be seen as a way to change and empower community. When we expand the definition of community to include voices of youth as changemakers, then we hear from the most vital members of the community. These voices often go unheard because these youth are excluded on the basis of their age, the way they look or their background. Their insights can lead to meaningful change.

The impact of this one session has forever changed my 30-plus years of perspective as a mediator and restorative justice practitioner.

We see time and again that youth are resilient. The most heartening thing was the way in which they communicated with me. I often find that lacking in other groups. I continue to be concerned about restorative justice being dominated by whites, and primarily white women. So often the participants are people of color and the issues involve the uniqueness of our lives, therefore, it makes more sense that people of color be able to guide these conversations.

Many whites still do not fully understand our differences in communication and experience and often practice "tone policing." This, more often than not, causes participants to stifle themselves.

There is also the issue of power dynamics. There is still an unexamined assumption that for someone to truly be in charge or an expert they must be white—even if the issue pertains to someone else's lived experience. Because of the racial dynamics in this country, people of color often view whites as agents of the system that oppresses us.

There is an inherent power and comfort in having facilitators or circle keepers who more closely resemble the participants.

In the years that I have been using this video no one has expressed the clarity of understanding that these young men, who are often dismissed by others, brought to the discussion. In this time, when we are looking for an authentic path to racial wholeness they bring a compassionate, understanding that we cannot do without.

Youth of color must be at the forefront of restorative justice practices so as not to diminish their voices. Youth need to be in positions of power to lead conversations that affect the future we expect them to lead. They need the practice of decision-making with empathy.

As practitioners, we must check our positions of power and recognize when to be a leader versus when to be an ally. Remembering always that the most valuable principle of restorative justice is empowering people to decide their own fate.

Can Restorative Justice Make Young, Black Lives Matter in Schools?

Johonna R. McCants-Turner

I am standing outside a government building in Washington, DC, in the heat of the summer with a group of about 15 people; most are African American teenagers. My own chocolate brown forehead is reflecting the glorious light of the summer sun, and my brow is furrowed something serious. Tawanda, one of the teenagers, standing next to me, is holding a clipboard with sheets of paper that contain her prepared remarks. This is the scene that was captured in a photograph that appeared on the front page of the *Washington Post* about 15 years ago. The accompanying article reports on the press conference that the Justice 4 D.C. Youth Coalition (JDCY) is holding on the steps of Washington, DC's City Hall as part of a city-wide youth-led campaign. Named by the Black and Latinx youth at its helm, the "Stop the War on D.C. Youth!" campaign sought to block a package of proposed policies that would increase young people's contact with the criminal legal system, resulting in increased rates of youth incarceration. Later that year, DC's City Council passed an omnibus juvenile justice bill into law that included most of the alternative policies that we, as members of JDCY, demanded, including the closure of DC's then-infamous youth detention center and the creation of community-based alternatives to incarceration (D.C. Law 15-261, Omnibus Juvenile Justice Act of 2004).

Much more than challenging policies, the "Stop the War on D.C. Youth!" campaign sought to challenge the mainstream story that cast Black and brown youth as perpetrators of violence and promulgated the dominant logic that public safety is premised on policing and punishment. In contrast, the story advanced by our activism pointed to the criminalization and detention of young people of color as a real threat to youths' safety and security. We also told a very different story about violence than the one advanced in mainstream media— a story that highlighted the violence that young people of color experience as a result of institutional oppression, rather than the mainstream story of "youth violence" (McCants, 2009).

Today, organizers in the Black Lives Matter movement continue to advance very different stories than what is reflected in mainstream discourse about what is necessary to ensure the safety and security of Black people and Black communities. Similar to JDCY's grassroots organizing campaign 15 years ago, contemporary movement stories also point to the criminal-legal system as an instrument of war and proclaim that safety and justice is not advanced through carceral expansion. These stories also illustrate a vision of a society in which the dignity and sanctity of Black life is upheld:

where "institutions that inflict violence on Black people" are "replaced by institutions that value and affirm the flourishing of Black lives"; where the "experiences and leadership of the most marginalized Black people" are centered "including but not limited to those who are trans and queer, women and femmes, currently and formerly incarcerated, immigrants, disabled, working class, and poor"; and where "the current systems we live inside of [are] radically transformed." (Movement for Black Lives, 2021)

This vision, according to the Movement for Black Lives, is at the center of what it means to make Black Lives Matter. In 2016, the Black Lives Matter at School Network was launched. The network has four demands of which the first is an end to zero-tolerance policies in schools and the implementation of restorative justice (BLM at School, n.d.). As schools and school districts respond to these demands, it is imperative to amplify understandings of restorative justice emerging from Black youth and other young people of color, increasing the likelihood that restorative justice will contribute to the creation of schools in which young, Black lives are valued and kept safe (Stith, 2018). This essay responds to this need, joining a litany composed by activists, organizers, and scholars including the contributors to the anthology, *Black Lives Matter at School: An Uprising for Educational Justice* (Hagopian & Jones, 2020).

Can restorative justice make young, Black lives matter in schools? The answer depends in large part on whose version of restorative justice. In this essay, I argue that it is imperative to center the visions and narratives of restorative justice articulated by Black, Indigenous, young people of color organizing for restorative justice in their schools. Youth organizers articulate the promise and potential of restorative justice concerning their own school-based experiences of state-sponsored racialized violence. Unlike dominant narratives of restorative justice in education, their stories reflect the harm caused by racialized neoliberal disinvestments in education. Their stories not only challenge dominant frames and discourses of restorative justice in education but also construct new frames and discourses that link the movement for restorative justice in education directly to the demands and goals of the Black Lives Matter movement. Moreover, youth organizers envision restorative justice as one aspect of broader social, political, and institutional transformations that will usher in an educational future in which poor and working-class Black, Indigenous, young people of color can learn and grow unfettered.

I was introduced to youth organizing when I became involved with the Justice 4 D.C. Youth Coalition during graduate school. Youth organizing is the process of bringing young people together to collectively analyze and win solutions to problems that affect them and their communities, dismantle structural inequality, and build movements for social justice (Listen, Inc., 2003; McCants, 2007). A new period of youth-led organizing emerged in the

United States in the early 1990s in the context of an increasing shift toward a neoliberal political economy characterized by widespread disinvestments in social welfare and the proliferation of repressive discourses and punitive policies at federal, state, and local levels, including schools. As those primarily affected by underfunded schools and community programs, rapidly declining economic opportunities, and increased surveillance and policing, poor and working-class youth from Black, Latinx, Asian, and Indigenous communities fought back together, resulting in the formation of youth of color as a political identity (Kwon, 2013). Through collective analysis, participatory action research, community education, public speaking, and direct action and other activities, youth organizers contribute their unique gifts and visions to broader racial and social justice movements.

Through youth organizing, young people are advancing restorative justice to dismantle the school-to-prison pipeline, challenge systemic violence in their schools and neighborhoods, and advance education equity and justice. While many see the academic, administrative, and advocacy work led by educators, scholars, and policy advocates as the locus of efforts to bring restorative justice in schools, I see the activism and organizing led by young people of color as the heartbeat of the contemporary movement for restorative justice in education. From my earliest experiences with youth organizing, I was positioned as an adult ally and quickly learned that one of my most important roles was to amplify the voices, visions, and analyses of the young people whom I organized alongside. Although quite removed from the frontlines of youth organizing in my day-to-day work as a college professor, I approach my essay in this spirit, seeking to learn from and amplify the stories of youth organizers working for restorative justice in their schools as part of broader movements for educational justice.

Ethnic studies scholar Daniel Hosang (2006) has written how "youth-led activist groups use community organizing to contest the discourses used to define and explain social problems and crises, and to imagine the world through alternative logics, ideas and frameworks" (p. 5). This essay builds on this understanding. I will specifically reflect on the contributions of youth organizers in a national alliance of educational justice organizing groups called the Alliance for Educational Justice (AEJ). Founded in 2008, AEJ is a national network of over 30 youth-led and intergenerational groups organizing to end punitive school policies and practices, advance restorative justice, and catalyze educational equity (Stith, 2018). Through AEJ, youth organizing groups active at the local level in their own cities work together to create shared strategies, campaigns, and frameworks and shift national education policy. The founding national organizing director of AEJ is veteran education justice organizer Jonathan Stith. I came to know Stith as a friend and colleague in Washington, DC, through our leadership roles in the Justice for D.C. Youth Coalition and the D.C. Chapter of Building Leaders Organizing Communities

(BLOC), a collective of social-justice-oriented youth workers. The stories and perspective in this essay grew out of our conversations and collaboration over the past several years including a workshop that we facilitated together at the Association for Conflict Resolution Conference in 2017 titled, "Can Restorative Justice Make Black Lives Matter in Schools?" During the workshop for conflict resolution scholars and practitioners largely unfamiliar with youth organizing or students' experiences of harm in schools, Stith shared stories from AEJ's organizing, particularly their growing campaign against police violence. This essay integrates these stories and the collaborative analysis that we shared, but even more so centers and promotes the analysis of youth organizers in AEJ and the education justice movement.

In the next section, I define restorative justice and discuss the need for new narratives of restorative justice. I also introduce the concept of a "restorative justice narrative," a term that builds on critical race theorists' understandings of counternarratives and their societal functions. Then, in the following two sections, I share two snapshots of youth organizers' creation and deployment of restorative justice narratives that differ from and contest dominant narratives. Finally, in the conclusion, I suggest ways that these new narratives can be deployed by scholars and practitioners to align our work for restorative justice in education with the demands at the center of the Black Lives Matter movement, in concert with the work of youth organizers.

Toward New "Restorative Justice Narratives"

Restorative justice is a philosophy that emphasizes healing and accountability to repair harm and injury, build healthy relationships, and create thriving communities (Turner, 2020). The philosophical roots of restorative justice can be traced to indigenous communities around the world that hold worldviews that center on interconnectedness, healing, and collective well-being. Calls for restorative justice in schools build on generations of antiracist advocacy and organizing to end the school-to-prison pipeline. Many advocates of restorative justice in education insist that restorative justice is necessary to provide a more appropriate and corrective response to student misbehavior than racialized exclusionary discipline measures, particularly zero-tolerance policies, an approach reflective of broken-windows policing in which the most minor infractions (e.g., broken windows) are regulated and severely punished. Some calls for restorative justice in education go beyond envisioning restorative justice as a disciplinary reform to the wholesale transformation of school culture and pedagogy. By and large, the body of mainstream rationale for restorative justice in education, despite its reformist intentions, overwhelmingly reinforces the idea that the primary harms that need to be addressed by restorative justice practices are the harms that *students* are inflicting on one another, and on educators.

In other words, dominant narratives employed to advocate for restorative justice in schools often name students' behavior, and particularly the "bad behavior" of Black and brown students, as the primary problems that restorative justice solves, particularly when introduced into urban schools. The story continues by naming some of the reasons for students' misbehavior, including traumatic home lives and environments. Many of us retell this narrative. For example, I recently attended a talk by a progressive young Black theologian who reiterated that restorative justice is necessary to address students' behavioral problems caused by multiple forms of trauma. But even when we point to a myriad of veritable root causes for students' harmful behavior, we still unwittingly advance the story that the bad behavior of students, and especially that of Black, Indigenous, students of color, is the *primary* site of harm that restorative justice practices are instituted to resolve.

Additional sites of harm experienced by youth are missing from these stories. Narratives of restorative justice in education are also missing accounts of the students who are largely responsible for bringing restorative justice policies and practices into their schools and school districts as a result of their advocacy and organizing efforts (Stith, 2021). Moreover, mainstream stories of restorative justice in education are largely devoid of the understandings, frameworks, narratives, and visions that these students develop and promote in the process. While dominant understandings have enabled important educational reforms, they also constrain the liberatory potential of restorative justice in the lives of Black students, in particular. We need new narratives of restorative justice.

Critical Race Theory highlights the power of counternarratives to deconstruct and subvert dominant stories that have harmful, racialized impacts, and advance emancipatory analysis. Counter-stories are also critical for addressing gaps in agendas for liberal reforms, identifying unintended consequences, and broadening platforms for social justice. Informed by Critical Race Theory, I am particularly interested in the points at which youth organizers' analyses diverge from the discourses reflected in dominant narratives, or stock stories, of restorative justice in schools. Historian and criminologist Howard Zehr has posited that holding a restorative philosophy of justice leads one to ask, "What harm has been done?" "Who has been hurt?" "What are their needs?" "Who has the responsibility to meet these needs?" and "What is the appropriate process to involve those impacted in an effort to make things right?" (Zehr 2002). Translating these questions into a theoretical lens informed by Critical Race Theory, I call stories that contain responses to these questions "restorative justice narratives." In the next two sections of this essay, I share two examples of how youth organizers construct and communicate restorative justice narratives—significant moments at which they advance their critical perspectives on the harms and needs students experience at school, those responsible for meeting the needs engendered by harms, and the appropriate processes to facilitate healing and repair that involve those most impacted. As these snapshots illuminate, youth organizers articulate restorative justice narratives within the context of organizing for safe and nonviolent schools that position restorative justice as a philosophy and practice that encompasses intersectional racial justice.

The Philadelphia Student Union "Protests All Forms of Violence"

The Philadelphia Student Union (PSU) was started in 1995 by 12 Philadelphia high school students to give public school students a voice and leadership in improving the quality of their education by changing educational policy and practice. PSU organizes direct action campaigns that have led to increases in public school funding and resources, the implementation of restorative justice practices and student-led training of police officers in their school buildings, among many other major impacts. In 2008, PSU became a founding organizational member of the Alliance for Educational Justice (AEJ).

On Martin Luther King Day in 2009, PSU launched the Campaign for Nonviolent Schools to transform school safety policies (Dzurinko, McCants, & Stith, 2011). Three major incidents to which PSU responded were critical in the formation of the campaign: a lockdown at one high school in which "three dozen armed police flooded the building," the existence of a form of corporal punishment at another high school, and a series of attacks on Asian immigrant students by some African American students at a third high school. In an article published in 2011, co-authored with then-PSU executive director Nijmie Dzurinko and AEJ's national organizing director Jonathan Stith (2011), we discuss how PSU developed a vision of school safety built from an intersectional analysis of violence that names and connects police abuse, disinvestment in schools and communities, fights among students, and student abuses by school staff. Drawing from Dr. King's holistic analysis of violence and nonviolence, PSU's youth organizers defined violence as "power that hurts," nonviolence as "power that helps"; and through the latter, situated their own organizing efforts as forms of nonviolent resistance. Later, they expanded their definition of violence to "the power to hurt someone's chances at survival." PSU advances these reframed understandings of school violence and safety through the narratives they tell while organizing for nonviolent schools, a vision that encompasses restorative justice.

On December 14, 2014, students from PSU and two other local organizations, Boat People SOS, and Asian Americans United staged a die-in in front of the headquarters of the Philadelphia School Reform Commission, which governed Philadelphia's public schools from 2011 to 2018. Over 200 students lay on the ground together in the aftermath of grand jury decisions not to indict the police officers responsible for the deaths of Eric Garner and Michael Brown. Earlier in the month, students at high schools throughout Philadelphia held die-ins for the same reason in solidarity with similar protests happening in other cities. However, on this occasion students lay on the ground for six minutes to also honor and bring attention to the story of Laporshia Massey, a sixth grader who died of an asthma attack that she had at school. Because there was no school nurse, the 12-year-old was sent home after she told a school volunteer, "I can't breathe." The Philadelphia Student Union released a statement about their action entitled, "Philadelphia Students Die-In to Protest All Forms of Violence." In the statement, they say:

> We, at the Philadelphia Student Union, define violence as "the power to hurt someone's chances at survival." Violence can take place interpersonally, but it can also happen in a system or institution. When Darren Wilson shot unarmed 18-year-old Mike Brown, that was violence. When our "justice" system refused to indict the killers of Mike Brown and Eric Garner, that was violence. It is violence not because it shows that the justice system does not work on behalf of Black people, but rather because it proves that this system was never designed to protect Black people. . . . This system does not rehabilitate, it destroys Black lives and breaks apart black families. Our education system, too, is broken and violent.

They go on to place Laporshia's death in this continuum of antiblack state violence.

> Laporshia's death was a result of a state government that refused to provide adequate funding to its Blackest school district. Laporshia's death was a result of the actions (and inaction) of local politicians and school district officials committed to the privatization of our schools and city, regardless of the costs on human lives. When our schools are intentionally lacking nurses, counselors, books, all the things we need to be successful and safe, it is not only criminal, it's violence. Cuts to education don't happen in a vacuum, decisions to cut resources from school is systematic and it is disproportionately affecting Black students.

They close the statement by listing their demands including increased funding for counselors, nurses, and social workers, and an end to school closures, new prisons, and prison expansion in Philadelphia and the state of Pennsylvania. Youth organizers from PSU and other groups in the Alliance continued to recount the story of Laporshia's death in their efforts to shift debates and approaches to school violence and safety, while demanding that the budgets for school police be redistributed to pay for school nurses and medical supplies in schools, mental and emotional health staff, afterschool programming, and restorative justice specialists. However, Masssey was not the only child who died at a Philadelphia public school after a health crisis ensued and there was no school nurse present to provide medical assistance (Lee, 2014).

PSU's accounting of anti-Black violence is a restorative justice counternarrative that explicitly links neoliberal disinvestments in education, police violence, and carceral expansion. Critical theorists have argued that carceral expansion and neoliberal economic policies marked by privatization, deregulation, and public disinvestment are "two sides of the same political coin" (Wacquant, 2010). While restorative justice is on the surface mobilized to interrupt the neoliberal-carceral policies and practices, dominant discourses of restorative justice in schools that over-emphasize individual "responsibilization" and "student accountability" risk reification of racialized neoliberal logics and co-optation by neoliberal school reform agendas (O'Brien & Nygreen, 2020). In addition, an exclusive focus on racialized disciplinary policies obscures additional means by which students are hurt by institutional violence linked to racial neoliberalism and carceral expansion. PSU's protest against "all forms of violence" centers student voices demanding that state institutions change the conditions that threaten students' survival. It also designates institutional and social change, particularly investments in resources that support students' well-being and disinvestments in policing and prisons, as the most appropriate processes for healing and repair.

The Alliance for Education Justice and the #AssaultatSpringValley

As a national network, the Alliance for Educational Justice reflects the analysis and vision of local organizing groups like the PSU, providing a platform where student-led organizations working at the local level can learn from one another and build power. National campaigns are one of the mechanisms through which AEJ's local organizers work toward common goals developed through collective analyses and vision. In September 2017, AEJ launched a national campaign for police-free schools. Rooted in students' direct experiences with violence at the hands of school police, the campaign was launched after a series of police assaults against students from 2015 through 2017, beginning with the assault of a 15-year-old girl by a school resource officer at Spring Valley High School in Columbia, South Carolina.

The campaign faced major obstacles amid increasing efforts to put more police in schools and arm school staff in the wake of the mass shooting at Parkland Florida's Marjory Stoneman Douglas High School in February 2018. Despite these challenges, in November 2018, AEJ released a report and action kit co-authored with the Advancement Project, a civil rights organization, called, "We Came to Learn: A Call to Action for Police-Free Schools" (Advancement Project and Alliance for Educational Justice, 2018). The report narrates the historical advent of policing into US schools in the mid-20th century as attempts to suppress rising Black and Chicano student movements. It also presents case studies of school police violence against Black students' and youth organizing groups' responses, and a mapping of 58 known assaults perpetrated on students by school police officers from November 2010 to March 2018. The map is a product of a connected campaign that AEJ created and called the #Assaultat-campaign, an effort to track and bring increased awareness to students' experiences of police violence in schools as part of their efforts to increase student safety by removing police and resourcing schools to meet students' physical, psychological, and social needs. With each assault, they develop a new hashtag with the name of the school where the student was violated by a school police officer (#Assaultatcampaign) to circulate the stories. As part of the campaign, they developed an interactive map and website to track police assaults against students in schools.

October 2015: The #AssaultatSpringValley

The #Assaultat campaign was created after Niya Kenney, a student at Spring Valley High School in South Carolina, recorded a police officer assaulting her fellow student, Shakara, in their math class. Their teacher called an administrator to report that Shakara did not put away her cell phone in class when asked to do so. The administrator then called in the school resource officer, Ben Fields. I have chosen not to recount the horrendous and gruesome details of the white police officer's brutality against Shakara, a 16-year-old Black girl, which has been circulated widely on the news and over social media. As the police officer began to brutalize Shakara, Niya yelled out, "Isn't anyone going to help her?" "Y'all cannot do this!" Both girls were charged with "disturbing schools," a misdemeanor in South Carolina. There were many beautiful and powerful means by which people responded to support these two students, particularly youth organizers in AEJ. I will share one moment. In November 2015, Niya Kenney was honored at a national gathering for youth organizers organized by the Funders Collaborative for Youth Organizing. After she told her story on stage, AEJ members read and delivered her letters of love and solidarity shared by youth organizers from around the United States (Stith, 2021). AEJ youth organizers' restorative justice counternarratives include the story of Shakara *and* Niya as a focal point.

AEJ defines police-free schools as "Dismantling school policing infrastructure, culture, and practice; ending school militarization and surveillance; and building a new liberatory education system" (Alliance for Educational Justice, n.d.). Within the context of their campaign for police-free schools, AEJ's youth organizers emphasize how school staff responded to Shakara having her cell phone out in class. This, youth organizers attest, is evidence that restorative justice is necessary because Black, Indigenous, young, people of color are being harmed by racist and demonizing interpretations and institutionally sanctioned violent responses to normal student behavior. Whereas dominant narratives of restorative justice often implicate punitive responses to student behavior, youth organizers' counternarratives go much further to also implicate how their behavior is being defined through the lens of antiblack racism and connected systems of oppression including adultism, heterosexism, ableism, and patriarchy. Their claim is also consistent with research that identifies "noncompliance," "willful defiance," and "insubordination" as the primary reasons cited for the suspensions of Black, Indigenous, students of color in US schools, particularly Black girls (Morris, 2016).

Significantly, AEJ's organizers chose to center the story of a young woman assaulted by the police as they narrate the problem of police violence in schools, in contrast to dominant narratives of police violence that center on cisgender Black men. In *PushOut: The Criminalization of Black Girls in Schools*, scholar-activist Monique Morris describes how Black girls, more than any other student group, are excluded from or arrested in their schools, often quite violently as in the case of Shakara, for behavior that educators deem "irate," "insubordinate," "disrespectful," "uncooperative," or "uncontrollable" (Morris 2016, 11). It has been suggested that the confluence of racialized and gendered expectations by school staff predominantly comprised of white (cisgender) women, the school-to-prison nexus, and the apparatus of school policing lead Black girls to be especially vulnerable and targeted. Emphasizing resistance and resilience alongside repression, AEJ's youth organizers also center the role of Niya to amplify how students are already acting to intervene in racialized state violence in their schools, despite the risk. This narrative choice is also consistent with the Black Lives Matter movement's vision of centering the leadership and experiences of Black people who are most marginalized, including Black women, girls, and femmes.

The Black Lives Matter movement has also brought greater public awareness to Black people killed by police after engaging in mundane behaviors and actions like jogging, sleeping, taking out a wallet, or getting a traffic ticket. A popular but unattributed post circulated on social media in the summer of 2020 read:

> We can't go jogging (#AmaudArbery).
> We can't relax in the comfort of our own homes (#BothemSean and #AtatianaJefferson).
> We can't ask for help after being in a car crash (#JonathanFerrell and #RenishaMcBride).
> We can't have a cellphone (#StephonClark).
> We can't leave a party to get to safety (#JordanEdwards).
> We can't play loud music (#JordanDavis).
> We can't sell CDs (#AltonSterling).
> We can't sleep (#AiyanaJones).
> We can't walk from the corner store (#MikeBrown).
> We can't play cops and robbers (#TamirRice).

We can't go to church (#Charleston9).

We can't walk home with Skittles (#TrayvonMartin).

We can't hold a hairbrush while leaving our own bachelor party (#SeanBell).

We can't party on New Year's (#OscarGrant).

We can't get a normal traffic ticket (#SandraBland).

We can't lawfully carry a weapon (#PhilandoCastile).

We can't break down on a public road with car problems (#CoreyJones).

We can't shop at Walmart (#JohnCrawford).

We can't have a disabled vehicle (#TerrenceCrutcher).

We can't read a book in our own car (#KeithScott).

We can't be a 10-year-old walking with our grandfather (#Clifford Glover).

We can't decorate for a party (#ClaudeReese).

We can't ask a cop a question (#RandyEvans).

We can't cash our check in peace (#YvonneSmallwood).

We can't take out our wallet (#AmadouDiallo).

We can't run (#WalterScott).

We can't breathe (#EricGarner).

We can't live (#FreddieGray).

This accounting not only reflects the demonization of Black drylongso in and around our homes and neighborhoods but also in the hallways and class-rooms of our schools.

AEJ's youth organizers construct restorative justice narratives that define exclusion, criminalization, and police violence experienced by Black students engaged in mundane teenage behaviors—like having a cell phone out in class—as among the primary harms that they face in schools. These narratives, such as the #AssaultatSpringValley, have been central to the development of their vision for police-free schools, which they see as an obligation of school districts and state governments to provide to make schools safer for students who experience racialized state violence. AEJ also lifts up the story of the Toronto District School Board's removal of police from public schools in 2017 and the long-term racial justice organizing that led to this change (Stith, 2018). This story from Toronto, Canada, also presents community organizing as a necessary process to work for repair, as well as sustained participation in intersectional and transnational racial justice movements. As the snapshots in this essay demonstrate, student organizing for police-free schools began long before the increased visibility of calls to defund police in the wake of the vigilante murder of Ahmaud Arbery, and the police murders of Breonna Taylor, Tony McDade, and George Floyd. By the end of 2020, at least 100 school districts had pledged to move police out of their district's school buildings. Youth organizers laid the foundations for these wins over many years—creating and promoting new narratives about safety and justice through their campaigns, education, research, and media.

CONCLUSION

Youth organizers' restorative justice narratives disrupt the invisibility of racialized state and structural violence against youth that is commonplace within schools. They center how not only young men but also young women are targeted by police violence in schools; they also share how gender-expansive and gender-nonconforming youth, youth with disabilities, and gay, lesbian, bisexual, and transgender youth are especially impacted by state violence in educational institutions. In addition to the state-sanctioned violence students face at the hands of police in schools, youth organizers' restorative justice narratives challenge the erasure of structural violence in schools from narratives of school violence. Their narratives also link the absence of necessary resources for students to the presence of school resource officers. Through neoliberal economic shifts, money spent on policing is diverted away from what students need to be physically and emotionally healthy including school nurses, school counselors, and school psychologists. Youth organizers' restorative justice narratives of harms, needs, responsibilities, and repair make visible the racialized harms done to entire communities of students, particularly Black youth. Arising from youth organizers' multifaceted analysis of anti-Black violence, removing police from schools, providing students with access to necessary resources and services, and institutionalizing restorative justice practices are all necessary, complementary, and corollary actions to uphold the dignity and sanctity of Black life within educational institutions.

Youth organizers' restorative justice narratives point to three narrative shifts that are critical when scholars and practitioners tell stories about restorative justice in schools. First, when we ask, what is the harm and who has been impacted, we must shift from telling stories that name student deviance as the primary and most substantial harm to stories about institutional domination and oppression. We must tell stories that call attention to the racialized forms of state and structural violence that students experience in schools. Second, when we ask, what is the process to bring people together to make things right, we must shift from telling stories in which young people are merely the recipients of benevolent action by school officials and adult advocates to those in which students appear as agents of change. We must center the stories of youth organizers that are primarily responsible for bringing restorative justice to their schools. Third, when we ask, what is needed to make things right, we must share the emancipatory visions of youth organizers: visions of nonviolent schools, of police-free schools, and of antiracist schools.

Restorative justice must not be introduced as a more effective "management" strategy or as a solution to student disciplinary problems but as a paradigm that helps schools to center the voices of young people, end racial and gendered violence, and heal the harms of educational injustice. In the words of my brilliant friend and colleague Jonathan Stith (2021), "RJE [Restorative justice in education] practitioners must see themselves as politicized healers, view restorative justice in education as the antithesis to the school-to-prison pipeline, and understand restorative justice as a prefigurative practice place of the society we seek to transform." Reflecting on their student activism to reframe debates on immigration and incarceration, a group of undocumented college students along with their professor wrote, "*Living* counternarratives—those that take shape in the real world—cannot be constructed and sustained only by scholars working on theory, but rather in practice by grassroots action and collectives of people whose work is driven primarily by lived experience and necessity" (Dominguez et al. 2009). With this in mind, let us amplify the living counternarratives of youth organizers and activists who define and envision a restorative justice that has the potential to make Black lives matter in schools.

CHAPTER 24

Hope and Healing

···

mily Dickinson pictured hope as "the thing with feathers that perches in the soul, and sings the tune without the words, and never stops at all." Tupac Shakur noted hope as the persistence of the rose growing through cracks in concrete.

Against a backdrop of urban political machinations, manipulated racial tensions, and systemic injustice, Gerson Ramirez and Henry Cervantes, both Chicagoans, reflect on possibilities for hope.

—Mary Adams Trujillo

· ·

Politics of Hope and Healing: Lessons from Chicago

Gerson Ramirez and Henry Cervantes

Gerson: My interest in the politics of hope is grounded in my experience growing up in a working-class neighborhood, Albany Park. As a child of Guatemalan immigrants and deeply religious parents, I was constantly reminded to live with hope and to believe in the possibility of a better future.

As a child, my neighborhood school lacked resources. There were times when students like me didn't have a proper classroom, so we jumped from the lunchroom to the basement and to closets at times. Through dealing with other factors that played a role—the local gangs, the poverty, and violence in my neighborhood—it seemed there was little hope. I spent most of my time as a high school and college student working on grassroots campaigns and community organizations because I believed that a better future was possible. I realized that to bridge that gap required more than hoping it to be possible. Seeking more tools to problem-solve and improve Chicago's impoverished people's conditions, I enrolled in the master's of public policy program at the University of Michigan in 2018. There the concept of hope reappeared, and I realized I had it all wrong. Hope is not solely about believing in a particular outcome. Hope is a multidimensional concept with an imperative social component. Hope is

···

a relationship with a community, believing in the desired outcome, and most importantly, working to build that future together.

One of the major factors that contribute to Chicago's hopelessness is its political culture created by "The Machine." The Machine is a hierarchical organizational system, a semiformal political network that reaches down through neighborhood and local organizers to respond to the problems of individual neighborhoods, or even families, in exchange for loyalty during elections. This is not exclusive to Chicago, as machine politics exist throughout the nation. In Chicago, it was a result of explosive immigration and migration to many cities in the 19th century. This sort of system has been fundamental to maintaining, and at times enforcing gun violence, segregation, and a culture of corruption. This problem of corruption is known to any person in Chicago who watches the news. The leaders in government are consistent in doing unscrupulous acts that produce anger, fear, cynicism, and lack of the trust that is needed to build any kind of hope in the community. A political system concerned only with maintaining power ultimately produces a culture of despair, an absence of trust. Trust within the community must be built with a shared vision of progress that is worth hoping for. This kind of relationship must transform into a covenant, meaning the community needs to hold each other accountable and commit to working on the shared vision of progress.

Chicago has 77 neighborhoods and a lot of the neighborhoods are identified by their ethnic identity. However, it is not a coincidence that Mexicans live together, but separate from Puerto Ricans, and the Irish separate from Italians. In 1934 when Congress created the Federal Housing Administration (FHA), they were charged with administering funds to assist people with their mortgages. As they administered a program to help people buy homes, they did so with a grading system that rated risk factors. Real estate companies created maps that showed green areas, which were rated as "A," to indicate "in-demand" neighborhoods. These neighborhoods were considered excellent prospects for insurance and investment. However, the neighborhoods where black people lived were rated "D" and were usually considered ineligible for FHA support. Black people were viewed by the FHA as devaluing property values and increasing risk. The US federal government was not alone in practicing redlining as a tactic to segregate the public. The private sector also created maps and were hesitant to give loans to black buyers.

Today there are 18 neighborhoods where more than 90% of the population is black. It's easy to forget that many of the tools to analyze real estate and racial data were created in Chicago and other cities looked to see what Chicago was doing. Tools like restrictive covenants were created in the city to legally limit type of people who can own property. These contracts were not only legally binding but they were used as a tactic to continue segregation into the 20th century. Years later, the marks of segregation and systemic and structural racism can be illustrated by gun violence faced today, mostly concentrated in working-class neighborhoods where the concentration of people is largely black or Latino. Most of the violence is away from the Loop, which is the downtown area where most economic activity occurs.

Henry: Due to the history of segregation in Chicago, Black and Brown communities neighbor one another. Yet, the forces of oppression always seek to turn neighbor against neighbor so that a real community is not possible. This was true between my neighborhood of Little Village, which is a Mexican immigrant neighborhood, and North Lawndale, which is a Black neighborhood. Youth and community activists mobilized several types of demonstrations to bring the Greater Lawndale community together to address anti-Blackness that resurfaced in my community as a result of looting that occurred during the Black Lives Matter protests following George Floyd's murder by police. That is the history of humanity, the constant struggle among peoples to form part of a beloved community.

As a Mexican American growing up in Chicago, I often wondered why we are referred to as the "inner city" in the first place, when Black and Brown communities make up the majority. We are the city!

In Chicago, Black and brown communities have been devastated by decades of systemic oppression, disinvestment, and neglect. It is no secret that the violence and devastation caused by those social evils often define our communities to the outside world. But violence is the direct result of oppression. Our ghettos, neighborhoods, and barrios are seen as dangerous and decaying places in the "inner city." Currently in Chicago, the communities with the highest rates of COVID-19 infections have been those zip codes with majority Black and Brown residents. According to data published by the Latino Policy Forum, my neighborhood of Little Village and neighboring North Lawndale rank first in death rate due to COVID-19 compared to all other zip codes in Cook County, Illinois. Moreover, in Illinois, the Black and Latino population has contracted COVID-19 at over two and three times the rate of the white population, respectively. The virus has made visible what has always been hidden in plain sight: the huge racial disparities of health and wealth in American society. As the impact of COVID-19 rises, so does the violence in our neighborhoods. How do we begin to heal the wounds of such traumatic and violent realities that continue to plague our neighborhoods?

GR: To apply the conventional version of hope in this context would be to overlook the pain that the neighborhoods have faced. There is anger, frustration, and fear in the community, so it is wrong to ask people to simply change their attitude to be more positive, or to act as if the experiences and suffering does not exist. "Hope" is thrown around so loosely that some think the word is interchangeable with a positive attitude and expectation. So, it is fair for people to be skeptical, but the skeptic might confuse hope with optimism or naivete. Applying optimism is more of an attitude, and a sense of confidence that the situation will get better. Hope has very little to do with attitude of the individual or community. It would be naïve to ignore the dire circumstances in a situation. True hope does not do that—true hope is an existential relationship that is instituted in the trust of another person and their shared vision of future conditions. This means that constructing hope is a covenant that bonds the individual and their vision of progress, with the collective. False hope is telling a fourth grader that they will score well on standardized tests despite having to rely on substitute teachers and the lack of services to support their instruction. Or, telling neighbors that the gun violence will stop after a gang war was initiated. This false sense of hope is how many understand the word. I am not simply arguing that the people who have witnessed gun violence, segregation, or corruption should change their attitude toward their living conditions. What I am asking is after the *politics of despair* becomes the status quo, and I believe that is the case in Chicago, like many other cities, what should the witnesses, survivors, and spectators do? How can struggling communities overcome anger and fear-based politics of despair that fuel gun violence, distrust of new arrivals in the neighborhood, and feeling of powerlessness.

HC: Angela Davis once said, "It is in collectivities that we find reservoirs of hope and activism." To me, this means that thinking as a collective, thinking in terms of we, us, and ours can help us find the hope and the courage to transform reality. It can encourage us to find our collective power. Hope, just like fear, are the greatest motivators.

The good news is that faith, belief, and hope can help us build community amid such chaos.

For those of us who believe and have hope in Jesus, it is not enough to just believe, we must act and do as if our hopes depended on how we live our lives. I would say that hope is not just wishful thinking, it is actually hard work. It is knowing that how we live our lives are our testament of our deepest hopes. I remember a friend of mine once wearing a baseball cap with the words "Hope Dealer." Apart from being the coolest cap I'd ever seen, I thought to myself, we need more people dealing in that type of work. To have hope and deal in hope is to be bold in this world.

GR: I emphasize the relationship component because in communities that suffer, entrusting is a difficult task. So, building hope is first about building trust with and within the community. From trust, one can construct a shared vision of the improvement of conditions. The shared vision of improvement is the covenant in which the actors are responsible for keeping. But how can survivors and witnesses who have directly and indirectly experienced the pain of gun violence, corruption, segregation, and other forms of systemic and structural racism have hope?

HC: What brings me great hope is the ancestors who came before us, the ancestors who waged their own struggles for our liberation. Our black, brown, and indigenous ancestors who taught us ways to continue the struggle for social change. There is a remarkable history of Black and Brown unity, dating back to the Great Migrations of African Americans and Mexicans to Chicago. These communities have always lived side by side, sharing an often hidden heritage of Black and Brown solidarity and healing in our movements for change and social justice. Our local history remembers names like Lucy Gonzales Parsons, Fred Hampton, and Rudy Lozano, who dedicated their lives to racial solidarity, struggle, and healing. Black and Brown cultural resistance work continues in Chicago to this day.

We try to bridge Black communities like Englewood to Brown communities like The Back of the Yards. For the past several years, we have organized Black and Brown Unity events in the form of African and Aztec healing ceremonies held within communities impacted by violence. We do this with the support of local community members and organizations.

Our ceremonies are one way to unify Black and Brown communities through cultural racial healing.

The pandemic isolated many of our people who are struggling to meet their basic needs. Part of those needs are also emotional and spiritual. Our ceremonies are one way to unify Black and Brown communities through cultural racial healing. This is embodied in a saying: *La cultura cura*, or culture heals. In 2020, during the pandemic, African and Aztec dance groups, Xochitl-Quetzal, and in collaboration with two local organizations—Healing Every Youth and Culture Saving—often held ceremonies along the dividing lines between Black and Brown communities. In this way, our cultural resistance work continues to hold sacred space in places for healing.

These songs and dances connect healing practices to the broader movement, the oral tradition, and spiritual resistance of our peoples' lives.

GR: What hope should Chicago have? When time and time again people work to build hope to only have it be destroyed by systems like machine politics. I remind myself that hope is like (plants) striving to reach the horizon, the horizon which keeps getting further from me as I walk toward it. While we never fully reach the purest version of this hope, at least I walked and I did so with my neighbors. Ultimately people (we) have to see that our progress is tied to each other. We can we grow and learn from our collective struggles. Our empathy and action build relational covenants that reinforce hope. So, as simplistic as it may sound, the communities of Chicago, and other struggling districts, we are roses and yes, we have bruised petals but we as communities must learn to celebrate our tenacity and our inherent ability to grow. Ultimately, every community has to recognize and acknowledge that its goals and struggles represent one people working and hoping together striving to improve everyone's quality of life, starting with the most vulnerable.

HC: When I think of hope, I think of volition, the desire and motivation that drives us to make something better a reality. Most importantly how do we bring that into existence?

We host the ceremony at the intersection of Ogden and Lawndale Avenue, the dividing line between North Lawndale and Little Village. On that intersection is a corner store and an auto body shop with a mural of Martin Luther King Jr. and Cesar Chavez. In these businesses, Black and Brown people work together every day. These ceremonies are rooted in healing rituals dating back to before the enslavement of African peoples and the conquest of Mexicans in North America. At these ceremonies, African and Aztec dancers smudge each other with traditional copal and sage, herbs to heal each other, in a sign of respect. The drummers gather to play rhythms and songs that have existed for many centuries. The ceremony begins with an offering of thanks to the four cardinal directions, thanking the ancestors for passing on these traditional ways to each generation. Talking circles provide a sacred space for community members to gather to speak, reflect, process, and heal. Dressed in ceremonial regalia, the dancers form a circle and take turns offering their prayers in forms of dance. The ritual helps tell the stories of our survival, I am amazed at how the instruments used in African and Aztec dances are so similar—the drums, ankle shakers, even the beadwork on the regalia, with their bright colors and patterns sharing similar characteristics. The structure of the dance groups are similar, as well as the dance formations and the fact that it is mostly women who are keeping these cultures alive. These common traits connect these dance traditions, despite the geographic distance between their origins.

Portions of this article were previously published on the website Waging Nonviolence, reprinted with permission of the owners: https://wagingnonviolence.org/2020/11/cultural-rituals-healing-solidarity-black-brown-communities/.

CHAPTER 25

Credible Witnesses and Testimonies

. . . .

R*ayshauna Gray and Hasshan Batts offer reflections and radical strategies to become "we/us/ours."*

—Mary Adams Trujillo

. . . .

Heart Work

Rayshauna Gray

In 2017, I created something that would help more people than I could've ever imagined. I was working at Harvard Business School and my imposter syndrome was raging. I won't rehash everything, but all the old standards showed up.

Self-doubt? **Present!** Depression-induced forgetfulness? **Here (not)!** Anxiety? **Here first!** My struggles were an issue. And it was clear that I couldn't move forward until I faced them.

I am a person with no college degree who's helping her mom live a full and meaningful life. Somebody with a father serving a life sentence in the Florida prison. Grandkid of sharecroppers, but I'm literally influencing how policy gets made on a federal level because certain people listen to me. And I never thought it. At some point, it was a self-esteem thing, because I still don't have a college degree. Who would have guessed, but I really took stock of what my own energy brings to life. It just, felt like everyone else had energy. And it was my existential or common cosmic homework to try to deal with it or interpret it. I've become the person who has gathered so much as a result of how fervently she saw it. People ask me stuff. And suddenly, I'm telling folks that I think of us as cultural beneficiaries, agents, and eventual ancestors, even if we don't have kids. And I think about how we inherit a world but, we are in another one that'll be released

. . . .

in a couple of episodes. We're not just wrestling with the world that we inherited, but we also have to be held accountable for what we allow to still grow.

Needing to find a healthy way to process my anxiety, I developed my #The HeartWork framework and started having difficult, transparent conversations about everything from shame to fear to workplace myths like meritocracy, and all the insecurities, -isms, and -phobias one could imagine with anyone who'd chat with me.

I was aware of the connection between our personal lives and our politics when I designed The Heart Work, but it was beautiful to see a room of people use it to interrogate personal wounds, reflect on their communities, and cultivate lasting positive change.

There we were in August 2019, all 40-something of us, unpacking what we'd been told about our "pathologically broken" neighborhoods and the convenient cultural narratives that allowed some of us to internalize it. There we were, countering those mistruths with what we know about areas of disinvestment. There we were doing the hard but necessary work of healing ourselves and ultimately our communities . . . starting with our stories. Because what's more powerful than the stories we tell ourselves about ourselves?

As I prepped for my November 2019 session with the Obama Foundation's Hartford cohort, I considered my Roseland community back home in Chicago, my current home in Cambridge's historic district, and all the things I'm equipped to do because of how much I love both.

Over 90 minutes, the 43 of us worked through my framework highlighting what imposter syndrome tries to convince us of, how society bolsters those mistruths, and how we can do good work while being anchored in love for ourselves and our communities.

When I first created my framework, I had a broken heart and a fractured sense of self. I literally weep with joy each time I facilitate. I'm honored every time. Growing up, folks said, "Teach from your scars, not your wounds." While I agree when it comes to certain circumstances, the radical vulnerability we embody when sharing our healing processes can be so cathartic.

I've become a healer by taking a cold, hard look at my story and empowering others to do the same. Something magical happens when a group of people enter a room and choose to unfurl the tightly coiled personas and stories they deal in every single day.

People come to my sessions because they are often ashamed, seemingly "alone," and exhausted. Then, something magical happens. I walk people through the underside of my life in eight columns, launching into my deepest "stuff" (responsibly and nimbly) so that others can see how I process, diagnose, and choose to structure my (un)learning and healing. They perk up, they cry, they marvel at themselves and one another. They pour into one another, offering tangible support and encouragement. They shake off isolation by choosing to heal in the community. And I don't know about you, but I'm better able to engineer the spaces I want when I'm motivated by love, sustained by a healthy sense of self, and firmly rooted in my values.

. . . .

Radical Welcome

Hasshan Batts

I was 11 years old when I found my grandmother dead on the kitchen floor. I was 11 years old when I was suspended from school, I was 11 years old the first time I was arrested. I was afraid, I felt alone, and I was angry. I wish someone would have asked me if I was okay. I know what it feels like to be rejected, kicked out, suspended, expelled, asked to leave, divorced, locked up, and placed in solitary confinement.

I was left back in kindergarten, left back again in the seventh grade. I spent three years in the ninth grade, and I was pushed out of high school after the 11th grade into prison. I'm a prison survivor, a son, a brother, a father, a husband, a grandfather, a neighbor, a healer, a storyteller. I'm a community epidemiologist and a community-based participatory researcher and what that means is that I've learned to listen to people and encourage and support you in telling and owning your own story, rather than telling your story for you, rather than commodifying, publishing and benefiting from creating solutions for people that possess the brilliance, passion, and creativity to produce solutions for themselves.

I worked in a juvenile justice facility with a young man named Rahim. He was a beautiful, brilliant, and charismatic young man, and Pennsylvania requires that youth sentenced for a violent crime write a victim impact letter prior to being released. Rahim vehemently refused to write the letter, extending his stay for months and possibly years. When I started working with Rahim as his therapist, I asked him why the resistance? Why was he refusing to write the letter? Rahim told me story after story of growing up in an abusive home and of living in a violent community where he had to fight bullies every day to get home safe to an unsafe environment. Rahim said to me with tears in his eyes, "Ain't no one write me no damn letter all the times I was a victim." Rahim's experiences led me to research and recognize that over 60% of violent offenders have been victims of crime. Imagine a world where Rahim and children like him were asked, "How can I help rather than be rejected, kicked out, locked up, or thrown away for expressing their pain?" Imagine if they were greeted with a radical welcome.

Imagine if Rahim were greeted with a radical welcome that affirmed his greatness, that affirmed he belonged and that reminded him that he was connected to a community that loved him and believed in him and believed in his best self. Radical welcome greets you with a radiating smile. It takes the time to learn your name, and perhaps the most radical part, it forgives you and welcomes you back into the community when you do harm, and don't show up as your best self. I knew the first thing we had to do was implement a no-reject, no-eject policy at the facility, a policy that states you are more than the worst thing you've ever done. A policy that states that we know that you will not always show up as your best self, but we will not vote you off the island, a policy that states that you are greater than your bad days. My colleagues and I intentionally created a space where accountability and compassion could co-exist. A space where Rahim and youth like him could share their pain and experiences and at times act out and not be othered or voted off the island.

What we learned is that lessons like compassion, respect, forgiveness, and empathy are not taught, they're modeled through a radical welcome that creates connectivity and safety and a sense of belonging. And we know that when people feel welcomed, they show up different. When I was at my worst, Mama Batts would lean down and whisper in my ear, "Baby, when you decide to put half of the energy you put into doing the right thing that you put into doing the wrong thing, you're going to change the world." When I was at my worst, and I got a little bigger, she would tippy-toe and reach out to me and say, "Boy, when you decide to put half of the energy you put into doing the wrong thing into doing the right thing, you're going to change the world."

Everyone needs a Mama Batts in their life that will see past our errors and see greatness in us and tell us our true story. But Mama Batts wasn't enough to keep me safe, because I was born into a world that hated and rejected me, and naturally, it taught me to hate myself. When our children attend schools with police officers instead of counselors, when they're followed around stores, suspended, judged, and further rejected for expressing their pain, they will find welcome and belonging in other ways, often through gangs, crime, promiscuity, and drugs.

Tupac Shakur spoke for a whole generation of rejected urban youth when he suggested that he hung around the thugs despite their dealing drugs because they "showed a young brother love." Even with a mother that stepped in when the rest of the world stepped out, I went astray, because we need a radical welcome that extends beyond that one caring adult that every child deserves. We need a community that internalizes and epitomizes, we all belong. We need a community where our worth and greatness are constantly being affirmed from the moment we walk in the door, to the moment we leave.

I recently spent two weeks in Senegal and learned firsthand about what's called Senegalese *teranga*. *Teranga* is a Wolof word that means extreme hospitality. There's no English equivalent because it doesn't exist here. It's the way you get off a plane and people embrace you like you've known them your entire life, and they smile and tell you welcome home upon finding out that you're an African American. You know how we walk down the street face in our phone and ask someone how are you? And we really don't care. We don't want to hear about the grocery list, we don't want to hear about your sciatica and we definitely don't want to hear about your hemorrhoids. Well, in Senegal, I experienced a genuine interest and concern for my well-being from strangers. It felt like a sense of belonging, when constantly welcomed with a smile, a warm embrace, invited to share a large meal out of a communal bowl with strangers. Senegalese *teranga* didn't appear overnight, it was developed during times of colonialism and postcolonialism to fight the racism of the French. It was developed because the Senegalese knew that difference has the power to other and destroy us. And they knew that all the ethnic groups that were dealing with the oppression and white supremacy during that time from the French would split, and it would develop a hatred among them if they didn't begin to work together. During the 15th and 16th centuries, the collective trauma of the black Holocaust in Africa empowered the groups to join and to learn to create an identity that was centered around welcome so that difference did not set them apart. It is so ingrained and institutionalized in Senegal that their soccer team is called the lions of *teranga*. Leaders across Senegal knew this. And to this day, they stay committed to it and you can feel it everywhere you go, in everything they do, because they epitomize a radical welcome. They showed me what it feels like to experience the critical questions that are at the heart of it. How are you? Are you safe? Are you okay? How can I help? I couldn't help but think about feelings of rejection I had experienced as a child and witnessing the countless youth and adults like Rahim in the detention centers, mental health facilities, and programs and community settings in which I worked and resided. And I wondered, what would our lives have been like, had we been greeted with a radical welcome?

Let me share a story of what a radical welcome looks like in practice. Jose is a community college student that I learned about from his business professor while he was finishing a 14-year prison sentence for drug possession. His professor would call me every week and tell me about Jose's progress, about his 3.9 grade point average and that he wanted him to come to our agency when he returned home. We were the only ones that he felt would greet him and accept him the way that he needs to be accepted because he has spent half his life incarcerated and decades as a veteran gang member.

The day Jose was released his professor personally drove him to the center where he was greeted with a radical welcome. He was greeted with that smile. He has been back every day since. He mentors youth, he walks youth home that are being bullied, he has a desk and support to finish his homework. He's a leader in our community, because he's found a place where he can return, he found a way that he can help the children and families in the community he contributed to destroying. He has found a place that welcomes and recognizes the best parts of him, a place where he can be restored, and teach and epitomize restorative practices. And if you ask Jose, what did he find? He'd say he found a home. He'll tell you, it's kind of like an episode of *Cheers*. When Norm walks into the bar, and everyone screams "Norm!" Imagine had Jose found radical welcome in school, imagine had he been greeted with a smile and encouragement, rather than being told he'd never amount to anything, that he would die in a pool of his own blood in junior high school. The people, the places, and how we show up stick with us and we often live up to the expectations of those that we encounter. Imagine how the most vulnerable among us would show up, if when at school, the library, and the mall we were treated like we belonged, like people were genuinely excited to see us, like we had a place and we are part of something larger than ourselves.

Radical welcome heals, it warms and inspires us to be our best, it increases accountability and reminds us that we are bigger than something than just ourselves. Imagine a world in which we practiced radical welcome, rather than reinforcing the behaviors that lead to criminal activity in a search for belonging. Imagine a world where the police aren't being called on a neighbor for playing their music too loud, when someone needs to use the bathroom and can't afford to buy a cup of coffee and the police are being called, or a young Black man wearing a hoodie can eat a pack of Skittles in peace because he belonged. I work with an organization called the Promise Neighborhoods at Lehigh Valley. And we're primarily led by volunteers that are prison survivors, formerly incarcerated, criminal justice involved, or who have been negatively impacted by the prison industrial complex. And what we learned in our work on our quest to help youth get from cradle to career is that safe and stable communities are critical to successful educational, health, and life outcomes.

We learned through surveying thousands of our community members, key stakeholder interviews and focus groups, that safety is of primary concern, regardless of race, age, socioeconomic level, or zip code. Our theory was that by practicing radical welcome, by creating an environment that fosters a sense of belonging, that embraces *teranga* and restorative practices we could decrease violence, and increase connectivity, and perceptions on safety.

What we learned from the 120 families that we partnered with in community-driven focus groups is that smiles matter, that names matter, and that greetings matter. We learned that people feel most welcomed in places with friends or family, in doctors and dentist's offices, in churches and bodegas. Our suspicions were affirmed that when people feel welcomed, they show up different. Our theory was that by practicing radical welcome, by creating an environment that fosters a sense of belonging, that by embracing and promoting *teranga* and restorative practices, we could decrease violence, and increase connectivity, and perceptions on safety.

My research and work within vulnerable and oppressed communities have taught me that there are three critical questions that our neighbors in crisis, often wish someone would ask. These three questions reinforce radical welcome. These three critical caring and compassionate questions sound kind of simple and they are. It begins again, with a smile, not a regular, small, but uncomfortably large smile. And by learning someone's name, it includes active listening, committing to what's important to the people that we encounter in the places that we show up every day. It's how we treat people like Rahim, Jose, and me when we don't show up as our best selves. It's how we define our neighbors that have made mistakes. I again invite you to imagine what would it look like every day to show up in the places that you show up every day with a radical welcome in all that you do? Imagine a world where every child, every struggling adult, every neighbor in wrestling with loneliness and isolation, every neighbor in recovery has someone that believes in them, sees the best in them and asks, "Are you okay? Are you safe? How can I help? Are you okay? Are you safe? How can I help? Are you okay? Are you safe? How can I help?" Rejection, zero tolerance, and retribution are the imperatives of our time. I propose we reimagine a world centered in radical welcome, healing, forgiveness. restorative practices, a world in which mistakes are forgiven and allowed to be made.

CHAPTER 26

Walking by Faith

···

H ow does a field whose ostensible aim is to make the world better and more equitable for all untangle and extricate itself from historic injustices, power imbalances, and hegemonic practices? For some, faith informs belief and action. As a follower of Jesus, my personal commitment is to walk out the work of reconciliation. In this case, "walking out" has meant writing collaboratively and in community, experimenting with diverse forms and formats of presentation, and prayerfully hoping this book will serve as encouragement and a guide for those seeking justice in many different walks of life. In the final articles, justice practitioners and ministers Cherice Bock and Velda Love provide examples of how faith, action, and contemplation work together.

—Mary Adams Trujillo

···

Fierce Love: Friends, Racial Justice, and Policing: A Biblical Economy of Care

Cherice Bock

Excerpts from an Address to Friends Committee on National Legislation
Annual Meeting and Quaker Public Policy Institute (November 2020)

I'm going to tell you about a few of my experiences at Portland's racial justice protests in these last several months, and I do so not so you'll be impressed by me (although it's a mark of my privilege as a white person that you might be), but because I think it is incredibly important for white people to tell these stories and do the emotional labor of trying to communicate about police brutality, its links to racism, and the bigger links to economic access and natural resources. I realize not everyone here considers themselves a Christian, but I hope it will still be meaningful to you to hear about a biblical economy of care, about ancient societies that were trying to set themselves up in a way that was just and caring to the most vulnerable individuals in their midst. Finally, I will share a few of the high points of my learning about my own internalized white

···

supremacy and settler colonialism as I've noticed my own reactions these last several months. While this is in many ways a conversation I'm addressing to white folks, I hope it is also shows solidarity with Friends of color.

I was arrested and detained for several hours at the Immigration and Customs Enforcement or ICE facility in Portland for tying a balloon to a gate. It was a silver star balloon, and it was one of 193 carried by protesters that night as we marched through the streets, chanting, "No justice? No peace," and, "Whose streets? Stolen land." Each balloon represents a life lost in ICE custody since the agency began in 2003. As we approached the building to deliver this symbol, federal agents emerged from the building and arrested several of us, seemingly at random, and pepper-sprayed the group—we had just arrived at the facility, and most of us had not yet donned our respirator masks and goggles, which have become standard protest equipment in the months since the murder of George Floyd. As the Department of Homeland Security officer held me down to put zip ties around my wrists, I watched my silver star balloon float away, eerily similar to the soul it represented.

Although surprised to be arrested for that nonviolent direct action, I did not feel particularly scared, which is a mark of the privilege I hold in my white skin and my citizenship status. I was inconvenienced for a few hours, and I spent those hours knowing I shared the building with those who are being detained—many without trial—for indefinite periods of time. I experienced minor police brutality, being thrown to the ground and feeling a bit of pepper spray drift. This punishment was hugely disproportionate to the alleged crime of not obeying the "lawful" order of moving away from the building immediately when asked. And this is why I was out there—I can put my white body on the line to show up the injustice and disproportionately violent reaction of law enforcement. But it is easy to see how this kind of law enforcement behavior, done in full view of members of the press and legal observers on nonviolent protesters, is magnified and intensified when they're not being watched, and when they're dealing with folks without the correct legal papers, or who are treated as less valuable in our society because of the color of their skin.

There is fierce solidarity in the group of interfaith clergy I was representing. Sometimes protesters ask us why we're out there, and often thank us for being there. Some get it, and say things like, "It makes sense, Jesus was killed by the state!" Exactly. For those of us who are white, although Friends generally did not support slavery or taking land from Native Americans, we benefited from cheap access to property and other economic benefits, and folks of color have tried to communicate about the injustices we're helping perpetuate. Although those of us who are white are often sympathetic and feel bad about this harm, we tend to have a hard time actually doing anything to change the systems of oppression we're participating in. When the required changes feel like they would be uncomfortable economically, socially, or in terms of our accustomed lifestyles, it seems to me like we often have a hard time sticking with the conversation long enough or with enough openness to our own need for change to actually make it work. I hope and pray that is not the case this time. I have personally learned and grown in my understanding of racial justice this summer and fall. There are places where I've seen glimpses of the Beloved Community emerging among the counterculture of the protest activists, and places where I've felt myself running into my own internalized white supremacy and settler colonialism. If you get nothing else from this message, know that what I am essentially trying to communicate here is that: *When we say, "There is that of God in everyone," when we say, "Black Lives Matter," when we say we stand in solidarity with those who are marginalized, these are intensely relational and profoundly economic and ecological claims that place on us a responsibility of care.*

I told the story about my arrest for trying to place a balloon on a gate because it shows the utter absurdity and arbitrariness of the laws and the way they are enforced. You can see law enforcement officers are protecting their building, the laws that the building represents about who belongs in this country, and the value (or lack thereof) of the lives of those they say don't belong. You can also see clearly the issue of protection of property over people in the police killings of George Floyd and Breonna Taylor that sparked this most recent energy in the protests for racial justice. George Floyd was arrested for being suspected of having used a counterfeit $20 bill. For this, he was murdered—without evidence, and even if he had used counterfeit money, the legal punishment is not death. In the case of Breonna Taylor, when the verdict came out regarding the officers' use of deadly force, the only charges that were found to be enforceable were the ones about the damage to the property of her neighbors. The officers could not be convicted for killing her, but they could be held liable for damaging property. Their job is to protect property: the property of the store owner who thought the bill was counterfeit, the property of homeowners or landlords—and in order to protect that property, they can use lethal force against human beings, particularly those most historically associated as property and with commodity production.

But I think it is easy for most of us to say with our mouths that Black Lives Matter, and to believe it, and to care about racial justice, but when it comes to actually changing the economic, social, and ecological systems that prop up white supremacy in this country, and imperialist ideologies of wealth and status upon which white supremacy is based, we have a hard time actually doing the transformative work, if we benefit somewhat from the system as it is. It's hard work to change the system, and I don't actually have to think about it all the time, as a white person, because it doesn't seem to be visible—it's hidden from me unless I'm paying attention.

Some of this, I believe, comes from a failure of imagination, of vision and awareness, and some of it comes from fear, because there is the very real concern that if we no longer fit our lives to the economic model as it is, we will be destitute. We have no social safety net as a culture, we have no assurance that we won't simply fall down enough rungs on the hierarchical ladder that we will no longer be able to afford food and shelter, that we will have to work until we die with no retirement savings. In this way, each of us is eternally struggling to be worthy of being treated as a human being, each of us competing, each of us showing we are valuable because we are still producing. This is how the economic and social hierarchy of our society dehumanizes us all, treats us as interchangeable inputs of labor, to be used and discarded, but keeping us at different strata so that at least we're better off than "those" people, whoever is lower on the ladder than we are. In this model, we must live in a constant state of underlying terror, with little room for empathy. We must believe we got to the rung we are on by merit, that the laws that keep us with at least the level of comforts and privileges we enjoy must be just and correct, because otherwise we may lose the level of privilege we do manage to have.

Every once in a while, something breaks through this facade for white folks, like the combination of the pandemic and George Floyd's murder. We recognize injustice, and that this is no way to live, and that we're all in this together. We yearn for a society in which no one has to fear, in which we are all taken care of and we care for one another, and where we recognize the humanity of each one, and our own inherent value.

Although I was raised a Quaker and was taught our denominational history of abolition with pride, and although my family members participated in the civil rights movement, although I have devoted my career to studying and teaching about biblical justice issues and I've done community organizing around environmental and climate justice, I realized this summer and fall I still have a lot to learn about my own internalized white supremacy and settler colonialism.

This brings me to the biblical economy of care, because it is this same vision that I believe the Bible points us toward, both in Jesus' vision of a kin-dom of God and in the shalom community to which the Israelites were invited in the Hebrew Scriptures.

Jesus says his message is primarily good news to the poor, to prisoners, to the blind and the oppressed (Luke 4:18–19). Jesus sets this up as his mission statement, the message around which he shapes his ministry. His message is of meeting the needs of real people, feeding them and healing them, inviting them into community when they had been cast aside. And this is a message that threatened the religious and political leaders of his day, for which he was killed, because it unmasked and refused to follow the systems of power that legitimated their roles in society.

I think what happens is we get too stuck on the laws and the rules, and we forget about the humanity of one another, we forget about simply caring for one another as human beings. So, in whatever political and economic and social and ecological system we find ourselves, we can practice an economy of care for one another—and in whatever system we're in, if it's one that tends toward empire, it will try to separate us, make us afraid, and keep us from trying to care for one another. So that is our work, to build an economy of care.

This summer I have seen something beautiful emerge in the streets of Portland, something that looks an awful lot more like a church than a lot of churches (or meetings) do. It is messy and it is decentralized and I often wish there was more order to it, but I have seen so much kindness and generosity, so much mutual care, so much genuine concern for one another. Everyone is still human, and there are annoying things that happen, and there are power grabs, but there is also connectedness and the emergence of a new Beloved Community. I share in what follows some reflections about what I'm learning about an economy of care through the protests, and how I'm faced with my own internalized white supremacy and settler colonialism. I share these in hopes that they will encourage and challenge you, too.

As the protests began outside the Justice Center in downtown Portland, folks noticed there were people living there, and they began bringing food and supplies to feed those who made their home in the park. Other protesters could eat, too, and folks could pay what they were able, and everyone got enough. People organized into mutual aid groups and began circulating around the protest group with supplies such as hand sanitizer, earplugs, wipes for getting tear gas out of your eyes, and even respirator masks and new filters. Other groups brought snacks and water bottles (and plenty of hand sanitizer), and a snack van emerged. Medical teams formed, wearing red crosses to identify themselves. I saw countless medics helping folks out of clouds of tear gas, helping them recover as they coughed, vomited, and cried the tear gas out of their systems. (I was initially concerned about protests as vectors of the coronavirus, but after research started coming out that protests do not seem to be problematic spreaders, since everyone is wearing masks and being careful, I decided this was a worthy enough reason to venture out of my otherwise tight coronavirus bubble.) A group called jail support collects donations and brings snacks and coffee to those being released from a night in jail, and helps ensure that each person gets safely home, even if their car keys and phones have been confiscated and sent to a different facility.

Additionally, there is now a variety of service-oriented "blocs" popping up all over Portland. Each week there are numerous groups offering their services, such as mending bloc, mechanic bloc, and art therapy bloc. Groups with a special interest or skill set up in a park and people come to learn, get help, and heal.

When major wildfires occurred in Oregon in September, the mutual aid groups switched from providing food and supplies for protesters to organizing necessities for those displaced by fires.

Protesters have been monitoring a Black-owned home for the last several months to make sure its owners cannot be evicted due to foreclosure, citing gentrification and anti-Black housing policies in the past and present. When raids by white nationalists or law enforcement happen in encampments of people without homes, the protest community is alerted and people arrive to stand in the way, to de-escalate, and to at very least bear witness.

This reminds me of early Friends, who did not intend to become a denomination known for social justice, but who went about their own business, acting as faithfully and equitably as they could, and for this they were imprisoned. Going to prison themselves, their eyes were opened to the deplorable conditions, and lack of education and economic opportunity, and they began working in practical ways to help, as well as in using their voices to speak truth to power in the political realm.

Today's protest community can be challenging: there are grifters, there are those who want to use the protests to build their own personal brand and political influence, there are every once in a while outside agitators trying to make protesters look bad. The people are human and the situations are stressful, and we're in the middle of a pandemic with tremendous economic impact. Many protesters are employed, but many are struggling financially and still trying to show up and stand up as best they know how. This is the Beloved Community, a group of misfits and outsiders, folks who make mistakes and think too highly of themselves, and folks with kind and genuine hearts who refuse to give up on justice.

The first criticism you are likely to hear about the protests are about violence and looting. I have seen broken windows (but no one taking anything from inside) and trash fires. I have bumped into major feelings of discomfort around this, and I've learned a lot. First of all, notice that you may have thought of broken windows and trash fires as violence, but this is actually property destruction. I think this tells us something about ourselves when we start to notice what we consider violence, and what we think of as justifiable to do to human beings in response to property destruction. Maybe you don't think police violence is legitimate either way, because you're likely a proponent of nonviolence in all circumstances, given the folks who are likely to be at an FCNL (Friends Committee on National Legislation) gathering, but you can see this happening in society, and I imagine many of you have thought of the property destruction as violence. This shows us that we're equating property with people. I have heard a lot of outrage over broken windows, and quite a bit less about police brutality against human beings, as white folks get bored with the conversation and want to move on.

As a Quaker with a commitment to nonviolence, this conversation has stretched me, as I imagine it may have many of you. Part of the critique I hear is about how the protesters don't look, sound, and act respectable. We imagine that if the protests only looked respectable, if we felt comfortable with them, then they would work, and society would change. This is a way of blaming the victims of violence, akin to blaming a woman for her assault because she's dressed provocatively. It allows those of us who are white to be spectators who have not yet been moved enough by others' suffering—we do not yet consider them deserving of our sympathy.

Furthermore, I have been challenged to recognize the intersectional nature of the civil disobedience protesters are engaging in. Although it's easy for me, as someone who benefits from property rights as they are, for the most part, to condemn acts of property destruction, it is quite different when looked at from the perspective of those Indigenous to Turtle Island and those whose ancestors worked the land for others' profit. Who made these laws about who has a right to what property, and who do these laws benefit? As discussed earlier, the economic aspects of racism are clear. By continuing to make visible both the economic impact and the brutality of police response, protesters are keeping us focused on these topics. You may not like their tactics, but for me, I've been challenged to come face-to-face with my own white supremacy in my thoughts about my and others' right to the land and the economic benefits we enjoy. I work hard and I honestly barely get by financially, but I'm educated and I'm able to own property because of my ancestors owning real estate before me, and passing down inheritance and connections. My Quaker forebears bought into the idea of Manifest Destiny, that this land was a gift and a blessing for us—"This land was made for you and me," not for those from whom we stole it (this implies)—and in so doing, we participated in stealing the land. I've been confronted with my own lack of any actual entitlement, and the falsehood of my presumptions about what is fair in terms of property rights. While it does no one any good to feel shame about any of our ancestors who are of European descent, we can recognize the harm that has been done, and that it has yet to be righted. Civil disobedience to point this out continues to call us to recognize the injustices upon which we're basing our lives and identities, and speaks truth to *us* and the power we hold.

For those of us with some power in the system as it now is, how will we respond when we are the ones to whom truth is being spoken? Will we respond by recognizing others' humanity and just claims? Or, when the query becomes economic, will we get caught up in our learned patterns of white supremacy, assuming we have a right to this land and its resources?

I have learned a lot about my white privilege in the area of policing. I have come face-to-face with police brutality, its basis in dehumanizing people and protecting property over people, and the racist practices law enforcement perpetrate. I've witnessed excessive and unnecessary use of force on peaceful protesters, and I've witnessed times when white nationalists are present with weapons, and law enforcement stand facing racial justice protesters, protecting white nationalists. I saw this in Salem, Oregon, last weekend, and it was on clear display yesterday in videos from DC. (This was about a week and a half after the 2020 election when white nationalists descended on Washington, DC, for demonstrations during the day, attacking bystanders by night.) When white nationalists threaten, physically harm, and mace racial justice protesters, law enforcement officers do not intervene, or appear in normal uniforms on bikes. Contrast that with the armored vehicles and riot gear with which they show up to nonviolent racial justice protests. While I understood in my head that police brutality was occurring, and that it occurred more often against people of color, experiencing this myself has been eye-opening. I have been surprised by the level to which the social and economic status quo requires control of property, including people viewed by our economic system as property, but this is only news to me because I'm white and I've had the privilege of being able to ignore it.

If you are white and you notice yourself feeling uncomfortable with this message, I invite you to listen through your discomfort and see how you may be asked to stretch, grow, and transform as you wait in the power of fierce love.

. . . .

Morning Musing

Velda Love

6:32 am. Time to rise.
Time to collect myself for a long day of virtual contact
without being physically present.
Time to recognize where my help comes from and give thanks.
Time to shine a light on 4 billion years of known existence-
    prehuman to the present.
Time to facilitate conversations with grace,
prepared study, and acknowledgement that even 6 hours is just
    scratching the surface
Time to dive into very muddy & multilayered topics involving how
    a group of humans decided to elevate themselves for profits at the
    expense and elimination of other people groups whose presence
    on earth predates their ancestors.
And will I still rise ?
I rise to be an instrument.
WE will rise to be instruments.
We will rise to be useful human vessels
delivering small antidotes of corrective narratives about segments
    of human history,
Relying on a Spirit that has been gifted to us
to face realities
for the good
through the pain
So I call on that great Spirit
and the ancestors who believed in freedom.
May love, grace and wisdom guide us this day.
Peace

. . . .

Conclusion

··

J ust as the contributors to this volume represent different constituencies and points of view, we expect that the readers of this volume will also differ in their life experiences and perspectives. As you have read, we hope that these differences have required you to reach beyond that which is familiar and comfortable. Our goal has been to facilitate new relationships between individuals, ideas, and communities with the desired outcome of eliminating racism within our professional practice of conflict resolution.

We have communicated this goal through the use of language, often a source of conflict in itself. We encourage practitioners to recognize that, whether in the agreements we write or in the tones and sounds we use, language delivers, creates, impacts, reflects, and transforms conflict and culture. May you be encouraged to examine and adjust personal and professional language, so that our words become tools of liberation, not of oppression.

The collaborative process of developing this book through a year of social upheaval, global pandemic, natural disasters, as well as personal triumphs and tragedies, has included moments of great joy, painful conflict, sadness, frustration, and satisfaction. Sometimes our ways of thinking and doing collided. Nevertheless, we persisted, trusting our intention, and committed to bringing this volume from conception to birth.

Even so, despite our best intentions, we recognize that there are many necessary voices still unrepresented. We encourage you, beloved community, to persist as well. Let's reach out to find and promote those voices, especially those that make us most uncomfortable, the ones that seem to make no sense or challenge our sense of self. Understand their context. As authors, we are confident that each thoughtful contribution to the collective achievement of a society, indeed a world, where all of humanity thrives, is not only in our best interest. It is possible.

Lexicon

··

Words . . .

A poet once said to me, as if it were common knowledge, "You know, language and thought continually reinforce and transform each other." I have said this phrase so often that I think of it as my own thought. Language is like that, simultaneously a tool and engineer of culture. Without conscious recognition, we make language our own, perhaps not recognizing the multidimensional power we have brought into our minds. For this reason, this volume includes a lexicon of words used in this book; in some cases, we include multiple definitions, reflecting multiple spheres of meaning. We invite you to examine your use of these words, perhaps trying them out in multiple communities to broaden your understanding.

Lexicon: A consideration of language frequently used in communities of practice, often with multiple meanings, but rarely interrogated in depth. Examples include:

Antiblackness: An often subliminal component of racism manifesting as internalized oppression, overt racist speech, and action, or even a subtle denial of the significance or validity of Black experience. See chapter 1 for examples.

Antiracist: Practices that move beyond mere awareness of racism, to develop a just and equitable society. An example is the work of Ibram X. Kendi.

Arbitration: An established form of alternative dispute resolution (ADR) where outcomes are decided by designated persons. If arbitration is binding, parties agree in advance to abide by decisions. Some arbitrations are non-binding. Binding arbitration agreements often occur in consumer contracts.

BIPOC: Black, Indigenous, and people of color; not white; a sometimes problematic shorthand that equates an intrinsic sameness of the experiences and oppression of Black, indigenous, LatinX, Middle Eastern, Asian people. Has the potential to "lump together" nonequivalent experiences. Note that this label may be offensive to some "BIPOC." Ask first.

Corea: Spelling the country's name with a "C" acknowledges usage prior to Japanese colonization and reflects a contemporary international movement to decolonize language.

··

Decolonization: Intentional unlearning of a mindset of oppression based on historic cultural domination; a process of re-minding to "liberate" thinking. See work by Tuck and Yang (2012) that further expounds on "settler colonialism" and the necessity of repatriation considerations.

LatinX/Latin(X): A presumed egalitarian means of naming people whose common ancestry would have been called Latin or Latino; eliminates the gender-specific aspect of the Spanish language. Some people whose primary language is Spanish may object to this designation. Ask first.

Mediation: A voluntary process involving a third-party neutral who helps the disputants come to a mutual agreement. Examples may include peer mediation in schools, landlord-tenant, or divorce mediation.

Punctuation: A social convention reflecting cultural impositions on human thought; domain in which dynamics of dominance are embodied in historical changes in linguistic usage. In this volume, for example, some authors capitalize "White" as a reference to light-skinned people of European heritage; others do not. To capitalize "Black" but not "white," for example, may suggest that white is assumed or normal, Black exceptional. Where in that grammatic hierarchy lies B/brown?

The editors asked one of our contributors, tom kunesh, to explain why he writes his name all in lowercase letters. His reply provokes deep reflection about how power is embedded in the most ordinary of daily rituals:

> my casual response to questions about my writing my name in all lower case is that i'm not a capitalist ;) and though it's good & true, it's not the real reason. it's a combination of a lot of factors, including a lot of foreign language study and practice writing (german, russian, spanish, greek, lakota) and realization that we as adult individuals are masters of our first language, and can and should be 'able'/'allowed'/ to write it as masters as we wish without the conventions of *Webster* or the *Chicago Manual of Style* or our high school english teachers or european linguists of 'aboriginal' languages. it was a realization that -somebody- takes charge of the language (like the Real Academia Española) and says what -they- think everybody else should do . . . and that all of the languages treat their nouns and pronouns and adjectives differently. And that some writers could do it and be respected (ee cummings, Don Marguis).
>
> so i figured that with my newfound knowledge of languages, i could control my own name & how to write it & its meaning. so i do. my use of lowercase in my european name indicates that my family is mixed-blood white and lakota.
>
> my first 'foreign' language was german—they capitalize _ everything_, it seems. then russian—they only capitalize pronouns.

then spanish—the same. which made me wonder,—why does english capitalize itself & so many other words? . . . just like german . . . this was 40 years ago, . . . and then came the study of proto-indo-european language development and the politics of linguistic empire-building and marxist critique. my BA was in spanish—at the early time of computer labs. then my MA thesis used some more languages and better Macs and i wanted the words displayed in their languages correctly—enter the age of Macintosh computers and multiple language fonts & making it good-looking . . . which led me into my side job of typesetting & design. and mastery over the printed word. . . . it's been a fun ride.

i use lowercase for languages since they're common nouns & adjectives, not victorian Proper Nouns. lakota wasn't a written language until europeans started transcribing it using roman/latin characters . . . my response to 'Sioux Nation' is lakota oyate. place names i consider names and worthy distinguishing as special.

Race: A social construction based on skin color and presumption of biological characteristics; sometimes used interchangeably and erroneously with ethnicity. Examples of race include black, white, and Asian. Examples of ethnicity may include Greek, Ugandan, and Mexican.

Racism: A deeply held belief in the superiority of or that favor the "white race." Typically, systemic racism is associated with systems and structures of power and ability to carry out these beliefs. Individuals may also express racist beliefs and can enact these interpersonally. An example might be a white person who calls the police on a black person they assume is breaking into their own car. (True story.) Organizations may develop policies and practices that are **systematically** racist when they judge applicants by their (black-sounding) names or who hold "people of color" employees to a standard not applied to white employees. Can "people of color" hold beliefs about the superiority of white people (internalized oppression)? Yes. Can people of color hold beliefs about the superiority of their own race and ethnicity? Yes. A major difference is the ability of people of color to create or benefit from these systems and structures of privilege and power.

Reconciliation: A hope and movement toward elimination of injustice; a peaceful resolution and restoration of harmonious relationships.

Restorative justice: A system of practices whose objective is to repair harms (bring justice) to individuals and communities by bringing together those most affected by the harms; the ultimate hope is for reconciliation.

Trauma: In Greek, trauma is a wound that overwhelms or seriously impairs the individual's as well as the community's ability to cope. These traumas can exist at primary, secondary, and tertiary levels. Examples include intimate partner violence, violence against trans people, police brutality, sexual assault or abuse, psychological abuse, and racialized terrorization. Example from Tomi Nagai-Rothe in chapter 21: "For me being (re-)traumatized means tightness in my stomach, an inability to focus, fatigue, fear and sadness from the uncontrollable replay of traumatic memories."

White supremacy: System of values, beliefs, and practices created to justify kidnapping, enslaving, and exploiting African peoples to build the economic system of the United States; justification of the destruction of indigenous cultures and lands; demonization and exploitation of people from Central and South America, the Caribbean, and Asia to access labor and resources. Today, this system and its accompanying values, beliefs, and practices are used to justify racial discrimination and violence against the descendants of the aforementioned.

References

···

Advancement Project and Alliance for Educational Justice. (2018). We came to learn: A call to action for police-free schools. The Advancement Project. http://advancement project.org/wecametolearn/

Alcoff, L. M. (2003). Latino/As, Asian Americans, and the Black-white binary. *Journal of Ethics, 7*(1), 5–27.

Angelou, Maya. (2014). The Maya Angelou quote that will radically improve your business. https://www.forbes.com/sites/carminegallo/2014/05/31/the-maya-angelou -quote-that-will-radically-improve-your-business/?sh=50d421d8118b

Appiah, K. A. (2018). The myth of meritocracy: Who really gets what they deserve?, Long Read. *The Guardian*. https://www.theguardian.com/news/2018/oct/19/the -myth-of-meritocracy-who-really-gets-what-they-deserve

Arao, B., & Clemens, K. (2013). From safe spaces to brave spaces: A new way to frame dialogue around diversity and social justice. In L. Landerman (Ed.), *The art of effective facilitation: Reflections from social justice educators* (pp. 135–150). Stylus Publishing. Retrieved from https://www.vanderbuilty.edu/oacs/wp-content/uploads /sites/140/From-Safe-Spaces-to-Brave-Spaces.pdf

Baldwin, James. (2021). Confronting History: James Baldwin. https://www.kinfolk .com/confronting-history-james-baldwin/

Barnes, C. W. (2019). *I bring the voices of my people.* Eerdmans.

Blackwell-Johnson, J. (1998). African American activists in the Women's International League for Peace and Freedom, 1920s–1950s. *Peace & Change, 23*(4), 466–482.

BLM at School. (n.d.) *The demands.* BLM at School. Retrieved March 8, 2021. https:// www.blacklivesmatteratschool.com

Bowland, S.Y. (2008). What is justice in conflict resolution? In M. A. Trujillo, S.Y. Bowland, L. J. Myers, P. M. Richards, & B. Roy (Eds.), *Re-centering: Culture and knowledge in conflict resolution practice* (pp. 303–318). Syracuse University Press.

Bridgeford, E. (2020). Or it can swallow you whole. In S. Terry (Ed.), *More justice, more peace: When peacemakers are advocates*, pp. 19–33. Rowman & Littlefield.

Bush, R. A. B., & Folger, J. P. (1994). *The promise of mediation.* Jossey-Bass.

CDC. (2019). https://www.cdc.gov/media/releases/2019/p0905-racial-ethnic-dis parities-pregnancy-deaths.html

Chang, A., Basey, D., Carey, V., Coleman, A., & Hoban, K. (2008). Race, (in)justice, and conflict resolution: Injustice in the African American community, effects on community, and the relevance of conflict resolution. In M. A. Trujillo, S.Y. Bowland, L. J. Myers, P. M. Richards, & B. Roy (Eds.), *Re-centering: Culture and knowledge in conflict resolution practice* (pp. 108–127). Syracuse University Press.

Chinook Fund. (2015). https://chinookfund.org/wp-content/uploads/2015/10/Sup plemental-Information-for-funding-Guideline-pdf

Chow, K. (2017). 'Model Minority' myth again used as a racial wedge between Asians and Blacks. NPR.org. https://www.npr.org/sections/codeswitch/2017/04

···

/19/524571669/model-minority-myth-again-used-as-a-racial-wedge-between-asians-and-blacks

Davis, B. G. (2020). American diversity in international arbitration: A new arbitration story or evidence of things not seen. *Fordham Law Review, 88*(6), 2143–2154. https://ir.lawnet.fordham.edu/flr/vol88/iss6/3

Davis, D., & Maldonado, C. (2015). Shattering the glass ceiling: The leadership development of African American women in higher education. *Advancing Women in Leadership, 35*, 48–64.

D.C. Law 15-261, Omnibus Juvenile Justice Act of 2004.

Desmond Tutu Quotes. (n.d.). BrainyQuote.com. https://www.brainyquote.com/quotes/desmond_tutu_106145

Dobbins, F., & Kalev, A. (2020, October 20). Companies need to think bigger than diversity training. *Harvard Business Review*, 2–10.

Dominguez, N., Duarte, Y., Espinosa, P., Martinez, L., Nygreen, K., Perez, R., Ramirez, I. & Saba, M. (2009). Constructing a counternarrative: Students Informing Now (S.I.N.) reframes immigration and education in the United States. *Journal of Adolescent & Adult Literacy 52*, 439–442. https://doi.org/10.1598/JAAL.52.5.8.

Döringer, S. (2020). The problem-centered expert interview: Combining qualitative interviewing approaches for investigating implicit expert knowledge. *International Journal of Social Research Methodology*, https://doi.org/10.1080/13645579.2020.176677.

Drakulich, K., Wozniak, K. H., & Hagan, J. (2020). Race and policing in the 2016 presidential election: Black Lives Matter, the police, and dog whistle politics. *Criminology, 58*(2), 370–402. DOI: 10.1111/1745-9125.12239.

Dugan, M. (1996, July). A nested theory of conflict. *A Leadership Journal: Women in Leadership—Sharing the Vision 1*, 9–20.

Dzurinko, N. McCants, J. & Stith, J. (2011). The campaign for nonviolent schools: Students flip the script on violence in Philadelphia. *Voices in Urban Education, 30*, 22–30. http://vue.annenberginstitute.org/sites/default/files/issues/VUE30

Edwards, D. (2020). Beloved communities for all. In S. Terry (Ed.), *More justice, more peace: When peacemakers are advocates*, pp. 193–208. Rowman & Littlefield.

Ely, R., & Thomas, D. A. (2020). Getting serious about diversity: Enough already with the business case. *Harvard Business Review, 98*(6), 115–122.

Faulkner, W. (1929/2015). *The sound and the fury*. London: Vintage Classic.

First, J. M., Danforth, L., Frisby, C. M., Warner, B. R., Ferguson, Jr., M. W., & Houston, J. B. (2020). Posttraumatic stress related to the killing of Michael Brown and resulting civil unrest in Ferguson, Missouri: Roles of protest engagement, media use, race, and resilience. *Journal of the Society for Social Work and Research, 11*(3), 369–391.

Folger, J. P., Bush, R. A. B., & Della Noce, D. J. (Eds.) (2010). *Transformative mediation: A sourcebook—Resources for conflict intervention practitioners and programs*. Association for Conflict Resolution and the Institute for the Study of Conflict Transformation.

Fusch, P., Fusch, G. E., & Ness, L. R. (2018). Denzin's paradigm shift: Revisiting triangulation in qualitative research. *Journal of Social Change, 10*(1), 19–32. DOI: 10.5590/JOSC.2018.10.1.02

Gee, Michael. (2018, February 28). Why aren't Black employees getting more white-collar jobs? *Harvard Business Review*, 2–6. https://hbr.org/amp/2018/02/why-arent-black-emplouees-getting-more-white-collar-jobs

Goens-Bradley, S. (2020). Breaking racism's insidious grip on restorative practices: A call for white action. In E. C. Valandra & W. Waphaha Hoksila (Eds.), *Colorizing restorative justice: Voicing our realities* (pp. 37–54). Living Justice Press.

Gray, A. (2019). The bias of "professionalism" standards. *Stanford Social Innovation Review Special Issue*. https://ssir.org/articles/entry/the_bias_of_professionalism_standards

Green, M. Z. (2017). Reconsidering prejudice in alternative dispute resolution for Black work matters. *SMU Law Review, 70*(4), 639–680.

Guest, G., MacQueen, K. M., & Namey, E. E. (2012). *Applied thematic analysis.* Sage Publications.

Gunning, I. R. (1995). Diversity issues in mediation: Controlling negative cultural myths. *Journal of Dispute Resolution,* (1), 55–93.

Hagopian, J., & Jones, D. (2020). *Black lives matter at school: An uprising for educational justice.* Haymarket Books.

Hairston, C. D. (1999). African Americans in mediation literature: A neglected population. *Mediation Quarterly, 16*(4).

Hairston, C. D. (2008). Reflections on "African Americans in mediation literature: A neglected population." In M. A. Trujillo, S.Y. Bowland, L. J. Myers, P. M. Richards, & B. Roy (Eds.), *Re-centering: Culture and knowledge in conflict resolution practice* (pp. 159–164). Syracuse University Press.

Hairston, C. D. (2016). The professional is personal. *Transforming from the inside out.* The Institute for the Study of Conflict Transformation.

Harmon-Darrow, C., Charkoudian, L., Ford, T., Ennis, M., & Bridgeford, E. (2020). Defining inclusive mediation: Theory, practice, and research. *Conflict Resolution Quarterly, 37,* 205–324.

Harris, A. P., & Gonzalez, C. G. (2012). Introduction. In G. G. y. Muhs, Y. F. Niemann, C. G. Gonzalez, & A. P. Harris (Eds.), *Presumed incompetent: The intersections of race and class for women in academia.* Utah State University Press.

Hewlett, B. (2012, June 13). Herding Cats: Quote of the Day. https://herdingcats.type pad.com/my_weblog/2012/06/q.html

Hikido, A., & Murray, S. (2015). Whitened rainbows: How white college students protect Whiteness through diversity discourses. *Race Ethnicity and Education.* doi:http://www.tandfonline.com/action/showCitFormats?doi=10.1080/13613324.2015.1025736

Hinton, M.D. (2018). Inclusion and social justice as peacemaking within higher education. *Journal of Social Encounters, 2*(1), 1–6. https://digitalcommons.csbsju.edu/social_encounters/vol2/iss1/1.

Hoffman, D. A., & Stallworth, L. E. (2008, February/April). Leveling the playing field for workplace neutrals: A proposal for achieving racial and ethnic diversity. *Dispute Resolution Journal,* 37–46.

Hooker, D. A. (2020). A story of a journey: From resolution beyond transformation. In S. Terry (Ed.), *More justice, more peace: When peacemakers are advocates,* pp. 159–176. Rowman & Littlefield.

hooks, b. (1994). *Teaching to transgress: Education as the practice of freedom.* Routledge.

hooks, b. (2001). *All about love: New visions.* William Morrow.

Human Rights Campaign Fund. (2020). "Fatal Violence Against Transgender and Gender Non-Conforming Community in 2020." https://www.hrc.org/resources/fatal-violence-against-the-transgender-and-gender-non-conforming-community-in-2021

Izumi, C. (2010). Implicit bias and the illusion of mediator neutrality. *Journal of Law & Policy, 34*(4), 71–155.

Izumi, C. (2017). Implicit bias and prejudice in mediation. *SMU Law Review, 70,* 681–693.

Jennings, W. J. (2020). *After whiteness: An education in belonging.* Eerdmans.

Johnson, J. M., & McGowan, B. L. (2017). Untold stories: The gendered experiences of high achieving African American male alumni of historically Black colleges and universities. *Journal of African American Males in Education, 8*(1).

Johnson, M. E., & LaRue, H. (2009). The gated community: Risk, aversion, race, and the lack of diversity in mediation in the top ranks. *Dispute Resolution Magazine, 15*(3), 17–20.

Kean, B. (2020, November 15). The elasticity of racism: Why arriving immigrants to America succeeded where Black Americans didn't. *Medium*. https://medium.com/our-human-family/the-elasticity-of-racism-e0ea24833aa4

Khan-Cullors, Patrisse, & Asha Bandele. (2019). *When they call you a terrorist: A Black Lives Matter memoir*. St. Martin's Press.

King, M. L., Jr. (1964). *Why we can't wait*. Signet Books.

King, S., & Kinzler, K. D. (2020, July 14). Bias against African American English speakers is a pillar of systemic racism, Op-Ed. *Los Angeles Times*. https://www.latimes.com/opinion/story/2020-07-14/african-american-english-racism-discrimination-speech

Konrad, A. M. (2018). Denial of racism and the Trump presidency. *Equality, Diversity and Inclusion: An International Journal, 37*(1), 14–30. DOI: 10.1108/EDI=07-2017-0155.

Kwon, S. A. (2013). *Uncivil youth: Race, activism and affirmative governmentality*. Duke University Press.

Lang, C. (2020, June 26). The Asian American response to Black Lives Matter Is Part of a long, complicated history. *Time*. https://time.com/5851792/asian-americans-black-solidarity-history/

Listen, Inc. (2003). *An emerging model for working with youth: Community organizing + youth development = youth organizing*. Funders Collaborative on Youth Organizing.

Lopez, G. R., & Parker, L. (2003). *Interrogating racism in qualitative research methodology*. Peter Lang.

Lederach, J. P. (2003). *The little book of conflict transformation*. Good Books.

Lee, T. (2014, March 22). Another Philadelphia student dies at a public school with no nurse. MSNBC News. https://www.msnbc.com/msnbc/another-student-dies-school-no-nurse-msna334541

Liu, S. R., & Modir, S. (2020). The outbreak that was always here: Racial trauma in the context of COVID-19 and implications for mental health providers. *Psychological Trauma: Theory, Research, Practice, and Policy, 12*(5), 439–442.

Lorde, Audre. (1984). *Sister outsider: Essays and speeches*. Crossing Press.

Lorenzi, M. (2006). Power: A radical view by Steven Lukes. *Crossroads, 6*(2), 87–95.

Low, S. C. (2008). From volunteerism to vocation: Challenges in breaking into professional mediation. In M. A. Trujillo, S.Y. Bowland, L. J. Myers, P. M. Richards, & B. Roy (Eds.), *Re-centering: Culture and knowledge in conflict resolution practice* (pp. 265–272). Syracuse University Press.

Lowndes, B., & Press, S. (2016). Ally-ship and dispute resolution practitioners: A continuum. *Mitchell Hamline Law Review, 42*(5), 1572–1599.

Lugo-Lugo, C. R. (2012). A prostitute, a servant, and a customer-service representative: A Latina in academia. In G. G. y. Muhs, Y. F. Niemann, C. G. Gonzalez, & A. P. Harris (Eds.), *Presumed Incompetent: The Intersections of Race and Class for Women in Academia*. Utah State University Press.

Mabry, C. R. (1998). African Americans "are not carbon copies" of white Americans: The role of African American culture in mediation of family disputes. *Ohio Journal on Dispute Resolution, 13*(2), 405–460.

Maher, C., Hadfield, M., Hutchings, M., & de Eyto, A. (2018). Ensuring rigor in qualitative data analysis: A design research approach to coding combining NVivo with traditional material methods. *International Journal of Qualitative Methods, 17*, 1–13. DOI: 10.1177/1609406918786362.

Manakem, R. (2017). *My grandmother's hands: Racialized trauma and the mending of our bodies and hearts*. Central Recovery Press.

Mandela, N. (2014). *Long walk to freedom: The autobiography of Nelson Mandela*. Paw Prints.

McCants, J. (2007). Youth organizing and activism. In G. Anderson and K. Herr. (Eds.) *Encyclopedia of Activism and Social Justice* (pp. 1506–1509). Sage Publications.

McCants, J. (2009). *Re-visioning violence: How Black youth advance critical understandings of violence in climates of criminalization.* Doctoral dissertation, University of Maryland. http://hdl.handle.net/1903/10211.

Minefee, I., Rabelo, V. C., Stewart, J., & Jones Young, N.C. (2018). Repairing leaks in the pipeline: A social closure perspective on underrepresented racial/ethnic minority recruitment and retention in business schools. *Academy of Management Learning & Education, 17*(1). https://doi.org/10.5465/amle.2015.0215.

Morris, Monique. (2016). *Pushout: The criminalization of Black girls in schools.* New Press.

Mosley, D. V., Hargons, C. N., Meiller, C., Angyal, B., Wheeler, P. Davis, C., & Stevens-Watkins, D. (2020). Critical consciousness of anti-Black racism: A practical model to prevent and resist racial trauma. *Journal of Counseling Psychology.* Advance online publication. http://dx.doi.org/10.1037/cou0000430.

Movement for Black Lives. (2021). Who we are. https://m4bl.org/about-us/.

Myers, L. J. (2008). Toward a fuller knowledge in peace management and conflict resolution: The importance of cultural worldview. In M. A. Trujillo, S.Y. Bowland, L. J. Myers, P. M. Richards, & B. Roy (Eds.), *Re-centering: Culture and knowledge in conflict resolution practice* (pp. 20–31). Syracuse University Press.

Nader, L. (1993). Controlling processes in the practice of law: Hierarchy and pacification in the movement to re-form dispute ideology. *Ohio State Journal on Dispute Resolution, 9*(1), 1–25.

O'Brien, D., and Nygreen, K. (2020). Advancing restorative justice in the context of racial neoliberalism: Engaging contradictions to build humanizing spaces. *Equity & Excellence in Education, 53*(4), 518–540.

Ogbolu, M. N., Singh, R. P., & Wilbon, A. (2015). Legitimacy, attitudes and intended patronage: Understanding challenges facing Black entrepreneurs. *Journal of Developmental Entrepreneurship, 20*(1).

Oluo, I. (2020). *Mediocre: The dangerous legacy of white male America.* Seal Press.

Onwuachi-Willig, A. (2017). Policing the boundaries of whiteness: The tragedy of being "Out of Place" from Emmet Till to Trayvon Martin. *Iowa Law Review, 102,* 113–1185. https://scholarship.law.bu.edu/faculty_scholarship/292.

Perry, A. M. (2020). *Know your price: Valuing Black lives and property in America's Black cities.* Brookings Institution Press.

Phelps-Ward, R., & Kenney, J. (2018/2019). Surviving whiteness and white people: The coping strategies of Black, entry-level student affairs professionals. *Journal of Student Affairs, 28,* 121–132.

Phillips, F. P. (2009, Spring). Diversity in ADR: More difficult to accomplish than first thought. *Dispute Resolution Magazine,* 14–24.

Press, S. (2011). Court-connected mediation and minorities: A report card. *Capital University Law Review, 39,* 819-851.

Rogers, N. H. (2015). When conflicts polarize communities: Designing localized offices that intervene collaboratively. *Ohio State Journal of Dispute Resolution, 30*(2), 173–232.

Roy, B. (1999). *Bitters in the Honey: Tales of hope and disappointment across divides of race and time.* University of Arkansas Press.

Santana, V. J. (2020). Restorative justice through a trauma-informed, racial-equity lens. In E. C. Valandra & W. Waphaha Hoksila (Eds.), *Colorizing restorative justice: Voicing our realities* (pp. 243–260). Living Justice Press.

Schmidt, C. (2018). Decentering whiteness. *Group, 42*(4), 311–329.

Scott, D. T. (2016). Recruiting and retaining African American male administrators at predominately white institutions. *Urban Education Research and Policy Annuals, 4*(1), 39–46.

Scott, K. M. (2003). Exploring the intragroup conflict constructs and behaviors of African-American public school children in an inner-city conflict resolution education (CRE) program. *Conflict Resolution Quarterly, 21*(1), 95–113.

Sherrod, B. (2020). Your silence will not protect you. In E. C. Valandra & W. Waphaha Hoksila (Eds.), *Colorizing restorative justice: Voicing our realities* (pp. 55–64). Living Justice Press.

Smith, L. T. (1999). *Decolonizing methodologies. Research and Indigenous peoples.* Zed Books Ltd.

Stanfield, J. H., II. (1994). Ethnic modeling in qualitative research. In N. K. Denzin & Y. S. Lincoln (Eds.), *Handbook of Qualitative Research* (pp. 175–188). Sage.

Stith, J. (2018). #EndWarOnYouth: Building a youth movement for Black lives and educational justice. In M. Warren and D. Goodman, (Eds). *Lift us up, Don't push us out! Voices from the front lines of the educational justice movement.* (pp. 82–91). Beacon Press.

Stith, J. (2021). Bigger than an RJ circle: Youth organizing for restorative justice in education. In T. Lewis and C. Stauffer (Eds). *Listening to the movement: Essays on new growth and new challenges in restorative justice.* (pp. 67–76). Wipf and Stock. https://zehr-institute.org/publications/docs/chapter-5.pdf

Stulberg, J. B. (2020). Mediating disputes that divide communities: What constitutes "success"? *Mitchell Hamline Law Journal of Public Policy and Practice, 41*(3), 241–264. https://open.mitchellhamline.edu/policypractice/vol41/iss3/7.

Sue, D. W., Capodilupo, C. M., Torino, G. C., Bucceri, J. M., Holder, A. M. B., Nadal, K. L., & Esquilin, M. (2007). Racial Microaggressions in Everyday Life: Implications for Clinical Practice. *American Psychologist, 62*(4), 271–286.

Thurman, Howard (1996). *Jesus and the Disinherited.* Beacon Press.

Tillman, L. C. (2002). *Black fatigue: How racism erodes the mind, body, and spirit.* Berret-Koehler Publishers.

Torres, G., & Pace, K. (2005). Understanding Patriarchy as an expression of whiteness: Insights from the Chicana movement. *Washington University Journal of Law and Policy, 18.*

Trujillo, M. A. (2008). Why research matters: The reciprocal nature of knowledge. In M. A. Trujillo, S.Y. Bowland, L. J. Myers, P. M. Richards, & B. Roy (Eds.), *Re-centering: Culture and knowledge in conflict resolution practice* (pp. 67–92). Syracuse University Press.

Trujillo, M. A., Bowland, S.Y., Myers, L. J., Richards, P. M., & Roy, B. (Eds.). (2008). *Re-centering culture and knowledge in conflict resolution practice.* Syracuse University Press.

Tuck, Eve, & K. Wayne Yang (2012). Decolonization is not a metaphor. *Decolonization: Indigeneity, Education & Society, 1*(1), 1–40

Tudy-Jackson, J. (2011). "Non-traditional" approaches to ADR processes that engage African-American communities and African-American ADR professionals. *Capital University Law, 39.*

Turner, J. (2020). Creating safety for ourselves. In Valandra, E. (Ed.). *Colorizing restorative justice* (pp. 291–321). Living Justice Press.

Tutu, Desmond. (2017). Quotations, O. E. (2017). Desmond Tutu 1931–South African Anglican clergyman. https://www.oxfordreference.com/view/10.1093/acref/9780191843730.001.0001/q-oro-ed50016497#:~:text=Desmond%20Tutu%201931%E2%80%93&text=If%20you%20are%20neutral%20in,will%20not%20appreciate%20your%20neutrality

Valandra, E. C., & Yazzie, J. R. (Eds.). (2020). *Colorizing restorative justice: Voicing our realities.* Living Justice Press.

Wacquant, L. (June 2010). Crafting the neoliberal state: Workfare, prisonfare and social onsecurity. *Sociological Forum 25*(2), 197–220.

Waging Nonviolence (2019). https://wagingnonviolence.org

Waldron, I. R. G. (2020). The wounds that do not heal: Black expendability and the traumatizing aftereffects of anti-Black police violence. *Equality, Diversity and Inclusion.* https://www.emerald.com/insights/2040-7149.htm. DOI 10.1108/EDI-06-2020-0175.

Walker-Barnes, C. (2019). *I bring the voices of my people.* Eerdmans.

Wilson, S. (2020). Calling out whiteness. In E. C. Valandra & W. Waphấha Hokšila (Eds.). *Colorizing restorative justice: Voicing our realities* (pp. 103–114). Living Justice Press.

Wing, L. (2008). Whither neutrality? Mediation in the twenty-first century. In M. A. Trujillo, S.Y. Bowland, L. J. Myers, P. M. Richards, & B. Roy (Eds.), *Re-centering: Culture and knowledge in conflict resolution practice* (pp. 93–107). Syracuse University Press.

Winters, M. F. (2020). *Black fatigue: How racism erodes the mind, body, and spirit*. Berret-Koehler Publishers.

Wu, E. D. (2015). *The color of success: Asian Americans and the origins of the model minority*. Princeton University Press.

Yoo, J., & Koudela, P. (2014). Sesŭmmu, distinction, debate and features of Hereditary Mudang in Korea. *Aceta Ethnographica Hungarica: An International Journal of Ethnography, 59*(2).

Young, M. D. (1958). *The rise of the meritocracy*. Thames & Hudson.

Zehr, H. (2002). *The little book of restorative justice*. Good Books.

Zuberi, T. (2001). *Thicker than blood: How racial statistics lie*. University of Minnesota Press.

Index

....

court mediation
    Bowland on, 112, 198
    Hairston on, 12
COVID-19 pandemic
    Bock on, 276–78
    Ciccone (James) on, 168
    Davis on, 72
    Gee on, 211
    Hairston on, 6, 13
    Melaku on, 147
    and prison programs, 242
    Ramirez and Gerson on, 262, 264
    Roy on, 199
Covington, Tonya, 244–46
Crawford, John, 257
creativity, Gee on, 214–15
credentialing
    Davis on, 68
    Hairston on, 15
    Lederach on, 196–97
    Patterson on, 210
credibility
    Chené on, 194
    Lederach on, 193
credible messenger
    Batts on, 123
    Bowland on, 117, 123
    Volpe on, 117–22
criminal background, Bowland on, 198
criminal justice system
    Charles on, 179–80, 183
    McCants-Turner on, 247
    Wade on, 144–45
Critical Race Theory, 251
Crutcher, Terrence, 257
cultural appropriation, Moore on, 88–92
cultural sensitivity
    and mediation, 76
    Tafoya on, 22
culture, Ramirez and Gerson on, 264
Culture Saving, 264
curiosity, Jones and Trujillo on, 226
curriculum
    Lum on, 201
    for prison program, 233

Dalai Lama, 220
dance, Ramirez and Gerson on, 264–65
Davis, Angela, 236, 263
Davis, Benjamin, 61–73
Davis, Jordan, 256
Dayton shooting, Gee on, 213–14

decentering Whiteness
    Davis on, 61–73
    definition of, 59
    Hairston on, 7
    Hitchcock on, 127–28
    Iyer on, 59–60
    Lum on, 205
Declaration of Independence, 181
decolonization
    Childers on, 169–71
    definition of, 284
    jiche on, 152–63
    kunesh et al. on, 135–37
Democratic Party, Charles on, 181–82
denial, Roy on, 109–10
depression, jiche on, 156
Diallo, Amadou, 109, 257
dialogue
    Chené on, 46
    Gray on, 267
    Jamison on, 30–31, 33
    Trujillo on, 188
    See also continuous dialogue
Dickinson, Emily, 260
dignity, Ciccone (Diane) on, 140–44
Discovery, Doctrine of, 70, 177, 180
diversity
    in classroom, 227
    Lum on, 201–2
divorce mediation, critique of, 81
documentation, Lum on, 207
dominance
    Chené on, 38–51
    Roy on, 191–92
Dominguez, N., 259
Donald, Jenoah, xv
Dorsey, Carl III, xv
double consciousness, Bowland on, 207
drama therapy, 212
Dzurinko, Nijmie, 252

Ebonics, 28
economic issues
    Bock on, 277–78
    Ciccone (Diane) on, 143
    McCants-Turner on, 249, 254
    Tafoya on, 20
editorial conventions, xix–xx, 284–85
education
    Beeman on, 148
    Covington on, 245
    Davis on, 67–68
    Garcia on, 97–99

immigrants
　Iyer on, 53–60
　Melaku on, 146–47
　Ramirez and Gerson on, 260–61
Immigration and Customs Enforcement
　　(ICE), 274
imposter syndrome, Gray on, 266–67
improv, Gee on, 214
inclusion
　Batts on, 268–72
　Ciccone (Diane) on, 140–44
　Ciccone (James) on, 167
　Hairston on, 10
　Jamison on, 23–37
　Tafoya on, 21–22
　Volpe on, 120
　Wilson on, 122
indigenous peoples
　Bakr et al. on, 240–41
　Bock on, 279
　Charles on, 175–85
　kunesh et al. on, 135–37
　Lederach on, 193–94
　Moore on, 89–92
　and restorative justice, 250
　Tafoya on, 18–22
individualism, 86
　Charles on, 180–81
infant mortality, 186
information technology, in arbitration,
　　72
infrastructure, Tafoya on, 20
insight, 111–16
Institute for the Study of Conflict
　　Transformation, Inc., 5
institutional racism
　See systematic racism
intent, Jamison on, 28–29
intercultural communication, Covington
　　on, 244
internal neutrals, Patterson on, 210
International Criminal Court Arbitration,
　　65–66
internet, Ciccone (James) on, 166, 168
internships, Davis on, 69
intersectionality, Bock on, 279
interviews
　Chené on, 41–45
　Hairston on, 8–9
invisibility
　Ciccone (James) on, 163–64
　Garcia on, 93–107
　Hairston on, 5, 7–8

Iyer on, 57
Tafoya on, 21
See also making visible
Iyer, Pushpa, 52–60

jail support, 277
Jakes, T. D., 34
Japan and sexual slavery
　jiche on, 153–62
　resources on, 157
Jarvin, Sigvard, 65
Jefferson, Atatiana, 256
Jennings, Willie James, 231–32
jiche, 134–37, 152–62
Jig Is Up! Movement, 128–31
jobs in conflict resolution
　Hairston on, 10
　Roy on, 81
Johnson, Amir, xiv
Johnson, Dion, xiv
Johnson, Mychal, xiii
Jones, Aiyana, 256
Jones, Anthony, xiv
Jones, Barbara L., 222–30
Jones, Corey, 257
justice
　Armster on, 132–33
　Davis on, 72–73
　Hairston on, 14
　Roy on, 2
　See also peace and justice work;
　　restorative justice
Justice 4 D.C. Youth Coalition, 247, 249

Kang, Christopher, 157, 159
Kellogg (WK) Foundation, 40–50
Kendi, Ibram X., 31, 205
Kenney, Niya, 255
Khan-Cullors, Patrisse, 236
Kim-Gibson, Dai Sil, 157, 159
Kim Hak Sun, 157
Kinard, Daverion, xv
King, Martin Luther, Jr., 6, 62, 182, 252
knowledge
　Patterson on, 209
　Trujillo on, 224
　Volpe on, 117–22
knowledge production, 4–17
　Melaku on, 147
　Roy on, 75
Koudela, Pál, 159
kunesh, tom, 135–37, 284–85
Kwanzaa, 143

Whiteness
    in academia, Iyer on, 53–60
    calling out, Hairston on, 7
    See also decentering Whiteness
White people and antiracist practice,
        108–10
    Clifton-Soderstrom on, 236–37
    Hairston on, 15
    Hitchcock on, 125–28
White privilege
    Bock on, 274–75, 278–79
    Jamison on, 29, 33
    Roy on, 109
White supremacy
    Bock on, 273–76, 279
    Charles on, 179–80, 183
    Ciccone (James) on, 165–66
    definition of, 286
Wilson, Darren, 253
Wilson, Dwight L., 122–23
Wilson, S., 12
Wise, Tim, 31

Woodard, Wilbon Cleveland, xiii
working with versus working for, Chené
        on, 42, 46
Wright, Daunte, xv
writing
    Ciccone (James) on, 163–69
    Patterson on, 208–11
    Wilson on, 122–23

Yang, K. Wayne, 135
Yaun, Delaina, 218
Yoo, Jinil, 159
youth
    Batts and Garcia on, 94–107
    Covington on, 244–46
    Gee on, 216
    McCants-Turner on, 247–59

Zehr, Howard, 251
zero-tolerance policies, 250
Zia symbol, 89

About the Contributors

....

Dr. **Mary Adams Trujillo** is a conflict transformation strategist who offers consultation and coaching for individual, organizational, and community transformation. As a researcher, mediator, and spiritual director, she has provided almost 40 years of service to clients who wish to increase skills and knowledge in the areas of communication, culture, and conflict. She is a frequent speaker and presenter at professional conferences and has authored and co-authored several books and articles related to conflict, culture, and faith. Dr. Trujillo received her BA from the University of Illinois in 1973, her MA in rehabilitation counseling from the University of New Mexico in 1975, and her PhD in communication studies from Northwestern University in 2004.

Michelle E. Armster is the Executive Director for Mennonite Central Committee (MCC), Central States. She has many years of experience in meditation, facilitation, conciliation, restorative justice, arbitration, victim/offender mediation, antiracism, and alternatives to violence. Michelle graduated from Lancaster Theological Seminary's MDiv program in 2007 and served as a co-pastor of St. Andrew United Church of Christ in Lancaster, Pennsylvania, as well as associate pastor for community outreach at Blossom Hill Mennonite Church in Lancaster, Pennsylvania. She presently resides in Wichita, Kansas, and is active with Wichita Griots, an African American Storytellers organization, and a member of National Association of Black Storytellers, member of the African American Council of Elders, Wichita/South Central Kansas, Inc., and an adjunct professor at Bethel College in North Newton, Kansas.

Jamal Bakr, who is of Mexican and Palestinian heritage, was raised in the "Back of the Yards" neighborhood located on the south side of Chicago. Beginning with his own understanding of violence and systemic oppression, he writes as an advocate for healing in his own and other affected communities. He is a student in the North Park Theological Seminary's School of Restorative Arts and is a frequent contributor to *Feather Bricks*.

Hasshan Batts is a prison survivor, healer, son, father, grandfather, brother, husband, and friend. In addition, he is a community epidemiologist, activist scholar,

....

community-based participatory researcher, leading expert on trauma-informed care, reentry and community engagement, and a dynamic motivational speaker. Hasshan is the founder and president of the Prison Survivors Network, Executive Director of the Promise Neighborhoods of the Lehigh Valley, adjunct professor, Lehigh University postdoctoral Research fellow, Rider-Pool Collective Impact fellow, distinguished Robert Wood Johnson Culture of Health Leader, Pennsylvania Commissioner on the Governors' Advisory Commission on African American Affairs, member of the Pennsylvania Reentry Council, founding board member of the Lehigh Valley Justice Institute and board member of Resurrected Community Development Corporation. Hasshan holds a master's in social work from North Carolina A&T University and a postgraduate certificate in Global Health and Doctorate in Health Sciences from Nova Southeastern University.

Angie Beeman is an associate professor in the Marxe School of Public and International Affairs at Baruch College and an affiliate professor in the Black and Latino Studies Department. Her research examines the evolution of racism and how this process affects institutional practices, identities, and interracial organizing. Her forthcoming book, *Liberal White Supremacy*, presents a model for evaluating differences between liberal and radical organizing and how progressives silence racial and class oppression.

Cherice Bock is a Quaker minister living outside of Portland, Oregon, on the traditional lands of the Kalapuya (now the Confederated Tribes of Grand Ronde). She holds an MDiv from Princeton Theological Seminary and an MS in environmental studies and is completing her PhD from Antioch University New England. She speaks, writes, and engages in activism at the intersection of religion, social justice, and the environment. Bock leads Oregon Interfaith Power & Light.

S.Y. Bowland was born and raised in Harlem, New York. She is known for her contributions to conflict resolution and restorative practices. She has been an educator, trainer, organizer, facilitator, and practitioner. She is a cofounder of Practitioners Research and Scholarship Institute, which is a collaboration of multireal people in the world of conflict resolution and peacemaking. She was a co-chair of the National Conference on Peacemaking and Conflict Resolution. She co-edited *Re-Centering Culture and Knowledge in Conflict Resolution*. SY has served on the faculties of Tuskegee University, Columbia College, and Morehouse School of Medicine Family Practice Development program. She credits her most valuable education to the streets of Harlem.

Celeste Brock: For 82 years, I've loved a diverse crowd of humans, animals, and birds. I read early, voluminously, voraciously. With an English Lit/Psych B.A., I worked in substitute teaching and social work, as well as 25+ years of academic editing (my business for professors/worldwide students) My experiences include many Quaker years with La Jolla Meeting/San Diego Meeting; spiritualist training/ordination; loving Mother Earth; choir singing (including temple choir); two marriages; multiple deaths; two daughters. Especially my half-Pacific Islander (adopted) son opened my heart and mind, expanding my healing empathy.

Henry Cervantes serves as manager for The Peace Exchange, a program of Holy Family Ministries, and has trained activists from around the world. Cervantes volunteers as a nonviolence trainer at the Cook County Jail in Chicago as part of the Sheriff's Anti-Violence Effort (SAVE) and is adjunct professor for North Park Theological Seminary at Stateville Correctional Center. Cervantes is an Anti-Defamation League 2021 Glass Leadership Institute Fellow and an Illinois Humanities Road Scholar.

Mark Charles is a dynamic and thought-provoking public speaker, writer, and consultant. The son of an American woman (of Dutch heritage) and a Navajo man, he teaches with insight into the complexities of American history regarding race, culture, and faith to help forge a path of healing and conciliation for the nation. He is one of the leading authorities on the 15th-century Doctrine of Discovery and its influence on US history and its intersection with modern-day society. Mark co-authored, along with Soong-Chan Rah, the new book titled, *Unsettling Truths: The Ongoing, Dehumanizing Legacy of the Doctrine of Discovery* (IVP, 2019). Mark ran as an independent candidate for the US presidency in the 2020 election.

Roberto M. Chené, MA, is a private practitioner in intercultural leadership and conflict resolution from Albuquerque, New Mexico. Roberto has degrees in philosophy and theology, and has done postgraduate work in Social Welfare Policy at Brandeis University. He has deep roots and extensive experience in social justice work within the Chicano-Latino community. His work includes the exploration of the leadership and relationship-building capacities that are integral to creating authentic intercultural community, especially the facility in sharing power that is fundamental to achieving racial equity and healing. His work is based on the view that the challenge we face is to construct a paradigm of relationships where the differences are not reconciled through dominance as is dictated by the current diversity model, but through negotiation and facilitated participation.

Laurie Childers is a visual artist, ceramics teacher, songwriter, and storyteller in Oregon. She grew up moving between the different planets of the civil rights–era Deep South and the antiwar, freethinking, feminist West Coast. In the 1980s, seeking to save forests, she provided technical support for fuel-efficient cookstove projects, working alongside traditional potters and artisans on five continents. Friendships and observations have made her a committed advocate for peace and justice.

Diane Ciccone's nearly 50-year career includes a BA from Colgate University and a JD from Hofstra School of Law. As an attorney she has worked in the courts, government, and law firms. She is an arbitrator, mediator, and currently an administrative law judge. Early in her career, often the only Black woman in the room, she developed a reputation of excellence and a woman to be respected. She is also a filmmaker and author.

James Ciccone is an American novelist, lawyer, and educator. He is perhaps best known for his Western novels, *Stagecoach Justice* and *A Good Day to Die.* He wrote *The Rituality of Jazz as Composed by John Coltrane* in his youth, and his seminal research on Everett Holmes, New York's first black mayor, is cited by the *Harvard Guide to African American History.* He served as pro bono general counsel to the ATA, the nation's oldest African American tennis association, and wrote the ATA Constitution. He was inducted into the Black Tennis Hall of Fame in 2017 by unanimous vote.

Michelle Clifton-Soderstrom is Dean of Faculty and professor of theology and ethics at North Park Theological Seminary. She authored *Angels, Worms, and Bogeys: The Christian Ethic of Pietism* and co-authored *Incorporating Children in Worship: Mark of the Kingdom.* Michelle was also the architect of North Park's School of Restorative Arts—a master's degree program in restorative justice ministries for incarcerated men and women. She is ordained to word and sacrament in the Evangelical Covenant Church.

Tonya Covington was appointed by the Mayor of Albuquerque to bring restorative justice to the city. She is the immediate past president of the New Mexico Mediation Association. Tonya has been a trained mediator and teacher of mediation since 1988. She has expertise in restorative justice and workplace, family, transformative, cross-cultural, postal (REDRESS), divorce, and elder mediation.

Emeritus Professor of Law **Benjamin Davis** joined the University of Toledo College of Law faculty in 2003 and retired on January 31, 2021. Earlier, he was a director at the International Chamber of Commerce (ICC) in Paris; the American Legal Counsel at the ICC International Court of Arbitration; a strategic business consultant and development consultant in France and West Africa. Professor Davis is the creator of fast-track international commercial arbitration and a former chair of the American Bar Association Section of Dispute Resolution.

Jeani Garcia is a community organizer with over seven years of helping her community heal from trauma. After having lost her precious son Kareem to gun violence in 2012, Jeani has dedicated her life to helping teenagers and young adults who are transitioning out of gangs. She has also started the support group Mother2Mother; she has been at the side of mothers and families who have also lost a loved one to gun violence.

Jada Gee is a theater major with an interest in psychology and sociology at the University of Dayton in Ohio (Class of 2023). She aspires to be a certified drama therapist and was honored as a W.S. McIntosh Scholar. She currently works as a volunteer mediator, and intern at the Dayton Mediation Center to explore the world of transformative mediation. Jada is also a part of the Common Good Players, a drama troupe that specializes in pedagogy, social justice, and devised theatre. Additionally, Jada serves as the Native American Committee Chair for the Multicultural Programming Council at University of Dayton. Whether she's led to a practice or a stage, Jada hopes to help and support others.

Rayshauna Gray is a creator, researcher, and policymaker currently affiliated with the Massachusetts chapter of the National Organization for Women, the Boston Book Festival, and Harvard University. She supports research, historic preservation, and economic development efforts in Cambridge, Massachusetts, and her hometown Chicago. She looks forward to pursuing similar work in her ancestral home of Mound Bayou, Mississippi.

Cherise D. Hairston is a 25-year veteran of the conflict resolution field working primarily in the area of community mediation, conflict management teaching and training, team development, and conflict coaching. She is a Certified Transformative Mediator™ and Fellow with the Institute for the Study of Conflict Transformation and a National Association for Community Mediation Board of Directors Elder. Cherise is a certified professional coach with the Co-Active Training Institute for the International Coach Federation.

The poems and short stories of **Frank Eugene Hall** explore connections between inner landscapes of the human spirit and outer landscapes of nature. A descendant of Europeans and Native Americans, he takes a global historical view. Frank started in Florida but has spent most of his life in Oregon, where he lives under oaks and solar panels in Corvallis. He is a member of Portland Ars Poetica and Poetics Corvallis.

Jeff Hitchcock is cofounder and executive director of the Center for the Study of White American Culture, a nonprofit organization that performs training, organizational consulting, and publishing activities on decentering whiteness and building multiracial community. He is author of the book, *Lifting the White*

Veil: A Look at White American Culture, and an editor of the book *Accountability and White Anti-Racist Organizing: Stories from Our Work.* Jeff currently lives in Graham, North Carolina.

Pushpa Iyer is an activist, scholar, and practitioner of conflict resolution and diversity, equity, and inclusion. Dr. Iyer is currently an associate professor and director of the Center for Conflict Studies at the Middlebury Institute of International Studies. Currently, she is developing Compassionate Courage, an intervention approach designed for identity-based conflicts. She holds a PhD in conflict analysis and resolution from George Mason University and an MBA from the University of East London.

Cheryl L. Jamison, JD, is a belonging and connectedness consultant. She gained her professional experience and personal insights from positions including director of both nonprofit and government organizations, legislative director for a member of Congress, and research analyst for the Missouri House of Representatives. She is the program director for Paralegal Studies at Columbus Technology College. She is on the faculty of the University of Maryland Global Campus and Tufts University.

jiche is a freedom artist, poet, and earthkin agitator and teaches literature and critical theory in Chicago using mind-body and restorative social praxis.

Barbara L. Jones is a community dispute resolution specialist, social justice activist, and youth-violence prevention advocate and faculty member in Detroit, Michigan. Barbara serves as program director in higher education, K–12 settings focused on community engagement, conflict resolution, and social justice activism. With over 20 years of media advertising experience, Barbara has worked for various media organizations, her teaching experience spans from transformational conflict resolution; diversity, equity, inclusion; social justice activism; marketing; advertising; and college to career readiness.

tom kunesh is from a large Catholic family in Minnesota. His mother is/was a member of the Standing Rock lakota oyate, grandfather born on the Fort Berthold reservation in North Dakota. tom joined the Navy, served in the Persian Gulf and Indian Ocean as a russian & farsi linguist, BA in spanish, MA in religious studies, Mdiv in Uuism & atheism, activist on indigenous issues since 1993, currently pushing decolonizing curricula, and being in a family.

John Paul Lederach is Senior Fellow at Humanity United and Professor Emeritus of International Peacebuilding at the Joan B. Kroc Institute for International Peace Studies at the University of Notre Dame. He works extensively as a practitioner in conciliation processes, active in Latin America, Africa, Southeast, and

Central Asia. He is widely known for the development of culturally appropriate approaches to conflict transformation and the design and implementation of integrative and strategic approaches to peacebuilding. He is the author and editor of 24 books and manuals, including *Building Peace: Sustainable Reconciliation in Divided Societies* (US Institute of Peace Press) and *The Moral Imagination: The Art and Soul of Building Peace* (Oxford University Press).

Rev. Dr. **Velda Love** serves as the United Church of Christ Minister for Racial Justice in Cleveland, Ohio. Velda develops antiracism curriculum, trains clergy and laypersons, leads reparatory racial justice workshops, develops training resources, and faith-based online educational platforms. Her work centers on addressing historical and contemporary injustice resulting in systemic, structural, and individual racism impacting local communities, and national and global policies and practices.

Grande Lum is the provost and vice president of Academic Affairs at Menlo College. Mr. Lum was director of the Department of Justice's Community Relations Service in the Obama administration. His latest book is *America's Peacemakers: The Community Relations Service and Civil Rights* (co-authored). He earned a bachelor's in psychology from University of California, Berkeley, and a law degree from Harvard.

Dr. Johonna McCants-Turner is associate professor of Peace and Conflict Studies at Conrad Grebel University College, University of Waterloo. Her scholarship intersects restorative and transformative justice, narrative peacebuilding, and contemporary social movements. As an educator-trainer, convenor, and co-learner, she has contributed to visionary organizations and projects around the world. Dr. McCants-Turner is a founding advisory member of Life Comes From It, which funds BIPOC-led restorative justice, transformative justice, and Indigenous peacemaking initiatives in the United States.

Tsedale M. Melaku is a sociologist and author of *You Don't Look Like a Lawyer: Black Women and Systemic Gendered Racism*, which reflects the emphasis of her scholarly interests on race, gender, class, intersectionality, workplace inequities, diversity, and organizations. Dr. Melaku's work has been featured in numerous outlets such as *Harvard Business Review*, *New York Times*, *Washington Post*, *Bloomberg Law*, *Forbes*, *Fortune*, and *CBS News*.

Laurene Miller-Patterson, inspired by liberation stories of the generation before her in human and civil rights, believes humans can create peace, equity, intercultural respect, greater kindness, and true responsibility to the ecological systems that hold us. She was fortunate, and remains forever grateful, to the like-minded and far more talented people who brought her along to be a witness to what we can accomplish with the clear intention to be better in all ways.

Johnnie P. Mitchell is a native of Hilton Head Island, South Carolina, and founder of the historical celebration of National Freedom Day. She is a graduate of Spelman College, with a master's degree from the University of South Carolina. She leads The Jig Is Up! movement from Charleston, South Carolina, based on her Book: *The Jig Is Up: We Are One! Race Is a Hoax That FAILS American Education*. She has two adult children and four grandchildren.

With over 35 years of experience, **Lucy Moore** is a facilitator, mediator, trainer, and consultant, specializing in complex, often confounding, natural resource conflicts. Based in Santa Fe, New Mexico, she learned about working across cultural boundaries while living and working in the heart of Navajoland. With this background, most of her cases today involve tribal issues and parties. Working with a culturally diverse team of practitioners she strives to build understanding and create alliances across racial and ethnic divides.

Jorge Morales was born in Chile and attended missionary school for elementary and secondary education. He attended college at the University of Pennsylvania and graduate school at Stanford University. He's had a lifelong interest in mysticism and after some years in academia and industry, he trained at a Zen Buddhist temple in the eighties and was involved with a Sufi order in the nineties. He clerks his monthly meeting and liaisons with Mexico City and Pacific Yearly meetings.

Tomi Nagai-Rothe (she/her) lives on Lisjan Ohlone land, in the San Francisco Bay Area. She is an Asian American and Pacific Islander person of Korean-Japanese descent, a mother of two and grandmother of two, a Friend (Quaker), writer, and activist working to improve her community. Tomi uses healing movement to help ground people, foster community connection, and a deeper connection to Nature. She is an internationally certified instructor of Shintaido, a spiritual martial art.

Diego James Navarro is a Hispanic/Latino community college educator who works with formerly incarcerated and other adult students using a liberatory/social justice research approach creating a culture of dignity. Diego teaches college faculty in affective learning approaches and developed the Academy for College Excellence Five-Day Experiential Learning Institute to help faculty and staff experience mind-body approaches to embodied teaching and employ noncognitive learning activities to create psychologically safe learning environments.

Gerson Ramirez is a proud Chicago native. His engagement with hope is grounded in his experience growing up in a working-class neighborhood. He believes hope is created through relationships with a community that believes in the desired outcome and, most importantly, constructing that future together. Gerson earned his BA in sociology from North Park University in 2016 and a master's of public policy at the University of Michigan in 2020.

A co-editor of *Re-Centering Culture and Knowledge in Conflict Resolution Practice* (Syracuse University Press, 2008) and the current volume, **Beth Roy** focuses both services and writing on social change. Among other works, she is the author of *Some Trouble with Cows* (UC Berkeley Press, 1992) and *Bitters in the Honey* (University of Arkansas Press, 1999) as well as *41 Shots . . . and Counting: What Amadou Diallo's Story Teaches Us About Policing, Race, and Justice* (Syracuse University Press, 2009). In recent years, she prioritizes mentoring young champions of justice, writing, grandmothering, and enjoying the beauty of New Mexico.

Nadine Tafoya, MSW, LCSW (Mescalero Apache), is a wife, mother, and grandmother. She lives in a rural Pueblo village in northern New Mexico with her husband and family. She was born and raised in New Mexico, under the guidance of her father and grandfather, both Servant Leaders of the Apaches. She founded Nadine Tafoya & Associates in 1999, an independent consulting firm, specializing in behavioral health prevention and treatment, program evaluation and community development initiatives, decolonization, creative conflict management, and intercultural peacebuilding.

Maria R. Volpe, PhD, is a professor of sociology at John Jay College of Criminal Justice, City University of New York, and director of the CUNY Dispute Resolution Center. An internationally known scholar, Dr. Volpe has lectured, trained, and written extensively about dispute resolution processes, has been widely recognized for her distinguished career, has administered dozens of grant-funded projects, and conducted research on police mediation, varied diversity-related concerns, and ADR responses to disasters.

Mary Wade: In 2005 I founded the organization Building Respect in Community. The mission is to engage the community in training and activities to restore respect. We have gone into schools and held a Teacher's Appreciation event. We uplifted Appreciation for Elder where we paired young adults with their parents or grandparents to learn their history. We have held many youth activities culminating in the bi-annual Youth Peace Olympics, which were started in 2011 and focus on spirit, love, respect, honesty, peace, and combining education and recreation. Besides major family commitments, I am active in NewCore, a New Conversation on Race. I have continued to write poetry, teach, and speak on Spirituality and Conflict Resolution and am currently teaching workshops on

Dr. Howard Thurman through the Alternative Seminary. My life is very full as I soon reach 81 years, as God wills.

Jonathan Webb, MPH, MBA, is the CEO for the Association of Women's Health and Obstetric and Neonatal Nursing. He has spent more than 15 years in the public health space at local, state, and national levels promoting equity, improving community health outcomes, addressing the social determinants of health, and tackling several epidemics including maternal and infant mortality, childhood obesity, diabetes, and cardiovascular disease. He serves on several national boards and committees.

Dwight L. Wilson has published historical fiction including *The Kidnapped: A Collection of Stories* and *The Resistors: A Collection of Stories*, and six books in the series *Esi Was My Mother*. He also writes modern psalms. Current books include *Modern Psalms in Search of Peace and Justice* and *Modern Psalms for Solace and Resistance*. His writing is fed by his Quaker faith and a lifetime of social activism.

CPSIA information can be obtained
at www.ICGtesting.com
Printed in the USA
LVHW020051240922
729134LV00001B/27